Behind the Seams

Behind the Seams

Women, Fashion, and Work in 19th-Century France

Susan Hiner

BLOOMSBURY VISUAL ARTS
LONDON • NEW YORK • OXFORD • NEW DELHI • SYDNEY

BLOOMSBURY VISUAL ARTS
Bloomsbury Publishing Plc
50 Bedford Square, London, WC1B 3DP, UK
1385 Broadway, New York, NY 10018, USA
29 Earlsfort Terrace, Dublin 2, Ireland

BLOOMSBURY, BLOOMSBURY VISUAL ARTS and the Diana logo are trademarks of Bloomsbury Publishing Plc

First published in Great Britain 2023

Copyright © Susan Hiner, 2023

Susan Hiner has asserted her right under the Copyright, Designs and Patents Act, 1988, to be identified as Author of this work.

For legal purposes the Acknowledgements on p. vi constitute an extension of this copyright page.

Cover design by Adriana Brioso
Cover image: *With the milliner* (pastel 0; 91 × 0; 75) by Edgar Degas, 1898. (© Orsay Museum/ Christophel Fine Art/Universal Images Group/Getty Images)

All rights reserved. No part of this publication may be reproduced or transmitted in any form or by any means, electronic or mechanical, including photocopying, recording, or any information storage or retrieval system, without prior permission in writing from the publishers.

Bloomsbury Publishing Plc does not have any control over, or responsibility for, any third-party websites referred to or in this book. All internet addresses given in this book were correct at the time of going to press. The author and publisher regret any inconvenience caused if addresses have changed or sites have ceased to exist, but can accept no responsibility for any such changes.

A catalogue record for this book is available from the British Library.

A catalog record for this book is available from the Library of Congress.

ISBN: HB: 978-1-3503-3980-4
PB: 978-1-3503-3979-8
ePDF: 978-1-3503-3981-1
eBook: 978-1-3503-3982-8

Typeset by RefineCatch Limited, Bungay, Suffolk
Printed and bound in Great Britain

To find out more about our authors and books visit www.bloomsbury.com and sign up for our newsletters.

Contents

Acknowledgments vi

Introduction   Behind the Seams 1

1   Veiling Women's Work 9

2   Fashion's Fingers: Immodest *Modistes* 41

3   Fashion's Voices: "*Modistes des Lettres*" 89

4   Fashion's Eyes: Painting in the Mirror 147

Epilogue   *Midinettes* in Motion 199

Notes 203
Works Consulted 241
List of Illustrations 253
Index 257

Acknowledgments

I began working on this book in 2013, and over the course of a decade, the project evolved and the number of people and institutions whose support I relied upon expanded. I would like to thank Frances Arnold of Bloomsbury Academic, who enthusiastically supported my project, along with her able staff, who shepherded it to completion; the anonymous readers of the manuscript who offered insightful comments; Susan Johnson and Piper McDonald, whose editorial assistance and image sourcing helped me finalize the manuscript.

I'm grateful to the many organizations that supported my project: the National Endowment for the Humanities, which awarded me a generous fellowship that helped get the book underway; the American Library in Paris, which, early on, hosted me for a month of productive research in Paris; the Bard Graduate Research Center, and specifically Michele Majer, who invited me to present my research; Maude Bass-Krueger and Sophie Kurkdjian, the organizers of the "Séminaire Histoire de Mode," run under the auspices of the IHTP/CNRS, who gave me the chance to share my research with a Paris audience; Cecilia Novero and her colleagues in the Research Seminar at the University of Otago, for engaging with this material and offering excellent feedback; Laurent Cotta of the Paris Galliera, who accompanied me in my exploration the astounding trove of artwork produced by the Colin sisters; Nadine Stewart, for her millinery expertise; and the librarians and archivists at the Archives de la Ville de Paris, the Bibliothèque de l'Arsenal, the Bibliothèque Forney, the Bibliothèque historique de la Ville de Paris, the Bibliothèque nationale de France, and the Cabinet des Arts Graphiques of the Musée Carnavalet.

I was fortunate to have been included in two collaborative events that moved my project along. Heidi Brevik-Zender organized a symposium on "Fashion, Modernity and Materiality" at the unforgettable Château de la Bretesche in Missillac, Brittany, where some of my early thinking for this project, enhanced by discussions and champagne with my co-participants, developed. In addition, Grace An and Alicia Walker organized and hosted an AALAC workshop on the topic of "Women's Bodies as Sites of Social Negotiation" at Bryn Mawr College, and a follow-up workshop took place at Oberlin College. The stimulating intellectual environment the hosts created and the vibrant interactions with participants from different disciplines, in particular Mireille Lee and Greggor Mattson, advanced the development of my final chapter and helped crystallize the overall shape of the book.

My thanks extend as well to my home institution, Vassar College, and to the many people there who have supported this project: Judith Dollenmeyer, who helped me identify grants and refine my proposal in the book's early stages; Chris Johnson and Gary Hohenberger of the Vassar Grants office; Amanda Thornton and Lori Buckey for their efficient administration of grants I was awarded through Vassar's Gabrielle Snyder Beck Fund; Steven Taylor, who was so generous with his time and skill in helping me with images; and the Vassar Library community, who were always ready to help, no matter how arcane the request or how overdue the book—particularly, Debra Bucher, Rebecca Burwell, Gretchen Lieb, Ron Patkus, Dean Rogers, and Lydia Smith.

I offer my heartfelt gratitude to my Vassar colleagues, whose moral support and advice have been important along the way—Betsy Bradley, Anne Brancky, Bill Hoynes, Cynthia Kerr, Lydia Murdoch, Thomas Parker, Vinay Swamy, and Susan Zlotnick; and to my colleagues in Vassar College's Historic Costume Collection, who helped me experience the material reality of historic clothing—Kenisha Kelly, Arden Kirkland, and Holly Hummel. I offer a special word of thanks to Mita Choudhury, who generously helped me navigate the Paris archives with her historian's expertise and was always willing to step out for an *apéro*. I cannot overestimate the support I received from my amazing writing group at Vassar—Sophia Siddique Harvey, Jeffrey Schneider, Joshua Schreier, Silke von der Emde, and Eva Woods-Peiró. We have been working together for many years now, and my book is so much the better for the invigorating and kind discussions we share. I offer my sincere thanks to my students, especially my dedicated research assistants, Andrew Snyder and Suchen Zhu, and others who performed key on-site research tasks in Paris and London—Hannah Tatar and Emily Selter—and those who, like Alexandra Figler and Kevin Choe, have been superb interlocutors throughout the evolution of this project. Many other students, among them Athena Randall, and especially those who have taken my seminar on "Fashion's Empires" at Vassar over the years have contributed mightily to my thinking about the book through their questions, observations, and perspectives.

I was also fortunate to have several sharp readers and creative thinkers outside of my institution engage with my work. I wish to thank my dear friend, Kaudie McLean, for her expert editing from early days. Our shared pleasure studying French literature with the magnificent Millicent K. Ruddy shaped an early friendship that continues to be nourished by our mutual affection for our teacher and what she taught us to appreciate. Pauline Le Ven provided generous assistance in locating images, and Sylvie Mercier thoughtfully sent me fashion ephemera from a *vide-grenier* that helped me visualize what I was analyzing. Gwen Grewal and Valerie Steele provided stimulating discussion of all things fashion, especially welcome during pandemic months.

My superb colleagues in the Nineteenth-Century French Studies community have also played an important role in the completion of this book—from conference presentations, informal conversations, and enlightening virtual book discussions to reading and critiquing my work, this group of scholars has given me a vibrant intellectual home. I especially thank colleagues who read portions of the book, helped me locate materials, or fielded questions—Elizabeth Emery, John Finkelberg, Michael Garval, Rachel Mesch, Bénédicte Monicat, Raisa Rexer, Victoria Thompson, and Alexandra Wettlaufer. Several dear friends and colleagues have given considerable time and intellectual and emotional energy over the years reading and critiquing multiple drafts, helping with translations, asking the right questions, and always believing in my project: I offer my profound thanks to Masha Belenky, Carolyn Betensky, Marni Kessler, and Lise Schreier, each of whom brought their discerning eyes and brilliant minds to bear on my manuscript. Although she is not here to see the final product, my friend and mentor Priscilla Ferguson's wit and wisdom, along with her excellent example of generous scholarship, continue to guide me after her untimely death.

Finally, I offer my deepest gratitude to my family—John and Nora—who have been patient and supportive throughout, genuinely interested in what I was writing, and always willing to wordsmith or talk through ideas.

I dedicate this book to my grandmothers, my mother, and my sister—Ruby Pauline, Martha Estelle, Mary Elizabeth, and Laura—whose work, both visible and invisible, helped make mine possible—and, finally, to my extraordinary daughter, Nora.

* * *

Portions of some chapters derived in part from the following earlier essays: "Becoming (M)other: Reflectivity in the *Journal des demoiselles*, which appeared in *Romance Studies*, 31:2 (2013), "The Modiste's Palette and the Artist's Hat" in *Degas, Impressionism, and the Paris Millinery Trade*, Exhibition Catalogue, edited and co-curated by Simon Kelly and Esther Bell (St. Louis Art Museum and Fine Arts Museum of San Francisco, 2017), "Fashion Animation: Heads, Hats, and the Uncanny Work of Fashion," in *Fashion, Modernity, and Materiality: From Rousseau to Art Deco*, ed. Heidi Brevik-Zender (SUNY Press, 2018), and "Femininized Commodities, Female Communities: The Colin Sisters and the Stealthy Work of the Fashion Plate," *French Historical Studies*, 43:2 (2020). I am grateful to the editors for permission to use this material. Unless otherwise indicated, all translations are my own.

Introduction: Behind the Seams

The dress ... almost always has a fitted coat attached with bows and decorated with a charming plait or an invisible thread.[1]

According to Balzac, the less respectable the lady, the more visible her dress seams and the more visible anything "seamy" those gaps might reveal. A disreputable woman was easily identified by her "badly fastened hooks that expose the mesh through an opening in the back of the dress, worn leather shoes, used hat ribbons, a too-puffy dress, a too-tight skirt."[2] By contrast, a well-sewn dress, custom-made to serve as a second skin, denoted the seamless elegance of respectability. The literal seaming of a dress thus expressed both social and moral distinctions. The pins and hooks, thread and stitches holding together the elaborate garment were artfully concealed under yards of silk, lace, velvet, or wool. The social construction of femininity, its processes, mechanisms, and raw materials, hid behind a similar ideal of seamlessness, leaving the impression that effortless elegance was innate, natural.

In my previous book, *Accessories to Modernity: Fashion and the Feminine in Nineteenth-Century France* (2010), I focused on the *femme comme il faut*, a specifically nineteenth-century figure whose mission was to incarnate the principles of feminine respectability, largely through her clever deployment of fashion signals.[3] The present study extends that discussion, returning to the metaphor of seams—only now as it concerns those women on the production side of the increasingly important fashion economy in nineteenth-century France. Seamlessness in fashion served and reinforced the increasingly pervasive ideal of feminine bourgeois respectability, and the women who created fashion were instrumental in the production of all it implied; they were potentially both complicit and oppositional. Not only were their methods and tools of fabrication often unseen, but so too was their labor spent creating fashion. Both garment and idealized femininity magically materialized, fully formed, in the gorgeous, hand-colored pages of the fashion press, described and promoted in weekly chronicles of fashion's exploits, which also strove to conceal the processes of their production.

The women working "behind the seams" of France's nineteenth-century fashion economy were largely concealed from view: the seamstress who cut and sewed, the *modiste* who trimmed the dress and created an embellished matching hat, the women columnists who chronicled fashion's vagaries week in and week out, and the female fashion illustrators whose renderings created models that sped around the globe. Increasing the invisibility of their labor, contemporary scholars have tended to focus on consumption alone.[4] These women workers have also been erased by disproportionate attention to literary texts, such as Balzac's, which constructed a certain form of visibility to the exclusion of others. Traces of their work remain, nonetheless, in voiceless archives: in wardrobes, of course, but also in fashion magazines, in popular literature and prints, in the daily press, and even in legal and civil records. *Behind the Seams* recovers these women's often tacit participation in the production side of a fashion economy by attending to these understudied archives. The book thus turns the metaphor of seams inside out to consider what their interstices reveal about a less visible nineteenth-century France.

The seam is a rich and perplexing metaphor. It implies sewing, joining, and making, but it also suggests ripping, undoing, and hiding. It is at once a space of opening that is sealed, a point of vulnerability, and a line of expansion that makes creation possible. Most importantly, in the context of the present book, it is a sign of work—work that often tries to conceal itself. In fact, the seam was a sign of specifically female work (hence seamstress, in French, is *couturière*).[5] For historically, before the nineteenth century, only male tailors had the legal right to cut expensive fabric, and it was the seamstresses, frequently the tailors' wives and daughters, who assembled the pieces of cut cloth, sewing them together to create, and usually to conceal, the joining seam.[6] The seam and the seamlessness to which fashion aspired form an overarching metaphor for this book's project. I focus on three groups of women, mostly working-class and bourgeois, both real and imagined, working in the nineteenth-century fashion industry, who led relatively invisible lives while the commodities they created achieved hypervisibility. The tangible work of these women was masked by mythologizing, anonymity, and marginalization.

Its mythologies notwithstanding, fashion was a powerful regime that depended on women's expert manipulation of its raw materials. The delicate finger work of seamstresses and *modistes* yielded elegant dresses and ethereal hats; the subtle, persuasive rhetoric of written chronicles resulted in savvy, targeted marketing campaigns of goods and behaviors; and the stylized visual splendor of the detailed drawing, engraving, and painting of fashion plates fed an aspirational fantasy that ended in consumption. Yet this fashion regime paradoxically excluded many of the women on whom it depended by hiding their labor. At the same time, however, some women harnessed the possibilities offered them by the growing fashion economy, channeling the feminization of fashion and their own expertise with the tropes of idealized femininity to forge careers. In other words, we might say that they collaborated with this same regime to create pathways to professionalization largely unavailable to women in other sectors of the economy. The pun of my title thus also refers to a kind of performativity: one of the key themes of the book is the duplicity some nineteenth-century women learned to negotiate in order to become successful professionals, sometimes simply in order to work.

Even as their products were ubiquitous—globally disseminated, marketed, and sold—and their lives sensationalized, whether through eroticizing mythologies or through idealizing bourgeois ideologies of respectability, these women's actual work lives remain obscure. With this dialectic of hypervisibility/invisibility in mind, Marx's concept of the commodity fetish haunts the book, both in its most literal forms as well as in its less conventional meanings. Not only hats and other consumables, divorced from the labor of their creators, but also the studied leisure of the fashion column, precious pearls of wisdom that conceal the class and labor of the women who wrote them, and the commoditized fashion plate, both marketing tools of the industry, were all produced through a laborious process that diminished the artistic identities of their creators.

These women—some workers, others entrepreneurs, and still others freelancers—crafted their agency through negotiation at every step, developing strategies and counter-strategies to make lives for themselves. While they certainly did achieve success, contributing dramatically to the identity of nineteenth-century Paris as the "capital of fashion," it would be a mistake to see these women in a simple, binary way, that is, as either purely subversive of or purely collaborative with the system within which they worked. Likewise, mediated by a representation imposed by a patriarchal culture, their success was never an undiluted victory. Nor were they purely victims. Instead, their negotiations were complex, involving a constant to-and-fro and a systematically ironic positioning vis-à-vis their own identities and place within the emerging fashion system. Challenging the monolithic idea that women were primarily fashion's victims (either as brainless consumers or exploited labor), then, I try to show how these women—certain fashion workers, fashion chroniclers, and fashion-plate artists—worked within an oppressive system to forge successful careers, at least by nineteenth-century standards. To illuminate a more nuanced picture of these women's extensive contribution to France's most important economic sector in the nineteenth century, I work with lesser-known literary texts, such as vaudeville plays and panoramic literature, press and legal documents, the burgeoning women's press, and the vibrant and ubiquitous visual print culture of nineteenth-century France.[7]

By engaging with these documents, I explore the representation and the counter-strategies of these women workers, in particular, *modistes*, fashion writers, and fashion illustrators, the three groups engaged in the production of fashion's fantasy. Working in an active network with each other, a network that encompasses elements of both the fashion industry and the fashion business (which also elaborated a rich cultural ecosystem—what Barthes would later term the "fashion system"), they achieved both agency and influence within a cultural system that exploited working-class women and denied employment opportunities to bourgeois women. While these women made significant professional contributions, their actual work often remained hidden behind predominant myths about the working woman and the entrenched and powerful ideals of bourgeois womanhood. Although fashion had significant negative impacts on women in the nineteenth century—as it still does—it also gave some of them opportunities for lives of productive work. That is the story I want to tell in the chapters that follow.

Chapter 1, "Veiling Women's Work," explores the ways in which women's work was hidden in the nineteenth century. First, I consider the power of the fashion commodity—whether material, discursive, or visual—to conceal the work of women in the fashion industry. These women include fashion workers, the legendary working-class *grisettes*, whose image and reputation as carefree, sexually available young women were celebrated in literary and popular culture throughout the nineteenth century.[8] However, bourgeois women worked in the fashion industry too—among them journalists and painters—who also produced commodities that were essential to the success of the industry.

Further, I propose that a kind of discursive and representational veiling worked in tandem with the commodity's power to cover their work. Marni Reva Kessler has explored the cultural history of the veil and its particular valences in Second Empire Paris, illustrating its function as an artistic device as well as its multiple metaphorical significations for a changing cityscape and the women inhabiting modern Paris. In a different formulation, Béatrice Craig has also developed an important discussion of what she terms the "discursive veil" to refer to the ways in which cultural ideologies around women distorted perceptions of their lived experience.[9] Like the seam, the veil, as Kessler has amply demonstrated, is a rich metaphor linked to fashion; but unlike the seam, the veil does not signal work; rather it is a distorting screen that obscures what it ostensibly protects. The metaphorical veil surrounding the *modiste* (and, by extension, other women fashion workers), for example, took the form of a cultural mythology that imbued her craft with a pervasive image of eroticism. Similarly, a domestic ideology surrounding the bourgeoise that bound her to a life centered on motherhood, leisure, and household management veiled the work of middle-class women. Both ideological systems concealed the real work of working-class and bourgeois women alike and found expression in powerful visual representations—the first in a prolific popular print culture and the second in the widely disseminated fashion plate—in addition to discursive forms; these women were not merely hapless victims of an exploitative system.[10] Indeed, in this chapter I also introduce what I identify as the collusion of these women with the commodity, a willed participation in their own veiling process, through which women fashion workers—whether *modistes*, *chroniqueuses*, or artists—sometimes themselves adopted strategies to distort or conceal their real labor to achieve professional goals that might otherwise be out of reach.

Chapter 2, "Fashion's Fingers: Immodest *Modistes*," centers on the "aristocrat" of fashion workers. *Modistes* enjoyed more autonomy and higher social prestige than any other fashion worker and so, potentially, had more opportunities for social mobility than their sisters of the needle. They were primarily known for artistic hat creation, but they were typically also skilled seamstresses, designers, and stylists in their own right. They were without a doubt the most eroticized of all the female fashion workers, and, perhaps because they possessed as much autonomy and visibility as they did, often marketing their goods on their persons and in their wide shop windows, they had achieved some measure of independence as women workers early in the history of fashion. Furthermore, their business throughout the course of the nineteenth century was booming. The greater the threat a woman posed, however, the more likely she was to be negatively mythologized through sexualizing images and quasi-literary representations of her frivolity.

A visual fantasy world thus proliferated around *modistes*. Countless prints and popular literary texts repeat the same tropes of the sexy *modiste*, posing rather than working, the object of a typically male gaze. She became kind of a stand-in for all of the urban women working in the fashion industry—and they were generally understood to be disreputable, aiming to seduce a man from a higher class in order to marry and escape their working-class life. *Modistes* were particularly troubling for the social order in this regard because apprentices with enough skill could rise through the ranks and achieve a degree of independence—through the hierarchical system of the *atelier* and because of the lucrative possibilities of the expanding industry. However, the sexual autonomy emphasized by the print culture surrounding the *modiste* actually covers for what was perhaps a more disturbing entrepreneurial autonomy.

My aim in this chapter is to balance the visual and literary mythology surrounding the *modiste* with an analysis of other types of contemporaneous documents that have been little studied. For example, there was some resistance in the popular culture to the lascivious and mercenary image of the *modiste* ubiquitous in the press and visual and literary culture. As a counterpoint, then, to this mythology, I also consider several vaudeville plays—a genre whose audience included *modistes* themselves and other working women—that present alternative views of *modiste* figures. Other, non-literary archival texts also reveal alternative portrayals of the lived experience of women workers such as *modistes*, a work history that is obscured by the prevailing mythology. I thus examine newspaper articles and bankruptcy records to get closer to the lives of these women. These archival documents show that the rapid expansion of the fashion industry meant that girls from the country could come to the city, apprentice in an *atelier*, and possibly, eventually succeed. The *modiste*'s profession was indeed thriving throughout the 1800s and, by the end of the century, the industry employed tens of thousands of female workers. Newspaper records from the business sections also indicate how entrepreneurial many of these women were; while many of the records are often poignant, recording business failures and other losses, they also point to the scope of the industry and can offer a glimpse into a non-mythologized work life.

If the first part of the book centers on the representation of "fashion's fingers," or the world of *les petites mains* (little hands), a charming yet tellingly reductive epithet for the low-level makers of the material objects of fashion, the next two chapters turn to what might be called "fashion's eyes and ears." Here, I examine the *chroniqueuses de mode*, or women fashion writers, some anonymous, others pseudonymous, and some named, as well as fashion's first important female illustrators, the Colin sisters, and the essential product of their labor—the fashion plate. These tastemakers and product placers recorded fashion's continuously changing cycle week-by-week in the leading fashion publications of the nineteenth century. The power they wielded, the agendas they pursued, and the products they placed as they labored weekly to convey the spectacle of fashion—these are the concerns that structure this section.

Chapter 3, "Fashion's Voices: *Modistes des Lettres*," develops an analysis of the creators of fashion discourse, the tastemakers, who were sometimes referred to as *modistes des lettres*.[11] They wielded the power of the fashion system discourse, making or unmaking trends, and serving as cultural intermediaries in an extended period when society was reinventing itself. These women journalists at work in the early fashion industry were not the typical working-class women of the *ateliers*. Rather, they were educated and familiar with the dominant bourgeois ideology of domestic femininity. Now usually, in nineteenth-century France, educated bourgeois women were not entrepreneurial, as work for bourgeois women ran counter to the prevailing view of appropriate femininity. Like their working-class counterparts, however, some bourgeois women also found inroads to a reputable work life thanks to the fashion industry. Each of the three women I study—Jeanne-Jacqueline Fouqueau de Pussy (1786–1863), Olympe Vallée (la vicomtesse de Renneville) (1811–90), and Emmeline Raymond (1828–1902)—developed appealing and distinct media personae that belied the fact that they were actually paid for a living, a fact that was difficult to reconcile with an idealized bourgeois feminine identity. This obfuscation was essential to their ability to remain oracular goddesses to the aspirational readers they reached, for they became models for the class to which their readers aspired, a class that styled itself as leisured, worldly, and domestic. Each journalist had a different niche, and all three engaged in a strategically tailored discursive veiling.

These and other women like them emerged as the premier tastemakers to the aspiring—and expanding—bourgeoisie over the course of the nineteenth century. Each in her own way, and in her own historic moment, was a deft businesswoman who grasped the potential of the modernity of illustrated fashion journals. These fashion writers concealed, shaped, or transformed their identities in their columns to mediate directly between products and reader-consumers, and their invented identities invariably hid the labor they expended to keep the journals churning week after week. Women such as these shaped both fashion trends and female behavior and, through strategic product placement and the masterful manipulation of the cultural fantasy of the feminine, fostered consumer culture and practices within the male-dominated world of publishing and pioneered innovations in the fashion journal—a mediating ecosystem bridging text and image. By cultivating personalized relationships with readers, they expanded their readership and developed loyal followings, supporting the major publishing houses for which they worked. They also, it goes without saying, worked in tandem with the makers of fashion, like the *modistes* whose shops they visited and promoted, and with the illustrators, who were dispatched to shops by publishers to produce exquisite images that served both as pseudo-advertisements as well as dreamscapes for aspirational readers, viewers, and shoppers.

Chapter 4, "Fashion's Eyes: Painting in the Mirror," turns to this third group of women working in the fashion industry as it was forming: the fashion illustrators. Here I focus on the two most prolific and accomplished fashion-plate artists of their day: Héloïse Leloir (1819–73) and Anaïs Toudouze (1822–99)—known today as the Colin sisters—who essentially cornered the market on fashion illustration in the second half of the nineteenth century. It was a field that had been dominated by male artists, who typically only did commercial work to make extra money.[12] Unlike their male counterparts, however, the Colin sisters had to flip that model, since as women, it was much harder for them to pursue professional fine arts careers. Trained by their father, a respected Romantic painter, the sisters share a professional biography similar to that of many aspiring women artists of the nineteenth century. Shut out of the École des Beaux Arts, they made careers in the commercial art world of fashion illustration. Ironically, their fashion plates were much more widely disseminated and collected than any of their artist father's or half-brother's works.[13] Prints of the sisters' pictures were sent around the world and made their way into albums and picture-frames. Attesting to their claim on professional artistic identity, and unlike many fashion-plate artists, they signed their works, making their gender apparent. They were, in short, omnipresent in the domain of fashion publication, sketching and painting on tight weekly deadlines to illustrate the latest fashions and promote shops and styles.

Nevertheless, what we see in their work product is a fantasy of fashionable leisure, motherhood, and female companionship—the traditional themes of nineteenth-century fashion plates. This was the fantasy lifestyle to which bourgeois readers aspired, but not necessarily the life these artists lived. Veiled in the image is the painstaking process and real labor that lay behind its creation; also shrouded is the significance of these illustrations to the success of the fashion industry. The chapter thus considers the work process of the sisters, who elevated the fashion-plate genre, and whose archive of sketches and watercolors reveals that their commercial art involved much the same skill sets as so-called high art. Sketching on site (that is, in shops) meant that, like the fashion editors and journalists with whom they worked, they visited stores and their adjacent *ateliers* to see and study what was being fabricated. There they would make sketches, and then at home in the studio, recreate or embellish according to their own fancy the fashions to be publicized, eventually, through the reproduction of lithographs created from their renderings in watercolor, the sisters' principal medium. Scholars have rightly celebrated the modernity of Impressionist painters depicting everyday scenes in spaces such as shops and *ateliers*, inspired in part by fashion-plate artists such as the Colin sisters.[14] Perhaps we might reframe the terms of that comparison and consider how artists such as the Colin sisters were engaged in a similar artistic practice.

In the hands of the Colin sisters, the fashion plate serves as a visible but silent archive of the spectrum of female labor that was so often hidden in fashion production—from the artist-illustrator to the fashion worker. Fashion illustration permitted the sisters to have professional art careers at a time when a successful career as a noncommercial artist was, for most women, out of reach. Like the fashion journalists, who disguised their real labor to appeal to the leisured aspirations of their readers, and like the *modistes*, whose eroticized reputations overshadowed their work accomplishments, these fashion illustrators are virtually unknown in spite of the pioneering work they did in the fashion industry and the pathways they opened for bourgeois-aspirational and middle-class women in the workforce.[15]

A brief epilogue, "*Midinettes* in Motion," returns to the story of the Parisian fashion workers with which the book opens. These women workers were evolving in tandem with the booming *fin-de-siècle* fashion industry. As work in the city for girls with needle skills became ever more plentiful, many young women otherwise destined for a life in service or as the wife to an impoverished provincial husband moved to Paris to seek employment. Some of them brought with them their folklore traditions, which would morph into new rituals, appropriate to a new independence and increased visibility. Tradition dictated that when a girl turned twenty-five and was still unwed, she was required to make offerings of bonnets for Saint Catherine (*coiffer sainte Catherine*), the patron saint of unwed girls (and also of needleworkers).[16] This practice marked her passage into spinsterhood and also offered a melancholy consolation: she would possess saintly celibacy, unless, of course, a suitable fiancé saved her from this fate. Young girls recited prayers to Saint Catherine, and cards were sent to the *catherinettes* wishing them luck in their inevitable pursuit of a husband. Many such girls may have seen fashion work in the metropolis as an alternative to this trajectory, however.

Indeed, by the end of the nineteenth century, Parisian fashion workers, known as *midinettes* because they left their *ateliers* at noon (*midi*) each day to grab a quick bite from a *dînette*, had appropriated the November holiday, making it a celebration of women's work in the needle trades, in particular, millinery.[17] Alongside the *course des catherinettes*, which entailed an annual race through the streets of Paris in light-hearted celebration, these *midinettes* also took to the streets in strikes, demanding higher pay and decreased working hours, which they won in 1917. The Parisian fashion worker, whose visibility had been defined primarily through a lasting mythology of her elegance and *légèreté* (loose morality), was now being recognized as an important contributor to France's luxury economy, and to its modernization. For, notwithstanding the persistence of this mythology, which continued to haunt popular representations of fashion workers, the *midinettes* managed to harness the subversive energies nascent in vaudeville representations of the early nineteenth century to lead 10,000 fashion workers in the *grève joyeuse* (joyful strike) that would crystallize a model of solidarity already perceptible in the nineteenth-century *atelier*.

Behind the Seams centers on women's involvement in fashion production in nineteenth-century France and expands upon the metaphor of seams to reveal a story more complex than previously acknowledged. By focusing on the intersection of the culture of fashion in nineteenth-century France and other cultural forms, and by considering the impact of this nexus on the idea of the feminine, *Behind the Seams* ushers these women and their work out of obscurity and asks also that we rethink women's relation to fashion as one not only of passive consumption, but also, importantly, of productive agency and self-determination.

1

Veiling Women's Work

It was a gauzy lilac bonnet, with straw braids around the wide brim, and then a bouquet of poppies, wheat and cornflowers, amidst shell-shaped ribbons, tilted to the right of the form on the brim.[1]

In his "Story of a Bonnet" (1832), published in one of several Paris literary guidebooks popular in the mid-nineteenth century, Antoine Fontaney, a minor man of letters, seizes upon the trendiest and most coveted of women's fashion accessories of his day—a *capote*—to evoke both the fleeting fragility of fashion and, in a metonymic echo, the equally ephemeral affections of Parisian women.[2] From his liminal perch at the window of his mistress's salon on the rue Vivienne, a street known as much for its prostitutes as for its theaters, fashionable shops, and *ateliers*, the *flâneur*-narrator, a fictitious Englishman by the improbably ludicrous name of "Lord Feeling," describes a series of scenes he witnesses at the intersection of consumption and production, visibility and invisibility, art and industry. With the satirical wit typical of the panoramic genre, Fontaney manages both to ridicule the naïve outsider-narrator and to critique the frivolous nature of *Parisiennes*—shoppers as well as mistresses. However, this text also stages the transformation of a fashion product into the proverbial Marxian commodity fetish *avant la lettre*. For Fontaney narrates the lifecycle of a "magical" commodity decades before Marx even coined the term—an overdetermined bonnet, which begins as an amorphous collection of unglamorous raw materials, passes from the hands of the *modiste* who created it to its spectacular display in the shop's "animated" vitrine, and ends up on the delighted bobbing head of an eager shopper.[3] Fetishized, the *capote* loses all trace of the *modiste*'s labor as it enters society and becomes a focal point of admiration. In a rainy instant on the streets of Paris, however, the hat is destroyed, but not before wielding its mystical power and seductive allure over all who behold it.

The story unfolds in several scenes that magically transform the *modiste*'s labor into the spectacle of the commodity. As Lord Feeling waits for the unfaithful Madame de Saint-Clair to perfect her *toilette* for their evening's outing, he casts his voyeuristic male gaze through the curtainless window of the *modiste*'s shop across the way. If he cannot enjoy his mistress's company, the working girls of the *atelier* are an able substitute: "I trained my eyepiece on them [the shopgirls]."[4] Undetected, he penetrates the private workspace of the *modistes*, peering "behind the seams" to observe these *charmantes filles* as they socialize after their evening meal, chatting and laughing. What most captures his attention, at first at least, is the one young woman who is set apart, pensive, with an air "of distinction and superiority"[5]— the *première demoiselle*. Presented as a singular creative artist, she seems to mirror the narrator, himself a stand-in for the male artist-writer, who observes and weaves his narrative from his superior, apparently omniscient perspective. Spotlighted by an author who presumably wishes to emphasize the unique skills of Parisian artisans (this text was written for a "guidebook," after all, no matter how ironic), the *première* is thus acknowledged, however fleetingly, as possessing creative agency, and her work is thereby elevated. This *modiste* will, however, shortly be overshadowed by the very commodity she produces; and a powerful cultural mythology surrounding female fashion workers would also do its work to eclipse her identity.

In the *atelier*, each girl knows her place within the hierarchy of workers as they labor together to produce the exquisite object that is the lady's hat, but the *première*—the most talented *modiste* and, typically, the successor to the *maîtresse*, who owns the shop—earns this rank through her gift for inventing fine new fashions.[6] The voyeur-narrator devotes several paragraphs to the creation of an enchanted work of art: this hat is *not* a *chapeau de commande*, he states, meaning a hat commissioned by a client; rather, it is the product of the *modiste*'s own creative imagination, and it exerts the power to initiate fashion trends. It is "the improvised hat, the one that dictates fantasy, that can coif only a head never before seen by the artist, but is rather imagined."[7] It is as if the *modiste*—much like the master-marketers, fashion journalists and illustrators—were engaged in the very invention of the consumer. To do so effectively, as we shall see, these women ultimately had to disappear behind their own spectacular creations, since nineteenth-century ladies' fashion depended upon an ideal of leisure and domesticity that precluded work. By showing us the space where the commodity is born, however, Fontaney/Lord Feeling perhaps unwittingly reveals key information about the ways in which women's labor was occluded. For a brief moment, before the commodity assumes its autonomous powers, readers seem to have access to the creative agency of a woman—a *modiste*—who will all but disappear by story's end, erased by the magic of the commodity she has created, along with other forces. By apparently disenchanting the commodity, then, Fontaney's text exposes the magic trick—that is, he reveals the labor behind the commodity. Or does he? This is a question to which I shall return.

If, as Alice Kessler-Harris and Sylvie Schweitzer have both persuasively documented, "women have always worked" ("les femmes ont toujours travaillé"), why was that work consistently concealed?[8] This is the vexed question informing this chapter, which examines both the mechanisms of concealment and the powerful ideologies that drove it. The masking of nineteenth-century women's work—whether behind ideological veils of appropriate femininity, the glittering spectacle of the commodity, or, most remarkably, by women's intentional concealing strategies—is at the heart of my inquiry. The force behind this masking was a formidable, vigorous, and pervasive class-inflected ideology that resisted the notion of women at work—an ideology that took different but related forms for middle- and working-class women. Bourgeois women were yoked to a model of femininity that resonated with images of leisure, domesticity, and respectability.[9] This was an ideal that precluded imagining such women as working to earn money, an ideal that, for married women at least, was even underwritten by the law itself.[10] Working-class women, on the other hand, were subject to a different form of the same ideology, which appeared as opposite to the one applied to their middle-class sisters but which was actually deeply intertwined with it. In the case of working-class women, this ideology was frequently expressed in the form of a widespread cultural myth concerning the supposed rampant sexuality of the female fashion worker, who was thus repeatedly represented—in both print and image—primarily as erotic and seductive rather than as hard-working. This representation, because it was both easily reproduced and titillating, became culturally monolithic.[11]

There is, to be sure, ample evidence that both working-class and middle-class women worked in the nineteenth-century fashion industry,[12] but their labor was mostly overshadowed by its own fruit, obliterated by the sheer power of the commodity itself. Marx's familiar concept of the commodity fetish is useful in unpacking the process through which women's labor was obscured, and I draw on his idea to illustrate the magnitude of the commodity's grip on social experience. He develops his discussion of the "fetishism of commodities" in terms of a "secret," and his analysis is in many ways an attempt at demystification.[13] Alternating between the synonymous descriptors "mystical," "enigmatical," and "mysterious" to characterize the product, he depicts the process of its transformation, or animation, as a commodity.[14] Crucial to this description, the social relations among the people who create the products are transferred to the objects they have created; these products, then, as commodities, assume, fantastically, social relations among themselves. The essential human element that is rendered invisible by this transfer to the commodity is the labor expended in its production; but "traces of [that] exploited labour" remain, perhaps in that "living" quality the commodity seems to exude.[15]

Commodities in the world of fashion, however, can be understood to include more than hats and dresses. Here I propose to stretch the notion of the commodity fetish to consider the ways in which fashion products broadly conceived—whether material objects such as ladies' hats, published fashion columns inspiring consumer behaviors, or collectible fashion plates promoting aspirational fantasies—obscured the very real, but mostly invisible, female labor required to produce them. In this sense, we might speak of discursive and representational commodities as well as material ones, all of which contributed to the construction of a shimmering spectacle of fashion behind which fashion workers, journalists, and illustrators, primarily women, labored. Discursive commodities like fashion columns and representational commodities like fashion plates exerted enormous power over consumers in ways similar to their material cousins—all of them collaborating in a mutually reinforcing network, akin to Barthes' fashion system.[16]

The power of the commodity, however, was not the only process through which women's work was hidden. For, ironically, these women's labor was also intentionally concealed by their own strategies of dissimulation, workarounds for an ideological system that distorted or erased their labor. The women who produced these commodities—whether material, discursive, or representational—also frequently participated in the very processes of masking that enhanced the power of these commodities, strategically gaining access to an emerging capitalist regime through a kind of covert professionalization. Before exploring these women's collusion with the commodity system, the central claim of this book, I will foreground the reasons for that collusion and examine what I term, following historian Béatrice Craig, the "ideological veils" that hid or diminished women's work.[17] Class-inflected ideologies around women working prevented a clearer view into these women's actual productivity. By exposing what was at stake in the concealment of women's labor, we can begin to uncover the mechanisms of that concealment—how the commodity's power erases labor and produces enchantment, modeling in the material realm a process that would emerge both verbally and visually as well in a complicit network with the women producing those commodities. It turns out that the very process of concealing the labor of the commodity in a consumerist society also required labor, which, especially in the marketplace of fashion, itself also needed to be actively concealed.

Ideological Veils

Labor historians interested in gender have shown how forms of historical amnesia have erased women's work in consequential ways. Maria Tamboukou asserts, for example, that for nineteenth-century working-class women, a "class amnesia" may partly explain why we do not have more detailed records of the lived reality of women's work in the 1800s. Practical realities that characterized working-class women's lives, such as illiteracy, also explain why so few accounts, such as memoirs or letters, exist to offer an insight into the real lives of nineteenth-century working-class women,[18] but Tamboukou also points to the fact that working-class women erased *themselves* as they strove for higher status and escaped the working class, leaving little or no trace of their previous working-class lives. Furthermore, she suggests that the historian must at times take a "narrative approach to archival research" to reconstruct the story that the archive sometimes resists.[19]

Other scholars point to the very construction of the archive itself, arguing more broadly that the silences of the archive around certain histories are the result of the ways in which the historical narrative is shaped through power. Hazel Carby, for example, states that "the inequalities of power in the production of sources, archives, and narratives" determine whose stories are recorded and thus remembered.[20] Arlette Farge's exploration of Paris archives relating to eighteenth-century life, *Vies oubliées*, further refines this position by considering what she characterizes as unclassified or "leftover" archival materials. Her eclectic collection of shopping lists, letters from prison, notices of abandoned children, among other documents, fires the imagination and offers a partial glimpse into past lives. By valorizing incomplete or undefinable materials, her approach transforms the *déchet* (waste) into *relique* (relic), thus proposing a new understanding and appreciation for "that which has escaped knowledge."[21] Indeed, examples across a wide range of fields illustrate that generalized deficiencies or opacities of the archive pose obstacles to accessing certain kinds of knowledge, often pertaining to women and other marginalized subjects. For many working-class women such as those I consider in chapter 2, but also for the middle-class women considered in subsequent chapters, the historical record is often thin, fragmented, or even nonexistent.[22]

In addition to these impediments, however, or perhaps simply ancillary to them, other forces contribute to obscuring the work lives of nineteenth-century women. The work of women vanished behind what Craig has termed a "discursive veil" to illustrate the historical and cultural erasure of female labor in nineteenth-century France.[23] Craig invokes the metaphor of the discursive veil to explain a "widespread cultural amnesia" around women in business and "their ability and willingness to be economic agents"; and while her focus is geographically and chronologically restricted, her argument can be applied more broadly.[24] Importantly, Craig widens our understanding of the middle classes, which she pluralizes to acknowledge the diversity of the bourgeoisie; she thus includes "trading classes or commercial classes," among whom some *modistes* could certainly be counted—in particular, those who managed to achieve ownership of their own shops.[25] Further, she explains the late nineteenth century's erasure of women's entrepreneurship as the result of later historians' reliance on an overly broad and unnuanced "separate spheres ideology" and their attending focus on the paternalistic agenda of industrialists.[26] While Craig excludes milliners from her analysis, arguing that, because they participated in a "quintessentially nineteenth-century female craft," they were thus exempt from the erasure experienced by women in more masculine-coded businesses, I contend that the *modiste*'s work was indeed hidden beneath such an ideological veil. As Tilburg has shown for the *midinettes* of the *fin de siècle*, "the enticing nature of the midinette type has made her so familiar to scholars of nineteenth- and twentieth-century France as to become hidden in plain sight."[27] Like the *midinette*, the *modiste*'s actual work—from the labor in the *atelier* to the entrepreneurship of the *maîtresse*, who achieved a degree of professionalism and ownership—is consistently concealed by a flirtatious image that endured from the emergence of the figure of the *modiste* in the late eighteenth century into the early twentieth century.

Fashion's female creators were hidden behind ideologies responding to the perceived social and moral threat posed by women working that became pervasive in post-Revolutionary France. These ideologies, rooted in a patriarchal system that devalued women's work and often actively kept women out of the public workplace, while class-based, adopted visual and discursive stories that either diminished the acknowledgment of women's work or erased it altogether.[28] In the case of bourgeois women, the notion of work directly conflicted with the familiar ideology prescribing their role as domestic homemakers, mothers, and/or leisured ladies.[29] In a parallel but different way, in the case of working-class women, this response took the form of a mythology that frequently converted their honest labor into sexual promiscuity: women fashion workers were thus invariably viewed as venal in the popular cultural imaginary. In either case, the underlying ideology transformed both groups of women—middle-class and working-class—into fetishized commodities themselves, as domestic goddesses or eroticized strumpets. Below, I will briefly describe the contours of each of these ideological veils in turn to explore the causes for the concealment of women's work across class.

In the case of middle-class women, work was controversial for a variety of reasons emanating from the driving ideology of appropriate bourgeois femininity perpetuated by ladies' fashion itself. The social valorization of ideas governing bourgeois feminine respectability, perhaps best expressed in the frequently invoked separate spheres ideology, gripped nineteenth-century France from its crystallization with the Napoleonic or Civil Code in the early decades into the Belle Époque.[30] As James F. McMillan explains, in the aftermath of the Revolution, aristocratic women began to adopt a "family-oriented strategy" and an ideal of domesticity as a form of rehabilitation for what was perceived as the decadence of the old regime aristocracy.[31] Seeking models of behavior, middle-class women aligned themselves with this ideal as well, and found resources in the many etiquette manuals and fashion journals that insisted upon the centrality of marriage, motherhood, and domestic duty to a proper woman's life. To suitably fulfill the social role this ideology defined for her, then, a bourgeois woman did not work.[32]

One of the most prominent and widely diffused representational tools of the idealization of bourgeois femininity was, of course, the fashion plate. Like the many etiquette manuals that also proliferated throughout the nineteenth century, the discourse that supported the fashion plate, the fashion column, repeated in discursive, descriptive form what the image pictured. As a pendant to the imagery surrounding the sexy *modiste*, the fashion plate encapsulates and reiterates in seemingly infinite variations the key contours of a bourgeois feminine ideal. In image after image, we find elite women, usually in pairs, but sometimes in groups with children, enacting the domestic life of leisure that constituted respectable womanhood. Significantly, some of the early male fashion plate artists, like Louis-Marie Lanté, Achille Devéria, Numa, and Gavarni, created prints both for the satirical and/or popular press, such as those picturing *modistes*, as well as for the fashion press.[33] This overlap reinforces the fact of a single ideology underpinning perceptions and expectations of women, no matter their class: these perceptions and expectations emerged, however, in distinct, but intersecting visual registers.

The visual rhetoric of bourgeois feminine respectability is most readily on display in a print such as the one pictured in figure 1.1, in which two female ball-goers, with near identical features, enact their roles even as they advertise a trendy dressmaker's skill. With the same plump arms, sloping alabaster

Figure 1.1 *Anaïs Toudouze, Le Follet, Paris, 1856–7, Rijksmuseum, Amsterdam (http://hdl.handle.net/10934/RM0001.COLLECT.483629).*

shoulders, brunette hair, and faintly rosy cheeks, these two women, dressed by "Camille" and coiffed by "Normandin," are ornamented with flowers from "Chagor aîné" (the elder). The artificial flowers that decorate their hair and dress bodices repeat the "real" ones gracing the ballroom, creating an equivalence that converts these represented women into interior ornaments; for they, too, resemble flowers in frothy, inverted urns. They converse, at least apparently, the one gesturing while the other gazes out vacantly, perhaps awaiting an invitation to dance, but in any case, showcasing the silhouette of her three-tiered gown, whose fabric emanated from a shop called "Filles de France," and whose lace and ribbon embellishments were created by the *couturière-modiste* "Camille." The spectacular inactivity of these women reiterates the ethos of leisure that underwrites bourgeois femininity.

Countless other plates depict similar pairs engaged in visiting, examining art prints, strolling, shopping, admiring children, arranging flowers, etc., and almost always feature two or more women of the same class staging scenes typically associated with domestic leisure. Only occasionally do we find a mixing of classes, such as in figure 1.2, depicting a philanthropic visit—one of the few productive activities officially sanctioned for bourgeois women. Even here, in the squalid garret of a sickly mother no longer able to properly perform the duties of motherhood, the bourgeois subjects central to the image's vignette reproduce domesticity, the one gesturing towards a plate of food, and the other holding up garments for the bedraggled child to try on. I will consider more fully the functions and meanings of the fashion plate in chapter 4, and the discursive power of the fashion column in chapter 3. Here, I wish only to signal the subtending ideology of domestic leisure that is reproduced in the fashion plate, an ideology that was packaged in fashion, globally disseminated, and widely consumed by an eager and growing middle-class public.

Like a mirror, the fashion plate reflects the ideology of bourgeois femininity back onto its feminine beholder; similarly, the lady's hat offers an overdetermined example of that same ideology at the material level, as a wearable object. Ladies' hats were assimilated to women themselves through their fragility and beauty, key attributes of an idealized femininity that did not sacrifice these qualities to work. For all of their ethereal delicacy, like so many other fashion accessories of the period, ladies' hats were weighty signifiers; and, perhaps more than any other accessory, they signaled the respectability that was required of nineteenth-century femininity. Proper women did not leave home *en cheveux* (hatless) lest they be mistaken for women of another sort. Indeed, for centuries propriety had dictated that women cover their hair (an erotically charged feature) in public from as early as the age of twelve, and especially once married.[34] This moral imperative distinguished ladies' hats from those of their male counterparts, who primarily wore hats simply for protection against the elements or to signal their profession. By contrast, ladies' hats, including those with functional value, were decorative objects designating beauty, charm, and virtue. Even the most practical of ladies' hats, the *chapeau de paille* (straw hat), typically wide-brimmed enough to protect white female skin from the sun's effects, was

Figure 1.2 *Héloïse Leloir,* La Mode illustrée, *1870, Rijksmuseum, Amsterdam (http://hdl.handle.net/10934/ RM0001.COLLECT.490704).*

fabricated with the same seamlessness associated with the respectability required of those made of fabric; the best straw, from Italy, achieved its superior reputation precisely because, in its fine suppleness, it appeared to be fabric and not straw. Beyond this moral signifying value, however, the lady's hat also embodied, as we have seen, the delicacy of idealized femininity, the prized possession of patriarchy.

In contrast to the bourgeois male *haut-de-forme* (top hat), nineteenth-century women's hats were elaborately decorated with expensive trimmings—ribbons and fruits, flowers and feathers. Unlike the uniformly recognizable top hat for men, for women there were infinite hat styles, shapes, and materials, a gendered difference quite apparent in the image in figure 1.3. The print, entitled "La Voix de la foule," or "the voice of the crowd," is captioned with exclamatory descriptions about the objects in the window: "What delicious hats!! What ravishing caps! Such taste . . . such lightness . . . it's perfect . . . it's divine . . ." Notwithstanding the comic incongruity of depicting conventionally dressed bourgeois *men* thronging uncharacteristically before a lady's hat shop and exclaiming over the goods displayed there, the print serves to emphasize the gender divide that fashion, and particularly hats, illustrated and perpetuated. Above the dozen or so top hats, practically indistinguishable from each other, we find a wide array of *capotes* and *bonnets* propped on stands in the window.[35] Some are structured and stiff with wide brims and ornamented with lace, ribbons, and flowers, while others, the *bonnets* on the outer edges of the vitrine, are soft, their fabric and ties hanging loosely. This variety contrasts with the uniformity of the male spectators' top hats and illustrates the ever-shifting trendiness of women's fashion. Hats for women, more than any other dress accessory, became the chief emblem of fashion's zeitgeist. Indeed, the many variations of women's headgear in the nineteenth century amplified the bourgeois woman's function as embellishment, excess, surface, and luxurious ornamentation.[36]

Less obviously perhaps, nineteenth-century working-class women, like middle-class women, were also subject to a gendered order that preferred to imagine women in domestic and maternal roles rather than in the public spaces that work increasingly implied. Working women earned lower wages than their male counterparts, an inequity that was justified by the belief—legally institutionalized by wage laws—that male breadwinners, as heads of households, should be paid wages able to meet family subsistence, thus casting women workers as dependents on husbands and fathers and further reinforcing their domestic role.[37] As numerous historians have illustrated, the question of women's work, particularly in the garment trades, became a fraught social problem in nineteenth-century France.[38] There was no dearth of discussion of the plight of the woman worker; and chief among its commentators, as both Scott and Coffin show, was politician and social commentator Jules Simon, whose widely read *L'Ouvrière* (1860) articulated the moral dangers of women's industrial work and famously deemed *l'ouvrière* (the female worker) the opposite of a woman.[39] Unlike the sheer inconceivability of bourgeois women working, however, the problem of working-class women, subject to the same domestic ideal, lay in their *need* to work. Because of this necessity, they were also, by

Figure 1.3 Anon. "La Voix de la foule," n.d., Musée Carnavalet, CC0 Paris Musées/Carnavalet Museum—*History of Paris.*

definition, thrust into a morally suspect category, as they no longer remained in the domestic realm to fulfill foremost their family obligations. These two applications of the ideology in many ways defied logic and reality, and yet they remained powerful and pervasive throughout the century, reinforcing a cultural imaginary that conceived of all middle-class women as ladies of leisure and all working-class women as belonging to the same category as ladies of the night.

According to contemporary commentators, working-class women, particularly those in the needle trades, the most common industry for women, were especially susceptible to lapsing into venal behavior, both because of their poverty and because of their proximity to and supposed desire for luxury.[40] Three decades after the publication of the influential *L'Ouvrière*, Simon supplied the preface to a primer for working-class schoolgirls written by L.-Ch. Desmaisons and titled *"Tu seras ouvrière."* It is clear from Simon's tone and references in this short preface that his view of the woman worker had not much evolved by century's end.[41] In spite of his characterization of Desmaisons's book as *aimable* (helpful, pleasant) and despite his endorsement of the trajectory of its wholesome protagonist towards a professional life in the fashion sector as a model for young working women, his preface ends with the same sentiment that had dominated his bestseller from the mid-century: "I don't find them [women] much to my taste except at home, taking care of others rather than themselves, charged with making them happy through their care and making them virtuous through their lessons and examples."[42] The tenacity of this domestic, maternal ideal cannot be overstated, even if the primer itself offers the story of a working woman's pathway towards successful professionalization. Tellingly, the story ends in marriage.[43]

The didactic narrative doubles as a school manual whose intended use was to inculcate moral behavior in young girls aspiring to become successful dressmakers, seamstresses, or *modistes*. The story, shot through with lessons in history, botany, geography, and other school subjects (it was, after all, a school primer), describes the life of Jeanne Bernard, a fictionalized peasant girl with whom young female pupils could identify, and who would serve as a moral example and a model for girls to emulate in order to succeed in the profession. Taught to sew by her grandmother, Jeanne apprentices first with the village seamstress, but when her extraordinary skill becomes apparent and surpasses the needs of her village's consumers, she is taken on in the neighboring town of Périgueux by a *vieille demoiselle modiste* (106). This descriptor offers a key detail that reflects an important relationship between women's civil status and their propensity to work professionally. Mademoiselle Irma Chardon's characterization as a *vieille demoiselle* ("old maid") indicates that her civil status is unmarried. Craig and others have pointed out that marriage inhibited women from pursuing work goals, as married women were legally prohibited from working unless expressly authorized by their husbands; unmarried or widowed women thus had more freedom in this regard.[44] Indeed, laws governing work and in particular restricting married women's rights to work had been initiated with the Code Civil enacted by Napoléon I in 1804. "Under the Civil Code, unmarried women (widows and spinsters) could manage their affairs as they saw fit once they were of age (21). Married women, on the other hand, fell under the *puissance maritale*—their husband's authority, which for all practical purposes meant they were retrograded to the status of a minor."[45]

It seems likely that there is a causal link between the contrasting situation of married and single women and the high percentage of singles among working women.[46] As Sweitzer has elaborated, the *femme majeure* (unmarried adult woman) and certain widows had more autonomy than their married counterparts, and this may explain in part the non-traditional civil status of many of the working women I discuss in this book. As we shall see in chapter 2, many *modistes* of the nineteenth century, whether fictional or historical, were indeed either single or widowed. Likewise, the civil status of the three journalists I study in chapter 3 is also instructive in this regard: one was divorced, another separated, a third never married.[47] Finally, of the two artist-sisters I write about in chapter 4, one, Anaïs Toudouze, was widowed, and the other, Héloïse Leloir, the wife of an artist, likely did not face the same rigid social codes of women's professional behavior that most bourgeois women would have endured. In any case, women who were not restricted by the legal implications of marriage were more apt to successfully pursue professional careers in all three areas of the fashion sector, thus suggesting that some kinds of work possibly offered favorable alternatives to marriage.

In Mademoiselle Chardon's shop, it becomes clear not only that Jeanne's skill exceeds that of the other workers in the *atelier*, but also that her moral rectitude distinguishes her as superior. Indeed, before Jeanne even leaves her village, we learn that she has been deeply influenced by her teacher, Mademoiselle Vallette, who, having learned about life in the *atelier* from her seamstress mother, warns Jeanne to "choose her friends well," presumably knowing from proximity "what it costs to be weak, lazy, loose and flirty."[48] Jeanne succeeds in Périgueux, and moves to Paris, where, after struggling to find steady work (here the text takes on the piecing system), and by proving her skill and morality once again, Jeanne eventually rises to become the *patronne* (boss) of a large couture house. It is, of course, an unlikely tale, but one that was nonetheless possible, as Simon insists, with a dash of brutal realism thrown in: "Yes, my girl; there has been someone for whom this beautiful dream was a reality; the same adventure could recur; but you must not believe it will recur often. Most workers remain workers."[49]

The primer repeatedly reiterates the twin keys to Jeanne's success—her unparalleled skill with a needle and, perhaps with even greater emphasis, her moral righteousness. This insistence begs the question of contemporary views of these women's moral standing and exposes the power of the stereotype. As Jeanne's apprenticeship progresses, she is repeatedly and favorably compared to the other young girls of the *atelier*, many of whom are described as morally lax: "There were young workers, flirty and vain, who had no scruples about measuring off a piece of ribbon from their clients' belts and cutting lace to save a piece for themselves."[50] Their vanity is directly linked to the petty theft they repeatedly engage in. In Paris, when first hired in a large fashion enterprise, Jeanne apprentices again in the different departments of the business. Notably, her experience during the three months she spends with the *modistes* in the *atelier* confirms the by now standard view of *modistes* as the most flirtatious of fashion workers: "In the workshops of the big cities, young women imagine that they prove their taste by their exaggerated coquettishness. They are sorely mistaken. This belief is especially widespread among *modistes* and flower makers ... These women tarnish their own reputations and even that of the house they work for."[51] The text suggests that *modistes*, in particular, intentionally engaged in flirtatious behaviors and adorned themselves coquettishly in order to present themselves *both* as fashionable *and* as transmitters of fashionability. In other words, the suggestion is that, no matter how frowned upon by the pious author of the primer, this behavior was in fact a marketing strategy. This explanation, grounded in these women's own entrepreneurial self-interest, was eclipsed, however, by the pervasive myth that fashion workers, and *modistes* in particular, were more interested in seducing middle-class men than seducing potential (female) customers into making purchases.

In the epilogue, the narrator reiterates the underlying moral lesson of his primer, insisting that Jeanne's moral rectitude and sober self-presentation are more common among women workers than they may realize. For these successful, morally upright, skilled dressmakers and *modistes* are not less numerous, just less visible than their "looser" sisters: "For those who aren't so loud show themselves rarely. You don't meet them in the street in dresses of garish colors, talking at the top of their voice and laughing loudly to attract attention."[52] Unlike the flirtatious and flashy fashion workers, these righteous girls and women supposedly remain silent and out of sight. In reality, however, righteous or not, they are overshadowed all the same by the very pervasive stereotype that made all fashion workers into women who were always, somehow, at least potentially sexually available, thus reinforcing the stereotype.

For working-class women, then, and for *modistes* in particular, who are the working-class subjects of my study, in addition to the processes of capitalism's veiling, the veiling of work proceeded from the presumption of the fashion worker's sexual promiscuity, her reputed laziness and unproductive flirtatiousness. A caricature from 1826, entitled "Ex-Modiste," aptly illustrates this presumption and spotlights the ambitious *modiste*, who has achieved her presumed goal of consumer status by ensnaring a man with status, even as it preemptively illustrates a scene from Fontaney's 1832 tale (figure 1.4). In this image, with a "decorated" officer at her side, the former *modiste* seems to have acquired all the accoutrements of a well-heeled and respectable urban female shopper: in short, she has crossed over to the other side. A cashmere shawl and a parasol are toted by her gallant companion, a servant follows at a discreet distance to carry her new purchases, and, as her crowning glory, an extravagant blue feathered *toque* hat is artfully tilted on her head.[53] This hat is an embellished version of the plain pink and blue *toques* that the *modistes* are placing on stands for their window display. Now on the outside looking in, this *ex-modiste* catches the gaze of her former colleagues at work in the shop in a kind of mirroring that stages the aspirational mythology of the *modiste*. In a gesture that connects the circulating commodities of the image, from within the *atelier*, the *modistes*, unmistakable in their black work aprons, point and stare through the vitrine at the glorious apotheosis of their presumed social fantasy.

Figure 1.4 S. Paul, *"Ex-modiste,"* Scène Parisienne, *no. 2. Paris, 1826, The British Museum.*

The cultural myth surrounding this figure—that she was flirtatious and pursued social advancement through sexual relations with powerful men—was so omnipresent throughout the nineteenth century that it recast these women's real lives of work and their professionalization as sensational and sentimental tales. Theirs was a work life that can nonetheless be documented, however faintly, in alternative archival materials, which I will consider in chapter 2. As Desmaisons's primer, idealized though it is, nonetheless demonstrates, sexual liaisons and marriage possibilities were not the exclusive pathway for such women to achieve social mobility. The visual and textual mythology of the *modiste*—the kind of representational veil on full display in figure 1.4—obscures other narratives, however. Just as the elaborately constructed and ornamented hat concealed its own constructed-ness, reinforcing the seamless elegance of the consumer who possessed it and disavowing the female labor that produced it, so too did the myth of the *modiste* conceal the fact of her labor. The hidden seam of fashion thus transforms the leisured consumer into an object to be seen and admired; the labor that made it possible must also remain hidden so that the commodity object can be seen as seamless and effortless.

While that myth, propagated in pictures and texts, exercised a mighty and lasting influence over perceptions of the fashion worker, other mythologies, reinforced both discursively and visually, made it nearly inconceivable that bourgeois women might work. In its affirmation of bourgeois femininity, the fashion plate served as a reversed pendant of the prolific print culture surrounding the *modiste*, which promulgated the erotic mythology that defined this figure for a century. Taken together, both of these representational veils, similar to their discursive companions, occluded the productive labor that women of both classes engaged in. The power and prevalence of these ideological forms notwithstanding, the women accomplishing the work sometimes engaged in concealing practices of their own, however. Before turning to this ironic veiling—the ways in which these women strategically participated in the dissimulation of their own work—I will return to the commodity exemplified in the "magical" object staged by Fontaney in his story of a bonnet.

Fetishizing Commodities

Thus far, I have been focusing primarily on the ideological motivations for the concealment of women's work. I turn now to the self-veiling mechanisms through which that concealment occurred: first, by considering the ways in which commodities themselves—whether material, discursive, or representational—often functioned to hide the construction of fashion by women working in the industry; and second, by considering the complicity of the very women performing the labor to make fashion's products. Both literary and visual culture illustrate that the object of production in a consumer context, particularly a fashion product, assumed powers that allowed it to overshadow, and sometimes even erase altogether, the workers who made it. The commodity—whether an ethereal hat, an authoritative editorial, or an exquisite fashion plate—exerted enormous power over consumers, who were often also collectors of these products, a gesture that further increased the fetishistic power of the object. The concealment of labor was key to amplifying fashion's mystique, its magical power, for the seamlessness of fashion's creations conformed to the presumption that those who indulged in it were also seamlessly fashionable.

Fontaney's tale illustrates the seamless fabrication of the fashion product and the transfer of that coveted seamlessness to the consumer. Back in the *atelier*, after a whirlwind of frenetic measuring, twisting, and gathering of the gauzy fabric, the *première modiste* cuts with confidence, while her attendants, the *demoiselles de magasin* (shop-girls), who are sometimes referred to, in a metonymic reduction that creates anonymity, as *petites mains* (little hands), take up the various tasks she gives them—forming the cap, the frame, and the borders of the *capote*, those isolated components of what will shortly become an artistic whole.[54] In a kind of pre-industrial and semi-mechanized production line, each of the nameless *agiles travailleuses* (nimble workers) has a task to complete, using scissors and long needles to manipulate cardboard, rough canvas, and metallic braiding into the "frame and scaffolding" upon which the *modiste* will realize her artistic vision.[55] While the narrator's description mentions the labors of the fashion workers and suggests that at least seven of them are involved in the construction of this object, only the *première*, the author tells us, is capable of "giving it the breath of life."[56] The narrator thus implies that the expert *modiste* has the power to *animate* the inanimate, a feat that communicates both the *modiste*'s skill and the outsized importance of this particular fashion object, the lady's hat, to the successful *toilette* of the respectable female consumer. Within fifteen minutes, the hat has taken shape; the *modiste* makes the final adjustments, and with her large needle "succeeds in indissolubly uniting with a few stitches the two main parts of the hat."[57] To finish, she attaches floral and ribbon embellishments to her creation.[58]

For all of her artistry and her superiority to the other fashion workers of the *atelier*, this is not the story of a *modiste*. Rather, as its title signals, "Story of a Bonnet" is the tale of a *capote*, and in a larger sense, it is also the story of hidden but potent female labor in the nineteenth century, the story I wish to tell in this book. No sooner has Fontaney-Feeling placed our *modiste* at the center of his description than does she recede behind the hat as if to illustrate the ascendancy of the commodity. Indeed, once this creation has been placed on a stand in the window after its tumultuous birth, its life force takes on even greater proportions when it enters the realm of consumption. Along comes a couple, and when the young wife spots the extravagant hat in the window, Lord Feeling, "in a single glance had discovered the secret relations of affinity that existed between the young woman and our lilac tulle hat."[59] The commodity fetish has been identified. Convincing her reluctant and stingy husband to make the purchase, the young woman succumbs to "the seduction of this magic headpiece," whose power only increases as it exits the shop on her head, her old straw hat discarded at the shop. More seductive than any man, the commodity's power expands as it enters the public space: like a young socialite, it is "launched." As the husband strolls from the shopping hub of the rue Vivienne to the center of masculine financial activity, the place de la Bourse, his "pretty wife on his arm," he gazes at her indulgently, pleased to show her off like his own accessory attesting to his social and financial success. "This fragile headpiece that we just witnessed being formed thread by thread, ribbon by ribbon, flower by flower—there it is now launched into the world atop such a charming head, but one having barely more brains than the *modistes*' dolls."[60] The affectively charged hat, which is greater than its component parts, has not only usurped its creator, but it also eclipses its wearer and assumes an important position in society as it swallows up the young woman, who is reduced to her head alone and assimilated to a *modiste*'s inanimate doll, or head form (*marotte*)—a tool that serves in the creative work of millinery.

The tale ends with a dramatic flourish and a classically misogynistic message. Lord Feeling is promptly dismissed by Madame de Saint-Clair's maid, who claims that her mistress is indisposed; but as the *flâneur* makes his way along the street, a sudden rainstorm interrupts his progress, forcing him to shelter in the doorway of the same *modiste*'s shop he had spied upon earlier. His perspective disconcertingly reversed, Lord Feeling observes the tragic dénouement of the *capote*, now reduced to tatters by the downpour—"it was no longer a hat, it was nothing"— as the once eager shopper, her new purchase ruined, returns to the shop to retrieve the modest straw hat she had replaced with the magical *capote*. Simultaneously, our narrator spots his two-timing mistress dressed for an evening at the Opéra, as she hops into a carriage with "a very handsome Polish officer."[61] He philosophically concludes that the fragility of women's emotional attachments is equivalent to that of their delicate and beautiful hats: "Madame de Saint-Clair had loved me for three days. The tulle hat had lasted three hours."[62]

Beneath the comic social satire that ensures the panoramic genre's popularity, however, lies a more complex set of messages, not necessarily intended by the author of this light-hearted text. Lord Feeling, omnipotent at the story's beginning, is cast away by its end, rejected by a *woman* who has the power to replace him—as if he were an outdated hat—with a shiny new model. Counter to the trope of women as exchangeable commodities in a patriarchal economy, a reading that reaches beyond Lord Feeling's misogynist conclusions suggests the theme of female agency just beneath the surface of this tale, revealing that it is here actually Lord Feeling who is reduced to a replaceable commodity. With the realization that he has become interchangeable, even disposable, our narrator turns to a kind of defensive projection through which he reduces women (consumers of hats, consumers of lovers) to *marottes*, that is, inhuman dolls—a far cry from the artistic, pensive, and creative force that defined the *modiste* at the story's outset. The commodity has successfully usurped male power, as well, then, for women are seduced by and desire these commodities more than they desire men. The "secret relations of affinity" between consumer and commodity have effectively replaced actual human relations. The hapless husband, Lord Feeling's bourgeois double, exists merely to provide the money for his wife's purchase, which he initially resists but to which he ultimately succumbs. Likewise, Lord Feeling naïvely awaits his mistress, serving as a placeholder until he is supplanted by the more handsome Polish officer, a rejection that he is powerless to prevent. Lord Feeling's feelings having thus been bruised, he finds solace in dehumanizing and demoting women—both producers and consumers of fashion—by animating and elevating the hat. His defensive narration thus reveals that it is not much of a leap to find a motive, however deeply buried in a cultural unconscious, for the erasure of the autonomy and creativity that potentially animated some women's labor.

Yet the run-of-the-mill misogyny of this story masks something more unusual here. We have seen how this text illustrates the transformation of the fashion product into a commodity fetish, revealing that fashion's success depends in large part on the commodity's erasure of the labor expended to produce it. However, the commodity is not acting alone, as it were. Whatever hint of female agency might have seemed possible is quickly shut down, just as the *modiste* as creative agent disappears from view as she leaves the shop to meet her boyfriend. For the strong cultural bias against women working and potentially achieving some degree of autonomy and expertise through that work produced forms of masking that obscured working women's important place in the fashion economy. Fontaney's fictionalized depiction claims to offer an objective window into the activities of the *atelier* and the material reality of the components of hat making: he literally peers through their wide vitrine. But what seems to be a window is, in fact, a perceptual veil, gauzy and distorting, created by Lord Feeling's own distinctly male subject position. It is an ideological position that repeats the preeminent mythology of the *modiste*, a mythology that, as we have seen, relies upon the well-worn cliché of the sexy fashion worker and that inclines us to see only her erotic commodification rather than her productive labor. For the story's *modistes*—whether *petites mains* or *première*—have all become erotic objects of consumption for the voyeur-narrator who presents the spectacle of women as commodities in his narration: "There were eight young, beautiful girls, some sitting nonchalantly, nearly sleeping, others standing, fresh-faced, with bright eyes, roaring with laughter, singing and chatting with abandon."[63] Lovely, unguarded, they appear through the window as so many pretty hats to be admired and purchased. Even the *première*, we learn, has left the shop for the evening for a tryst with her *calicot* boyfriend, thus doubling Madame de Saint-Clair's own amorous rendezvous; indeed, Madame de Saint-Clair, living as she does in the rue Vivienne, might even be perceived as the *ex-modiste* herself, the figure the *première* and all the other *modistes* of the shop presumably aspire to become.[64]

Thus, in a familiar discursive move, Fontaney's description of the work environment of the *modistes* offers no discussion of squalor or long hours, no mention of harsh mistresses, nothing about sexual predation, nor any description of the arduous labor of stitching tiny, fragile decorations onto a stiff fabric.[65] Instead, *modistes* and their work are idealized—in fact, the hat seems to materialize out of thin air—and the hat-commodity quickly effaces its creator, disavowing her labor and the conditions surrounding it, to become "magical," a descriptor that would permeate discourse about hats for over a century. In fact, the hat becomes a *phénomène vivant*—a living phenomenon—as the illustrator Numa's caricature (figure 1.5), published in the same year as Fontaney's story (1832), aptly demonstrates. This

Figure 1.5 *Numa (Pierre Numa Bassaget), "Phénomène vivant," 1832, Elke Rehder Collection.*

caricature exposes the disproportionate power of fashion commodities to usurp their human wearers, not to mention erase their human (mostly female) creators, and, in so doing, to express and enact social relations.

Numa's illustration exposes a process similar to that of Fontaney's story, except that here, rather than showing the interior of the workspace, all eyes are focused on the other side of the vitrine, the social space of the consumer where labor is no longer pictured at all. The image depicts three bourgeois subjects—one man and two women—apparently enjoying a chance social encounter while strolling in a park-like urban environment, as signaled by paving stones and distant trees. Numa's lady's hat, worn by the smugly smiling woman who is the focal point of the image, takes center stage and is clearly the *phénomène vivant* designated by the title of the picture. For the lady in the small *capote* draped in a blue shawl ignores her smiling acquaintance, focusing all of her straining attention instead on the towering hat. She leans forward with an upward gaze approaching adulation, her hands open as if supplicating this extraordinary object. The gentleman escorting the fantastically hatted lady seems to enjoy the hat's effect as much as his companion does, as he looks on with prideful pleasure. He replicates visually the husband of Fontaney's story, who seems to accept the extravagance of his purchase once he pridefully strolls the streets, displaying his female accessory as he makes his way to the Bourse. Admiration for the hat ultimately redounds to him, even as it graces his wife's head. Like Fontaney's story, Numa's image illustrates how social relations are fully mediated through the commodity.

The hat itself warrants the designation of *phénomène*, which suggests "extraordinary," "rare," rooted in the Greek "that which appears," and it thus parallels the "magical" apparition of the hat in the *atelier*. This hat too is a feast for the eyes: apparently constructed of fine straw, its *calotte*, or cap, is exaggerated into a large tubular point and is decorated with two immense blue ribbons, one at the tip and the other jauntily set to the side, artfully placed to complement the hat's crowning glory. Three white feathers, one simply enormous, protrude from the blue bow, adding approximately three feet to the lady's height. The manipulation of scale is typical of caricature, whether verbal or visual; if, in Fontaney's story, the hat's powers are verbally exaggerated ("utterly resplendent and utterly glorious"; "this magical headpiece"), in Numa's illustration, the artist performs a similar operation by graphically representing a hat that exceeds the bounds of realistic size and decoration.[66]

Numa's caricatural hat reveals what is actually lurking under the surface of a typical social encounter: while posing as occasions for small talk and polite admiration, such encounters are in fact occasions for gawking with both envy and desire. The "living" (*vivant*) aspect of this hat dwells partly in the residue of life referenced by the elegantly swaying feathers, one of which is a *plume d'autruche* (ostrich feather), the most coveted of hat ornaments. For hats were routinely festooned with "natural" embellishments—flowers, feathers—and made to look as though they were organic objects. Also, and more important, the entire hat overwhelms—even commandeers—the identity of the lady who wears it, such that her female acquaintance no longer sees *her* but only the "living" thing atop her head.

Numa ridicules the excesses of contemporary fashion, and his punning title *phénomène vivant* applies equally satirically to the female subjects who fall under fashion's spell—akin to Fontaney's shopper recast as a *modiste*'s dummy. For the phrase *phénomène vivant* also denotes a circus attraction, and it is but a short step from the gawking consumer to the ogling spectator. This image thus encapsulates fashion's spectacle and points to the strength of the commodity to overwhelm the very people, and system, that produce and consume it.[67]

As the hat becomes a living thing, the woman who wears it suffers de-animation, or, at least, as the title suggests, extreme objectification in the form of a sideshow marvel. In this scenario, she becomes the accessory of her escort, even as he is ridiculously depicted as well with his dandified posture, corseted torso, and absurdly large lapels and collar. The fact that she, hyper-accessorized as she is, becomes *his* accessory is one of the morals of this visual story, as in Fontaney's. Here again, the fashion commodity may *seem* to remove men from the transaction; but ultimately, men are still the primary beneficiaries of women's assimilation to commodities.[68]

Gender is thus seen to reinforce fashion's dazzling spectacle. As a hyperbolic social symbol of femininity, the woman's hat offers a miniature, yet exaggerated, version of a dress. Like a dress, this luxury commodity, concealing its seams, pins, glue, and thread, is also removed from its conditions of production—it is thus the commodity fetish par excellence. Defying its use value through its excesses and hiding the labor expended to create it, we have seen that the commodity assumes a social dimension. Considered as such, it is endowed with powers (social, economic) that ought to accrue to the workers who made it but that are instead attributed to the inanimate object—a hat. It was the very seamlessness of a product such as a lady's hat that elevated its status; recall the invisible stitching of Fontaney's *modiste* as she attaches the *capote*'s brim to its *calotte*, the part of the hat that hugs the head.[69] As Desmaisons's primer details, the *modiste* must learn how to conceal her work: "There [in the *atelier*] she learned to size the lining of the hats' wide brims and to place it so that there would be no folds, in such a way that it seemed glued and not sewn to the form. She was taught how to make fabric tubes and smocking with tiny stitches so close together that once the hat was prepared in this way, it was impossible to know where or how it had been sewn."[70] Seams, folds, and stitches vanish; artificial flowers seem fresher than natural ones; realistic, if exotic, bird feathers suggest the object might even take wing; and straw is so delicate that it appears to be fabric. The apparent organicity of the hat is purely constructed, though, and its "natural" features contribute handily to the erasure of labor, producing the fantasy that the lady's hat, naturally occurring, has taken on a life of its own.

The erasure of the signs of the hat's fabrication and, indeed, of work more generally is equally striking in the many advertisements and illustrations of ladies' hats over the course of the nineteenth century in the fashion press, where the object is portrayed in all of its magical glory, divorced from the elements and processes of its creation, free-floating and often independent even from the heads of the

Figure 1.6 *"Costumes Parisiens,"* May 30, 1832, Bibliothèque nationale de France.

women who purchased it. This image (figure 1.6), like thousands of others, evokes just such an erasure. For here, fine lace, ribbons, feathers, and artificial flowers ornament each hat's *calotte*. All of these embellishing items would have been crafted by secondary artisans—lacemakers (*dentellières*), ribbon makers (*fabricants de rubans*), feather workers (*plumassiers*), and flower makers (*fleuristes*)—none of whom are credited with or appropriately remunerated for their laborious, and sometimes dangerous, artisanal work.[71] This labor had to be concealed so that the consumer would not suspect that she too—assimilated to the fashions she wore—was constructed and formed by a fashion system that disavowed its own manipulation of fantasy and aspiration.

The anonymity and thus the erasure of these fashion workers increased the mystique of the luxury commodity whose only signature it would bear (if any) was that of the *maîtresse-modiste*. Only the *maîtresse-modiste*—in this case, Madame Lepetit with a shop at no. 1 rue Grange Batalière—is identifiable; as the shop owner, she has ascended to a position of ownership, possibly having risen through the ranks of the anonymous *modistes* herself, as outlined in Desmaisons's primer.[72] Like the "magical" fashion product, the brand or label would also be commodified over time, usually denoted by a single name, termed *la griffe de mode* (literally, "fashion's claw") in early nineteenth-century French parlance.[73] For it was her task (or that of her *première*) to combine these dainty items in artful ways, explicitly hiding the processes of fabrication to produce a fashion article that seems to have effortlessly sprouted lace and flowers, feathers and silk, as if through a natural process. Thread and glue are invisible, concealed beneath layers of ruffles, bouquets of fake blooms, and exotic plumes; in later decades, whole stuffed birds would be arranged upon hats mimicking flight and offering an exaggerated example of the "ambiguity of in/animateness" characteristic of fashion.[74] Each of these fashion products seems to hover disconcertingly between natural and artificial, animate and inanimate, disavowing its own "created-ness" and thus, also, its creators.

The head is not shown in illustrations such as these, and yet the objects themselves, suspended in mid-air, are depicted in ways that suggest movement, animation, life. In fact, the object seems to be saturated with living qualities, thus enhancing consumer desire and allowing consumers to imagine filling the empty shells of hats and clothing. Thus, held out to the shopper is a fantasy that through consumption she will in fact *become* her hat, become the fashionable thing herself, the fetish object imbued with its power. As the hat acquires vitality, the consumer in turn becomes infinitely replaceable, in effect reversing the hierarchy between animate and inanimate. Ultimately, in a gesture that is only too familiar from contemporary fashion practices, both the producers and the consumers of fashion become interchangeable as the commodity itself gains importance.[75] Like a paper doll whose outfits can change with the fold of a flap, the consumer becomes a prop, a full-body *marotte* or mannequin.[76] The fashion worker, expert creator of lifelike accessories, who worked to enhance the hat's seductive powers, disappears behind the myth of the *modiste*, thus effectively collaborating with the commodity that supplants her.

Clothing items, or material commodities such as the lady's hat, however, were not the only commodities capable of exerting a powerful influence over the social and economic marketplace. Nor were *modistes* (and other fashion workers) the only women engaged in the creation of the nineteenth-century fashion system. Other key commodities, less apparently material but powerful nonetheless, also contributed to the wild success of the nineteenth-century Parisian fashion economy; and other women, concealed behind discursive and representational veils of their own making, worked to build that economy and make a place for themselves outside of domesticity, outside of the bourgeois feminine ideal their work aimed to promote and upon which it depended. Ironically, then, commodification in fact enabled certain women to achieve lives outside of the domestic sphere. It is to these other commodities—and these other working women—that I now turn.

Framing Material Commodities

Beyond the hats, dresses, and other wearable items that constitute fashion's principal commodities, visual and verbal commodities also operated within the nineteenth-century fashion system. Fashion plates (*gravures de mode*) and fashion columns (*chroniques de mode*) were also laboriously produced and consumed as valuable commodities, usually by women. Fashion plates functioned as virtual shop windows, displaying goods that could be purchased or commissioned, to be sure, but also conjuring aspirational fantasies that held their viewers in thrall. Further, such images achieved broad circulation and authority in the mid-nineteenth century, when professional illustrators perfected visual marketing to the extent that the plates themselves became nearly as valued and collectible as the garments and accessories they represented. These pictures offered visual fantasies that whetted burgeoning consumer appetites and circulated globally to consolidate the Parisian monopoly on nineteenth-century ladies' fashion.[77]

Likewise, fashion columns, which were originally penned by male editors, had by the 1830s become the domain of educated women forging professional career paths in fashion writing. Parallel to the fashion plates, these columns enjoyed a wide and loyal readership and exercised the power to create trends, enforce social behaviors, and significantly bolster subscriptions for their publishers. Readers hung on every word these "oracles" of fashion uttered, and fashion journals came into their own when publishers realized how lucrative the information they offered—priceless advice and insider tips—proved to their publishing houses. Both groups of women, fashion illustrators and fashion journalists, worked long hours and labored carefully over a product that appeared as seamless as a lady's hat. In both cases—illustration and journalism—the women who did the work did so ostensibly in the service of an ideal of bourgeois femininity that their own lifestyle contested. The work itself provided pathways to professionalism (entrepreneurship, art, writing) that would most likely otherwise have remained closed to them.

While not literally identifiable as commodities in the way hats or dresses could be, fashion plates and fashion columns as products nonetheless followed a similar logic of disavowing, or even erasing, the intensity of the work required for their production. Like bespoke clothing, these products also appeared effortless—seamless, as it were—and exerted tremendous power over consumers. The labor, both intellectual and physical, that produced fashion columns and fashion plates—research, travel, drafting, editing, choosing, sketching, painting, printing, supervising, and so forth—thus disappeared behind the discursive and representational power of these commodities. The women who for the most part created these commodities, fashion journalists and fashion illustrators, essential to the rapid, successful expansion of the nineteenth-century French fashion industry, were similarly hidden, remaining largely unacknowledged. At the same time, the fictionalized, glamorous personae and splendid visual scenes of bourgeois leisure, cultivated by each group of women, carefully concealed the work required to produce fashion's fantasy.

Fashion plates celebrated and constructed fashionable women as spectacular objects to be consumed. Their content repeats familiar scenarios: women's idealized bodies are posed in various spaces of nineteenth-century bourgeois leisure—parks, shops, museums, opera houses, balls, drawing rooms—dressed in order to evoke an activity, a season, or an event, and almost always in the company of other women (although most likely, there was only a single model posing for all of the women pictured).[78] They stage social negotiation in various vignettes—conversing, strolling, visiting, reading, child-rearing, flirting, ball-going, and even shopping. They also serve as social negotiators themselves among consumers and merchants and producers (of both plates and products). Plates usually depict multiple views of dresses to display the design skill of the dress and hat designers. The artist strove to recreate the sensuous quality of fabrics—velvets, silks, laces, feathers, etc.—thus increasing the desirability of garments that conferred status and beauty on their wearer. As aspirational images, then, fashion plates (re)produced beauty and behavioral ideals for a nascent consuming bourgeois public anxious to emulate those in upper classes.[79]

Most fashion historians agree that fashion plates represented the first form of fashion advertisement, inspiring desire and persuading purchase through their deft deployment of exquisite colors and accurate renderings of fabrics and cuts, while offering key textual information as well: names and addresses of shops and vocabulary for identifying trends, fabrics, and accessories.[80] They also exercised a directive or even a disciplinary function; while it is certain that fashion plates served to indicate which trends were popular, or about to become so, they also offered pertinent information to a widening group of bourgeois readers who were anxious to learn both how to dress and how to behave in social circles perceived as superior to their own. The discourse accompanying fashion plates often drove this messaging, with fashion chroniclers voicing strong opinions about what was or was not appropriate for various occasions and social settings, thus becoming, in effect, authoritative tastemakers for legions of aspirational readers.[81] These functions—persuasion and discipline—support the commercial aim of the plate, encouraging consumption by creating desire and dictating appropriate dress and behavior by modeling and reproducing these in vivid color.

As both advertisements and aesthetic objects, fashion plates were communicative, collected, and commodified. In their function as advertisements, they transmitted practical information, which is evinced by the descriptive captions typically found along the bottom edge of the images (see figures 1.1, 1.2, and 1.6). Fashion plates were also collectible, frequently removed from the journal in which they appeared for collection in albums or display on walls.[82] Some publishers of fashion journals recognized the value of the collectability of these plates and made albums available for purchase by wealthy subscribers. Marie Bonin, in her study of the Colin sisters, refers to plates in the archives in Rouen that show signs of having been tacked to walls as "decoration of personal spaces."[83] Demonstrating the degree to which fashion plates were cherished by consumers, or maybe manipulated by seamstresses, the plates themselves might even sometimes be embellished.

For example, as pictured in figure 1.7, a framed fashion plate by Anaïs Toudouze, printed for the journal *Le Magasin des demoiselles*, has been enhanced to include sewn fabric, lace, ribbons, and knots, to approximate a three-dimensional version of the print. This curious object attests to an avid interest in, and indeed fetishizing of, the plate itself.[84] In the lower right-hand corner, opposite the signature of the original artist Anaïs Toudouze (Colin), we find simply "Jeanne"—the name of the embellisher, we must assume. Remarkably, "Jeanne" inserts her own signature alongside those of the artist and the lithographer, thus adding her authorship, or creative identity, to her palimpsestic gesture of embellishment. The fashion plate artist has already asserted her authority and creative identity by applying a fine arts tradition (the signature) to commercial art. She thus resists the anonymizing process that typically characterized this genre, especially for women artists working in the field. The quite literal "material" embellishment of the visual object collapses material and representational registers and emphasizes the overlapping structures of fashion's networks, even as it illustrates in a most unusual way the power and pleasures of the commodity.

There can be no doubt that fashion plates were important drivers of the fashion industry, and their unusual patterns of collectability attest to the influence they exercised. Likewise, the fashion columns accompanying these images offered greater insight into not only the procurement of the pictured items, but also their social deployment. The journal itself became a commodity, and the journalists who labored to produce it hid their work behind other identities—personifications of the values the journal aimed to endorse and projections of the idealized imagined reader herself. Most often presented as an object created for and possessed by bourgeois and upper-class women, the fashion journal was a prized possession, signaling taste and distinction. In a column from the 1840s, Marie de l'Epinay, an early fashion journalist, demonstrates this positioning of the journal as a commodity

Figure 1.7 *Jeanne. Embellished fashion plate by Anaïs Toudouze,* Magasin des demoiselles, *Laura Gail Diamond and Judith Lipnick, private collection.*

indicative of status: "*La Sylphide*, with its tasteful fashion plates, its distinguished literary articles, has become the obligatory ornament of all libraries, and there isn't a single chatelaine who doesn't want to make room for it among the elite books that cover the shelves of the well-read turret of her manor house!"[85] These discursive commodities were thus also highly valued, and accounted for the success of numerous nineteenth-century publishing houses. The textual description was indeed crucial, and in the space between image and word, in the communicative dialogue between representation and discourse, aspiration could nearly be transformed into reality.[86]

The women who wrote these journals into existence, who ascribed value to goods, had the power to make or break the value of a fashion product, but what is less visible are the long hours spent meeting deadlines and visiting shops to evaluate goods. Rather than display their toil, they labored to make their work appear effortless, their columns simply a byproduct of their contrived lifestyle. The three representative fashion journalists I discuss in chapter 3—Jeanne-Justine Fouqueau de Pussy (J. J.), Olympe Vallée (*la vicomtesse de* Renneville), and Emmeline Raymond—each developed and maintained large fan bases or what we would view today as "followers." Their likenesses could be purchased, they sustained active correspondences with subscribers, and they were celebrated and mourned upon their passing. Raymond, editor-in-chief of *La Mode illustrée*, even cultivated a back-page column that anticipates today's social media in its brevity and bridging of public and private discourse.[87] Most important, however, in assessing the commodity value of their activity, their expert advice, both behavioral and fashion-oriented, was considered valuable enough to keep them at the helm of the fashion publications of some of the most powerful publishing groups of the nineteenth century: the Thierry family, *Le Figaro*, and the Didot-frères. Each journalist was selected by management, her reputation cultivated and authoritative.

Fashion journals and the women columnists and illustrators who animated them were central catalysts of the modern fashion economy. In the virtual space of their pages, products and prose interacted and delighted, exciting the consumer appetites of readers across Europe and over the ocean.[88] Their serializing strategies ensured a stable readership, and their advertising practices, a continuous flow of income and new goods to publicize. The journals themselves contributed to the production of these objects as commodities, since what was pictured or described on the page was presented as consumable and thus exchangeable, belonging to a lifestyle that was staged and promoted in the pages of the journal. Similar to the tangible, and relatively new, spaces of the urban department store, it was in the virtual marketplace of the fashion journal that these items gained currency, became fashionable, or fell out of favor. In the nineteenth century, fashion columns and fashion plates, then, were both commodities that adhered to a logic similar to that of other fashion products, such as the lady's hat. For, like fashion's material commodities, they too were laboriously produced, appearing seamless such that the labor expended to create them disappeared.

Like *modistes*, who in some ways manipulated the myth concocted by the cultural imaginary around their activities to ensure their success, women fashion journalists, the so-called *modistes des lettres*, also hid behind cultivated media personae that contributed, by design, to the erasure of their own labor.[89] Fashion plate artists engaged in a similar ironic move—working hard to promote a bourgeois feminine ideal upon which fashion's success depended, in their case producing a representational, rather than discursive, veil, all the while flouting that same ideal by working outside of the academy from which they were excluded, and in the process ensuring that their art would be widely disseminated and viewed. All three groups of women working in the world of fashion labored beneath ideological veils, but the labor of occlusion, of intentional veiling, was also crucial to fashion's success. For fashion's very ostentatiousness, its ornamentalism, was utterly dependent on the seamlessness it exuded and thus on the concealing practices that made seamlessness possible.

Women Crafting Agency

We have seen that despite the erasure of hats' producers, the myth of the *modiste* as coquettish and fashionable remained ubiquitous and, as the 1892 primer suggests, was sometimes even embraced as a strategy by *modistes* themselves in order to achieve professional goals.[90] Likewise, we have seen that fashion columns and fashion plates, through discursive and visual rhetorics, repeated and reproduced an ideology that tied bourgeois women to leisure and domesticity, activities that foreclosed paid work. However, the women who carefully deployed these rhetorics—fashion journalists and illustrators—did so precisely to produce desirable commodities to feed that very belief system. They did so ironically, if sometimes unknowingly, challenging that very ideology through the fact of their own work and participating in what they surely recognized as a burgeoning economy that could offer professional alternatives to marriage and domesticity, as well as gainful employment for those who needed it. Thus, in collusion with the commodity fetish, and in complicity with these forms of idealized femininity, which was both reason and mechanism for labor's concealment, there is an additional layer of concealing that depended entirely on gender.

To extrapolate beyond the magical qualities of the commodity of the lady's hat, so richly displayed in Fontaney's tale, the women working behind the seams—*modistes*, journalists, illustrators—actively engaged in forms of deceptive self-fashioning. In the following chapters, I show that *modistes* often traded on a cultural myth that eroticized them to achieve professional success, stamping the commodity with their erotic imprint. But they also navigated the mythological minefield of their own reputations to achieve quiet but successful professional lives. Women fashion journalists, as well, invented and cultivated sophisticated media personae that concealed their work lives, feigning conformity to ideals that their readers aspired to emulate in order to maintain the fashion system and their place within it.

Women fashion illustrators like the Colin sisters, excluded from the official art world, embraced commercial art careers, creating objects that drew on their fine arts skills while promoting the consumption of a bourgeois feminine ideal they themselves did not wholly enjoy. Because fashion was so closely associated with women, it gave cover to bourgeois women seeking employment as specialists, especially in fields from which they were traditionally excluded. In the nineteenth century the professional worlds of journalism and art were off-limits to women, just as the world of design, such as tailoring, had been closed to women in the previous century. Fashion was the domain where such women could "fashion" a life for themselves with the constricted agency they possessed. These women's collusion with the commodity, then, whether intentional or not, helped them develop their own professionalizing strategies.

In this chapter I have focused on the occlusion of women's labor by the spectacular commodity—in all of its forms—and the ideological veiling that made women's work look like other activities, or even no activity at all. The power of the commodity and of gendered ideologies is only part of the story, however. Other factors also contributed to rendering invisible the labor behind the product, notably women producers' own complicity, even if sometimes oppositional, with the commodity system that demanded their own concealment. The rest of the story is that of the agency of these women, which takes a variety of forms—from resistance and opposition to performance and even collusion. Women working in different occupations, and inhabiting different social classes, necessarily experience different levels of intentionality and exercise different strategies for accomplishing their goals. Simply by working in the atmosphere of a stifling cultural imaginary, *modistes* performed resistance; by engaging in deceptive written performances, women fashion journalists became complicit in the ideologies that excluded women from the very work they, ironically, performed; and by claiming their artistic agency through the signature and referencing "high" art in their commercial products, women fashion plate artists assumed a subtly oppositional position in relation to the image represented in the plates they produced. By studying these commodities and the women who made them, we can arrive at a greater understanding of how nineteenth-century French women were both authors of and authored by a culture that seemed to locate value elsewhere but which actually hinged on these women's passive and active coding. Let us now venture behind the seams to discover these women.

2

Fashion's Fingers: Immodest Modistes

> *Yes, I am a modiste*
> *And to please every Taste,*
> *Both virtuous and wild,*
> *I serve as an artist.*[1]

The fantasmatic world of the Parisian *modiste* is on full display in a satirical print published by Pierre de la Mésangère (figure 2.1) depicting *modistes* "at work" in their *atelier*.[2] Printed during the First Empire and published in *Le Bon Genre*, the picture contains important clues to the popular perception of these fashion workers, as well as the spaces they inhabited and the hats they produced. In this image, the *modistes* are coded as both elegant ladies and erotic objects—creative artisans and disorderly tarts.[3] Their tiny shoes and feet resemble those of popular fashion plates and thus indicate their fashionability as well as their eroticization.[4] But surely the dainty dancing shoes pictured here are not of a kind one would suppose workers could practically wear, in particular those who might have to walk a great deal in the streets, like the *trottin* (errand girl). Likewise, their long, sometimes fingerless gloves, which would certainly call attention to their hands—the primary instruments of their work—nonetheless raise questions about the productivity in which the *modistes* are supposedly engaged, for they wear smart accessories rather than gloves for sewing. How indeed could the *petites mains* of these fashion workers manipulate ribbon and glue, flowers and thread? The image disavows their work even as it claims to represent it.

The contrast between Mésangère's print and a print of 1769 (figure 2.2) shows a striking change of representation over time. In the earlier image, the demarcation between workers, merchants, and customers is clearly established by the counter between them, while in Mésangère's scene, the counter offers no clear demarcation between worker and client, between producer and consumer.[5] In the eighteenth-century print, hatboxes, or *cartons*, are stacked neatly on high shelves behind the workers, as are undecorated hat forms; but chaos seems to reign in the nineteenth-century *atelier*. The workers in the background of the earlier print embellish various models of headgear as other women show

Figure 2.1 *"Atelier de modistes,"* Le Bon Genre, *1802–14, The Trustees of the British Museum, London.*

clients completed models and possible trimmings. The scene is orderly, the shop tidy, even somewhat domestic, as the reassuring presence of the sleeping dog in the center of the picture suggests. By contrast, the later image illustrates on multiple levels the increased "instability," to borrow Hollis Clayson's word, of the *modiste* and the disorder that ensues.[6]

Elegantly dressed in paradoxically unstructured and form-hugging Empire fashions, each of the four *modistes* models a different "look" while engaging in a different activity. The *décolletage* of the standing woman's pink gown is noteworthy, especially as she carries a hatbox and wears a *capote*, two details that signal she is about to exit the *atelier* into the street, most likely on a delivery. She must be the so-called *trottin*, charged with transporting goods publicly; and as the artist has made clear by depicting her with visible, full breasts, the virtue of young women circulating in the streets is questionable at best. Indeed, she belongs to the genre of the *grisette*.[7] She seems to assist the seated woman on the left, who wears a blue shawl and adjusts a headpiece atop her trendy Titus haircut, as if trying on one of her own creations. This gesture blurs the line between producer and consumer of luxury goods and thus reinforces the uncertain social status of the *modiste*, which I explore in more detail below.

Figure 2.2 *"Les Marchandes de modes,"* n.d., CC0 Paris Musées/Carnavalet Museum—History of Paris.

Directly across from this seated worker, we find another woman, the only woman who is *en cheveux* (hatless), attaching feathers to a fashionable turban she is creating on the *marotte* that she holds provocatively between her knees. The visibly erotic overtones attending to this community of women workers would be exploited in many popular prints representing the *lever* (morning rise) and the *coucher* (bedtime) of *modistes*.[8] The *atelier* in such illustrations was quite often figured as a space of licentious behavior—as though offering to the male viewer, such as Fontaney's Lord Feeling, a window into the private world of eroticized women.

The fourth of these workers, perhaps the shop owner, or *maîtresse modiste*, is stylishly dressed in blue with a matching *coiffe*; she holds a book, perhaps her ledger, but she appears to be more engaged in the sociability of the *atelier* than anything she's reading. On stands (known as *pieds*, *montres*, or *champignons*), completed straw and fabric hats are displayed, while at the feet of one worker, wide-brimmed straw hat forms, purchased from vendors, await shaping and decoration, and a hat box escapes the frame of the image on the other side. Strewn across the table are the tools and elements of embellishment: ribbons, braids, flowers, scissors, tape measure, pins, and pincushion. Unlike the didactic eighteenth-century image representing the functional *atelier* and commerce of the *marchandes de modes* (fashion merchants), everything here is in disarray, from the scattered work materials to the appearance of the workers themselves, apparently unsupervised and absent the regulating presence of clients, who were often accompanied by male companions.[9]

The image presents multiple and competing vignettes and layers of signification, all of which weave a rich texture for the cultural representation of the nineteenth-century *modiste*. The hierarchy of workers is expressed in the variety of activities on view, from *maîtresse-modiste* to humble *trottin*.[10] The variability of fashions in hat wear is likewise visible in the wide range of hats on display; the tools of production bear silent witness to the creative process; and the embodiment of sexy elegance, together with the network of gazes staged by this print, work to broadcast an identity—or a fantasy of an identity—that would remain potent for more than a century.

Satire notwithstanding, Mésangère's spectacular print is a master image of both the actual tools and the activities of the millinery craft in nineteenth-century France. It also contains the elements of a mythology surrounding the complex figure of the *modiste*—a mythology that obscures her work while it would haunt the public conception of this fashion worker throughout the century. I do not use the word "spectacular" lightly, for this image, like so many others, at once celebrates and critiques, mythologizes and effaces the spectacle of the working woman, who is as much on display as her products. The ambiguity of the origins, status, and activities of the nineteenth-century *modiste* contributes to a more generalized instability regarding this worker, which in turn created an imaginative space ripe for mythologizing.[11] Mésangère's print offers up the myth of the immodest *modiste,* free to circulate publicly in the streets and resembling a fashionable and proper lady consumer, a persistent myth that worked to hide her actual labor, as I discussed in chapter 1.

Of the many fashion workers on display in the print culture of the early nineteenth century, the *modiste* stands out as a cultural riddle (figure 2.3). As the so-called elite of the vast array of female fashion workers in nineteenth-century Paris, *modistes* were widely celebrated in popular image and song and on the vaudeville stage. In spite of this apparent surfeit of visibility, or perhaps because of it, the *modiste* nonetheless remains the most mysterious, ambiguous, and potentially least understood of nineteenth-century female fashion workers. An artisan whose activities ranged from dress accessorizing and embellishment to styling and, of course, hat-making, the *modiste* was a liminal figure, not easily categorized. In this she incarnated a society in flux; her work was likewise more difficult to define as it became more specialized over the course of the century.

Modistes were often portrayed at work—either creating goods in their *atelier*s or delivering them to their clients. These portraits, however, tended to be much less intended for documenting their labor than for exaggerating their mystique. Because the myth encircling *modistes* overtook the historical record of their actual labor, it is important to note that the evidence of their resistance to the myth appears most clearly in the simple fact of their widespread presence in the workforce. As I will explore in this chapter, various journalistic genres and legal records attest to a substantial female working class in the nineteenth-

Figure 2.3 Charles Philipon, "L'Agaçante Modiste," No. 3 Têtes de femmes, 1828–9, Musée Carnavalet, CC0 Paris Musées/Carnavalet Museum—History of Paris.

century fashion industry. But such historical documents, obscure in comparison to popular representations of *modistes*, offer little information about their working conditions, about appropriations of the myth to their own advantage, or about forms of resistance apart from simply working. Thus, we are left to root out those moments when the popular representations themselves challenged the myth—perhaps reflecting the sentiments and activities of real *modistes*—and to speculate about how these working-class women, with far fewer resources than their working bourgeois counterparts, might have contested and even co-opted the stereotype surrounding their lives and identity.

When not working in the *atelier*, *modistes* often strode the streets of Paris to deliver their goods, contained in their trademark hatboxes—their passport to the freedom of movement. Typically, *modistes* were fashionably dressed and likely wore a hat from the *atelier* where they worked, perhaps even one of their own creations, to advertise their goods and the desirability of elegance in general. That they were stylishly dressed and walked about freely and unaccompanied—a clear divergence from the norm mandating that women travel in the company of men—gave significant cause for anxiety. The mere fact of the *modiste*'s solitary travel presented the troubling suggestion of personal agency independent from a father or husband, apart from the role of daughter, wife, or mother; and her fashionable attire raised the specter of economic agency while sounding the alarm of upward social mobility. Thus, *modistes* appeared to possess the trappings of the middle class while enjoying an independence that respectable bourgeois women did not possess. No wonder, then, that a mythology raising questions around the *modistes*' respectability while hiding the realities of their labor arose to greet this socially liminal figure—and keep her in her place.

As Barthes famously explained in the preface to *Mythologies*, in which he sets out to disrupt the hegemony of everyday mythic structures, his intention, born of a resentment at "seeing Nature and History confused at every turn," was to "track down, in the decorative display of *what-goes-without-saying*, the ideological abuse which, in [his] view, is hidden there."[12] Everyday myth, reinforced by the dissemination of stereotypes, is powerful in that it permeates every aspect of daily life: visible everywhere, it thus appears to be naturally occurring. What ideological work did the myth of the *modiste* attempt to accomplish? The "what-goes-without-saying" of the *modiste* was that she was a woman of loose morals, eager to snag a husband and steal into the middle class. The convention that *modistes* were actually prostitutes was a commonplace grounded in truth—the truth of work for women in nineteenth-century France—which was predicated on low wages, making it necessary to supplement a meager income.[13] This stereotype, however, also concealed the other work they did—fashion work, which was real, if poorly remunerated, and essential to an industry that was becoming a powerful economy.

We need look no further than *Les Français peints par eux-mêmes*, the compendium of nineteenth-century social types published in 1841, for the principal contours of this myth. Here, we learn, the *modiste* is corrupted by her desire for luxury and thus lapses into sexual wantonness. The author of "La Modiste," Maria d'Anspach, herself a former *modiste*, lends credibility to the narrative and offers a moralizing account of the *métier*.[14] "It is no surprise then that the *modiste* likes luxury ... [a] weak creature, living with both misery and opulence, the brilliant futilities that surround her are an enormous pitfall; her deprivation tries her morality. She spends half her life desiring."[15] D'Anspach insists that the surroundings and tools of the *modiste*'s trade lead directly to her moral defeat, as she is permanently in contact with luxurious materials she cannot afford to purchase. The danger is thus that the producer of luxury fashion goods imagines herself as the consumer of her own product, working as she does in a state of constant desire and having "in her hands, before her eyes, velvet, silk, flowers and feathers."[16] The sensuality of the raw materials of her trade reinforces the erotic subtext of her condition and potential for corruption associated with this *métier*.

D'Anspach corroborates the myth of the *modiste* by concluding that, both in the shop and on the street, the *modiste* sought to attract a potential husband. This working girl might pass as bourgeois and thereby transgress class lines; she could also, simultaneously, be easily seduced into profligate spending and consumption by her own work, possibly wasting the fortune of a would-be husband and his family. The *modiste* is thus doubly beset by the dangers of an emerging modern commodity culture: at once occluded producer and illegitimate consumer, her relationship to the luxury fantasy she herself creates is complicated by her necessary participation in the spectacle of the feminine. Yet D'Anspach herself became a writer, all the while internalizing and reproducing the official discourse surrounding the *modiste*. Her own biography undoes her mythologizing. Through her vocational trajectory, rather than through her commentary, D'Anspach reveals that there are fissures in the received wisdom about this figure and therefore that there is a potential for resistance to the tyranny of the stereotype.

Now, all working women, particularly those in the needle trades, were subject to this kind of slippage into prostitution in the popular imagination.[17] Indeed, as Alain Corbin's research on nineteenth-century prostitution has shown, it was true that many registered prostitutes were also fashion workers.[18] Why was the *modiste* especially susceptible to this type of suspicion? What was so particular about her work activity, her proximity to luxury, and her engagement in creation and commerce that made this fashion worker, above all others, the paradigmatic emblem of the cultural legend? Because of her mythic status, the *modiste* is at once the farthest removed in the cultural imaginary from her actual labor yet most visible in popular cultural production.[19] The *modiste*'s reputation developed throughout the nineteenth century, helped on its way by a flourishing print culture that frequently represented these workers as flirtatious girls surrounded by luxury items, as well as by a popular theatrical culture that regularly staged scenes of workaday life and romantic entanglements in the *atelier* of a *modiste*. How was the nineteenth-century public to make sense of the popularized image of a venal working woman creating a fashion object—*le chapeau féminin*—that was recognized as the single most important indicator not only of status, but, more ironically still, of female propriety?[20]

This chapter examines the myth of the immodest *modiste* as it was forming and tightening its grip on the cultural imaginary, but I also challenge that myth through a multidimensional consideration of this figure that juxtaposes popular visual, performative, journalistic, and legal documents. I explore the myth and its contestations by examining the iconography of the *modiste* in print alongside her representation in an understudied and ephemeral form of nineteenth-century popular culture where the *modiste* was ubiquitous: vaudeville theater.[21] As a corollary to these representational and popular genres, press clippings and legal documents appearing throughout the century nuance and sometimes contradict the narrative set forth and perpetuated by the representational texts and images so prevalent surrounding the *modiste* in nineteenth-century France. For the weekly press, with its *faits divers*, marriage announcements, juridical news, and business updates, presents an unexplored reality check on the widespread representational culture surrounding the nineteenth-century *modiste*.[22] Engaged in both luxurious creation and display, the *modiste* was an indeterminate figure freighted with greater complexity than is perhaps generally understood. Read in concert, the documents I consider here bear out that she was not in fact associated as exclusively with sexuality as her ubiquitous myth may insist.

The chapter is organized in four parts. First, a brief exploration of various historical treatments of the needle trades reveals that the *modiste* emerged as the elite member of this class of workers. In this section I offer a summary of the evolution of *modistes* from the dress embellishers and celebrity stylists of the late eighteenth century (such as Rose Bertin, *modiste* to Marie-Antoinette) to the milliners of the Second Empire and the early Third Republic, that is, from 1852. The second part examines what we might today call a viral visual culture surrounding *modistes* in the first half of the century. Many popular prints depict a demure *modiste* at work, in her *atelier* or delivering goods, such as the woman seen in figure 2.4, who modestly clutches her clothing around her; however, the majority, such as the *agaçante modiste* pictured in figure 2.3, suggest quite blatantly her association with sexuality. These competing visual representations further reinforce the instability of her status. The third part analyzes several representative vaudeville plays in which *modistes* feature as central or ancillary characters and considers the effects of this figure's cultural ubiquity. The plays both echoed and contested many of the visual representations of the *modiste*, thus further complicating a myth too mono-dimensionally linked to prostitution in the nineteenth-century texts we know. By pushing back against this mythology, vaudeville theater seems to give a voice to the mute *modistes* of print culture—allowing them in some measure to re-center work at the heart of their identity. Here, more than in other popular representations, we find portrayals of *modistes* as agents of their own lives, which may reflect the regular presence of real *modistes* in vaudeville's audience. However, because of the conventionality of the genre, the majority of vaudeville plays tend to support and maintain the normative understanding of this figure. A more direct counternarrative emerges through an examination of a series of press and legal documents from a variety of sources, which I take up in the final section of this chapter. Connecting texts, images, vaudeville productions, and ephemera from the press reveals a counter-discourse to be deciphered, which suggests there is far more to the *modiste*

Figure 2.4 *Louis-Marie Lanté.* "*Modiste,*" Costumes d'ouvrières parisiennes, *1824, Bibliothèque nationale de France.*

than the myth presents, and ultimately also challenges assumptions about the centrality of consumption in women's role in France's early fashion economy. For women were also key producers of fashion, and through that productive role, hidden though it often was, they forged professional pathways. By exploring work patterns and lived experience, I expose several forms of contestation of the ubiquitous myth of the immodest *modiste* and uncover hints of their agency.

A Liminal Figure

Before turning to the mythmaking surrounding the *modiste*, and the resistance to that mythology, let us first briefly consider this figure's somewhat peculiar place in the history of the needle trades. As Clare Crowston has demonstrated in her study of the seamstresses of the Old Regime, the *modiste* emerged at the end of the eighteenth century, when the long-restricted seamstresses' guild had finally gained some measure of autonomy from the male tailors' guild.[23] Already, *modistes* were asserting themselves and thus exerting some form of agency. This new exclusivity was due at least in part to the culturally potent influence of Rousseau, who, by insisting on the innately female talent for sewing, created a gendered discourse that suggested the effeminacy of male tailors and the natural predisposition of women to needlework, a discourse that would dominate the nineteenth century.[24]

As a result of this rise in status and expansion of the work scope of the seamstresses, other women fashion workers began to appear and stake out their territory, in particular the *marchandes de modes*, the entrepreneurial female fashion merchants, forerunners to the *modistes*, "who emerged from the shadows of the mercers' guild in mid-century and soon overshadowed the seamstresses in commercial status and prestige."[25] The *marchandes de modes* were responsible for decorating the seamstresses' product by artfully arranging laces, cloth, and other accessories (*garnitures*) to create a stylish package, such as the one caricatured in figure 2.5 for its excessive embellishment. The caricature's excess, however, reveals the scope of the *marchande de mode*'s work. The model disappears beneath layers of lace flounces and ruffles; her head is covered and exaggerated under piles of stitched cloth; and the *pièce de résistance* that confers style and exotic opulence, while adding a splash of color, is a red cashmere shawl. The individual has been completely swallowed by fashion and recreated as a fashionable object under the hand of her *modiste*.

By far the most celebrated *modiste* of her day was Rose Bertin, the "ministre des modes de Marie-Antoinette," to quote the subtitle of historian Michelle Sapori's 2003 study of this historical figure and the culture of the *marchande de modes*, in which Rose Bertin was deeply implicated.[26] In spite of the celebrity of a Rose Bertin, however, much mystery still surrounds the genealogy of the *marchande de modes*, as historian Jennifer Jones has emphasized, and this explains to a certain extent the continued

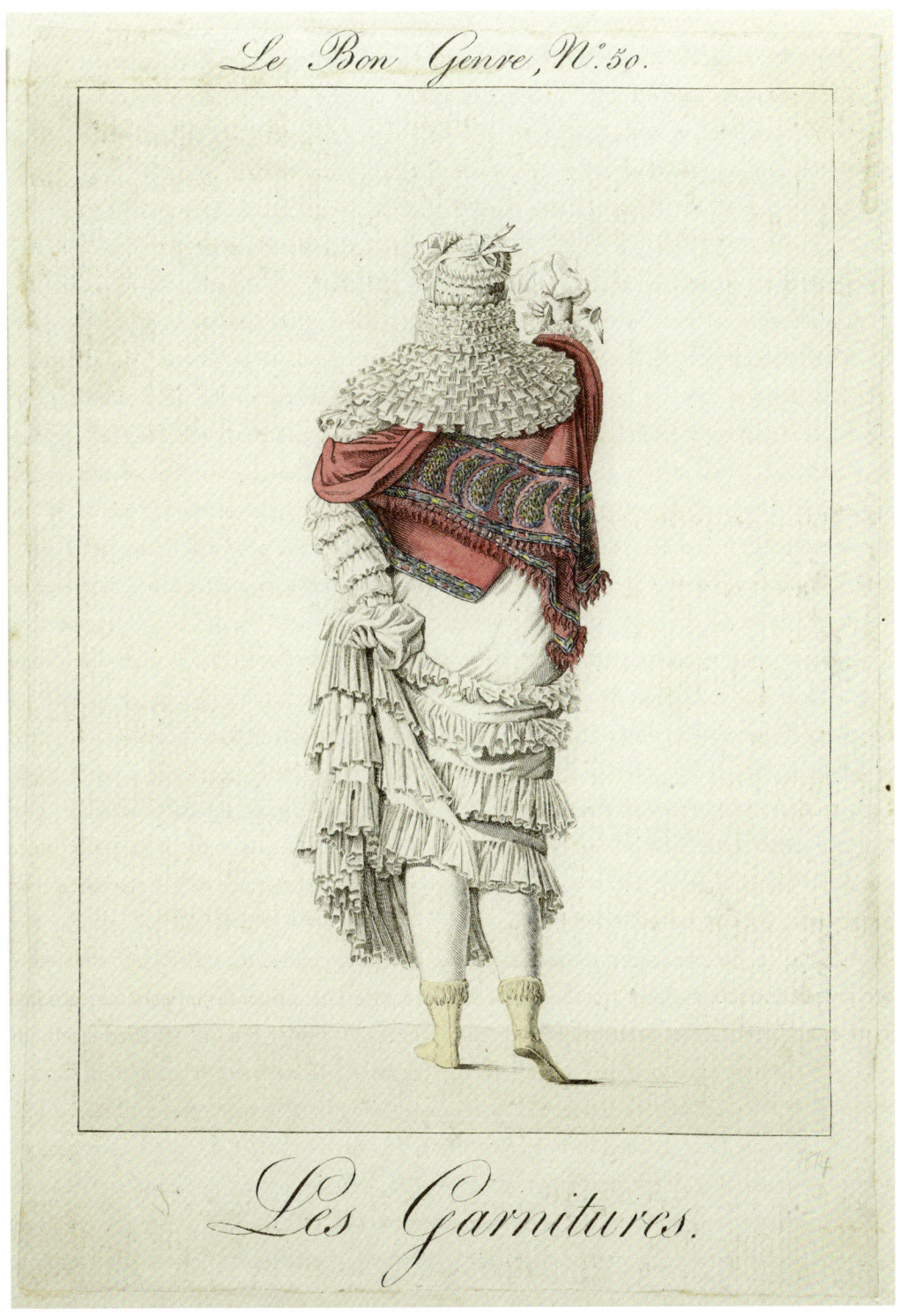

Figure 2.5 *"Les Garnitures,"* Le Bon Genre, *Paris, 1812, The Trustees of the British Museum.*

confusion over her evolution to *modiste* and narrowed specialization as milliner in the nineteenth century.[27] This uncertainty—regarding her origins, status, and activities—contributes to the more generalized instability around this figure especially in the late nineteenth century, creating circumstances favorable for mythologizing.

From the beginning, it would seem, the *modiste* inhabited a liminal space, occupying a "special position" like her ancestress, the *marchande de modes*, as Daniel Roche has indicated in his study of the fashion economy of the eighteenth century.[28] Tied in part to older practices of *ancien régime* extravagance, *modistes* were also progressive, their work combining old and new, thus literally allowing them to incarnate the paradoxical mechanism of fashion that both references the past and constantly reintroduces novelty.[29] They were contesting, apparently, the entrenched and gendered guild system, and their creative agency helped fashion develop into the powerful industry it became in the nineteenth century. The *modistes* also served as points of contact between consumers and producers, following fashion as well as creating new trends. Their *ateliers* doubled as shops for commerce, making workspace and marketplace interchangeable. The *modiste* was therefore poised in several respects on the threshold of multiple identities, spaces, and functions, and this liminality only increased the potential for mythmaking.

The task of the *modiste* was to invent the concept of fashion as a complex dance between old and new. Roche insists on the centrality of artifice in her creative process: "The domain of the modistes was arranging and changing; custom and fancy, taste and caprice inspired their activities and hastened their pace. The art of the fashion merchants . . . was the triumph of artifice."[30] Artifice, indeed, was key to the success of the *modiste* and of fashion more broadly, for creating the impression of newness—whether sprucing up an old gown or hat or envisioning, creating, and marketing a new "must-have" trend—depended on the *modiste*'s keen eye, imagination, and nimble fingers to create something beautiful from very little: bits of ribbon, artificial fruits and flowers, scraps of cloth and lace, and feathers, all mounted on what began as a nondescript hat form. More than any other fashion worker, *modistes* understood and commanded the rhetorics of artifice upon which fashion depends.[31]

By the 1820s, *modistes* became more fully associated with millinery, and hats for women were increasingly fashion's focal point in a period when fantasy and excess were requirements in a social landscape of visually signifying distinctions.[32] Hats and the *modistes* who made them thus stand out as particularly significant to fashion's engine: poised between production and consumption, between artisanry and art, the *modiste* created fashion's trends with the tilt of a brim, the addition of a feather, the color of a ribbon. Occupying a liminal position from these multiple perspectives, then, she was also deeply engaged in the manipulation of artifice in the service of perpetuating fashion. Her flirtatious persona and engagement with artifice express her creative agency, even as they reinforce her mythology; this play with ambiguity contributes to obscuring her agency. Because they were viewed as overly flirtatious women at best and as prostitutes at worst, *modistes*—enmeshed in the changing social landscape and socially unstable themselves—were therefore more productive of social anxiety than their more traditional sisters in the needle trades; they were thus also more susceptible to the mythmaking that would dominate much of the nineteenth-century visual representation produced to identify them.[33] The vast visual culture surrounding the *modiste* offers a window into the inherent contradictions associated with this figure and will help to map the ideologies governing gender and work in nineteenth-century France.

The Myth Goes Viral

Visual culture offered a primary conduit for the mythology surrounding the *modiste*. In jarring contrast to her dark apron, the traditional garment of the female artisan, the *agaçante modiste*[34] featured in figure 2.3 sports a jaunty plaid *toque* and a low-cut yellow dress with *gigot* sleeves, so popular in the 1830s, that draw the eye to the delicacy of her wrists and hands and the white slope of her fleshy shoulders and bare neck.[35] In her deep *décolletage*, which seems inappropriate for the workplace, dangles an oversized cross that professes a bit too much her virtue. What is most striking about the image, however, is not her provocatively fashionable dress—for *modistes*, who interact with consumers, needed to advertise their styling skill, much like fashion plates marketed clothing more generally. It is, rather, her coy glance, looking up and out at a viewer beyond the frame while her nimble fingers seem to continue working the wide satiny bow she drapes around the crown of the hat that sits atop a nearly invisible *marotte* in her lap. Is her occupation to embellish hats, or something else entirely? This *modiste* is a flirt, a tease, as the adjective *agaçante* tells us, and her workspace is a theater of seduction. According to the print, her flirtation is akin to her creative process: working in artifice (as opposed to inventing or innovating) to create something beautiful from very little, she teases out a design to produce a look. Portrayals such as this diminish any creative agency.

This image was published by Charles Philipon in 1834 for a series entitled "Costume des femmes de Paris." The series includes captions such as "La décente lingère" and "La piquante couturière," which trade on popular perceptions of these female working types and pun on the actual labor they perform.[36] The *décente lingère* (decent linen worker), who dealt in household and personal linens, created the fine white garments that displayed respectability and wealth; and the *piquante couturière* (sexy seamstress) pricked (*piquer*) the fabric with her needle as she sewed the seams of dresses. What of the *agaçante modiste*? In images such as this one, the product is hidden away, either literally within a hatbox or figuratively through the shift in focus from product to producer, deflecting the emphasis from labor and product and indeed making the *modiste*'s activity look nothing at all like work. The emphasis falls not on her embellishment of the hat, but instead on the provocative look of the pretty fashion worker with her exposed bosom, delicate fingers, fashionable clothing, and coquettish pose. She has become a product herself.

Simultaneously an artisan of luxury creations and a delicious object of consumption, the Parisian *modiste* thus occupied a peculiar and paradoxical space in relation to luxury and lust (*luxure*) in the popular imaginary. Whether working alone, as the *agaçante modiste* seems to be, in a community of other workers in the *atelier*, such as in figure 2.1, on the streets delivering her goods, or in the privacy of her sleeping quarters, we frequently find—in nineteenth-century prints created by many of the century's most popular male artists—that depictions of the *modiste* reinforce, through her sexuality, the troubling uncertainty that gives rise to her myth.[37] In turn, the myth draws the viewer's attention away from both her labor and her agency. An examination of images from each of these three conventional spaces—*atelier*, street, and bedroom—illustrates the "natural habitat" of the nineteenth-century *modiste*. Whether she is portrayed as venal or not, the elision of sex work with fashion work permeates her representations.

The visual grammar of this imagery insists on eroticizing the work and the feminized spectacle of fashion even as it reinforces the troubling liminality associated with a figure that is ill-defined and thus easily mythologized. For example, an 1822 lithograph by John James Chalon, "La Marchande de Modes," (figure 2.6), repeats some of the same tropes we see in the earlier *atelier* scene, only adding customers, which makes more explicit both the commerce and the spectacle implied in the earlier image. The workspace pictured here seems to be located in one of the *passages* of Paris, the early covered shopping malls—or arcades—famously analyzed by Walter Benjamin. The arcades exemplified the ambiguity of space, both indoor and outdoor, associated with new forms of commerce, and it is no surprise to find again the blurring of *atelier* and boutique. Here, the *modistes*, each more precarious than the other, are literally working (in) the streets. Once more, we find the expected set of objects and figures: hatboxes, a vast array of brightly colored, completed hats on stands, a head-form gripped between the knees of a fashion worker, and three pretty *modistes*—two engaged in creation, their fingers busy with needles, pins, ribbons, and flowers; and a third, perhaps the eponymous *marchande de modes* of the image's title, showing a finished product to a prospective buyer.

We also find some alarming additions, however: the head-form in the lap of the rocking *modiste* is oddly phallic, with an uncharacteristically elongated neck and eyes trained on the fashion worker's crotch; unlike her two colleagues, she is not wearing the traditional garment worker's dark apron. But for the work she is engaged in, we might mistake her for a consumer. As in the 1834 image of the *agaçante modiste*, here too, the *modiste*, whose fingers seem so busy with a pink hat, looks not at her work but instead directly at the male client, who returns her gaze, a gesture of looking emphasized by his monocle. Busy at once with her fingers and her eyes, the *modiste* is skilled both in fabrication and social stratagem. Accomplished in the artifice of fashion—the print suggests—*modistes* could easily impersonate their social betters, and the linking gaze between the fashion worker and the male client precisely expresses this "dangerous" potential circulation between classes. While his female companion studies the gold hat that would so nicely complement her yellow shawl, a hat proffered by the central

Figure 2.6 J. J. Chalon, "La Marchande de Modes," 1822, The Trustees of the British Museum.

figure, who leans back invitingly, Monsieur examines the eroticized workers, every bit as much on display as the hats.[38] Finally, commerce is signaled by the green cashbox centrally placed on a hatbox in the background, but the till is gaping open and unattended, thus emphasizing the troubling lack of regulation of this business. This set of images indeed illustrates an increasing sense of disorder that dovetails with the increasing instability associated with the *modiste*: where does she fit socially, morally, even spatially? Is she a fashion worker or is she a luxury good, or perhaps a sex worker, herself?

As Abigail Solomon-Godeau has proposed, "one of the most conspicuous features of commodity culture is its sexualization of the commodity," a move that lays the groundwork for the "homology between the seductive, possessable female and the seductive, possessable commodity."[39] Indeed, the commercial slippage between product and producer is even more evident, if rendered ambivalent, in a lithograph by Charles Vernier from the satirical series *Les Grisettes* (figure 2.7), printed in the mid-1840s (figure 2.7).[40] The print repeats the familiar visual tropes of the *modiste*'s *atelier*—hat stand,

Figure 2.7 Charles Vernier, "Les Grisettes," 1846–7, Musée Carnavalet, CC0 Paris Musées/Carnavalet Museum—History of Paris.

hat forms, work counter, *marotte*, hat in progress—and foregrounds the *modiste* herself as product. Pushed forward by her colleague, the *modiste* is on display as the commodity to be bought and consumed, while the hat languishes, forgotten, in the background.

The *atelier*, where clients interact with vendors and fashion creators, is portrayed here as a space for introductions; through this restaging of the commercial space of fashion, another—clandestine—commerce slips into view. The apparently virtuous pose of the foregrounded *modiste*—her hands clasped in prayer and exhibiting a worried expression of supplication—suggests perhaps that this *modiste* resists the role into which she is literally being pushed. Unlike the *agaçante modiste* of figure 2.3, this girl is prudently dressed for work, with her tidy hair and worker's apron worn over a simple and unadorned dress. While it is uncertain whether or not this *modiste* happily embraces the commerce her myth prescribes for her, it is certain that the space of the *atelier* is once again unmistakably sexualized.

If, in the iconography of the *modiste* in her *atelier*, we encounter repeated tropes that reinforce at once her commodification through the kind of slippage mentioned above as well as her identification with the consumer, a slightly different operation is at work on the street.[41] Removed from her traditional workspace, she is even less legible and potentially more subject to the mythmaking uncertainty fosters. Anne Higonnet offers a fruitful model for interpreting nineteenth-century visual culture in her discussion of an 1835 image of a milliner, in which the *modiste* is shown "delivering [her] goods (and not even to anyone) rather than producing them."[42] Removed from the standard indoor work environment, and walking unchaperoned in the street, the fashion worker is visually separated from her work and can thus be imagined as an erotic target rather than a working professional. A similar phenomenon is already apparent in an 1814 print from Mésangère's *Le Bon Genre* (figure 2.8). The two *modistes* in this stylized street scene of the early nineteenth century are easily

Figure 2.8 *"Rencontres des petites ouvrières,"* Le Bon Genre, *1814, The Trustees of the British Museum.*

identified by their hatboxes.[43] They are also quite clearly represented as the "sexiest" among this group of ambulatory workers, both with low-cut dresses, while the others are much more covered. The central *modiste* is perhaps asking for directions, given the fact that she and another of the women have fingers pointing, but all gazes, even that of the backward-glancing hatted figure, are turned on her, the focal point of the scene.

The representation of the *modiste* in the street participates in another popular theme for prints depicting the *petits métiers*, or itinerant traders, which offered vignettes of workers of the popular class, identifiable by their hawker's cries and also by their costumes and trappings.[44] While the two *modiste* figures are eroticized, thus referencing the anxiety associated with women working, particularly in the public space of the street, there is some ambiguity about her status. The *modiste*'s presence on the street is legitimized by a metonymy of her creation—the hatbox makes her mobility licit—even as her work as producer is hidden by the product and by her stylish elegance. Often conflated with the bourgeois consumer, whom she must impress with her creations, and thus potentially rising in social status and passing socially, the *modiste* suddenly becomes subject to the moral regulation of the *bourgeoise*, who was prohibited from walking publicly without a suitable companion.

The hatbox is the public signal of the *modiste*'s identity, and it also contributes to the suspicion associated with her. While allowing her a certain freedom of circulation, it nonetheless circumscribes her within an economy of luxury commodities. The product is hidden, but because of the distinctive shape and size of the box, its contents may be imagined by the viewer—the drab, simple hatbox expresses both the fantasy it contains and the fantasy work it activates. The hatbox is indeed a locus of desire, and the *modiste*, the only one who knows what is inside, controls its mystique. The inseparability of *modiste* and hatbox in visual culture signals that they are both packaged commodities, used to propagate fantasies on which fashion's success depended.

Just beneath the surface of these street scenes that trade on the presumed "easiness" of the unchaperoned, streetwalking *modiste* is the potential for her slippage into misery, if not violence. The *modiste* on the street is alluring and mysterious in an 1856 lithograph by Gavarni (figure 2.9). Her pensive look, the shimmering dark tones of her silk skirt and tightly wrapped shawl, and her respectably hatted head are offset by the centrality of her dainty foot and ankle and the white ruffle of her petticoat as, carrying her hatbox, she steps down from a bridge. Captured in isolation, she is a portrait of both mobility and mystery, her eyes downturned, unlike those of the *agaçante modiste*, but eroticized nonetheless by the display of her delicate, exposed foot. The peeking boot and ankle are visually aligned with the hatbox, the emblem of commerce and of hidden treasure: Gavarni thus links what was perhaps considered the most erotically charged (because alternately hidden and revealed) female body part of the nineteenth century with the artful fashions concealed within the ordinary hatbox. Other associations will also emerge.

Poised on a bridge, an urban structure denoting transition, this *modiste* has the freedom to change neighborhoods, as her errands and deliveries may require long trajectories, which is implied also by

Figure 2.9 *Paul Gavarni, "Porteuse de modes," 1856, © British Library Board (General Reference Collection DRT Digital Store 10172.e.14, between pp. 448 and 449).*

Figure 2.10 *Paul Gavarni, "La Chasse au trottin,"* Baliverneries Parisiennes, *1804–66, The Cleveland Museum of Art, Dudley P. Allen Fund 1925.1083.*

her umbrella. Forty or so years beyond the playful scenes from Le Bon Genre, this image attests to both the longevity of the representation of the *modiste* and the potency of its message. Here Gavarni, a fashion illustrator and one of the most celebrated engravers of his generation, hints at the complexity of the myth of the flirtatious *modiste* by rendering her in an ambiguous way.[45] Her appeal is at least in part her apparent vulnerability—she is alone, overburdened, and stepping downward—markers of her erotic objectification as she walks the streets of Paris and of her potential moral descent.

An earlier Gavarni lithograph (figure 2.10), entitled "La Chasse au trottin," makes even more obvious this eroticization and dehumanizes the *modiste* through its title, which transforms her, the *trottin*, a delivery or errand girl, into the prey of a bourgeois *flâneur*.[46] Slightly hunched and apparently fleeing, the little *modiste* appears to be stalked by the caped man—the hunter—whose gaze, however, no longer falls on her. Perhaps he has been rebuffed and turns away in disappointment; or perhaps, as the title indicates, he is embarking on his hunt as she fades into the distance. In either case, it is the uncertain status of the *modiste* that is foregrounded. Viewed from behind, curls escaping from her headgear, she is in motion, traversing the city with her identifying hatbox. The image encapsulates this movement through the airy drafting of her garments, which flow backward. The male is a darker, heavier, indeed, intimidating shape. Whether Gavarni's *flâneur* has been unsuccessful or is contemplating a hunt, the *trottin* is nonetheless designated as his prey, an erotic object for consumption by the male viewer/hunter. Even as the *atelier* scenes hinted at the commercial female community structure of the *maison close*, a government sanctioned brothel, her presence in the street reinforces her perceived availability, or perhaps it serves as a cautionary tale, meant to intimidate flirtatious *modistes* into modest behavior or warn her off her solitary movement. For the image clearly hints at potential violence—as a sinister man sets off to stalk his victim; it thus reminds us that behind the myth, there lay real danger and possible misery for working women, a reality that comes into focus with an examination of the press, as we shall discover further along.

Modistes are also frequently portrayed in their private quarters, into which nineteenth-century male viewers are invited to peer voyeuristically. A popular subgenre of the illustrated *petits métiers* is the illustration of the fashion workers' dormitories. Like the *atelier*, the dormitory was a communal space, in this case housing groups of workers for the evening. Over the course of the nineteenth century, we find recurring variations on "le lever" (morning rise) and "le coucher des ouvrières en mode" (bedtime for fashion workers), with *lingères, grisettes*, and *modistes* cycling through, rehearsing a genre that emerged at the end of the eighteenth century.

The communal bedroom scene typically depicts groups of partially clad, voluptuous women, some dozing, some dressing, and others attending to their toilette. Garments, boxes, and shoes are strewn across the floor, and, in the case of figure 2.11, a young boy arrives, apparently to deliver a letter, a *billet doux*, we must assume, being read by the woman at the far right. The space is eroticized on many levels—exposed flesh, semi-naked women in bed or at their toilette, and the careless presence of

Figure 2.11 *Dequevauviller, "Le Lever des ouvrières en modes," 1784, Bibliothèque nationale de France.*

unworn garments, all of which reinforce the voyeuristic quality of this type of image. Yet its composition mirrors that of the *atelier* scenes we just examined, which also depict the careless excess of fabric and elements of dress, groups of often scantily clad women engaging in a variety of activities, sometimes in the presence of an outsider. In the case of the eighteenth-century print, the "outsider" here is figured as an "innocent," whose gaze is purposely hidden; he is a stand-in, however, for the male viewer's gaze, invoking the titillation of sending the uninitiated into a brothel.[47]

In contrast to the late eighteenth-century print, the scene depicted in the 1830s image in figure 2.12 suggests a spatial downgrade for the *modistes* of the nineteenth century, signaled most obviously by the rank-looking, makeshift curtain and randomly placed chamber pot. Here, the workers seem to rebel against propriety and orderliness. Both images, however, signal the financial straits of the fashion workers—they sleep in an attic space, and the presence of hatboxes and tools in private quarters indicates

Figure 2.12 *"Dortoir de Modistes,"* anon., 1830s, Musée Carnavalet, CC0 Paris Musées/Carnavalet Museum—History of Paris.

that they must bring work home to supplement their income. The same elements that constructed the lifestyle of the eighteenth-century fashion workers are present here as well: suggestive and carelessly tossed clothing, tiny mules and slippers on the floor, a toilet table with mirror, beds, hatbox, and, of course, women socializing as they undress for the night. One of the women, her head bowed, perhaps in shame, appears to be pregnant—here, an overt signaling of the linking of *modistes* with extramarital sexuality.

Reinforcing the voyeurism of these scenes and the linkage in the social imaginary between the work of the *modiste* and her sexual life, a lithograph dating from the 1820s showcases the intimate interior space and its proximity to the space of commerce as a young gallant arrives to escort his *modiste* date to a ball (figure 2.13). Three fashion workers surround the figure of the top-hatted caller, two of them awoken from their slumber as they lie on their pallets in nightgowns and bonnets and a third dressed in chic masquerade ball attire. They sleep amid their work, as we see a hatbox, two hat stands, and a *marotte* on the shelf. In the adjacent room—the shop itself—we see outlines of hats on

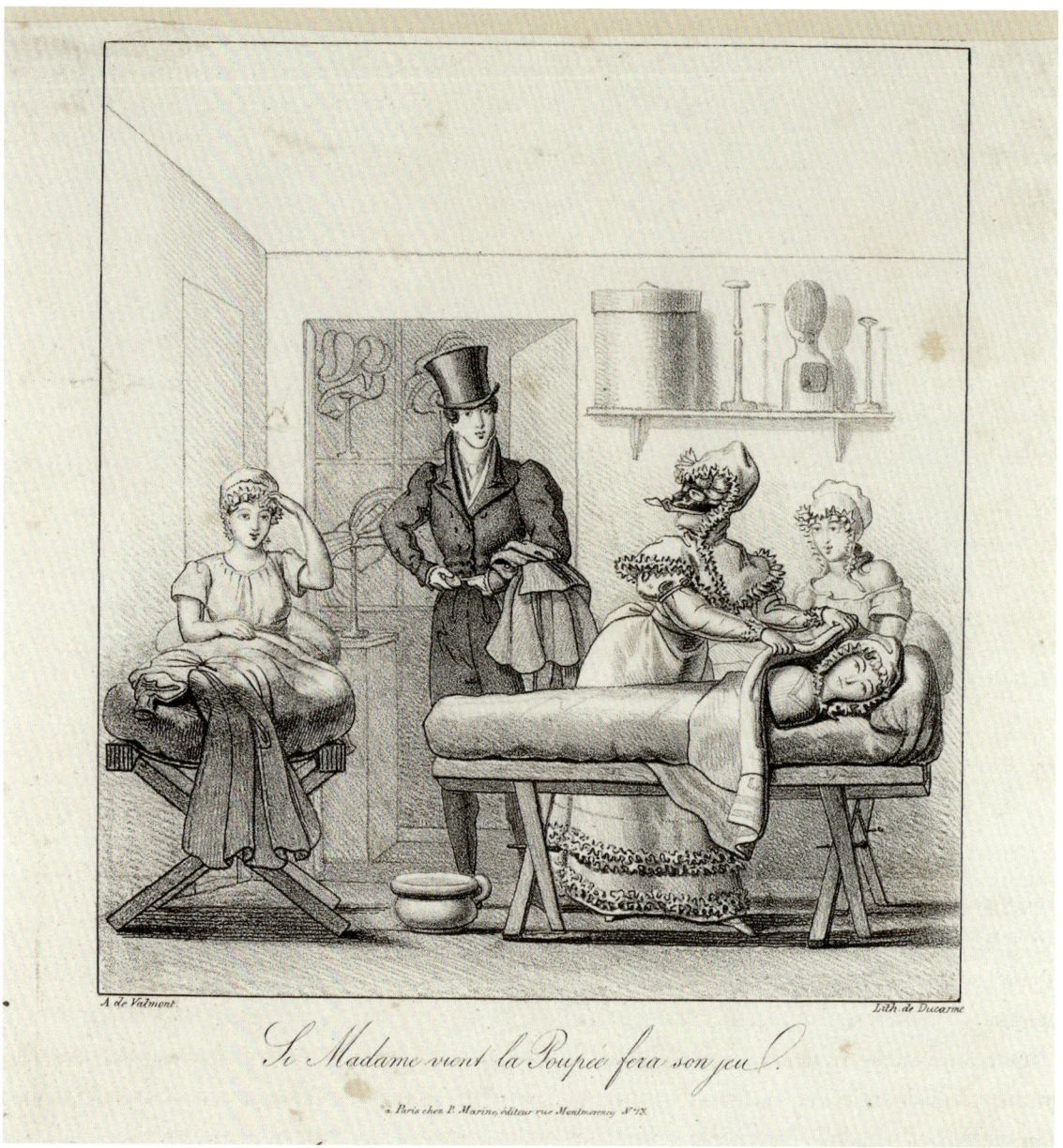

Figure 2.13 A. de Valmont, "Si Madame vient la Poupée fera son jeu," n.d., Musée Carnavalet, CC0 Paris Musées/Carnavalet Museum—History of Paris.

stands, poised to be sold. But most curious of all is the foregrounded scene, explained by the caption: "If Madame comes, the doll will play her part." The young *modiste*, eager for a night out at a ball, dresses a *marotte* in her nightcap and puts her to bed—should the mistress enter the dormitory, all heads will be accounted for, and the *modiste* can relish her illicit escapade.[48] The potential confusion of the *modiste* for the inanimate *marotte* allows her to trick her mistress and enjoy some autonomy. This same slippage, however, recurs throughout the print and theatrical culture of the period and calls attention to the dehumanization of the worker, particularly the female worker, at the same time.[49]

While the iconography of the private space of the flirtatious *modiste* clearly invokes the myth of venality associated with this figure, it also introduces elements of social commentary. These "dormitory" scenes present the male fantasy of the private world of the *modiste*, replete with lesbian overtones and the tropes of easy sexuality, even as they claim, through their matter-of-fact titles, to be realistic, universalizing snapshots of the day-to-day life of the female fashion worker. Popular images such as the one pictured in figure 2.13 suggest the slippery connection possible between venality and poverty.

In the 1827 lithograph reproduced in figure 2.14 (originally from 1817), entitled "Luxe et indigence," a working-class girl sleeps on a flimsy pallet in her decrepit garret while surrounded by the accoutrements of luxury. Unlike her shawl, repurposed as a curtain, her empty dress and bonnet are lovingly laid out and propped up on chairs to retain their form and resist wrinkling. They thus mirror the sleeping girl, who like the dress, seems to float on her flimsy bed. These objects also take on a certain animated quality, reinforcing both the power of clothing to create identity and the uncanny slippage between person and object frequently found in depictions of *modistes*. The girl is surely a *modiste*, we gather, from the ingenious transformation of her unmistakable hatboxes into a night table. Public and private selves are simultaneously revealed in this voyeuristic display of the *modiste* at rest. The *modiste* pictured in figure 2.14 sleeps alone, covered from head to toe, perhaps readying herself for another day of honest labor—she is a far cry from the bare-bosomed creatures of the *atelier*, even if she fulfills a voyeuristic fantasy allowing the viewer to peer into the private space of the sleeping worker.

One final image, contrapuntal to "Luxe et indigence," makes quite explicit this voyeuristic fantasy. In the "Modiste de la rue Vivienne" (1840), the anonymous artist converges spaces—private, public, commercial—in a pornographic image that literalizes the fantasy of the clandestine work of the *modiste* (figure 2.15). As noted in chapter 1, the rue Vivienne was famous for its *magasins de modes* and fashion workers, and in this image, there is no longer any ambiguity about the nature of the fantasy, even as the theme of liminality persists in the structure of the half-opened door.[50] Behind the semi-public space of the *atelier*, already suggestive of clandestine commerce, are the private quarters of the *modiste*, likely the *maîtresse-modiste*, given that her servant addresses her as "Madame" as she announces a (new) male visitor—"Monsieur le Baron," likely a client. Seated, with skirts removed and legs splayed, the *modiste* is exposed and "occupied" as it were, with her visibly aroused visitor. Instead

Figure 2.14 *"Luxe et Indigence." Le Bon Genre, 1827 (1817), The Trustees of the British Museum.*

of the *marotte*, the head form so frequently clasped between the *modiste*'s legs, we now find a whiskered gentleman, apparently eager to please.

Stylish as ever in spite of her state of undress, she has not removed her spotless white stockings or dainty black slippers, the recurring tropes of fashionability, consecrated in the fashion plates of the nineteenth century. This *modiste* incarnates the ease with which fashion reinforces eroticism.[51] The pornographic print thus crystallizes the erotic innuendo of the *atelier* scenes, the street scenes, and the dormitory scenes, literalizing the suggestive symbolism of the coy glances, the hatbox's concealment, and the half-dressed fashion workers as they prepare for work, not to mention the surreptitious night out on the town, with a head-form guaranteeing the girl's reputation. *Modistes* may well have been creating hats for women, but, clearly, they were being represented in visual culture by and for men.

The anxiety the *modiste* produced is palpable in the print culture I have been exploring, for, more than any other female garment worker, as the elite member of the needle trades with constant access

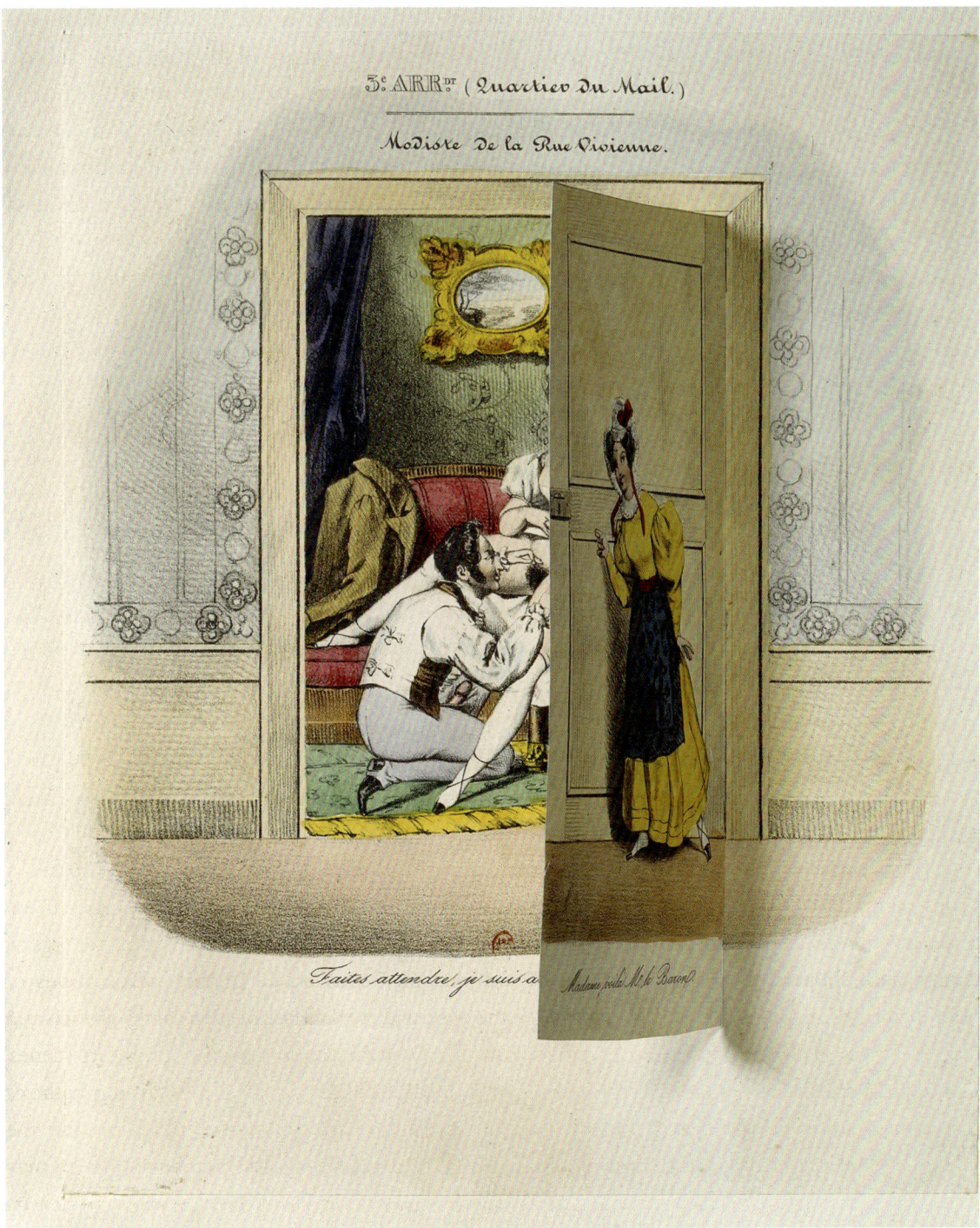

Figure 2.15 *"Modiste de la rue Vivienne,"* Portes et fenêtres, les Douze arrondissements de Paris, *1840,* Bibliothèque nationale de France.

to the luxury materials of fashion and over-the-counter communication with her clientele, along with professionally justified freedom of movement, she was well poised to enter the middle class almost imperceptibly. By proximity, then, and through her expert manipulation of costume, the *modiste* could perform elegance in ways that made her perilously indistinguishable from respectable bourgeois women. This flexibility also subjected her to moral imperatives that were unsustainable for working-class women (because of her need to walk unchaperoned to deliver her goods, for example), thus "confirming" her moral laxity. My analysis of the prolific visual culture surrounding *modistes* demonstrates the extent to which the myth that rose around her obscures her labor and thus her agency. However, traces of that agency are sometimes visible in spite of the myth, and these reminders of the *modiste*'s professional ambition find expression in other forms of popular culture as well, forms that occasionally offer greater visibility of her potential for agency.

The Myth Takes the Stage

We have seen the degree to which the *modiste* was entrenched as an object of spectacular display in the print culture of the first half of the nineteenth century. Shops themselves were configured to best display the goods produced, but also the pretty *modistes* as they trimmed their creations. Many shops, such as the one ostensibly run by the enterprising *maîtresse-modiste* of the pornographic print, or the one Lord Feeling spied upon, were located in the rue Vivienne, in close proximity to the Théâtre du Palais Royal and other popular theaters of the period. As Jennifer Terni has observed, theatrical performance was closely tied to other spectacular sites, like shops, and this proximity reinforced what she terms "associations" among various forms of commerce and spectacle.[52] It is not surprising, then, to find *modistes* being represented on stage in vaudeville replicas of the spectacular space of fashion shops. On the vaudeville stage, the flattened myth of the *modiste* was often projected and repeated, but it was also sometimes contested, in no small measure, perhaps, because the audience itself comprised many of the fashion workers the plays tried to capture. In her *Mémoires,* for example, Jeanne Bouvier, who worked primarily as a *couturière*, but also as a *lingère* and *modiste* over the course of her long career, always supplementing her income through piece work, describes treating herself occasionally to a night at the theater: "Thanks to the extra work I did and a salary of five francs, for ten hours of work, my situation was passably good. From time to time, I gave myself a night at the theater. L'Opéra comique was my favorite. A seat for twenty sous allowed me to amuse myself."[53] Vaudeville theater was a common, and relatively inexpensive, leisure activity for the working women of Paris.

Like the "restaurants, waiting rooms, drawing rooms, and offices" that Terni cites as vaudeville's favored settings because they allowed for "impromptu social interactions," the *atelier* was also a frequent set for vaudeville plays. Spaces of spectacle and consumption, *atelier*s and *magasins de modes* were also equipped with many of the instruments for slapstick humor and shifting disguise—precisely the definitive ingredients of vaudeville itself. The *quiproquo*, or infinite variations on mistaken identity and substitutions (of people and/or things) that create vaudeville's farcical humor, is particularly potent in plays set in fashion shops: here, the props of disguise are omnipresent, and artifice is crucial to the mechanisms of disguise. The props of the *atelier* that serve ostensibly to enact the work of hat-making provide the occasion to consider various forms of identity confusion: social, gender, and moral. They also remind a theater audience that *modistes* were workers, participating in a productive economy, even if those tools also served culturally or narratively symbolic purposes on stage.

Seizing on the familiar iconography popularized by print culture, vaudeville theater insists on the contradictions inherent in the figure of the *modiste*, rather than overemphasizing the monolithic stereotype that had become commonplace. This deeper complexity can be explained in part by the nature of vaudeville itself, which catered to popular and bourgeois classes and was closely entwined with mass culture and social commentary.[54] In addition, unlike visual representations, vaudeville plays were not static and could evolve with each performance. In play after play, plots revolve around a *modiste*'s attempt to redress the myth that unfairly characterizes her. While it is undeniable that vaudeville also participated in the work of mythmaking, it staged *modistes* who seem intent, whether self-consciously or not, on rehabilitating their image or succeeding in the world of honest commerce.

Competing visions of the *modiste* played out quite plainly on the vaudeville stage: sometimes modest and sometimes coquettish, the *modiste* was always entrepreneurial, a fact that was reinforced in the weekly press, which often inspired the plays themselves. As we shall see later, *modistes* appear in the pages of the press in a variety of contexts, notably, as businesswomen forming and dissolving partnerships. Indeed, the common thread running through the corpus of plays featuring *modistes* is less her mythic sexiness than her artisanal drive and spirited determination, in an expression of middle-class values that reinforces Mary Gluck's argument that vaudeville theater was predominantly concerned with reaffirming bourgeois culture.[55] This argument excepts, of course, that the middle-class values of work and entrepreneurship applied to men, and not to women; and therein lies a potential subversion by vaudeville's *modistes*. Frequently, their reputation for loose morals is challenged in these plays and their virtue vindicated by their professional ambition, suggesting that *modistes* also appropriate a role not typically assigned to their gender and class.

While often repeating and sustaining the mythic lax morality of the *modiste*, or at the very least, taking it as a starting point, vaudeville theater simultaneously offers a counter-discourse that, I propose, creates gaps in the conventional mythology, potentially making her a more active agent of her destiny. Vaudeville audiences were mixed, both in terms of class and gender; as I noted, there were *modistes* in the audience at many vaudeville plays.[56] While vaudeville's comic thrust depended on the flattening of characters into stereotypes, many of vaudeville's *modistes* defy the myth from the 1820s to beyond the 1860s. Before turning to several representative plays, let us briefly consider the place of vaudeville in French culture.[57]

Vaudeville was an oral rather than a written genre. On every title page, the date indicated is the play's first performance, not its publication; and each theater had its own particular clientele. Henri Gidel traces the history of vaudeville to popular song, explaining that the genre most likely emerged from the sixteenth-century *voix-de-villes*, collections of popular songs or "airs," easily recognized and repeated.[58] Vaudeville theater was thus an ephemeral and highly performative genre, relying more on recognizable character types matched with familiar melodies and slapstick pranks than on elegantly structured plots and psychological depth. For example, in the "air de la grisette," the transparent punning of a popular song from 1835 entitled "La modiste" reinforces the familiar mythology surrounding the type.[59] Each of the song's italicized words (*blondes, formes, faveur, cornettes, façon, posant, passe, plume, rubans*) refers to the trade of the milliner—the *blondes* are the type of lace she uses, along with embellishments like the feathers (*plume*) and ribbons (*rubans, faveur*); the *formes* are the unadorned bases for hats and might also refer to the rounded head, sometimes called a *tête à poupée* or *marotte*, on which the *modiste* creates the hat; the *cornettes* are ornamented cloth pieces, and the *façon* refers to her styling. However, these words also refer to the physical charms of the *modiste* and suggest a bawdy erotic subtext that reinforces the wantonness associated with this fashion worker: for *blondes* refers also to hair color, *formes* to voluptuous curves, *faveur* to the sexual act, and so on. The song insists on the interconnection of two types of work, both of which depend on the *modiste*'s skill with artifice. Thus, through the use of the "air," vaudeville does the work of mythmaking in a way similar to that of the reproduction and circulation of suggestive prints analyzed earlier.

From Eugène Scribe (1791–1861) to Eugène Labiche (1815–88), France's most prolific and successful vaudeville playwrights in the nineteenth century, but also in the work of many lesser-known vaudevillists, *modistes* are important recurring characters, many of whom acknowledge in some way their questionable reputation. As I detailed above, the *atelier* or shop was a frequent setting for vaudeville, which "capitalized, above all, on the things people try to hide in the social games they play."[60] The vaudeville stage was also a place to view and assess trends, where spectacle and fantasy could mitigate some of the tensions inherent in a rapidly metamorphosing society.

The play *Les Modistes* (1824) functions as a kind of vaudevillian double of the master image of the modiste's *atelier* analyzed above (figure 2.1). The play's characters illustrate the hierarchy of the *atelier*: a *maîtresse*, aptly named Mlle. Marabout (a *marabout* is a prized stork feather often used to ornament women's hats and hair), presides over four *modistes*, named and numbered according to their rank. At the bottom of the hierarchy, Louise, in fourth position, is the lowly, unpaid *trottin*; she arrives early, and is repeatedly shown carrying hatboxes and given the menial task of delivery. Beneath her, there is only the maid, Madeleine. Several love plots intersect in the *atelier*, as characters at each level of the hierarchy attempt to hide their romantic attachments from the others. The *maîtresse* is attached to a fake Englishman, but, as she is constantly admonishing her apprentices to "follow her example" and eschew romantic involvements for the sake of the shop's reputation, she must conceal him in an armoire when Madeleine appears. The maid has her own paramour, however, who also must hide in a second armoire when the *modistes* return to the shop. The *modistes* too have suitors who must pretend to be shoppers to conceal their intentions from Mlle. Marabout and subsequently must also be concealed under the counter when they inappropriately visit the shop. The *trottin*, Louise, ridiculed by her fellow *modistes* for loving a neighboring artisan and overworked by her mistress, both in trimming and delivering hats, is ultimately revealed as the virtuous heroine at play's end—rewarded with a happy marriage and freed of her servitude in the *modiste*'s *atelier*. Perhaps she will now enter a business partnership with her husband, a maker of men's hats and, since she is a skilled *modiste*, help him expand his business.

Les Modistes reveals the tropes of the cultural stereotype of the *modiste* now so familiar: driven by a desire for frivolous romances and hoping to bedeck themselves in finery for visits to the theater or to balls, *modistes* typically use their workspace not for work but for mercenary love affairs. Eminently conscious of their reputation for sexual misconduct, these *modistes* are eager to conceal their romantic entanglements; and, equally aware of the hierarchy within the *atelier*, they repeatedly remind Louise of her position. Louise, the one hardworking *modiste*, however, remains virtuous, signaled by her marriage, when she enters into an "appropriate" union with a fellow artisan. In this way, even if the majority of the play's characters conform to it, Louise refutes the conventional plotline that the *atelier* doubled as a bordello, and that all *modistes* were seductive social climbers.[61] Vaudeville could thus be a place to re-evaluate some of the received ideas about social types, even as it invariably reinforced those very ideas.

As we see in *Les Modistes*, where the *maîtresse* and her haughty *première* are exposed as hypocrites while the lowly Louise rises to the top, challenging the hierarchy of the power structure of the *atelier* is a frequent theme in vaudeville. Sometimes these plays simultaneously presented a more overtly oppositional view, staging self-conscious *modistes* who seem intent on rehabilitating their image or making it in the world of honest commerce. In a vaudeville play entitled *La Révolte des modistes* (1834), a group of young fashion workers rebel against their mistress's overbearing rules when she refuses to allow them to go to a ball with their boyfriends. One of the young men, Jéricho, not fleeing in time before the arrival of Madame Clément, must hide in the *atelier*. While claiming to search for her pin box, the antagonistic *maîtresse-modiste* is actually keeping tabs on the girls; she is the regulatory presence that signals the legitimacy of the myth, but the play stages the girls as honest and their suitors as potential scoundrels. Jéricho's sweetheart, Finette, hides him under the counter and proceeds to fabricate a hat on his head, using the traditional pose of the *modiste*, so as not to compromise her reputation (ironically, with a man's head between her legs). We find the key gestures both of slapstick humor and of identity play in the stage directions: "[Finette: 'Come here … and don't move …' (She positions Jéricho between her legs; a chair piled with fabric hides his back, she puts a hat on his head at the same time; she is supposedly holding a cardboard head-form)]."[62] He hides there, posing as her head-form, just as the *maîtresse-modiste* comes into the workroom to see what her workers are up to. Unhappy with Finette's work, the *maîtresse* rearranges the ribbons herself and pokes a pin straight into Jéricho's head, thus punishing him unwittingly for his illicit presence in the *atelier*. The tools of the *modiste* are often used in these plays to nuance and undercut her stereotype. The hatpin gag is a favorite with vaudeville's *modistes*—it allows for easy physical comedy, but it also literalizes the notion of retribution, punishing male characters for their complicity with the *modiste*'s mythic status. The onstage reproduction of the classic work pose of the *modiste*, her cardboard *tête* between her knees, here replaced by a live man, could not help but conjure the familiar imagery.

Now, as before, the mythic reputation is turned on its head. For Finette becomes an activist worker, demanding higher pay and fairer working conditions, even leading her small group in a strike.[63] In a mock workers' rebellion, the *modistes* pledge allegiance to Finette, their leader, swear vengeance with their hat stands held high over a hatbox in a satirical reprise of Jacques-Louis David's famous painting "The Oath of the Horatii," and bar all men from their "revolutionary dinner." As expected in a genre whose formula demands a happy ending, even if social structures do not necessarily remain intact, the plot devolves into a gender battle when the mistress (who figures surveillance) enlists the boyfriends to bring the girls back to work if she allows them to take the *modistes* to the ball. Only Jéricho manages to infiltrate the girls' dinner, now dressed as a woman. All returns to normal in the end, the *modistes* happily paired with their respective beaux and returning to the workroom. However, their rebellion did earn them a night out and better working conditions, and Finette emerges as an early spokeswoman, albeit in comic form, of workers' rights. Her reputation as a loose woman is just a theatrical pretext, then, to open up possibilities of slapstick humor and identity play; and by the drama's end, her dominant identity as a fair-minded worker all but erases the mythic reputation of the flirtatious *modiste*. Thus, popular literature pushes back against sexual stereotyping and questions of class mixing with a rebuttal of gender norms. From the mid-1820s through the Second Empire, vaudevilles staged *modistes* who had to overcome the problems of a precarious reputation.

Typically, it is an economy of virtue that organizes the action, and the restoration of respectability motivates each play's central dénouement. Another play, *La Modiste au camp* (1846), makes the power of the *modiste*'s ability to control her own identity its central plot device: a virtuous *modiste*, once again from the rue Vivienne, must outwit a whole army regiment by changing costumes and roles multiple times, thus becoming the figure of fantasy for each soldier to locate her fiancé and marry him. As before, this vaudeville also trades on the conventional reputation of the *modiste*, in this case Agnès, only to produce a scenario of mistaken identity and ludicrous costume changes, ending in Agnès's reward of marriage. Indeed, one of the most frequent thematic conventions of vaudevilles featuring *modistes* is the credulity of men in power who assume that the *modiste* is theirs for the taking. Their fantasies are repeatedly foiled by the *modiste*'s quick wits, and it is the shameful behavior of married bourgeois men that is often exposed.

The most familiar vaudeville play featuring a *modiste*, partially set in an *atelier* and featuring a hat on which the entire action turns, is no doubt Eugène Labiche's *Un Chapeau de paille d'Italie* (1851). Here, bourgeois marriage is exposed as the transaction it so often was through a set of improbable juxtapositions. The literal consumption of a hat (by a horse) sets up a series of absurd plots around a wedding, involving consumption of different kinds: the adulterous affair of the lady whose hat was eaten by the horse; the bridegroom's feeble attempts to purchase a replacement for the destroyed hat in the *atelier* of his ex-girlfriend, Clara, a *modiste*; the inebriation of the ambulatory wedding party; and the bartering of the bride by her father as the wedding party follows along intact, yet unaware, on the mad search for a replacement hat. The hat, whose disappearance signals adultery, is also the key to Fadinard's (the groom's) happy marriage, since, in the end, the wedding is complete and the bride receives a hat as a wedding gift.

However, the veneer of happiness in marriage that concludes the play, and which it thus seems to promote, is undercut throughout, and the character of the *modiste* plays a key role in revealing the actual target of the play's satire. Before the action of the play, Clara, the *modiste*, was Fadinard's victim, left to fend for herself in Paris after the caddish hero duped her. When he turns up in her shop, we learn that Clara has landed on her feet and worked her way up through the hierarchy of a *modiste*'s *atelier* to open her own establishment. She continues to struggle to distinguish herself from other Parisian *modistes*; unlike them, she insists, *she* is virtuous (much like Jeanne of the 1890s primer). Clara both defines and defies the myth: she is industrious, artistic, and entrepreneurial. Yet she also wants to keep Fadinard away from her girls, who, as fashion workers, would certainly try to flirt with him; and, in spite of his earlier deception, she still hopes to marry him, begging him to take her to the Ambigu—where she could watch . . . a vaudeville play.

The stage directions for Act Two, set in her shop, repeat the now familiar prop conventions: "To the left, a counter parallel to the side partition. Above, on a shelf, one of those cardboard head-forms used by *modistes*,"[64] and her monologue reiterates the undecidability of the *modiste*: "My workers are at work . . . everything is fine . . . It was a good idea I had to set up shop . . . It's only been four months and already I'm getting orders . . . Ah! It's because I'm not a *modiste* like the others, not me! I'm respectable, no lovers for me . . . for the time being."[65] Typical of vaudeville, which both reflects and satirizes social mores, Clara thus reinforces the myth of the *modiste*, but her success ends up being her shop and her enterprise, *not* a happy marriage. By the end of Labiche's play, Clara the *modiste* disappears from view, once more cheated by Fadinard, who had promised again to marry her; but we are left with the impression that she is better off without the cad, who is not redeemed in the end, and whose bride resembles, in her mute acquiescence, the head-form in the *modiste*'s shop. That Clara doesn't follow the typical *modiste*'s theatrical pathway leading to marriage is significant in a play that makes bourgeois marriage the central target of its satire.

Labiche was one of the most popular and prolific vaudevillists. Working in the mid- to late-nineteenth century, he was the clear heir to Scribe. His use of a hat plot and the character of a *modiste* places him in a tradition of vaudeville theater already commonplace by the 1850s. Labiche and the other vaudevillists consistently begin with the myth of the flirtatious *modiste* for vaudeville's own conventional ends: slapstick comedy, mistaken identity, reversal of fortunes. The location of many of these plays in hat shops or workshops invites disguise and cross-dressing, principal elements of comedy. In vaudeville, then, the myth still holds sway, and the spectator's leering gaze is multiplied in a packed audience; but it is transformed, and sympathy almost always enfolds the *modiste*, not her detractors. Moreover, by foregrounding the spaces, tools, and products of the *modiste*'s trade, this play, like so many others, emphasizes work for women as an alternative to marriage.

In an 1860 vaudeville entitled *Modiste et modeste*, performed at the Théâtre des Folies-Dramatiques, the myth of the "immodest *modiste*" is directly refuted by the hard-working Fifine. The play's action turns on the question of Fifine's marriage: will she be mercenary and marry a wealthy British suitor, or will she marry her more appropriately classed friend, the *petit-commis* (minor clerk) Adrien? Many of the standard clichés are at work in this play—references to the *modiste*'s moral laxity, props of hat-making, etc.—however, remarkably, here Fifine not only rejects the wealthy suitor, but she herself proposes marriage to Adrien. Her "modesty" is related at once to sex and to class: properly respectable, she will not sell herself to a wealthy bidder, nor will she reach for luxuries beyond the "modest" means of *petites ouvrières* (low-wage working women) and shop attendants. While fulfilling vaudeville's classic happy ending of marriage, and reaffirming class hierarchies by marrying within her station, Fifine's seizure and control of the very plotline of vaudeville nonetheless introduces a disruption of the bourgeois codes that gendered and classed behavior in nineteenth-century France.

Vaudeville's *modistes* are for the most part well aware of their mythical status, as evinced by some of their own comments about their suspect reputations. These plays also cultivate the other side of the working girl, however; her industriousness, her solidarity with other working girls, her drive to succeed, and her skill in creating fashion, the latter of which sometimes also becomes her survival mechanism, as in the case of Labiche's Clara, or even her escape hatch. What these plays share is the celebration of the subjectivity of a *modiste* who takes some control of her situation to determine her own destiny—not, as the myth of the *modiste* would indicate, either through prostitution or marriage, but through a mastery of her work and its prescribed artifice. I am not going so far as to suggest that vaudeville is the subversive antidote to the mythologizing print culture of the period. Rather, vaudeville has it both ways: the myth is preserved, thus satisfying the prurient interest of the bourgeois public in the sex appeal of the working woman and satisfying that same public's desire for moral delineation from the working classes; but the myth is also challenged by the *modiste* who defies her narrative and sticks it to bourgeois institutions and (often) masculine control.

Finally, a vaudeville called *Le Trottin de la modiste* (1847) will serve both to consolidate the comic potential of the *modiste*'s tools and to suggest how wide the gap was between myth and reality in the living conditions of these workers.[66] In this play, a hatbox, rather than a head-form or hatpin, becomes the centerpiece of the slapstick comedy and contains the secret to a family romance. Against her father's will, a young *modiste*, Aglaë, marries her seducer, Buridan, and bears his child. Her *modiste*-friend, Aphanasie, shows up with her *trottin*, a man called Loriot, who, secretly in love with Aphanasie, carries her boxes for her, signifying that she works in a high-end shop. The hatbox is excessively heavy, and Loriot can't resist opening it while Aphanasie is busy fending off the advances of Aglaë's new husband. It contains a baby's layette—clothes and accessories for the illicit baby have replaced a woman's hat. "Ah! You never know what's hiding in a *modiste*'s hatbox!" exclaims Loriot, expressing the fantasy that the hatbox represents and showing that it can be equated with desire.[67] As the plot advances, the hatbox becomes even heavier in a later scene and contains something that moves! Loriot quickly ties up the hatbox again and pokes it with a hatpin for an air hole. Then he loses it in a scuffle with the angry (grand)father, who is frustrated in his attempts to locate his daughter Aglaë. The hatbox now contains Aglaë's baby, who is eventually returned to its mother. In keeping with conventions of vaudeville, in the end, families are reunited, and fortunes and marriages are made.

This play exaggerates the function of the hatbox both to define identity and elicit fantasy. Because of its instant recognizability, this prop gives the *modiste* the cover to step out of her professional role and into supposedly illicit activity; and it also propels the plot forward through its role in signifying fantasy. Containing a variety of objects as it circulates through Paris and changes hands, the hatbox repeats the idea of the instability of the *modiste*'s identity; and yet, it also allows Aphanasie to orchestrate a solidarity narrative in which she can rescue her colleague. Through her wits, Aphanasie ties everything up neatly with husband, baby, and father's consent—and she herself is rewarded with love and fortune. Most importantly, this *modiste* gets a shop of her own: the ultimate reward is thus presented as autonomous work.

The happy ending of the vaudeville play, with its comic use of the most recognizable prop of the *modiste*—a hatbox—finds its tragic foil in the pages of the daily press, however, where we encounter an unhappy variation on a similar plot. The *fait divers*—or sensationalized news story—is a key coda to this slapstick comedy, given that vaudevilles were typically inspired by current events.[68] *Le Petit Journal* of November 1866, citing an incident recorded in the legal paper *Le Droit*, reports a dead newborn discovered in a hatbox at the Gare du Nord. After some investigating, the police arrested Marie B. . ., who admitted she has given birth out of wedlock. Claiming the baby was stillborn, she confessed to having placed the body in a hatbox and left it at the train station, where unsuspecting passengers took it to the lost and found. After several days, an odor signaled that the hatbox contained something other than a hat, and the girl was arrested; her ex-lover was not.[69] Of course, we cannot know if Marie B. . . was in fact a *modiste*, but her access to a hatbox and her low social status suggest she was at least engaged in fashion work. Like the hatbox, with its absence-in-presence signifying power, the mythic shell of the *modiste* is visible—her youth, romantic entanglement, and sexual activity all conform to the conventional traits of the *modiste*. Yet other elements, absent from the standard narrative—infanticide and desperation—are revealed in the *fait divers*. And while the *fait divers* criminalizes Marie B… to the benefit of her ex-lover, it also exposes cracks in a monolithic narrative. Marie B…'s tragic tale thus serves as a realistic counterpoint, or perhaps even a reality check, to the mythologizing surrounding the *modiste*, providing an alternative, non-ludic dénouement to the plot developed in the vaudeville play even as it recycles many of its conventional traits.

The Real *Modistes* of Nineteenth-Century Paris

While the genre of the *fait divers* often supports the romanticized mythology of the *modiste*, it also works against that narrative in some ways, exhibiting a kind of multifunctionality. Lionel Gossman argues for the inclusion of the *fait divers* in historical analysis, claiming that it "may provoke a reconsideration of what we believe we know about history and society and lead us to consider previously unobserved aspects of the past."[70] With respect to the figure of the nineteenth-century *modiste*, the *fait divers* offers material for a storyline that is both thriving and conventional—and a counter-story in the blank spaces of the text that invite questioning or speculation. In addition, the *faits divers* often shares the space of a single page with other press rubrics featuring *modistes*—columns whose sober tone and prosaic content present a quiet rebuke to the megaphone of myth. These less sensational columns in the daily and weekly press, such as marriage and business announcements, provide entirely banal counterpoints to the popular sensational image of the *modiste*.

Their typecast notwithstanding, real *modistes*—from the destitute *petites mains* and *trottins* inhabiting unventilated attic apartments to the *premières* and *maîtresses-modistes* who had risen to the top of their profession and were poking at the edges of the middle class—populated the city in increasing numbers throughout the nineteenth century.[71] An investigation into the weekly press from the 1830s through the 1890s affirms their presence under a variety of rubrics, corresponding to assorted activities and relative to their station within the hierarchy of the *métier*.[72] From crime stories and sensational *faits divers*, in which young workers are often featured as victims and perpetrators alike of crimes petty and serious, to discussions of commercial successes and failures, in which we find legal announcements of business ventures as well as bankruptcies, dissolutions, and debt collections, *modistes* from both ends of the professional hierarchy are frequent figures on the pages of the popular press.

The index of "reality" varies widely across these types of columns, with *faits divers* often intentionally embellished and sensationalized even if they may contain the kernel of a news event, while marriage announcements and business listings provided accurate, purely factual transmission of information in brief. Although the journalist is omniscient in both types of articles, in the *faits divers*, the point of view and voice are often discernible through word choice and tone, as we shall see. I briefly consider published marriage announcements and how they compete with the widely disseminated image of the flirtatious young *modiste*; afterwards, I consider a sampling of *faits divers* that pick up some of the key traits of the *modiste* and the themes of her narrative. In spite of their frequent conformity with the myth of the *modiste*, these articles nonetheless can reveal gaps or even present counter-narratives to the well-established image. I also examine the commerce rubrics and bankruptcy files that often appeared alongside the *faits divers* and which, when read in parallel, present alternative stories that not only contest the outsized mythology of the *modiste*, but also permit a glimpse into the lived realities of these working women.

Despite claims in the cultural imaginary about the *modiste*'s penchant for licentiousness—ranging from outright prostitution to the seduction of wealthy men from the upper classes in hopes of exceeding her social station—in many newspapers we encounter ample evidence of *modistes* leading respectable, even mundane, lives. Columns announcing marriages, for example, in which *modistes* are regularly listed as marrying within the ranks of their own artisan class, indicate how commonplace marriage was within one's own social class, despite a pervasive cultural anxiety evinced in visual and literary culture surrounding the imposture of the artisan into the upper classes. That these announcements even exist attests to some measure of control on the part of these working people, who would have actively chosen, and likely paid, to publish their wedding announcements. Unlike the ubiquitous representations circulating in other media forms and in *faits divers*, *modistes* actually exercised some agency over their own image in these nondescript daily columns.

Even a limited selection from the *Journal des débats* reveals, for example, that in March 1852, M. Roemer, "fabricant de pianos, rue de Marais, 10," married "Mlle. Schaale, modiste, rue de Grenelat, 49"; a few months later, in July, "M. Guillemot, tailleur, rue Lévêque, 6" married "Mlle. Albert, modiste"; and later that same month, a "lampiste, rue de Marais, 73," by the name of M. Flory, wed Mlle. Vitau, a *modiste* living in the rue du Faubourg-Saint-Martin.[73] As the press makes clear, it was a matter of course that *modistes* married dance instructors, pharmacy students, salesmen, engravers, cabinetmakers—among many other artisanal workers—routine facts located in the fine print of daily marriage announcements that puncture the stereotype of the immodest *modiste* who sought only to escape her condition through marrying up, if she married at all. Indeed, these wedding announcements doubly emphasize heteronormative respectability: both in the sense that these fashion workers were in large part marrying within their own class and that they were, in fact, marrying, since it was widely assumed that many of them, seduced and seducing and immoral, lived out of wedlock. The presumption of the *modistes*' universal precarity, then, so closely tied to an essential aspect of their stereotyped identity as fragile, young female prey, is undermined by the substance of the social status of their spouses. These *modistes* are socially liminal, situated above the proletariat and below the middle class; they are consistently skilled workers who marry artisans with solid professions, like Louise, the *trottin* from *Les Modistes*.

However, as indicated by the case of Marie B. . ., who left her dead infant at the Gare du Nord, many working women, some of them *modistes*, bore children out of wedlock and, if the press is any guide, were sometimes driven to infanticide or suicide. Unlike routine marriage announcements, this type of information was the stuff of *faits divers* and was certainly not narrated by *modistes* themselves. Importantly, in these press reports, which were primarily anecdotes sensationalized to attract prurient readers' attention, the subjects did not control their own image. Rather, the news stories were composed by male journalists; and although their content contained actual events pertaining to questions of social interest, the events were filtered through an increasingly powerful media. As Michelle Perrot explains: "[a] staging of private life, the *fait divers* is fed by social conflicts studied by journalists, mediators of collective feelings. Chosen, constructed, the *fait divers* is necessarily manipulated."[74] And similar to other contemporary popular media such as vaudeville plays, which themselves drew on *faits divers*, the press, and particularly the *fait divers* genre, used figures like *modistes* to appeal to readers by perpetuating the most sensational elements of their dominant cultural representation: youth and beauty, amorality, and a penchant for romantic entanglements.

Some of these stories contribute to the same type of mythmaking discussed earlier, while others leave space for speculation and empathy for the individual and the real-life conditions of working people behind the mythically sexy image. Reports in the juridical press and in *faits divers* abound, for example, in which a young *modiste*, often labeled *désespérée* (despairing) attempts suicide. Most frequently, the motivation behind these suicides and attempted suicides is ascribed to heartbreak. In one such instance of attempted suicide reported in *Le Figaro* in 1869, the narrative framing of the *fait divers* illustrates the pervasiveness of romantic upset as the key cause of such serious actions:

—A heartbreak once again has been the cause of an attempted suicide, which fortunately did not end in fatal results.

A pretty young modiste, Antoinette R. . ., living at 38 rue Folie-Regnault, threw herself around 2 o'clock down a well located in the courtyard of this house.

Misters Nicolas, wood carver, Biget, day worker, and Lavalette, cart-driver, who had seen her accomplish this desperate act, immediately organized the rescue of the unfortunate girl and pulled her out safe and sound.

Let's add that she has decided to no longer try to take her life.[75]

While the text's author seems to disappear behind journalistic objectivity, clues relating to a conventional male worldview are detectable. This *modiste*, like so many others, is visually pleasing to the male viewer—*jeune et jolie* (young and pretty), she is motivated by *désespoir d'amour* (despairing love) and is thus *malheureuse* (unhappy, unfortunate), and so conforms to the classic plot of romantic entanglement. She is, however, *heureusement* (fortunately) rescued *saine et sauve* (safe and sound) from a potentially fatal act by three working men who happened to be watching her in the courtyard. Male surveillance and voyeurism are coded here as heroism.

Readers, likely both disturbed and titillated by the potential violence, are reassured by the narrator who, in a rather condescending tone, adds a subsequent detail that everything is fine because, we are told, this *modiste* has "decided not to take her life anymore." Note the first-person plural form, *Ajoutons*, which at once includes the three male saviors in the concluding statement and re-objectifies the *modiste*, who is relegated to the third person. Like so many other such characters in *faits divers*, this *modiste* has no control over her story: we do not hear her speak, nor can we know why this love caused her such despair, other than to accept the journalist's vague, causal explanation. While he attributes her suicide attempt to heartbreak, however, it might just as easily have been the result of an unwanted pregnancy or abuse by her lover.

Another woeful tale describes the violent, self-inflicted injury with her own hatpin of a *modiste* named Germaine, inspired by her lover's announcement that his parents are forcing him to marry someone else. Entitled "Drame d'amour" (love drama), the story announces that "the young lady ... desolate, pulled a long pin from her hat and plunged it deep into her chest. She was going to stab herself again when her boyfriend grabbed her arm."[76] Promising to marry her, he bundles her, bleeding profusely, into a carriage as she assures the police arriving on the scene that, now that she has been promised marriage, "I feel better now, practically cured!"[77] Here, she is rescued by her lover, although his promise of marriage will hardly staunch the flow of blood. While this *modiste* is quoted, her words only confirm the stereotype of a lovesick girl, a trope of the conventional plot, with a propensity to self-harm.

In both stories, the *modiste* is young, and thus presumably an apprentice or low-level worker in an *atelier*. In both cases as well, her despair related to love drives her to a self-destructive act. For both girls, *malheur* (sadness, misfortune) becomes *bonheur* (happiness, good fortune) as the *modiste* is saved by a male hero. Each story also ends with the reassurance to the reader that all is well and that violence is past: the girl is "safe and sound" and "cured," respectively. But these stories conclude on a note of overzealous protestation from the journalistic narrator. For how can readers be sure that Antoinette is now over her heartbreak and that later, when three brawny workmen are not observing her, she won't simply try again? Likewise, how can we know that Germaine's generous suitor will keep his promise, especially given that he is no doubt financially beholden to his parents? Key to both stories are the journalistic framing and the repeated theme of heartbreak as driving these girls to self-harm. By removing their despair to the affective realm of romance, any other possible motives—poverty, physical or sexual violence, unwanted pregnancy—are effectively foreclosed. And the insincere, even mocking tone of this journalist, like so many others, along with the repeated theme of heartache as principal motive, suggests that these women are quite simply disposable; like their stories, they are a dime a dozen.

The journalist's imprint is often more legible in other *faits divers*, where the *modiste*'s perspective is occasionally reported but never inhabited. In a lighter version of the standard tale of heartbreak, for example, pejoratively entitled "Une nouvelle Dalila" (a modern Delilah) a *fait-diversier* (that is, someone who writes these stories) describes the vengeance of a *modiste* when she discovers her lover's infidelity:

> Mlle. Mélanie T..., a young modiste living in the faubourg Saint-Denis, having learned that her lover had been carrying on an affair for two weeks with another woman, and struck to the heart by jealousy, avenged herself in a cruel way. One night while her lover was sleeping, she armed herself with scissors and with the greatest of care cut off half of his mustache, his beard, and his hair; she then went out, leaving him a note explaining the motive for her vengeance. Didn't the very naive shorn man consider making a complaint to the police?[78]

Expertly wielding the tools of her trade, the scissors she would use to cut fabric or ribbon as she decorated a hat, Mélanie T... manages to exact a comic vengeance on her scoundrel of a lover, expanding her skill even, from *modiste* to *coiffeuse*. If his new haircut were not so humiliating and he could bring himself to report her, the story implies, Mélanie might well be cited or even jailed. Despite the *modiste*'s apparent agency in this *fait divers*, and her clever deployment of her particular skill set, it is important to note the heavy hand of the journalist. He essentially labels Mélanie a sinner by naming her after the famously emasculating biblical virago Delilah, identifying her gesture, albeit ironically, as *cruel*, even as he presents the betrayal that provoked it as typical, earning no other qualifications. Finally, we are told that the *modiste* writes her story in the form of a note; yet readers are denied unmediated access to her voice.

Countless stories such as these reinforce the familiar elements of the *modiste* mythology and make use of the material props associated with her narrative (hatbox, hatpin, scissors) to conjure the specificity of the *modiste*, always young, always pretty. But here, unlike on the vaudeville stage, the *modiste*-protagonist is likely to end up in jail, as in the case of Marie B..., in hospital, or worse still, the morgue, as in the case of Germaine, who may suffer blood loss, or Antoinette, who may yet throw herself down another well. Note that the names of lovers are carefully omitted. For while some degree of sympathy is solicited for the desperate, unhappy, or even jealous girl, guilt is never attributed in a meaningful way to the male perpetrators of the *modiste*'s woe; their behavior was, we must presume, neither sanctioned nor reproached to any extent.

Other *faits divers*, however, are less firmly attached to the romanticized view of a lovelorn fashion worker, allowing more space for a counter-narrative. One such anecdote describes the rescue of a *modiste* whose silence regarding her motives gives rise to speculation about the actual source of her despair:

A young *modiste* of eighteen, Pauline A..., living on Godefroy-Cavaignac street, went down, yesterday, at around four o'clock in the afternoon, to the banks of the quai Saint Bernard. After wandering for a moment on the quai, the young girl approached the edge and suddenly threw herself into the Seine.

A witness to this desperate attempt, a loading-dock worker named Laurent Allanche, rushed to her rescue and was fortunate enough to pull her from the water safe and sound.

The young *modiste*, who was taken to the hôpital de la Pitié, refused to share the motive that drove her to commit suicide.[79]

This *fait divers* repeats the recipe of many other such anecdotes. The key themes recur, along with a particular vocabulary, echoing and reinforcing the standardization of the narrative. She is young (*jeune*), an adjective repeated twice in this short description, and desperate (*désespérée*) and her act is sudden (*soudain*); and her rescue, by a robust male onlooker, leaves her "safe and sound." Here, however, although he has inscribed his voice forcefully through his lexical choices, the journalist does not, or cannot, for want of information, ascribe a motive to the *modiste*'s act, and while she hardly seizes control of her story, Pauline A...'s silence refuses the standard romanticized narrative of unhappy love and suggests other motivations, perhaps less palatable to a reading public, for her suicide attempt. Was she pregnant, starving, or both?

Right on script, another *fait divers*, published in *Le Petit Moniteur*, assumes heartbreak as the cause of suicide, but even a cursory glance begs an alternate reading: "Last night, around midnight, following a violent discussion with her lover, a woman named Blanchard, *modiste*, living at 14 Douai Street, threw herself from the window of her fifth-floor apartment. The poor thing was killed instantly."[80] Again, the formula is repeated: the journalist offers identifying information, a name, address, and time, which support the fact-based claims of journalistic writing. The standard elements of the journalistic approach situate the story in factual information, and readers learn the victim's profession, "*modiste*." Erasing himself behind a terse, matter-of-fact description, the journalist nonetheless controls the narrative by asserting a causal sequence of events: she threw herself from the fifth-floor window following an argument with her lover. One might just as readily assume, however, that this *modiste* was attempting to escape a dangerous relationship, or even that she was in that moment the victim of domestic violence when she suffered a fall from the window. Indeed, it is not far-fetched to imagine that she was pushed to her death in a fit of rage by the lover himself. According to the press, along with drowning, falling from a high window was a frequent mode of death for working-class girls.[81] Perhaps they were not so much lovelorn as impoverished or victims of violence.

Still other press stories tell of death or injury by asphyxiation, whether intentional or not, usually as the result of burning coal on portable stoves in unventilated apartments, under the rooftops, where the poorest lived. Jeanne Bouvier's account confirms the necessity of this type of makeshift stove, as the uppermost apartments lacked fireplaces and chimneys (and running water), and so to cook for oneself and keep warm, working girls would use a portable coal stove.[82] Accidents were frequent, but so too were suicides and attempted suicides, as an anecdote from *La République française*, entitled "Drame de la misère" (Drama of misery), recounts. Here, a mother resorts to attempted murder-suicide by asphyxiation: "A lady, Rose L. . ., *modiste*, living on Bouquet-de-Longchamps street, tried to kill herself last night, along with her six-year-old son. The unfortunate woman, driven by misery, had lit a portable stove in her room."[83] Saved by her neighbors, her son escapes danger, while the woman herself, perhaps widowed or abandoned by her partner, suffers a less hopeful prognosis. She remains hospitalized, but her naming indicates that a police report has been filed and that she may face prosecution if she survives.

Alongside these tales of desperation and misery, news stories also pick up other key themes so frequently repeated in the visual culture, as explored earlier, perhaps most notably the trope of the *modiste* as sexual prey and object of unwanted voyeurism. Just as Gavarni (figures 2.9 and 2.10) illustrated the allure for the male viewer of the *modiste* as she delivered her goods on the streets, and the innumerable images and narratives of modistes at work in the *atelier* crystallized an aesthetics of looking that figured the *modiste* as an available object of sexual desire, the *fait divers* genre performed similar narrative functions. An anecdote from *Le Siècle* (1857) recounts the tale of Mlle. Claudine G. . ., a *modiste* living, as expected, in a garret apartment, who, sewing one evening by her window, hears a strange sound. She discovers a young man blowing her a kiss from an apartment across the courtyard. When she ignores him, he sends her a missive attached to her cat's collar, announcing that, like her cat, he will make his way the next evening into her apartment, creeping across the rooftops and through her window, to offer his love in person. At first alarmed, Claudine decides to invite a friend over, perhaps hoping it might be amusing or planning, out of fear, not to be alone when the intruder arrives. But when they hear the sounds of someone approaching over the rooftops in the dark, events take a gruesome turn: the rooftop stalker slips and falls to his death in the courtyard below.[84]

While the anecdote exudes the sensationalism (tragic death) and narrative outlines (adventure, passion) typical of *faits divers*, it also contains details of the actual living and working conditions of young urban *modistes*. Claudine lives in an unlit apartment under the rooftops, so that she sits by the window at night for whatever meager light, and presumably air, might reach her, completing piece work to supplement her paltry income as a *modiste* at the bottom of the *atelier* hierarchy. In addition to these signs of hardship so common to working women, she is no doubt also harassed on the streets and in the shop by the likes of Gavarni's *flâneur*. Perceived through the eyes of the *modiste* herself, the anecdote reveals that she is also stalked at home by the voyeur next door. For all of its sensational appeal and evocation of sympathy for the hapless roof-creeping would-be lover, this *fait divers*, like so many others, inadvertently exposes less dramatic truths about the living and working conditions of urban workers such as *modistes*. Their glamorous image notwithstanding, in story after story, *modistes* are frequently the victims of crime, sometimes violent, in the streets, the *atelier*s, and their homes. A counter-reading, or even merely a careful reading, of the *fait divers* genre thus pierces the illusion propagated by the dominant mythology.

Indeed, as Michelle Perrot explains in her genealogy of the genre of the *fait divers*, as the descendant of the oral *canard*, in some cases "the *fait divers* thus becomes the gesture of hidden people and the reclaiming of their right to history."[85] If *faits divers*, read critically, help to fill in some of the gaps in the lives of the *petites mains* of the *atelier*, those youthful, potential *modistes* hoping to ascend the professional hierarchy to arrive some day at greater financial stability, another press rubric clarifies the entrepreneurial activities of the women at the other pole of the hierarchy, those more elite *modistes*. The business columns in a wide variety of dailies offer a glimpse into the successes and failures of countless fashion enterprises. These listings of legal acts and agreements, like the marriage announcements with which I began this discussion of the press, illustrate the degree to which the daily life of *modistes* carried on, despite the constant melodrama of the *faits divers* that was given more space on the page.

In the business columns, male and female entrepreneurs share coverage. Some arrangements are successful; others are not. Business associations, such as that in 1868 of "Mlle. Elisa Hermann, *modiste*, living in Paris, boulevard Malesherbes, n. 43, and Mlle. Constance-Louise Souprey, *modiste*, living in Paris, rue de la Pépinière, n. 6," are numerous, and the details, while certainly not as gripping as a *fait divers*, nonetheless shed light on the real-life circumstances and work of nineteenth-century Parisian *modistes*. In this case, we learn that Mlle. Souprey was a minor, but was "authorized to do business after receiving her father's permission" and that she would be an equal partner with Mlle. Hermann.[86] Their business partnership was set for ten years and was to be located at 43 boulevard Malesherbes, where Mlle. Hermann lived and worked. In another such announcement, "Mme. Joséphine Michel, spouse of Etienne Barthélémy, authorized, *modiste*" partnered with "Mlle. Eugénie Leroux, of age, *modiste*" to form a business under the name of "Barthélémy et Leroux."[87] In that same issue, indeed in the block immediately above, a *modiste*'s business partnership that should have continued for another four years was dissolved. Mlle. Léonie Guyot has ended a partnership with her unnamed business partner; a liquidation would follow.[88] Evidence of the establishment and the dissolution of business partnerships is frequent in these publications, leading to the conclusion that *modistes* were often pooling their resources to respond to an exploding consumer desire for the commodity they alone could produce.

These rather dry facts detailing creditors, addresses, names, and legal status are innumerable throughout the nineteenth-century daily press. The business columns are practically unreadable, given the size of the type in which they are printed, and they frequently appear in the back pages of the paper, nearly out of sight. If they lack the luster and drama of a tabloid story, they nonetheless reveal the steady work and entrepreneurial drive of Parisian *modistes* of the nineteenth century.

Bankruptcy records in the City of Paris archives help to further flesh out this story. Over the course of the entire century, sheaves of legal dossiers detail the dissolutions of *modistes*' businesses. While these particular records emphasize the failures of their entrepreneurial endeavors—that so many were even established and operated so continuously and steadily over the course of the century—bears witness to the importance of the industry.[89]

In these documents we find evidence of the variety of women working in the industry: widows, such as the Dame Veuve Bozon, who operated a *magasin de modes* on the rue du Caire, until her bankruptcy in 1879; or unmarried *modistes*, such as the two who ran "Demoiselles Desbarques et Cie" in the rue de la Chaussée d'Antin, Angèle-Hortense and Marie-Marguerite-Louise; and even married couples in business together, like Dame Sambon, wife of Paul Ernest Sambon, whose commercial identity, the eponymous name of her shop on the rue de la Ferme des Mathurins, was simply "Dame Paul." Some of these women are classified as *modistes*, while others continue to use the more archaic term *marchandes de modes*. Logic would imply that the vast quantity of bankruptcies of these industrious nineteenth-century women indicates the precariousness and perhaps the expense of the work, a succession of failures signaling the difficulty for women to make it in the world of commerce. While I certainly do not dispute this logic, the quantity of records and century-long pattern of bankruptcies of *modiste* shops also reveal traces of actual working women engaged in what was obviously a popular and highly competitive urban profession.

A final, brief exploration of several such cases helps to track the contours of the life's work of several *modistes* and shows traces, if faint, of their lived experience. The Gobley sisters, Élisa Anastasie and Clothilde Augustine, for example, *marchandes de modes* with a shop at 16 and 17 rue Vivienne, where they also lived, declared bankruptcy in March 1854. The bankruptcy documents reveal biographical and descriptive details that help to humanize women who are typically reduced by various nineteenth-century popular media to stereotypes, as I have shown throughout this chapter. Élisa was born in 1828, her younger sister Clothilde two years later, both in the village of Ancy-Le Franc in the Yonne, about 140 miles southeast of Paris. Here they lived with their father, a baker, and mother until they were seventeen and fifteen, respectively. In 1845, they went together to Paris to work for a *lingère* on the rue de Paradis Poissonnière and then returned to their village to open their own establishment. But when their parents died of cholera during the 1849 outbreak, the sisters returned to Paris, one working for a *modiste* in the rue Vivienne and the other for another *magasin*. With their inheritance, they eventually opened their own shop in the rue Vivienne, but "their business was not prosperous."[90] Their financial troubles began in 1851: their debts continued to mount and their accounting was not terribly accurate.

When the administrator of the bankruptcy (*le syndic*), M. Jobert, arrived to take stock of what remained of their possessions in March 1854, he found only twenty francs in the register, which he allowed the girls to keep to cover their personal expenses. The rest of the inventory amounted to

2,516.09 francs' worth of merchandise, industrial equipment and furnishings, and household items. The merchandise alone represented nearly 1,900 francs of the total value and contained a diverse array of raw materials and products that one would expect to find in a *modiste*'s shop: ribbons, satin fabric, black and white lace, and *blondes*, and embroidery, as well as finished products such as ribboned bonnets and eight hats, most valued at eight francs each, with one hat valued at eighty-eight francs. The tools and fruits of their profession were their most expensive possessions, indicating perhaps a prioritization of their commitment to work over their personal life. The breadth in valuation of hats tells us that they had a range of clients as well; at least one client might afford an expensive, even a spectacular hat.

More affecting than the remains of the young sisters' business, however, is the list of their household and personal possessions, from a smattering of kitchen objects and furnishings to their clothing. Here, much of it is in pairs: two poplin dresses, two silk aprons, two dresses in *jaconas*, a heavy cotton fabric, two silk hats, two pairs of booties, and one upright piano, rented from piano makers Veingartner and Becker, as a receipt proves. Each sister possessed only a few articles of clothing, a detail that paints a starkly different picture from that of the popular mythology, which dressed *modistes* in cashmere and taffeta (if they were dressed at all) as they partied all night with multiple suitors. It would seem, by contrast, that the Gobley sisters' preferred entertainment was a night at home together, taking turns playing the piano.

Another *modiste*, Dame Kirchleim, went bankrupt in 1864, and while the documents yield little in the way of a poignant inventory, they do reveal a trajectory quite different from that of the Gobley sisters and produce an equal share of empathy. Madame Kirchleim (we never learn her first name) was born in 1840 and educated at the Maison Impériale de Saint Denis, a detail that indicates that she was the daughter or granddaughter of one of Napoléon I's recipients of the Légion d'Honneur.[91] Like Élisa Gobley, she launched herself at seventeen but married a M. Kirchleim two years later, with a substantial dowry of 6,000 francs inherited from her father. Unfortunately, M. Kirchleim, who used his wife's dowry to open a *magasin de chapellerie* (hat shop) in the trendy Opéra neighborhood, was an inept businessman, forcing them to downsize dramatically shortly thereafter and move from their well-located shop off the boulevard des Capucines to a small room on a side street, where things continued to deteriorate. The husband fled the marriage and the country, leaving his wife to try to recover financially on her own by continuing to make ladies' hats. Ultimately, unable to pay the massive debts left behind by her husband's mismanagement, she descended into bankruptcy and moved in with her mother in the passage des Forges. Unlike the Gobley sisters, Madame Kirchleim started her adult life with a dowry and a husband, working as a *modiste* in tandem with her husband's *chapellerie*. But she was the victim of his mismanagement, and, equally important, of a social and legal system that mandated that her husband control her money.

A final example, from 1873, details the bankruptcy of Mlle. Lucie Desbordes, who, at thirty-two, owned and operated a *modiste*'s shop at 257 rue Saint-Honoré, one of the most exclusive addresses for

Paris fashion in the nineteenth century. Lucie was born in the town of Bourbon-l'Archambault in central France; and while we learn little more about her biography, the inventory of her possessions, both personal effects and merchandise taken at the time of bankruptcy, provides key insights into how she lived and worked. The inventory reveals, as with the Gobley sisters, more value in the merchandise from her shop than in her personal possessions. Along with various types of laces, embroidery, and fabrics, she also possessed sets of artificial flowers and ribbons, the remains of a once productive business that would now be sold to pay off her creditors. Her personal possessions were quite meager: a bed with bedding, linens, a table and two chairs, and *effet-usage de femme*, or "ladies' personal effects."[92] After losing her shop, where she had also resided, a typical practice for the shop owner, the bankruptcy administrator learns that Lucie Desbordes currently occupied a room on the sixth floor of a house on the nearby rue du Marché St. Honoré. Lucie had thus fallen from her position as shop owner to the condition of a poor fashion worker, ironically moving "up" to live in poverty under the rooftops even as she suffered social descent.

While these and many other bankrupt *modistes* of nineteenth-century Paris offer examples of failed entrepreneurship and indeed of hardship, they also recount narratives radically different from the conventional stories of the *faits divers*, the vaudeville stage, and the widely disseminated print culture around this figure. The vast quantity of bankruptcy cases on record in nineteenth-century Paris attests to the scope and competitiveness of the industry and reveals the variety of women engaged in the work. We find sisters like Élisa and Clothilde entering into partnerships with each other, perhaps full of excitement as they ventured back to Paris with their inheritance; or a woman like Madame Kirchleim, who, better off than many, sadly partnered with a good-for-nothing husband who squandered her small fortune; or Lucie Desbordes, who, at a fairly young age, built what must have been a successful business at one point, given that it was located on one of the hottest fashion streets in Paris. Each of these cases illustrates that the profession of *modiste* attracted different types of women who could enter into it from a variety of starting points. Even if their trajectories do not reflect success stories, they confirm a shared entrepreneurial drive, whether in young girls from the provinces attempting to make it in the big city or in a married *Parisienne* using the talents she possessed to survive a bad marriage and financial hardship.

Unlike the normativity of vaudeville, the drama of the *faits divers*, and the provocations of popular print culture, these business notices and bankruptcy documents offer a quiet testimony of actual activity and reveal traces of *modistes*' real work lives; this very fact of work presents some measure of resistance to the mythology that so dominated cultural perceptions of this figure. The daily and weekly press as well as legal records throughout the century prove deep archives for this stereotyped figure, depicted as either sexual prey or social predator, a frivolous artist with fairy fingers, whose actual labor vanishes behind a glamorized image that was duplicated and disseminated repeatedly by a dominant culture uneasy with the presence of real working women, especially those who, like *modistes*, moved about in public as part of their job and often resembled their social betters. Just as the hatbox expressed the recognizable and highly visible contours of a well-worn sign system and simultaneously concealed unexpected realities of lived experience, as removed from the glamorous luxury commodity of a lady's hat as can be, the signifying mythology of the *modiste* concealed lived and alternate realities that an examination of unexplored archives, such as journalistic and legal archives, can reveal.

These types of archives are precious, for they contribute a valuable human dimension to the stereotyped narrative and monolithic image of the *modiste* propagated by the popular media, a media perpetuating an ideology shaped by deep anxieties around working women, in particular, those who, like *modistes*, so closely resembled and potentially became bourgeois. What they lack in spectacular visibility, however, they make up for in sheer factual value, if we will but notice them. For they quietly tell the story of a booming industry, managed and worked almost exclusively by women, operating often in partnerships and laboring in *ateliers*, to build the economic powerhouse that was nineteenth-century Paris fashion.

Demystifying the *Modiste*

I began this chapter by asserting that *modistes* were cultural riddles, liminal figures who, in the nineteenth century, became a form of shorthand for the eroticization of fashion. Their reputation for coquettishness—a social form of artifice—was enhanced by their skill in producing fashionable creations out of the scraps of luxury. *Modistes* were walking advertisements for their products; indeed, they *were* the product, social creatures at the intersection of agency and fantasy, performing the consumable labor of the working class but looking the part of consuming bourgeois women. As such, the nineteenth-century *modiste* was an early avatar of modern consumer society. A cultural product, she reflected in visual culture the exquisite invitation to pleasure that fashion signified—the *modiste*'s apparently innate sexiness meant that her desirability could be transferred to the consumer who purchased her creations.

The cultural representation of the *modiste*, ubiquitous in print and on the stage, however, simultaneously conceals and reveals a more complex story. As we have seen, the myth of the immodest *modiste* both permeated popular culture and was propagated by it. Vaudeville theater, coterminous with the explosion of prints from the 1820s through the Second Empire, stages *modistes* who seem to speak back in a variety of ways to the fixed, repetitive, and silent imagery essential to the establishment and maintenance of myth. Like the "real" *modistes* of the daily press, vaudeville's *modistes* are cast as workers, engaged in the production of a polyvalent cultural product that lay at the very heart of fashion and the feminine—the lady's hat.

If the labor of the anonymous fashion worker disappeared behind the myth of the *modiste* visible everywhere in popular culture, the magical transformative potential of the objects she created would take center stage in both word and image in the fashion press of the era. Having a paradoxical status similar to the *modiste* in nineteenth-century French culture, the women active in the dissemination of fashion were also both highly visible and curiously obscured. As we shall see in the chapters that follow, women fashion writers, or *chroniqueuses de mode,* and women fashion illustrators, or *dessinatrices de mode,* were instrumental in creating and perpetuating an expanding fashion economy. Yet their real labor, like that of the *modistes,* was concealed under a veil of leisure, frivolity, pleasure, gossip, and hobbies. It is to the female disseminators of fashion, the tastemakers and marketers, the so-called *modistes des lettres* that I now turn.[93]

3

Fashion's Voices:
"Modistes de Lettres"

She subscribed to La Corbeille, a women's magazine, and to Le Sylphe des Salons. She would devour, without skipping anything, all the reviews of opening nights, of races and soirées, was interested in a songstress's début, in the opening of a shop. She knew about all the latest fashions, the address of the best tailors, the days one goes to the Bois and to the Opéra.

FLAUBERT, *MADAME BOVARY*[1]

While Emma Bovary was preoccupied with schooling herself in the fashions, pastimes, and best shopping destinations of Paris, the producers of journals like the real and imaginary ones she "devoured" each week were busy forming those like her through their deft invention and maintenance of consumer desire. By the 1840s, when Flaubert's novel was set, these magazines had become virtual shop windows for vicarious lifestyle sampling. Their editorial matter in particular was now not only indispensable insider information for the aspirational set but also a promotional space for the products and shops that were willing to finance the journals.[2] Such magazines were fashion's indefatigable churning engine—serializing not just fiction but also advice and fashion news. Reciprocally, fashion's rhythmic structure of seasonal renewal and endless *nouveautés* (novelties) worked to ensure a steady and ardent readership, eager to keep up, to belong, and to possess. While the newly minted female bourgeois consumer, as embodied in one of its most famous literary examples, has received a great deal of critical attention, my interest here lies in what Flaubert's evocation of the fashion press leaves out. How did publications like *Le Journal des demoiselles, La Sylphide,* and *La Mode illustrée* produce the likes of Emma Bovary? Appealing to variants of the "ideal" woman at different moments of her life, one journal might shape the *jeune fille* as she styled herself to become, eventually, an appropriate bourgeois mother, while other publications invoked the glamorous *Parisienne,* whose extreme fashion Emma adopts in a tragic misprision of the appropriate model for a provincial housewife.[3] Behind the success of such publications was a woman fashion writer—a *chroniqueuse de mode*—who worked hard to promote products and behaviors, to shape culture and identities, without ever appearing to lift a dainty finger.

These *chroniqueuses*, in concert with fashion plates and paid advertisements, were central agents in shaping consumers among the journals' readership, but their agency remained hidden behind a discourse that presented them principally as ladies of leisure. With their rhetorical panache and sometimes fabricated, sometimes embellished identities, it is easy to see why the metaphor of the *modiste* would be applied to these "literary milliners." Just as *modistes* might pass for bourgeois, these *bourgeoises* passed for elite women of leisure. Impersonating voices with perceived social authority, these women were functioning as "cultural intermediaries" well over a century before Bourdieu's invention of the term. For these columnists were "working at the intersection of culture and economy," doing the ideological work of defining taste and approving products for consumption in the crucible of the new industrial economy that began to emerge under the July Monarchy—the fashion press.[4]

If the task of the cultural intermediary is to shape consumer tastes and attach meaning to goods, then nineteenth-century fashion writers were doing precisely this in their weekly columns. For they possessed a level of expertise regarding products and markets and used their authority as leisured women to convey legitimacy of value by positioning themselves as refined arbiters, generously sharing their knowledge with a less-informed consuming public.[5] Whether writing pseudonymously or anonymously, dissimulating their identities behind initials or invented personae—or projecting an aristocratic origin that was likely specious—they regularly provided detailed descriptions of commodities and lifestyles for avidly aspirational readers. Yet the content of these columns disguised a prescriptive intent: the commodity of counsel, those precious pearls of wisdom that only the *chroniqueuse* could offer, accompanied the material commodities and their visualization as peddled by the journals. In the process of constructing her reader as a consumer, the fashion writer also directed the performance of gender and class with a firm pen.

The rhetoric of the fashion column, perhaps the most literal incarnation of what Cheryl Morgan refers to as the "rhetoric of the *chiffon*," is complex and paradoxical.[6] This chapter explores the ways in which that rhetoric worked to produce consuming women and affirm a dominant bourgeois ideology of the feminine. The *chroniqueuses de mode* had to embody, in their editorial identities, this dominant ideology, and the success of the journals in no small way depended on hiding the actual labor these women performed to create and maintain their personae and offer appropriate guidance to their avid followers. For as we saw in chapter 1, the stakes of hiding women's work were high, even if that labor (they were, after all, "literary *modistes*") was not as unseemly as working-class labor. The *chroniqueuses* were, to borrow another phrase from Bourdieu's lexicon, "need-merchants" engaged in the marketing of goods and behaviors and, consequently, in the fabrication of those "inarticulate longings" embodied in Flaubert's heroine.[7] Fashion writers were skilled at articulating and even at engendering such longings and were thus instrumental to the success of the journals and the objects they described and promoted—the fashions and the lifestyles those fashions supported. Feigning feminine camaraderie, these women writers influenced female readers and encouraged them to buy the magazine and the products they advertised. Yet in spite of their centrality to the project of the fashion press, and perhaps in part because they lacked the intellectual clout of writers for the feminist press, let alone the general (masculine) press, the *chroniqueuses de mode* have been largely overlooked by scholars.[8]

This chapter examines three of these writers—Jeanne-Justine Fouqueau de Pussy, la vicomtesse de Renneville, and Madame Emmeline Raymond—in their role as cultural intermediaries during a period of significant social transformation.[9] In each case, the three columnists, who, importantly, were also editors, wrote for different audiences in three overlapping but distinct time periods and thus adopted correspondingly different voices—voices that often presented identities at odds with their own lives as working women with deadlines to meet, shops to visit, and columns to write. Like the work itself, social position and perhaps the shared social standing between columnist and reader needed to remain hidden as the woman writer wrestled with the complexity of forging a commercial feminine voice in a genre that celebrated idealized bourgeois leisure, maternity, and domesticity as appropriate feminine behaviors and identities. This duplicity of identity is thus the central theme of this chapter. Carving out professional lives for themselves, they contested the dominant ideology in their lives and on the page, all the while concealing the extent of their labor.

While these columnists shaped fashion trends and female behavior through strategic product placement and expert manipulation of the cultural fantasy of the feminine, fostering consumer culture and practices within the male-dominated world of publishing, their columns also suggest that they sometimes quietly resisted fashion's hegemony and used their substantial platforms to create a space of genuine female community. The chapter also, therefore, explores moments of resistance to the very ideology their work purportedly constructed and celebrated. I suggest here that these fashion columnists, while participating in the dominant culture's self-promotion, sustained by the fashion economy they worked to build, occasionally voiced dissent, however discreetly, and sought alternative narratives for women, working through various forms of duplicity to accomplish this. Jeanne-Justine Fouqueau de Pussy, for example, whose professional life corresponded roughly to the period of the July Monarchy (1830–48), all the while pushing marriage as the endgame for her readers, spends the majority of her column enacting female friendship. Likewise, the vicomtesse de Renneville, who might be considered the *chroniqueuse* of the opulent Second Empire (1852–70), while certainly exuding the aura of a snob extraordinaire, occasionally engages in a self-conscious discourse that, at times, invites an ironic reading by pushing the limits of the credible with her high society ladies' behavior. Finally, Madame Emmeline Raymond, whose journal survived the Paris Siege and Commune (1870–1) and adapted to the new social landscape of the Third Republic (1875–1940), openly asserts the supremacy of the practical, which competes with the luxurious opulence on display on nearly every page of her journal, going so far as to flout the capitalist fashion market in which she participated by actively promoting what we would term today "sustainable fashion."

All three of these writers certainly used the fashion column to earn a living and promote their journals—carving out working identities for themselves *and* performing the function of cultural intermediaries. Yet as women working as writers and editors in the traditionally male industry of the press and publishing, they did not necessarily embody the ideal of bourgeois femininity even if their publications worked hard to pretend this was the case.[10] Indeed, each had a biography and civil status at odds with the ideal they themselves projected for bourgeois women of the period: Fouqueau de Pussy, the nurturing best friend, was divorced and childless; Renneville, the glamourous socialite, was a separated single parent; and Raymond, the domestic goddess, never married, becoming the proverbial spinster. Each needed to work to support herself, but concealing the labor expended to produce their columns and journals was essential to maintaining the fantasy of feminine leisure for which they served as surrogates.

The *chroniqueuses* I focus on wrote for three key journals spanning the July Monarchy and the Second Empire and into the Belle Époque—*Le Journal des demoiselles*, *La Sylphide*, and *La Mode illustrée*—all of which appealed to expanding bourgeois publics in Paris, in the provinces, and even abroad.[11] Morgan persuasively argues that women writers were forced to the margins through their association with the fashion press, suggesting that fashion writing thus delegitimized women's writing more generally. I propose here, however, that, notwithstanding Morgan's argument, women fashion writers nonetheless deserve deeper consideration, precisely because of the delicate balance they negotiated between work and the impression of leisure and between commerce and morality, and because, in their writing, they nuanced emerging feminine identities even as they invented the female consumer. How did these *chroniqueuses* attach meanings to goods, and what meanings were valued? What strategies did they deploy and to what end in their taste-making columns? Before turning to these exemplary journals and the women who penned their fashion columns and directed certain journals, however, let us turn to a brief historical contextualization of the fashion writer in nineteenth-century France.

From *Chroniqueur* to *Chroniqueuse*

As noted in chapter 1, fashion columnists, by the mid-nineteenth century, were primarily women, but this had not always been the case; indeed, the press in France had been dominated by men since before the Revolution, with a few exceptions.[12] The majority of fashion journals, write Bonvoisin and Maignien, "written and directed by men, began with an emphasis on literature or fashion. Their public was composed of several thousands of distinguished ladies, belonging to an aristocratic or bourgeois elite, the only classes of the population that knew how to read and had time to do so."[13] The original prototype of the nineteenth-century fashion writer was the eccentric ex-priest Pierre de la Mésangère, who took over sole directorship of *Le Journal des dames et des modes* in 1801 after the untimely death of his collaborator, Jean-Baptiste Sellèque, and oversaw the journal until his own death in 1831.[14] While the journal was founded (with Sellèque) by Madame Albertine Clément-Hémery, it was nonetheless Mésangère, nicknamed the "dictator of fashion" by Balzac himself, who fell upon the winning formula that kept it alive through the Directory, First Empire, Restoration, and into the July Monarchy.[15] This formula was, in the words of Annemarie Kleinert, responsible for "the conquest of feminine Europe" by the Parisian arbiters of fashion, and the *Journal des dames et des modes* paved the way for a host of journals to come throughout the century.[16]

Mésangère's original eight-page recipe combined detailed and authoritative fashion news, written mostly by him, cultural instruction and descriptions of social events, fiction, and one to two illustrations, usually drawn at the *marchandes de modes*, thus guaranteeing the authenticity of the design.[17] Fashion writing clearly was not just a matter of clothing styles but of taste more broadly, and the spectacle of consumption included music, theater, and literature, alongside dress and manners. This would remain the case throughout the nineteenth century, although some journals would focus more exclusively on fashion, especially later in the century. Fashion was therefore clearly a marker of class and respectability, which contributed to the need for the *chroniqueuses* to develop appropriately respectable personae.

The journal was primarily destined for female readers: Kleinert documents that, in two early prospectuses, the advertisements for subscription to the journal are addressed to "the lovely who will read me" and later "to the pretty women of Paris and the departments."[18] Indeed, expanding subscriptions to the provinces was crucial for business, and, as the fictional example of the voracious Madame Bovary attests, by midcentury, provincial readers were an essential source of revenue. If the audience of the early fashion press was understood as primarily female, however, its publishers and writers were mostly male. This was true for publishers throughout the century, even though the female fashion writer/editor gained traction and the fashion departments of journals became increasingly important to a publisher's success.[19] With its insistence on "objective" observation, fashion writing was coded male. As Margaret Waller has argued in her discussion of the fashion press during the Directory period: "While fashion itself was generally represented as women's work, writing about it—a relatively new and increasingly important activity—was nevertheless being claimed as a job for men."[20] This would change, however, during the July Monarchy, when magazine publishers actively sought out and hired women fashion correspondents, and the so-called "realist objectivity" of the male fashion observer would give way to female voices. These voices relied upon strategies of identification, even solidarity, with their female readers, to satisfy subscribers, but they also continued to use methods of realism, offering detailed descriptions and verifiable facts such as place names, addresses and social events, to give shape and, perhaps more significantly, to create consumer pathways to the material worlds they describe on the page.

At the time of its final run in 1839, the *Journal des dames et des modes* had established the norms of publication in what is known as the *presse féminine*.[21] The journal would be produced by a variety of contributors—writers, artists, engravers, and printers—and in its last three years, it was directed by a woman writer and fashion chronicler of some renown during the July Monarchy (1830–48), Marie de l'Epinay, a contemporary and rival of the more famous Delphine de Girardin, wife of the July Monarchy's most prominent journalist, Emile de Girardin.[22] While the choice to hand the pen to a woman to chronicle fashion may have been made by male publishers and editors, once these women began speaking (and writing), they gained prominence and power just as they earned the fidelity of countless subscribers.

Jeanne-Justine Fouqueau de Pussy became editor-in-chief of *Le Journal des demoiselles* at the time of its founding in 1833; while it was owned by the Thierry family, she was at the journal's creative center.[23] Likewise, the vicomtesse de Renneville (pseudonym of Olympe Vallée), while indebted to editor Hippolyte de Villemessant for giving her a start, became fashion's oracle during the Second Empire, and her fashion columns were a vital financial base for his papers.[24] Madame Emmeline Raymond, hand-picked by publishing giant Didot on the advice of Jeanne-Justine Fouqueau de Pussy herself, with her rigorous work ethic and personal devotion to readers, would attract more than a hundred thousand subscribers, making his journal a runaway success.[25]

The woman fashion writer, absent in the genre's early years, was by mid-century becoming a powerful force in the journals' success, and the three writers I examine here are exemplary of that power. During the July Monarchy and beyond, Jeanne-Justine Fouqueau de Pussy, who signed her columns simply "J. J.," would be editor-in-chief as well as the principal fashion correspondent for the *Journal des demoiselles*, dubbed "the bourgeois gospel" for two decades.[26] The vicomtesse de Renneville, so "baptized," as Villemessant put it, and thus engendered in a sense by her editor, was tasked with engaging readers through witty writing and social snobbery while at the same time actively animating the journal's soft advertisements. She did not disappoint—and wrote for the journal until 1857, when she launched and directed (with Villemessant's patronage) *La Gazette rose* (1857–84), a luxury fashion journal closely linked to the Second Empire and to Villemessant's own *Le Figaro*. By the mid-Second Empire and into the Third Republic, well after Emma Bovary's fictional suicide, *La Mode illustrée: Journal de la famille*, one of the most popular and widely disseminated fashion periodicals of the nineteenth century, launched in 1860, would be staffed by a predominantly female editorial team comprising fashion writers, *modistes*, designers, illustrators, engravers, and editors, headed up by the prolific Emmeline Raymond.[27]

I consider each of these women and their fashion columns in turn, beginning with J. J., whose journal was launched just three years after the beginning of the July Monarchy, when the press began its massive expansion.[28] Each woman crafted her own distinct identity with respect to her readership, an identity based, importantly, on female relationship and, to varying degrees, the performance of intimacy. Keen to increase subscriptions, these fashion writers developed a pseudo-confidence with their readers, often employing an epistolary conceit to summon a relationship of familiarity and comfort or recounting anecdotes related to society activities to satisfy provincial or aspirational class desires for vicarious leisure living. Eschewing the "dictatorial" male posture pioneered by Mésangère, Jeanne-Justine Fouqueau de Pussy, la vicomtesse de Renneville, and Madame Emmeline Raymond adopted individualized personae modeled on a kind of conspiratorial personal relationship rather than impersonal authoritarianism to reach an active new readership of consuming women.

I focus exclusively on these journalists for several reasons. First, all three were fashion writers for journals that had remarkably long runs. The *Journal des demoiselles* was launched in 1833 and ran until 1922; *La Sylphide: journal parisien* was published from 1840 until 1885; and, finally, *La Mode illustrée: Journal de la famille* ran from 1860 to 1937.[29] Second, all three women were not only fashion columnists but also founders and directors of journals; thus, they were more than merely fashion writers—they were decision-making editors and businesswomen actively engaged in all aspects of their journals' production.[30] Third, each of these journals created a different version of idealized femininity. Kate Nelson Best has loosely classified fashion journals of this period according to the feminine persona that was taking form in its texts and images—an aspirational reader, in a sense, but also a double for the *chroniqueuse* herself. One such figure was the *jeune fille*, incarnating the "cultural values of chastity, modesty, and naivety," to which the *Journal des demoiselles* corresponded; *La Sylphide* embodied the worldly, wealthy, sophisticated *Parisienne*; and *La Mode illustrée* related more readily to the bourgeois mother, "the chaste, moral arbiter of the family."[31] These distinct personae account in some measure for the specific "voices" adopted by each columnist: *la bonne amie*, or dear friend; *la reine des chiffons*, or dress queen; and *la bonne ménagère*, or good housewife. Finally, these journals were innovative in their practices, such as perfecting a studied intimacy with readers, using image and text powerfully to mutually reinforce each other and pioneering advertising practices. Yet each also deployed subtle resistance strategies, as we shall explore, introducing at least a sliver of doubt into the seamless narrative of fashion's idealized feminine. Each, through the deployment of a sort of duplicitous identity practice, paradoxically—if occasionally—perturbed that ideal.

J. J.: "*La Bonne Amie*"

Jeanne-Justine Fouqueau de Pussy, editor-in-chief of *Le Journal des demoiselles* during most of the July Monarchy and for a few years beyond, was born in 1786 in Orléans. Married in 1802, she divorced sometime before 1816, when divorce was made illegal in France, and kept her maiden name throughout her long professional career.[32] Not a mother herself, J. J. nonetheless performs motherhood in the pages of the journal, staging there a mother-daughter relationship and creating a virtual community to which she did not quite belong. For by the time she began her stint at the *Journal des demoiselles*, she was already forty-seven years old! This is remarkable because, for nearly twenty years, Jeanne-Justine effectively impersonated a teenager, ever touting the goals of marriage and motherhood month after month as she wrote her fashion column, which, as is typical of the genre, chronicled Parisian fashions and events, engaged in product placement, and provided instructions for home sewing, or *travaux des femmes*.[33] While her own life does not align with the expectations of her readers, J. J. nevertheless creates and embodies the persona of a young lady of a leisured class.

Unlike other contemporary fashion columnists, though, J. J. adopts an unusually intimate tone vis-à-vis her less fortunate *chère amie*, who was far from Paris. As Christine Léger-Paturneau observes, her "originality ... lies in the choice to present fashions for young ladies and advice for their realization written not anonymously in the third person as was the case for fashion periodicals at the time ... Here J. J.'s choice is to address her reader directly, as to a friend, a relation, speaking to her with the informal *tu*, which was quite audacious for the period."[34] Indeed, the intimacy she seeks to establish in this column was unusual; but the epistolary conceit was ingenious and, no doubt, appealing: she understood her audience. Of the three journalists I consider in this chapter, J. J. assumes the most personal mode, a stylistic choice that made sense, given the kind of relationship she aimed to form with her reader and the identity she chose: she assumed the persona of a *jeune fille—la bonne amie* writing monthly updates from Paris to her dear school friend. Never naming her interlocutor, for that would disrupt the identificatory experience she is building with her reader, J. J. refers to their time together at boarding school (*pension*) in numerous articles, dropping occasional references to shared memories and experiences. She thus establishes an ongoing correspondence with her dear school friend, one that she initiated after they left school and returned to their respective parental homes, J. J. in Paris and the anonymous friend in the provinces, to await inevitable and much anticipated marriage.

In her lively monthly column, entitled simply *Correspondance*, J. J. recounts the latest events of the capital, offers detailed instructions for a variety of sewing and other domestic projects, and describes the ball gowns, visiting dresses, coats, hats, hairstyles, and accessories of each passing season.[35] Her column typically follows a pattern: it begins with an anecdote or news item from which J. J. extracts a moral, then transitions (sometimes quite awkwardly) to detailed descriptions of handiwork—from sewing and embroidery to other household or artistic tasks; following this, the reader finds descriptions of Paris fashions, which occasionally promote J. J.'s favorite shops or brands, such as those of the *modiste* Mme. Séguin; finally, the author brings the discussion back to the intimacy of a personal letter, thus disguising any advertising behind the feigned sincerity of a fictitious friendship. Fashion writing, though, is always tied to other types of discourses in J. J.'s correspondence and is never purely descriptive. This would come later, when, after J. J.'s retirement in 1852, her successor (E. E.) began to focus her Second Empire column almost exclusively on fashion.[36]

If J. J.'s imagined correspondent, the mute and unnamed "dear friend," is the journal's imaginary ideal reader—then the decidedly bourgeois mother, reading over her daughter's shoulder, as it were, is both the journal's hidden reader and the aspirational model of the *jeune fille*. Desperate for Paris fashions, the young lady is also hungry for instruction on how to become accomplished enough to achieve the grand prize of marriage, or at least her mother is on her behalf. J. J. occupies both roles simultaneously, doubling the *jeune fille*-reader and dispensing motherly wisdom as editor-in-chief. Indeed, J. J.'s biography and self-casting as both mother *rédactrice en chef* and daughter *correspondante* position her on two sides of the relationship and as both-and, one-and-the-same, mother *and* daughter. For this is what bourgeois female adolescence was all about—becoming first wife, then mother.[37]

This ideal trajectory is illustrated in a lithograph published in an early issue of the journal, depicting in a triptych the dutiful wife, the contented mother, and, finally, the proud parent of a young lady—either preparing for her First Communion or, possibly her marriage (figure 3.1). Here, duty (*les devoirs*) is embodied in the tender care of one's husband, happiness (*le bonheur*) is achieved in family and needlework, and love and respect (*l'amour et le respect*) develop when the young lady emerges as a perfect replica of her mother, embarking on the same life cycle with the blessings of her family. The journal became an influential mouthpiece, exhorting young girls to "practice all the virtues, assigning them a moral and civic mission . . . Obviously, marriage is the single future of the young lady. And the future of the married woman is motherhood."[38] Because the *Journal des demoiselles* targeted an audience of *chrysalides*, or pubescent girls, it could capitalize on its young readers' desire to learn more about the mysterious state into which they were heading (marriage) and, simultaneously with the voice of authority, reproduce motherly wisdom.[39] In particular, J. J.'s seemingly intimate *correspondance* column in the long-running *Journal des demoiselles* confirms the degree to which ideals of feminine propriety and accomplishment were deeply enmeshed with fashion discourse and marketing.

J. J.'s first and last contributions to the journal, in 1833 and 1852, respectively, frame the rich correspondence in between and demonstrate succinctly the duplicitous identity of the *chroniqueuse*. The first piece, published in the journal's premiere issue in February of 1833, intimates the conceit of the correspondence and portrays J. J. as wily mother-marketer even as she presents herself throughout as daughter-consumer in solidarity with the young readers of the journal. Before fully inhabiting the identity of the Parisian teenager who writes to her provincial best friend, J. J.'s first contribution is a fictional dialogue between a mother and daughter, entitled "La Robe de bal." This is an allegorical piece that sets in motion the dialectical relationship between fashion and behavior, worldly elegance and social piety that would become the hallmark of the correspondence. She signs her name "Mme. J. J." and writes the column in the third person; she has not yet found her intimate persona, which would emerge by May of 1834. The entry reveals several clues to the role fashion will play in the modeling of behaviors for young ladies, however. First, here, fashion is subsumed under the broader category of "Arts," a traditionally appropriate domain for women; after this first issue, the *correspondance* as

Figure 3.1 Jules David, "Les devoirs, le bonheur, l'amour et le respect," Journal des Demoiselles, *1834, 2: 8, Bibliothèque nationale de France.*

category is inaugurated. Second, the footnote to J. J.'s story enjoins readers to consult the pattern, for the practical reason that readers could *voir le patron* (see the pattern) and use it to recreate the ball gown she describes; but this reminder also reinforces the symbolically resonant function of the *patron*, the pattern or model, which was to establish uniformly appropriate behaviors in young women. Indeed, the anecdote also provides a model for good conduct, just as the dress pattern is the material key to making the gown.

"La Robe de bal" stages the excitement of a young girl who learns from her mother that she has been invited to her first ball, a much-anticipated event in the life of adolescent girls, who depended on such invitations for their initiation into the world. Her mother advises in all things: "Look in my dresser, you'll find some white crepe, some white *gros de Naples*, some pretty white silk stockings and white satin slippers"; in addition to the dress, the stockings, and the shoes, all white, the young lady, adorned in white virginity, will carry a "bouquet and garland of white roses." While she dreams of feathers, necklaces, and earrings, her mother admonishes, "Believe me, my child, simplicity suits your age like the rose in the month of May."[40] What is appropriate attire for a married woman was not at all appropriate for a young lady, and the girl's mother shares key knowledge about the visual language of fashion for her uninitiated daughter.

Once the fashion lesson has concluded, the lesson in behavior begins, when a poor beggar woman, a regular recipient of the mother's benevolent charity, comes asking for an old blanket. Mother turns to daughter with a test: what is to be done, as there is no extra blanket to be offered? The daughter, clearly a model pupil, quietly proposes that she relinquish the pin money she would have used to pay the seamstress to make her ball gown, since she is surely accomplished enough to make and embellish it herself with the help of a pattern, fortunately provided by the journal itself.[41] The dutiful daughter delights in her own act of charity, which doubles as an act of self-promotion when, later, at the ball, upon receiving compliments on her dress, she proudly asserts, "I made it myself."[42] The pattern in question, to which readers have been advised to turn, shows how the overdetermined *robe à la Sévigné* could be made (figure 3.2). The journal is thus proven to be an indispensable guide, with its practical patterns and invaluable moral instruction, but also its more tangible reward—a beautiful, collectible *gravure de mode* (fashion plate), at once inspirational and aspirational.

The relationship between the *patron* and the *gravure* is crucial here: if the *gravure* represents the idealized product, the *patron* is the utilitarian modeling tool for achieving as close an approximation to the ideal as possible. However, there is a further layer of patterning at work in this inaugural story: Mother's good example and gentle suggestion model appropriate female behavior, which demands that virtuous girls *not* be consumed with fashion. Modeled charity thus marshals frivolous fashion, and *la robe de bal* is a pretext for establishing life patterns centered on charity rather than vanity. In the end, however, the fashionable dress has the last word, as the daughter basks in the compliments on her gown. Ventriloquizing both mother and daughter, J. J. has set the tone of the column for some

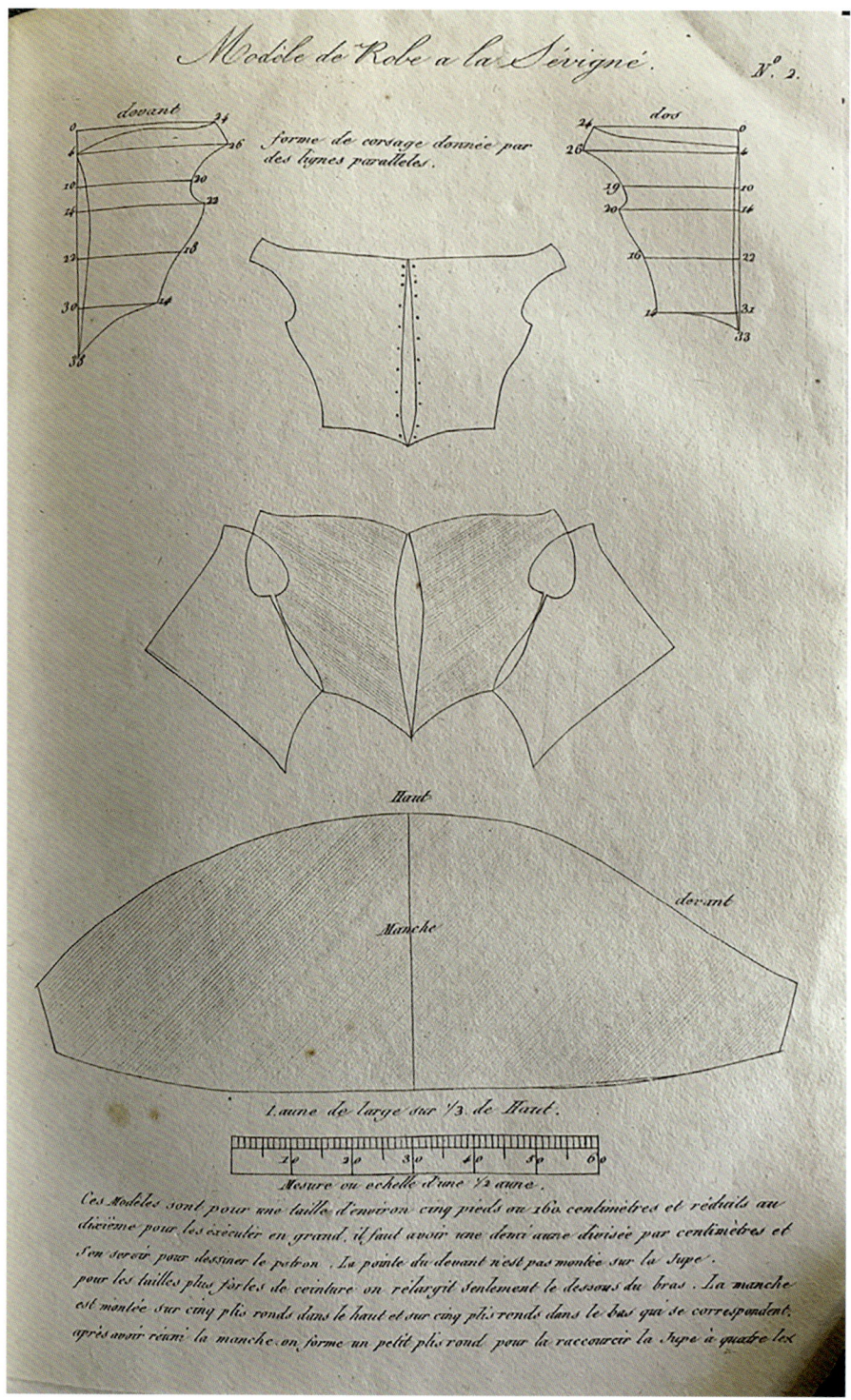

Figure 3.2 *"Modèle de Robe à la Sévigné,"* Journal des Demoiselles, *1833: 1, Bibliothèque nationale de France.*

twenty years to come. While it may be difficult to imagine that a young bourgeois home sewer could possibly be skilled enough to create the *robe à la Sévigné* herself, it was certainly not impossible. More important here, however, is the aspirational allegory that the story stages: driven by generosity and thus faithfully following her mother's model behavior, the young lady will be capable of following the material pattern that the journal proposes.

Most issues of the journal offer a lovely *gravure* illustrating a beautiful dress—perhaps the perfectly executed ball gown, as is the case in the journal's first issue; the plate is truly the "last word" of the journal, as it appeared at the end of the issue (figure 3.3).[43] In spite of the journal's penchant for moral didacticism, evident in the example of "La Robe de bal," the narrative was accompanied by a hand-colored fashion plate, which, as Sharon Marcus has pointed out in her work on feminine sociability in Victorian England, while not "overtly sexual," was nevertheless "designed to evoke erotic feelings in ways that a sewing pattern is not."[44] If the sewing patterns require dutiful reproduction and domestic economy in accordance with the mother's imperative, the luxurious plates make visible a girl's opulent fantasies. The tantalizing images were no doubt an important attraction for the journal's subscribers, a supposition further illustrated by the frequent decoupling of the plates and their textual companions: these pictures often ended up framed in bourgeois households or stored in collections, as we saw in chapter 1.[45] Instead of focusing on the practical benefits of sewing and encouraging productive business for potentially idle hands that could lead to charitable giving, the fashion plate produced desire, and possibly even anxiety, in the viewer—the desire to emulate, to see oneself reflected back in the hand-colored image, and the anxiety of possibly always falling short of that ideal.[46] In either case, the plate produced a form of reflectivity that was crucial to the marketing of a particular representation of bourgeois femininity and was one of the primary sales strategies of the fashion houses that advertised surreptitiously in the pages of this kind of journal. This mirroring suggested identification and could also be seen as an invitation even to inclusion within a female community, a tactic in which, as we shall see, J. J. was fully engaged.

In "La Robe de bal," Mme. J. J., as she signs this first column, successfully merges fashion with piety, propriety of dress with proper behavior. She does not efface fashion, but rather creates points of contact among various acceptable female practices, thus pleasing both mothers and daughters. The intimacy—signaled by the *tutoiement* (use of the familiar *tu*)—of the key mother-daughter relationship of instruction and obedience is modeled in this first issue; here, J. J. is aligned more closely with the mother figure than the daughter, but this will shift abruptly in the journal's second year as she adopts the identity of the youthful fashion correspondent, which she would maintain for the next nineteen years.

By June of 1834, Mme. J. J., who for several issues left the *Correspondance* column unsigned, began signing simply "J. J.," assuming the daughterly role with whom her readers could identify and invoking her own mother frequently as she writes to her dear far-away friend, whom, we learn, J. J. had met at boarding school.[47] We see this relationship enacted in an 1835 column, when J. J. closes her letter to

Figure 3.3 *"La robe de bal."* Journal des Demoiselles, *1833: 1, Bibliothèque nationale de France.*

her anonymous *bonne petite* with a word of advice from her own fictitious mother, who is hovering nearby: "Mother, who is reading this letter over my shoulder, tells me, 'Help yourself, and heaven will help you.' So that's what I'll do . . . Adieu!"[48] There is a clear resemblance between the bourgeois mother's role as educator and mentor in post-Revolutionary France and J. J.'s quasi-epistolary journalistic practice in her "Correspondance," even if her epistolary identity doubles that of her naïve readers. Daughter J. J. emerges as the primary voice in the issues running until 1852, but mother is always a presence—cited, obeyed, praised, and imitated: "And she's so right, Mother, I am so proud to understand and obey her!"[49] It is all the more crucial that "mother" remain "present" since J. J.'s fictive interlocutor, the unnamed dear friend of the provinces, is, we learn in the tenth issue of 1833, motherless ("You who have the misfortune of not having a mother").[50] The conceit thus allows J. J. to perform the role of mother and daughter simultaneously, occupying both roles as she offers countless instructions on how to make all manner of household and personal goods, usually modeled on something she has seen in a shop window, which she dutifully cites. Her writing thus straddles advertisement and individual industriousness, consumption and production as she exhorts her dear friend to follow her meticulous instructions on how to recreate, for example, a *tablier fort élégant* (very elegant apron), she has seen in the window of "Mlle Martin, galérie de l'Opéra," or to freshen or create a hat that will resemble the one displayed in the illustrated plate.[51]

J. J. cultivates industriousness in her readers, even as she tempts them to consume with her shopping anecdotes and descriptive paragraphs that offer further information about the colored plates. Nearly every issue includes detailed step-by-step instructions for various household or personal do-it-yourself projects, accompanied by intricate templates such as the one pictured in figure 3.4. Here, for example, we find four different pieces of a pattern for a cap that will be embroidered and embellished—the underside, the top, the *passe* (border), and the finished product. J. J. explains how to use the pattern: "You will size it five times longer and five times wider."[52] This pattern, like so many others involving intricate embroidery, cutting and measuring, multiplication and ratios, as well as code deciphering, bears witness to the real labor involved in developing the qualities of a proper young lady, a *demoiselle*. Indeed, the complexity and detail of the instructions J. J. offers over the twenty years in which she directs the journal presumes a level of skill possessed by at least some of her readers and certainly their seamstresses, with whom they likely often shared the patterns and instructions. Education and intelligence are dear to J. J., who recounts in one *Correspondance* column how, while embroidering with her mother one evening, as her father and brother were discussing history, she corrects her brother's mistake regarding a date. Her brother, indignant, labels her a *bas bleu!* (bluestocking) only to be reprimanded by *Maman*, who uses this opportunity to explain how the pejorative term originated as a critique of the salon of the estimable Lady Montague by political rivals. Mother comes to her daughter's defense, family harmony is restored, and J. J. finishes her letter with detailed instructions on how to make an embroidered *sac à tabac*, a worthy gift for a brother or father,

Figure 3.4 *"Planche VI,"* Journal des Demoiselles, *1836: 4: 6, Bibliothèque nationale de France.*

a *bonnet grec*, the colors for which would be decoded from the instructions, and a pattern for a percale undershirt with a set of measurements that would be converted to scale. She illustrates her faith in women's intelligence through her anecdotes as well as through her own industriousness.[53]

The link between the pattern and the fashion plate mirrors that of mother and daughter in J. J.'s configuration. Patterns, as we have seen, with detailed instructions for the reader to follow in order to create clothing items for herself, for her family and friends, or for charitable cases sometimes echo or support what we see in the *gravure*. All the while she is posing as a daughter, J. J. also channels the mother, as she frequently indicates that the finished product of the pattern she describes resembles the sleeve, skirt, hat, and so forth, that can be seen in the finely colored plate (*gravure*) representing the latest fashions.[54] A young woman's industry as well as her economy are to be praised, as in the inaugural anecdote of *La Robe de bal*; and the pattern, or model, should be understood as both a moral and practical one. As much as there is symbiosis here, there is also a tension built into the *correspondance*—a tension between moralizing mother and desiring daughter that is exemplified by the tension between the productivity of the home sewing projects (*patron/planches*) and the consumerism embodied in the *gravure* and associated with fashion. While the pattern is didactic, the *gravure* is an aesthetic spectacle tied to consumption. Just as J. J. cultivates the industrious economy of nineteenth-century French teens by echoing an imagined mother's voice reeling off complicated instructions week after week for the creations she proposes, she also offers the thrill of vicarious consumption to her avid young readers, for by the end of the 1840s, the *gravure*—and sometimes the text itself—indicated where dresses and hats could be procured rather than how they might be painstakingly recreated at home (figure 3.5). Most often, too, the women pictured in the *gravures* correspond to the *demoiselle* targeted by the journal, thus appealing to the identificatory consumer desires of the young readership of the journal and mirroring the fictional friendship that J. J. constructs. Occasionally, however, we also find what appears to be a mother-daughter pairing, thus reiterating the mentoring relationship J. J. celebrates and surreptitiously recreates on the page (figure 3.6). Even the *gravures*, then, appear to have been selected by the editor herself to reinforce the associations cultivated in the fashion correspondence over the years.

In her remarkable parting letter to her *chère amie* in December of 1852, J. J. bids farewell and summarizes what she has aimed to do in her column for these two decades. In *Le Journal des demoiselles*, the very first journal to target young people, she notes, her "goal was to teach you the skills that enhance the luxury of the salon and the more modest economies of the household" hoping to raise "you" as "the pride and joy of your family."[55] Finally shedding her fictional persona and even admitting that her good friend Florence, who often helped her describe *toilettes* and *gravures* in the later years as she continued to write to her anonymous provincial friend, "was only an imaginary character," J. J. at last acknowledges her twenty-year conceit.[56] "You believed in my friendship, and you gave me yours": the close relationship of friendship between two separated school friends—this "sweet sympathy"—is rather more like the relation of mother to daughter. Indeed, seemingly sanctioned by bourgeois mothers across France ("the approval and confidence of your parents"), this written performance of friendship encouraged charitable and domestically productive behaviors in young ladies by training them to work to emulate fashions on display in the gorgeous *gravures*. The patterns that reproduced fashion's latest trends shaped both bodies and behaviors, instructing young women in discipline, skill, and economy. In her final missive, J. J. closes the circle even as she enjoins her readers to continue the practice of modeling and reproduction: "Have your daughters copy you."[57]

J. J.'s final epistolary confession is both poignant and revealing of a benevolent duplicity that was required for a bourgeois woman like J. J. to work for a living. As a divorcée, later termed a "widow," as her ex-husband, Pierre Lerat, preceded her in death, she would likely have needed to support herself financially. Her lifetime of work involved much more than homemaking and needlework: she was engaged in reading and research, observation and interpretation, instruction, editing, persuasion, and,

Figure 3.5 *"Modes de Paris,"* Journal des Demoiselles, *1849: 17: 7, Bibliothèque nationale de France.*

Figure 3.6 *"Modes d'automne,"* Journal des Demoiselles, *1844, 12, Bibliothèque nationale de France.*

above all, writing. She wrote to transcribe into legible form the intricate steps of the *travaux de femmes* that she wished to teach her young readers, handiwork that would serve their future household needs, thus increasing their marriageability, and that would also perhaps enliven many a dull provincial afternoon otherwise spent in boredom at home. While it is possible to construe certain aspects of her instruction as lending themselves obliquely to work—sewing and embroidery projects, for example— it was clearly *not* intended to prepare young bourgeois ladies for work outside of the home as, say, a *modiste* or other professional in the fashion industry. Rather, establishing the irony of her life and career, she obfuscates her own labor in order to provide detailed fashion descriptions that initiated her readers into a lexicon of taste and brightened their monotonous domestic lives with pictures—in word and image—of the glittering capital of fashion.

J. J. retired from the journal in 1852, retreating to private life in her Paris apartment at 46 rue de la Victoire in the ninth arrondissement, where she would die eleven years later at the age of seventy-eight. Her death record from May 1863 lists her as the 'épouse divorcée du Sieur Lerat, décédé', survived by her nephew, who was present for the signing of the death certificate (figure 3.7).[58] In the obituary published in July 1863 in the journal she founded, her former colleagues offer a brief encomium of a spiritual and stoical woman who had suffered a long illness. She is fondly remembered for her gracious spirit, her practical good sense, her refined taste, and, of course, for her ageless animation of the "correspondence column" for nineteen years. While she served a community of readers, *amies inconnues*—born or aspiring to privilege, bourgeois mothers and daughters, urban and provincial—her life's work was a far cry from the daily activities and social engagements of her

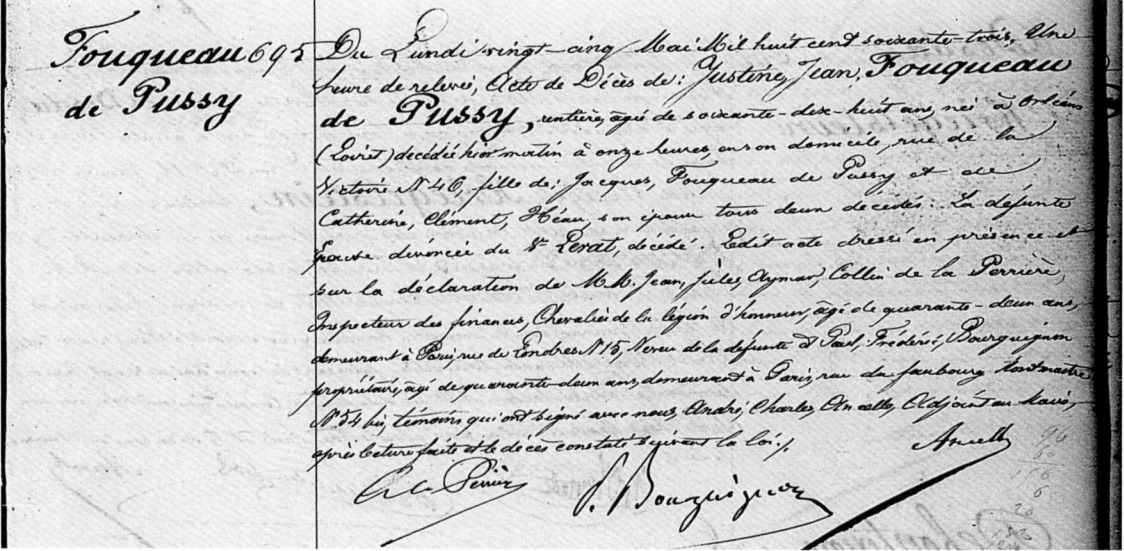

Figure 3.7 *"Acte de Décès: Fouqueau de Pussy"* 1863, 09, V4E 997, Archives de Paris.

readers. As Léger-Paturneau has elucidated in her moving account of the inventory of J. J.'s apartment at the time of her death, Madame Jeanne-Justine Fouqueau de Pussy may have lived comfortably, but certainly not luxuriously:

> She has few jewels and her clothes are generally fairly simple. One gold watch, one coral jewelry set, an antique fan and two modern ones, opera glasses indicating a worldly life. One black silk dress, the others in wool or wool muslin, many lace collars, a fur muff, a cashmere shawl, and a *marquise* parasol complete her wardrobe. No velvet headdresses, silk shawls, or *gros-de-Naples* dress as she had recommended to the reader of the *Journal*.[59]

While her bourgeois readers would have been engaged in creating or purchasing such fashionable garments and accessories, J. J., the writer, needed practical wool dresses that would stand up to weekly visits to various shops around the capital to evaluate goods, confer with her staff and publisher, and keep up with the cultural events she had to describe in her columns. Her single silk dress, cashmere shawl, and opera glasses attest not to a life of worldly pleasures, but rather to her engagement with the arts on behalf of her provincial readers, who could visit the Opéra, the Louvre, the fashion shops, and society salons only vicariously through their *bonne amie*, J. J.

Through her personalized correspondence, artificial though it may have been, J. J. thus offered a tantalizing taste of the world of consumable fashion that the *demoiselles* of her readership would eventually enter when they achieved their married destiny. Her ruse certainly had a commercial intent. Manipulating the principle of seriality, on which fashion also depends, she crafted a never-ending story that kept readers engaged and subscriptions healthy. She also aimed to guide young women as they entered society and adulthood to discover, perhaps as J. J., the divorcée, had discovered for herself, that dutiful marriage and happy motherhood could not be counted on to provide the fulfilling experiences depicted in both word and picture in the journal. J. J.'s protracted correspondence offers industrious creativity to readers who inhabit the limited domestic sphere of bourgeois femininity. But, more importantly, it offers female sociability as a relief, and J. J.'s work, which, after twenty years, had "exhausted [her] powers," had also engaged "all the thoughts of [her] spirit and [her] heart," occupying precisely the intellectual and emotional spaces that nineteenth-century bourgeois women usually reserved for their husbands and children.[60]

La Vicomtesse de Renneville: *"La Reine des chiffons"*[61]

In his multivolume memoir, Hippolyte de Villemessant, one of the most important and successful editors of the nineteenth century, describes his quest for an appropriate fashion chronicler for the society journal he founded in 1840, *La Sylphide*. He claimed to desire "not one of those carnival countesses or marquises whose title is borrowed from the pseudonym's dictionary, but a true society lady."[62] In other words, he seeks a "real" aristocrat, whose cachet of distinction would give her the authority to speak to readers nostalgic for, or aspiring to, the trappings and leisure of high society. It is hard to underestimate the magnetic power such prestige would hold, and again, Flaubert proves a worthy guide: Emma's brush with aristocracy at the Vaubyessard ball is marked by her rapture at all aspects of the aristocracy, no matter how corrupt or degenerate, and she subsequently names her only daughter after a fine lady whose name, Berthe, she had overheard someone call out over the ballroom's dance floor.[63] Access to fashion supposedly provided a window onto aristocratic mores; the journals were the conduit to a certain kind of cultural capital; and authentic femininity was thus perceived as decidedly aristocratic, particularly for aspiring bourgeois women.

Villemessant initially selected Madame Amet-Junot d'Abrantès, whose pedigree as the daughter of the writer Laure Junot, duchesse d'Abrantès, and the aide-de-camp of Napoléon, Jean-Andoche Junot, gave her the distinction presumably required of a reliable arbiter and disseminator of Paris fashions. She signed her columns *duchesse d'Abrantès*, signifying at once her authority and her distinction. Marie de l'Epinay, who had gotten her start at Mésangère's journal, subsequently began writing fashion columns for *La Sylphide* and was the principal columnist for the journal throughout the 1840s.[64] It was Madame Paul Descubes de Lascaux, née Marie Louise Olympe Vallée, renamed *la vicomtesse de Renneville* by Villemessant, whom he held in the highest esteem, however. This *vicomtesse*'s invented title flies in the face of Villemessant's original demands regarding the qualifications of aristocratic authenticity required of his fashion columnist, and he disavowed his earlier decisions for the sake of the journal.[65]

After her marriage to minor author Paul Descubes de Lascaux ended in separation, and with their son to support, Olympe Vallée went to work. In her memoirs, Madame la Comtesse Dash, a prolific author and acquaintance of Renneville's, recounts the unfortunate circumstances that had led the latter to her career:

> The two spouses didn't get along and they decided on a separation . . . The young woman, now a fortuneless widow, wanting above all to take care of her child, understood that she had to make her own destiny and that she could only rely on herself for her subsistence. She did the most honorable thing, the most difficult too for a woman accustomed to the comforts of life: she decided to go to work.[66]

The Comtesse Dash, observing that Olympe was separated from her husband, refers to her in the same breath as a "fortuneless widow," perhaps because the civil status of widowhood was more seemly for a woman than that of separation.[67] She also relates the episode when the young mother went to visit Villemessant and "explained to him her position with confidence and simplicity: he was interested in her."[68] Indeed, she appears to have impressed him, for, in his own memoirs, comparing her to a man,

Villemessant praises her for "the certainty of her speech and the frankness of her explanations."[69] In their 1862 history of the French press, authors Jules Buisson and Félix Ribeyre, however, describe the seduction of elegance she deployed on this man of the press. They write: "She wore a delicious pearl-gray outfit whose exquisite taste struck M. de Villemessant. He was looking for a fashion writer; he found her in the pearl-gray outfit" (figure 3.8).[70] Villemessant understood the subtleties of both class and gender dissimulation: rebranded with a title, rather than a simple *particule*, she ascended to a higher social status; and while she apparently wrote with a man's supposed wit, she beguiled in a lovely

Figure 3.8 *Nadar, "Vicomtesse de Renneville, Journaliste de Modes," Bibliothèque nationale de France.*

feminine package.⁷¹ Ironically, then, the *vicomtesse*, this separated, single parent, who *had* to work, would become the printed incarnation of the elegant, leisured *Parisienne*, marketing fashions selected with her own discerning eye and, like other fashion writers, using her rhetorical skills and emotional connection to subscribers to make money for the journal. She would join on the eve of the Second Empire, in 1850, and not once register the *coup d'état* of December 1851 that ushered in Napoléon III. In fact, her columns in *La Sylphide* would devote considerable attention to the Empress Eugénie, praising her impeccable taste and describing court attire and the Empress's entourage with zeal. In this sense, she chronicled the public spectacle of the *fête impériale*, selling its splendor to eagerly aspirational and nostalgic readers alike.

In a symbiotic relationship with Villemessant, who pioneered as yet unfamiliar but highly profitable advertising practices, Renneville mastered the art of the "advertorial," as Best aptly terms fashion editorials, even if she did not invent it.⁷² Primarily cast as descriptive rather than analytical, fashion columns frequently promoted the products and services of the purveyors who supported their journals through advertisement. Shops' or designers' names are regularly dropped right into the description, which was camouflaged as a conversational letter to a cousin or friend. Villemessant had famously negotiated Guerlain's acceptance to perfume the pages of early issues of *La Sylphide*. Later, though, Villemessant sought direct compensation and undertook "the conquest of the rue de la Paix; I went to find Mayer, Doucet, Capron, Chevreuil, who followed, without too much cajoling, the example of their neighbor Guerlain."⁷³ These same shops enjoyed direct advertisement in the fashion plates that accompanied each issue, on which shop names for clothing, as well as perfumes and other invisible goods, were inscribed in the image captions. The network of image, column, and advertisement is powerful through its repetition and the slippage it creates between one form of "objective" information (fashion plate, fashion chronicle) and another (advertisement). Fashion plates also contained promotions for merchants, as we shall see in greater detail below.

Under Renneville's clever pen, much like the *modiste*'s dexterous use of needle and scissors, the marketing of the journal itself as commodity hid beneath charming anecdotes, testimonies to good taste, and genteel tones. The raw transactional nature of subscriptions, publicity, and shopping was dressed up in depictions of aristocratic leisure or in delightfully witty exchanges, offering readers, between the lines, access to a classed world of goods. Keen to increase subscriptions, fashion writers like Renneville worked to create a pseudo-intimacy with their readers, often recounting anecdotes related to society activities to satisfy provincial or aspirational class desires for vicarious leisure living. However, Renneville, unlike J. J., was careful in every column to remind her readers of social class in both subtle and explicit ways, behaving less like a friend and more like a calculating opportunist, or what we might today call a frenemy.⁷⁴

Befitting her new identity, Renneville crafts a decidedly worldly column as she takes her readers shopping. Gone are J. J.'s meticulous instructions for various dress and craft projects, painstakingly labored over in a dim sitting room to yield gifts for others or respectable fashion items for oneself, for Renneville's readers seem, rather, to be primarily concerned with the pleasures of display and consumption.[75] Sewing and embroidery are activities reserved only for rainy days, when other, more exciting activities, namely shopping, are not possible. If sewing or embroidery are to be practiced, Renneville exhorts her subscribers to purchase chic patterns and materials from the high-end Parisian notions shop, Sajou: "When a young wife, or young lady goes to visit the magnificent needlework of the House of Sajou, she immediately becomes a little fairy."[76] Thus, even the *travaux des femmes* (women's needlework), traditionally understood as homemade and thus dissociated from shopping and fashion, has become commoditized.

Unlike the teen readers of *Le Journal des demoiselles* and their anxious mothers, eager for assistance in raising them correctly, the readers of *La Sylphide* aspire to belong to a more sophisticated crowd and are keen to be included in the fashionable society life of the capital, a life into which Renneville strategically inscribes herself. Like Emma Bovary, who famously longed either to die or to live in Paris, they yearn to become *Parisiennes*.[77] Renneville obliges by supplementing the formal *vous* she uses to address her readers, whom she often refers to as *mesdames*, *chères lectrices*, or *lectrices inconnues*, with the occasional use of the pronoun *nous*. While lacking the personal intimacy of J. J.'s *tu*, Renneville's *nous* gestures nonetheless rhetorically toward inclusion as she invites her readers to accompany her on conversational social and shopping expeditions. "But let's get back to the parties . . . Let's talk about ball gowns," she says, summoning her readers to participate, however distanced they may be, in the goings-on of high society.[78] As we shall see, this apparently inclusive *nous* is sometimes barbed, however, and plays into the social anxieties many readers must have brought to their perusal of the journal.

Acutely aware of all the most important social events, dropping names (of both merchants and aristocratic consumers), and, of course, describing in minute detail how anyone who mattered was dressed for a variety of occasions, Renneville deploys her "friendly" *nous* occasionally to erect a wall of exclusivity. At Longchamps, for example, in March 1850, she announces, "We know two lovely young women who imagined for Longchamps two gorgeous outfits that make all the beauty of this splendid lace stand out," suggesting, unlike the inclusive *nous* of the imperative, cited above, a society of women to which the reader does not (yet) quite belong.[79] While it may appear to be a *nous* of modesty, as it were, the echo of a "royal we" nonetheless lingers, and it pops up regularly when Renneville discusses her encounters with the aristocratic set. Balancing a welcoming inclusion with a snobbish exclusivity, then, Renneville thus markets her journal's distinctive voice of fashion—worldly, sophisticated, in-the-know—and she manipulates her readers' social insecurities to keep them desperately engaged, all the while impersonating a lady of leisure and thus distancing herself rhetorically from her necessary employment. Renneville's inclusion in her own royal we is presumed, even as it dissembles.

Likewise, distinct from J. J., the *vicomtesse de Renneville* always signs with her formal name and title ("V. de Renneville"), eschewing even the insertion of a first name. Also, in place of a uniform title for her columns, like J. J.'s *Correspondance*, which celebrated the intimacy of a "real" friendship even as it signaled the seriality of J. J.'s fashion chronicle—Renneville titles each of her columns individually, specifying the occasion or particular theme she plans to address, and thus privileging the worldly. Most frequently, however, she names her columns to coincide with fashion's seasonal shifts, thus supporting the newly instituted seasonality of the fashion business that imposed novel, or at least refreshed, fashions with each changing period—*Pendant le Carême*, *Longchamps*, and *L'Automne*, for example. In a column entitled *Code de la Mode* from October 1850, Renneville makes clear both her understanding and her approbation of fashion's relatively newly established rhythms: "Fashion, which has only pretty eyes to govern, and who knows how capricious blue and black eyes can be, has just renewed its code. Its laws follow the seasons' harmony, and live and die with the flowers. This is no doubt what ensures fashion's sovereignty and power."[80] Fashion's power is indeed also the journalist's power, which she harnesses week after week, as each latest event or weather shift demands—of women—the purchase of new goods. Renneville offers to crack the code for her eager readers just as she asserts the code's hegemony—and her own authority as decoder.

Expounding on the importance of the fashion economy, Renneville personifies *la mode* and often takes the coy position of fashion's staunchest defender: "Poor fashion, she is so unjustly maligned! Currently, fashion is the most serious principle we know, since she protects France's entire aura of elegance."[81] To fashion's detractors who would argue against luxury goods as an affront to class equality, she advances fashion's *benefits* to the working class: "These are all the thousands of nothings that rich women deem indispensable, which give industry and commerce so much prosperity and glory. Of course, one can dress without lace, lace is superfluous … but who weaves the lace? Who makes each design, each flower bloom? Is it the society lady? … No, it's the working woman who earns every day a living for her big family."[82] With a glib and confident disregard for the realities of working-class labor in the fashion industry, she uses her column to justify luxury consumption (it supports the French economy) and champions the burgeoning capitalist model of production: "Everything is interconnected in industry. Manufacture is its soul and the workers are its arms."[83]

She fails, however, to acknowledge her own role in this industrial chain, for the fashion chronicler, as primary marketer of fashion goods, had a powerful voice indeed, and she could obfuscate her undignified role as working (bourgeois) woman, preferring instead to perpetuate the fiction of her status as benevolent "code breaker" to her readers. This was, of course, purposeful, for to dwell on the labor expended on writing or editing a journal would tarnish the image that she, in fact, *works* hard in her columns to maintain. We know, however, that, like J. J. before her, Olympe Vallée wrote for a living, researching, writing, and editing her column three times a month to support her small family. The disavowal of fashion writing as work is a constant thread throughout fashion journalism in this period.

As important as social occasions and trendy outings are to Renneville's column, they are but pretexts for a continuous and repeated flow of soft advertisements, a precursor of the current practice of product placement. Even an evening at the theater, for example, is touted as an occasion to "observe" fashion's spectacle rather than an opportunity for cultural edification: "Let's pop into the Italians' to admire Mariton's hats."[84] Likewise, *Carême* (Lent), a time of abstention, and *deuil* (mourning), whose solemnity should be indisputable, both become occasions for rhapsodic fashion writing. Parties and social events, remarkably, do not stop for Lent, and Renneville tells us that: "Beautiful young women steal away toward pleasure, proud and happy! … Fashion should therefore not submit to Lent's austerities."[85] It is difficult to overstate how radical such a claim would have been in traditional, Catholic France, and how far a cry from J. J.'s this fashion advice would have been for proper ladies. Undaunted, in 1853, Renneville takes the time to invite her readers to "chat about church attire," posing the rhetorical question, "to go to church, is it a sin to primp and to dress with elegance?"[86] Her response is a resounding, "Not at all." In matters of clothing, she argues, cashmere, jewels, and lace are never a sin; but, she counters, if we were talking about feelings, *coquetterie* would be a vice.[87] She performs a deft rhetorical maneuver here, converting fashion's presumed shallowness and frivolity into an excuse for indulging in it; it is only in matters of deep importance, such as sentiments, that vain appearances should not prevail.

Even the presumably distressing occasion of mourning cannot dampen Renneville's enthusiasm for fashion: "The Dutchess of L… was in mourning, as were her two ravishing young daughters, but what a mourning! … and can we really call mourning that which gives greater sparkle to the eye and more freshness to a sweet face?"[88] In 1855, the *chroniqueuse* has found the ideal shop to meet the needs of refined shoppers for mourning wear: la maison Saran. Here, consumers can find elegance and coquetry to complement their loss:

> The house of Saran wishes, above all, that mourning should beautify, and that every mourning hat be made of cashmere, or jet-studded tulle, or be a charming headpiece, not a buggy hood. Some mourning wear shops neglect the coquetry and elegance of "all black," and maintain that a woman in mourning isn't paying attention, as if all women weren't Eve's daughters. What makes Saran successful is the tastefulness of its intimates, of its headpieces, of its fashion dresses. Many women go to Saran to buy their "all black" even when they are not in mourning.[89]

As with her apparently unorthodox inscription of coquetry in church fashions or her disregard for the cultural benefits of opera-going, here again, Renneville flips traditional wisdom while carefully tiptoeing within the outer boundaries of the appropriate. Because of their presumed respectability and the unstated absence of anxiety around class mobility, Renneville and her readers could take such a position. She concedes that fashion gives working women such as *modistes* an income and that working-class women make fashion possible. But the pervasive subtext of such discourse continues to be the distancing from work in the ideology of the feminine, the motivation for Renneville's need to position herself as leisured and to obfuscate her labor. A *modiste des lettres* is of a decidedly different social class from a *modiste*, and this difference is at play in Renneville's columns. Taste and elegance, qualities of all respectable ladies (read: bourgeois and upper class), must prevail, and women in mourning must be no less ladylike. Renneville legitimizes and promotes fashion, no matter the season, and orchestrates consumption, no matter the occasion. Indeed, under her pen, fashion seems to assume powers greater than art or religion, greater even than death!

While J. J. was intent on occupying idle hands with sewing and knitting needles, Renneville, also concerned with the dangers of indolence, which leads to *ennui*, but clearly more driven by a marketer's motive, proposes a different preventative measure: retail therapy. "Beware, Countess, of boring yourself too much in your boudoir, beware of wrinkles! Quick, call your maid, ask her to bring an elegant outfit; have the horses hitched to your carriage, and go visit all the most beautiful shops of Paris."[90] Shopping is thus rewritten not only as a leisure activity but also as an antidote to the physical and moral perils of boredom: "Perhaps you're sighing because you can't carry off or purchase all of the beautiful things you admire; but when you sigh, at least you're not bored (because you're desiring), and desire is the most chic of hopes."[91] Here Renneville celebrates and endorses shopping as both healthful and productive: among the bourgeois and upper classes, consumer desire, the materialization of which is the unspoken agenda of her column, is recast as an ethical, favorable feeling.[92] This is also beauty advice, for boredom's wrinkles are deemed ugly, which is antithetical to the feminine ideal that justifies the very existence of the fashion journal.

Offering her readers a vicarious shopping experience while also promoting her favorite shops on a near-weekly basis, Renneville is truly a master publicist for her favorite brands—or for those shops that have helped Villemessant to fund the journal. One exemplary column makes explicit Renneville's generalized strategy to detail a vicarious shopping expedition to promote certain shops and products. "Passe-temps de la mode" ("Fashion's Pastimes"), an article from November 1850, recounts the fictionalized shopping trip of just such a lady at risk of boredom, the "pretty Countess de P...," who visits each shop Renneville wishes to extol. "If you don't have anything else to do, let's follow the countess for a bit on her excursion and see if she deserves the reputation for good taste in fashion that she enjoys."[93] Renneville has just invited her readers, for whom this lovely countess serves as an aspirational double, to judge the good taste of an aristocrat. What could be more flattering? However, this is simply a rhetorical exercise, of course, and Renneville herself selects each shop: for lingerie, she visits la Crèche; for handkerchiefs, La Sublime-Porte; for dresses, Madame Flairin-Pelletier; for her *amazone* (riding costume), Lavigne, tailor and fabricant of human torso models; for "delicious hats," decorated with flowers and feathers by Zacharie and Cartier, Madame Soller; finally, on her way home, the improvised countess stops for a Belgian lace scarf at the French and Belgian lace depot. This trajectory evokes the routes that Emma Bovary traced with her finger on a map of Paris, and shopping expeditions such as this one frequently recurred over the seven years Renneville wrote for *La Sylphide*—which perfectly coincided with 1850–7, the period during which Flaubert composed his novel.

Toward the end of this rather lengthy and information-packed description, Renneville effects an important shift: we are no longer shopping *with* the imagined countess, but we *ourselves* are invited to step into her shoes—to *become* her. The vicariousness with which her readers have been exploring the shops of Paris evolves into a direct address, and the imperative *nous* of inclusion reappears: "Let's imagine, Madame, that you are going to the Opéra next Saturday. You smile, showing your little teeth, so white that you must be availing yourself of Camproger's coral powder."[94] Her reader, who has essentially assumed the rhetorical position of the imagined countess on her shopping excursion, is now praised for her good taste in beauty merchandise—teeth whiteners, perfumes, beauty creams, and hair-tinting products. The reader has not only stepped into the upper-class world of shopping, shadowing a "countess" as she selects the finest goods, but she has also acquired the authority of good judgment herself—a seal of approval that all but guarantees her (continued) purchase of the products she has been credited with using. That Renneville must promote, sometimes rather awkwardly, beauty and hygiene products like vinegars and tooth powder in the same space as high fashion and elegant accessories not only reveals the extent to which the journal is dependent upon soft advertisement, but it also offers key clues as to the actual social class of many of her readers and illustrates how challenging the *chroniqueuse*'s task of product placement actually was.[95]

We might again be tempted to picture Emma Bovary in the reader Renneville has generated in the column above, sitting in her dreary provincial home, fantasizing about Parisian hats from Madame Soller. And while a reader like Emma is helped to imagine such goods not only by Renneville's animated column but also by the *gravure* that accompanied the issue each week, illustrating many of the items the columnist describes (figure 3.9), it is also the case that less glamorous products were advertised in a more direct way—at the back of the printed issue (figure 3.10).[96] This advertisements page is in a sense a foil to Renneville's column, simply indicating, without rhetorical flourish, the names and addresses of shops mentioned in the article and announcing more pedestrian goods and services that the reading public might regularly buy. Here we find cosmetics, toys, toothpaste, and remedies advertised alongside services such as equestrian training, hair salons, gymnastics training, and childcare. Of course, department stores, shoemakers, *nouveautés*, and corsets also figure among the advertised services and products, but it is curious to compare Renneville's exquisite shopping excursion with the more mundane products tucked away at the back of the journal. While she might well use these products, the "pretty Countess de P. . ." would surely not be caught dead shopping for *dentifrice* (toothpaste) or *tonique anti-nerveux* (nerve tonic).

In the first issue of *La Gazette rose*, published in January 1857, founded and edited by Renneville and underwritten by her patron, Villemessant, the *chroniqueuse* announces that her new journal would be, unlike all other fashion journals past and present, free of excessive advertisements and

Figure 3.9 Héloïse Leloir, Gravure de Mode, "Chapeau de Mlle Soller," La Sylphide, 1855, Bibliothèque nationale de France.

Figure 3.10 La Sylphide, *December 1850, Bibliothèque nationale de France.*

publicity."[97] In her manifesto, or prospectus, which she calls "Le But de *La Gazette rose*," she rails against the degradation of fashion by advertisement and promises that her new journal will not resort to such corrupting practices. Of course, she can afford to say this only because the journal was underwritten by the monster success of *Le Figaro*, which also published her fashion columns; and, while placement for items as lowly as toothpaste disappeared, the pages of *La Gazette rose* continued to tout the same dressmakers, milliners, lace shops, and perfumers that *La Sylphide* had promoted. For all of her claims for the newness of the journal she edited, it replicated her columns in *La Sylphide*.

The advertising gap illustrated in *La Sylphide* exposes the duplicity of the fashion writer's identity as well as her rhetoric, returning us to the subtle use of pronouns discussed earlier, just as it exposes the truth about the journal's targeted customer. On the one hand, Renneville invites her reader to inhabit the lifestyle of a countess, implicitly attributing to her the social and cultural knowledge and good taste of such a figure. On the other hand, often in the very same breath, she offers the fashion advice and shopping instruction that only those who are not countesses, but who aspire to dress the part, would require. Some of her anecdotes even stage this moment of confrontation, enacting a virtual shaming of the excluded reader even as she is brought into the fold through precious fashion insights. For example, in 1856, she touts the invention of the *buste mécanique* (mechanical torso) of M. Bienvenu, which she claims gives the very best fit and relieves women of the drudgery of trying on clothes:[98] "—Do you, by chance, still try on your dresses? asks Madame de C... of a pretty little banker's wife who doesn't realize that *bustes mécaniques* exist.—But of course, the charming novice, blushing, replies. "You're so behind the times! I never try on my dresses. My dressmaker told me that I'm too well made for that."[99]

The pretty banker's wife, doubling the reader of Renneville's column, is both excluded and included; the price for unfamiliarity with fashion's "thousands of secrets that only a few initiates know" is, quite clearly, humiliation.[100] Of course, the so-called initiates are also mere fabrications, born of the brilliant collusion between the fashion writer and the manufacturer or purveyor of goods, both of whom profit from the economy of exclusivity upon which the fashion system rests. The vicomtesse de Renneville thus engages in a complex rhetorical dance with her readers: gossipy as she shares society's and fashion's secrets with her readers, she is also keen to keep them in their place—ever needy, always aspiring, not quite there. Impersonating the glamorous *Parisienne*, Renneville feeds the fantasies and the anxieties of thousands of readers eager to gain admission to a life of Parisian leisure and splendor.

When the vicomtesse de Renneville left *La Sylphide* for *La Gazette rose*, she had established her reputation as the "oracle of taste" (*l'oracle du goût*), but doubts around her gender, based on her witty, "masculine" style, persisted, as the countess Dash intimates in her memoirs.[101] The author of the *Revues des modes*, la marquise Athénie de la Sainte-Colombe, is quoted as responding to a query from a reader curious to penetrate the truth of Renneville's pseudonym: "It will always be time to *vicomtessederennevilliser*," she writes, "Madame la vicomtesse de Renneville is the pseudonym of

Madame de Lascaux, born Olympe Vallée."[102] More significant than this disclosure, however, which may well have been an open secret at the time, and more important than the celebrity that Renneville must have achieved to have inspired a verb referring to speculation around her identity, is the way in which this author exposes Renneville's duplicity, which was replicated in various forms by female fashion writers more generally. Although Renneville writes with great skill about the latest fashions, urging her readers to consume them, this author tells us, Renneville did not necessarily follow them herself:

> While talking to you about the charming and monstrous crinolines of the house of Ballonard, she [Renneville] knows how to skirt herself in reasonable measure and prefers—in springtime—a taffeta dress in the hue of a *frightened gray mouse* with a skirt of four flounces trimmed in broad taffeta bands of a *beetle wing* shade from the Corner Shop, to the silk tarlatans brightened with floral baskets and harvests from the Louvre Store. She does not wear the Louis XIII hat from Philibertine, but a regular hat, like everyone else.[103]

For all of its humor—the descriptions of clothing are clearly parodic and poke fun, in particular, at the French fashion industry's penchant for naming colors and styles in the most rarefied of ways—written with the sarcastic tone of a fellow fashion writer in the know, this account of the gulf between the fashions Renneville marketed and those she wore herself exposes the broader truth around double identities that characterized fashion writers in this period.

Renneville's identity as a social trendsetter and fashion oracle was part of a sophisticated marketing strategy, both for the sake of the journals for which she wrote and for her own financial stability; but it had its limits. Her obituary, published in *Le Figaro* in January 1890, reminds readers that she assumed her aristocratic title not out of vanity, but to "give pleasure—as she herself at least believed—to her clientele."[104] Still, her aristocratic patina would not survive the Second Empire. As would be expected, the journal whose general editor had given Renneville her start in the profession praises her as the "renovator of fashion journalism" even as she "bravely raised her family with the help of the journal," and this without the support of her estranged husband, "a determined bohemian."[105] Like her predecessor in fashion editing, J. J., and her successor, Emmeline Raymond, the vicomtesse de Renneville would become *rédactrice en chef* (editor-in-chief) of her own journal, *La Gazette rose*, whose exclusive tone and reproduction of social hierarchy sat well with the imperial aesthetic she praised. Her success, however, waned with time, and other, more technologically advanced and better funded fashion journals would eclipse "the somewhat dated attitudes of the poor vicomtesse de Renneville."[106] Indeed, the empire of the vicomtesse would cede to the good housekeeping of the bourgeois tastemaker, Emmeline Raymond, whose journal broke subscription records and pioneered new technologies, and whose voice merged J. J.'s Christian morality and home economics lessons with the vicomtesse's marketing savvy.

Madame Emmeline Raymond: "*La Bonne Ménagère*"[107]

In many ways, the director and fashion writer of *La Mode illustrée*, Emmeline Raymond (1824–1902), offered the unabashedly bourgeois counterpoint to Renneville's vicomtesse. In 1860, Raymond was recruited by publishing giant Didot *frères* to launch what would become one of the most popular women's magazines of the nineteenth century. According to a profile written by columnist Montclair for *Le Figaro* in 1890, Raymond had been recommended to Didot *frères* by none other than J. J. ("Madame de P…") of the *Journal des demoiselles*, with whom she had collaborated on the earlier journal.[108] Indeed, Raymond must have learned a great deal from J. J. and shared many of her concerns and interests; at the same time, she borrowed strategies from journals like *La Sylphide*, actively engaging in advertising and relying on the appeal of illustrations to help sell magazines. Published and sold at four different price points, the journal held wide appeal for every budget and, by 1890, boasted a readership of over 100,000 readers around the world (figure 3.11).[109] Widely disseminated in France and beyond (Raymond's columns were reprinted for *Harper's*, where she became the Paris fashion correspondent in 1869)[110] and a prototype for many of the women's fashion magazines we recognize today, *La Mode illustrée: Journal de la famille* was an eight-page weekly magazine appearing each Sunday that ran until 1937 (figure 3.12). Raymond retired (and died) in 1902, leaving behind thousands of fashion chronicles, detailed instructions for home-sewing and household craft projects—such as the turtle paperweight or toothpick- and match-holders made from lobster shells pictured in figures 3.13 and 3.14—and leaving also a voluminous one-sided correspondence that both documented in minute detail and influenced the rapidly changing fashions of an increasingly modern Paris, as well as the preoccupations and values of nineteenth-century French bourgeois society.

Her columns also incarnate a feminized bourgeois work ethic, however, that, in many ways, competes with the very engine of consumption that propels the journal she manages, edits, and cherishes. Under its veneer of bourgeois respectability and fashion advertisement, Raymond's columns often push back against the cyclical fever of the fashion system and advocate work—albeit safe, unpaid work within one's own parlor. Furthermore, through her own example of industriousness—as journalist, editor, and businesswoman—which receives little to no direct acknowledgement within the pages of the journal, she also left a legacy of female professionalization at once concealed behind the bourgeois ideology embraced and proselytized by the journal and perceptible in notable contradictions embedded in Raymond's discourse, which I will consider below.[111]

Through her weekly magazine, Raymond emerged as the premier tastemaker to the aspiring—and expanding—bourgeoisie in the second half of the nineteenth century. Indeed, expansiveness was a hallmark of the journal, not only in terms of its practical inclusivity that welcomed an ever increasing range of subscribers, attested to by the various price points, but also in terms of its literal size: *La Mode*

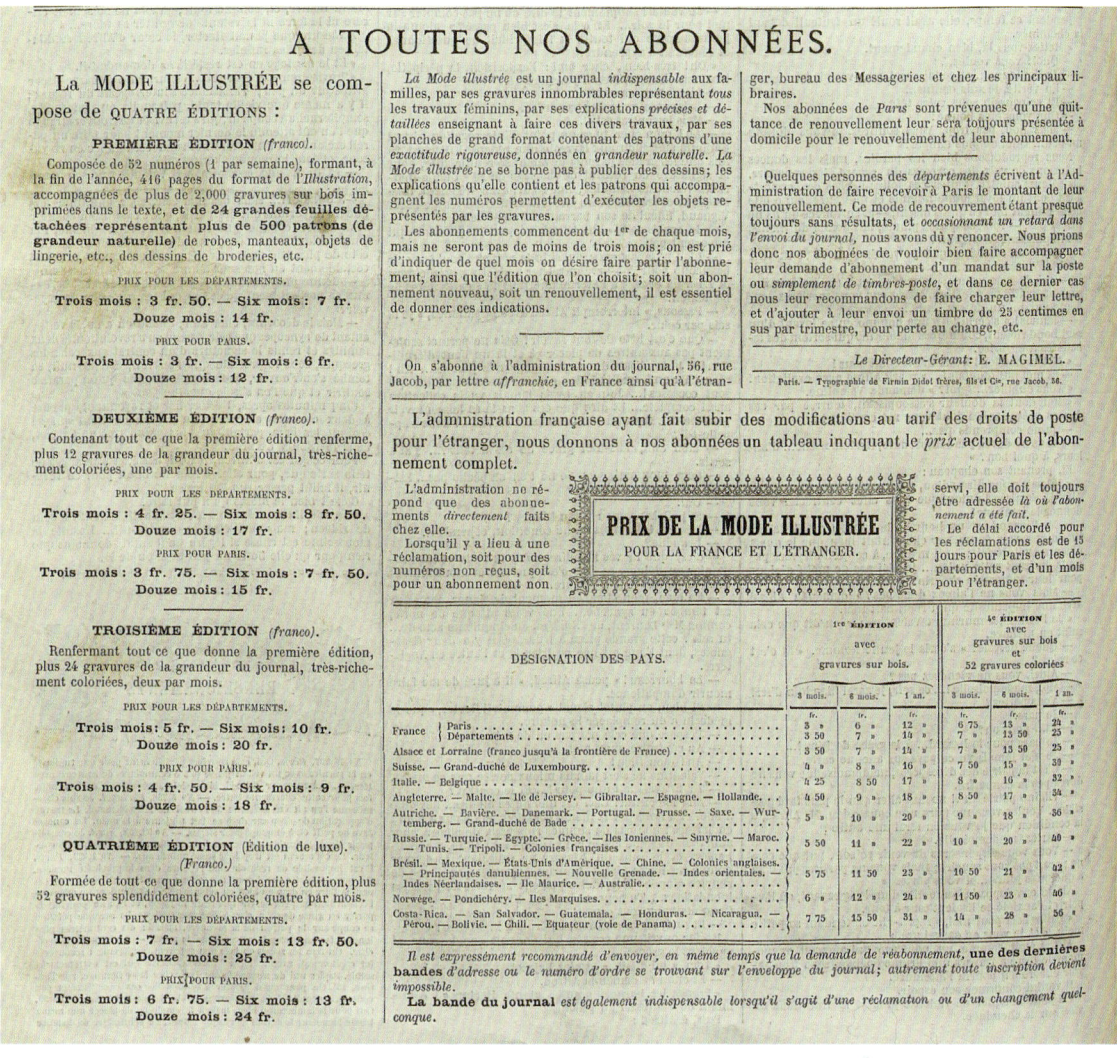

Figure 3.11 La Mode illustrée, *price scales, November 5, 1871, no. 45, p. 360, Bibliothèque Forney Digital Collection.*

illustrée was the first French fashion journal to adopt a large format. Raymond was a deft businesswoman who grasped the potential of the modernity of illustrated fashion journals in that, among other things, she never underestimated the intelligence and industry of her readers. Indeed, she increased readership not only through her fashion columns and household advice but also, like J. J. before her, through a weekly *Rébus*, or puzzle that played on the relationship between word and image, whose explanation would be revealed only in the subsequent issue, thus reinforcing the journal's seriality and appealing to both her public's interest in popular pastimes and their impulse to consume (figures 3.15 and 3.16).

Figure 3.12 La Mode illustrée, *October 27, 1872, no. 43, front page, Bibliothèque Forney Digital Collection, Ville de Paris/Bibliothèque Forney.*

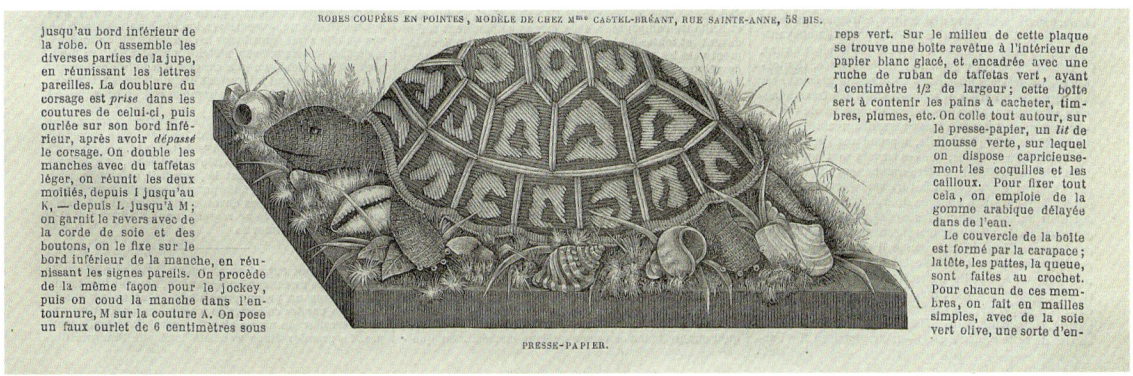

Figure 3.13 La Mode illustrée, *November 26, 1865, no. 48, p. 381. "Presse-papier" (paperweight), Bibliothèque Forney Digital Collection, Ville de Paris/Bibliothèque Forney*

Figure 3.14 La Mode illustrée, *December 16, 1866, no. 51. Toothpick and match holders made from lobster shells, Bibliothèque Forney Digital Collection, Ville de Paris/Bibliothèque Forney.*

Figure 3.15 and 3.16 *"Rébus,"* La Mode illustrée, *February 28 and March 7, 1869, nos. 9 and 10, pp. 72, 80,* Bibliothèque Forney Digital Collection, Ville de Paris/Bibliothèque Forney.

The visual effect of the journal was its greatest innovation, and, combined with Raymond's prose, which meandered in and around the illustrations to maximize the surface area of the page, *La Mode illustrée* was as much a feast for the eyes as an invaluable manual for all manner of household tasks. This juxtaposition—of practicality and visual splendor—sums up the journal's text-image strategy and embodies its core paradox of marketing fashion while preaching bourgeois frugality. Promoting consumption and breathing life into garments for readers to envision, images frequently offer disembodied fragments of outfits, as if the human form had been rendered invisible while the garment uncannily maintains its human shape (figure 3.17). Like two-dimensional clothes for paper dolls, which can be mixed and matched among subjects, swelling bodices for ladies and floating aprons for little girls share the page with a lampshade and a folding needlework stand. Fashions for family and home are assimilated on a single page. These images re-mediate the shop window in an eerie aesthetics of display, which both fetishizes the female body through decorporealization and animates the inanimate object.[112] They also, importantly, provide helpful visual aids with accompanying instructions for those who would prefer, or who only have the means, to create these items at home.

This technique of placing images directly onto the page surrounded by explanatory text—as opposed to the earlier practice of placing images, patterns, and diagrams as separate inserts to the journal—was introduced by the German magazine *Der Bazar* in 1855, five years before *La Mode illustrée* was launched, and was the result of advances in printing techniques. Wood engraving, instead of steel engraving, was a much less expensive technique and was adopted to multiply black and white images throughout the journal. The larger folio format was also already in use in the German publication, and it would appear that Raymond, who was multilingual and was no doubt quite familiar with *Der Bazar*, seized upon its superior, and cheaper, technology to help her journal achieve wider circulation. Indeed, as Marianne Van Remoortel's research has shown, journals like *La Mode illustrée* sometimes even used the same images as *Der Bazar*, commissioned from a German printer.[113] Raymond was savvy enough to adopt the technologies, even translating some of the German text describing images into French, without ever divulging their German origins, an irony noted by Van Remoortel and not to be dismissed, especially in light of the stridently anti-German columns Raymond penned during the Siege of Paris in the fall of 1870. Despite her deceptive "borrowing" from a German publication, however, Raymond should be credited with having created and directed a journal that far surpassed its original model and its international competitors in subscriptions and popularity. Her shrewd use of visual and textual strategies worked to construct and encourage an international female readership capable of responding appropriately to French modernity, for her fashion writing, as we shall see, encouraged individual choice within what often appeared to be a rigid morality in the pages of *La Mode illustrée*. In other words, Raymond exuded authority while simultaneously exhorting her readers to exercise personal autonomy in their choices.

By the Second Empire (1852–70), through a careful mediation by way of economies of homemaking, restraint, and reverence for the past, Raymond transformed fashion—and its most potent marketing instrument, the fashion magazine—into an indispensable engine of morality and productivity, without losing its elite edge—captured in the hand-colored plate.[114] The journal's title indicates as much: *La Mode illustrée: Journal de la famille*. Long figured as a frivolous aristocrat, fashion, under Raymond's

Figure 3.17 La Mode illustrée, *March 7, 1869, no. 10, p. 74, Bibliothèque Forney Digital Collection, Ville de Paris/Bibliothèque Forney.*

pen, would be redeemed by family values: the adjective "illustrée" refers then, literally, to the prolific and intricate illustrations of the periodical, as well as figuratively, to the anecdotes and advice on domestic virtue that contextualize the fashions on display—for these "illustrate" through example, similar to the ways in which J. J.'s "patterns" helped both figuratively and literally to shape female behavior. These moral imperatives thus temper the frivolity of fashion. Indeed, countering the excesses of Napoléon III's glittering imperial court, so celebrated by the vicomtesse de Renneville, Raymond proposes restraint and simplicity in dress. In the midst of the vertiginous upheavals of Haussmann's renovations to Paris, her columns advocate steady consistency, reforming fashion's requisite inconstancy and elitism as an inclusive practicality.[115] During the dark year of the Franco-Prussian War, the Siege of Paris, and the Commune (1870–1, *l'année terrible*), Raymond labored on, drafting columns and recording events—related to both fashion and politics—ultimately emerging with a clear mandate for *utilité* (usefulness), and even sustainability, in fashion.[116]

This usefulness had always been Raymond's driving mission. Indeed, in the "Prospectus de *la Mode illustrée*," published in the journal's first issue, the editor makes clear her guiding principle: "we consider it [work] the very goal of existence, the safeguard against all sadness and dangers . . . It is with this thought in mind [the value of work] that the journal was created. But next to the numerous useful tasks and talents the journal prepares for its readers, it also reserves a place in its columns to satisfy the need for healthy distractions . . . all the things a well-bred woman should know about."[117] Again, in her end-of-year letter to her subscribers in 1866, she reiterates the journal's purpose in a sentiment she would repeat frequently in later years: "Seven years ago on the same date, in the same place, I indicated the goal that the editors of *La Mode illustrée* proposed in creating this journal; I traced in a few lines the plan to which the editors wanted to conform and I added: 'We have the ambition, the dear ambition, to be useful, and who knows? . . . maybe we'll become indispensable.'"[118] Occupying bourgeois hands with domestic tasks, making industriousness appealing, Raymond intends to balance in her readers the desire to consume with the inspiration to produce. Usefulness—from how-to home economics lessons, sewing and household tips, to the names and addresses of shops and goods—was a strategy to embrace a newly consuming readership drawn from the ranks of the petite-bourgeoisie who were now shopping in department stores and discovering the pleasures of consumption.[119]

Distinct from her predecessors, Raymond magnifies the importance of morality and family, gearing her journal primarily to bourgeois mothers. With the expansion of *prêt-à-porter* and mass culture more generally, the market for *La Mode illustrée* was growing. Inclusivity thus prevailed in Raymond's journal as a smart business choice, whereas in Renneville's column, it was always checked by condescending rhetorical moves that subtly reminded readers of their place on the periphery of the inner circle. Contrary to Renneville's snobbish name-dropping and rhetoric of exclusion, Raymond seems to position herself as a demystifier of fashion's haughty secrets: this would be the "use-value" of her fashion columns. While Raymond's pronouncements could be terse and authoritative, her tone, particularly in the *renseignements* (queries) section, consistently reveals that she never underestimated her readers and strove to respond honestly to their needs and desires.

Along with hand-colored plates, dress patterns came with each issue, thus ensuring access (for a price) to the latest Paris fashions for even the most provincial of subscribers. While earlier publications like the *Journal des demoiselles* primarily showcased embroidery and embellishment as suitable occupations for idle female hands and typically offered scaled patterns or patterns for small articles of clothing, *La Mode illustrée* also included detailed stitching guides, patterns for clothing for the entire family, and how-to instructions for any number of household tasks—such as crocheting, sewing, embroidering and other needlework.[120] One could purchase the pattern book separately or order individual patterns from various pattern makers, including M. Leballeur, at 74 rue Taitbout, in 1863, or from Mme. Gérard, at 40 rue du faubourg-Saint-Honoré, in 1866. Several times a year, a *planche de patrons* (plate of patterns) would also be included in the issue itself. With the multiplication of household projects, the house itself could thus be "dressed," along with the lady of the house and her entire family. New also was the insertion of patterns, diagrams, and written instructions together on the same page, with words printed to fit alongside the images. This brought an immediacy to the reader's visualization of the items and meant that a wider range of goods, for a wider range of consumers, could be illustrated. In figure 3.18, as in so many other such images, text is placed in and around diagrams, offering detailed instructions accompanying the step-by-step pictures. Not only does this practice facilitate a reader's understanding and accomplishment of the project, but, perhaps more important, it meant that no space on the page was wasted, and the magazine thus embodied its own ideal of frugality.

A wealth of "useful" material was included in each installment of *La Mode illustrée*—thus threading through the notion of *utilité* as the principal objective of Raymond's discourse—and reinforced by creating visual links between fashion and household activities. Each issue of the periodical contained several standard rubrics, such as *description de toilettes* (description of fashion plates), *modes* (fashions), and *renseignements* (queries). The magazine also regularly featured beauty tips, hairstyle and hat decorating ideas, sewing patterns, detailed explanations of knitting, stitching, embroidery, and crocheting techniques, and household and cooking tips—all with detailed accompanying drawings (figures 3.18–3.20). Needlework, hair styling, and cooking are assimilated on these pages, which feature disembodied hands engaged in work to produce a well-crafted object. Sewing patterns, broken down into numbered parts and steps, mirror the numbered, step-by-step instructions for carving up a roast goose: both activities involve a sharp tool (figure 3.21) and, again, picture dainty hands busy at work, thus establishing a visual, and even material, parallel.

The journal thus showcases new ways of visually depicting female industriousness and competencies, and fashion, traditionally viewed as a tolerated frivolity, now becomes, through association with

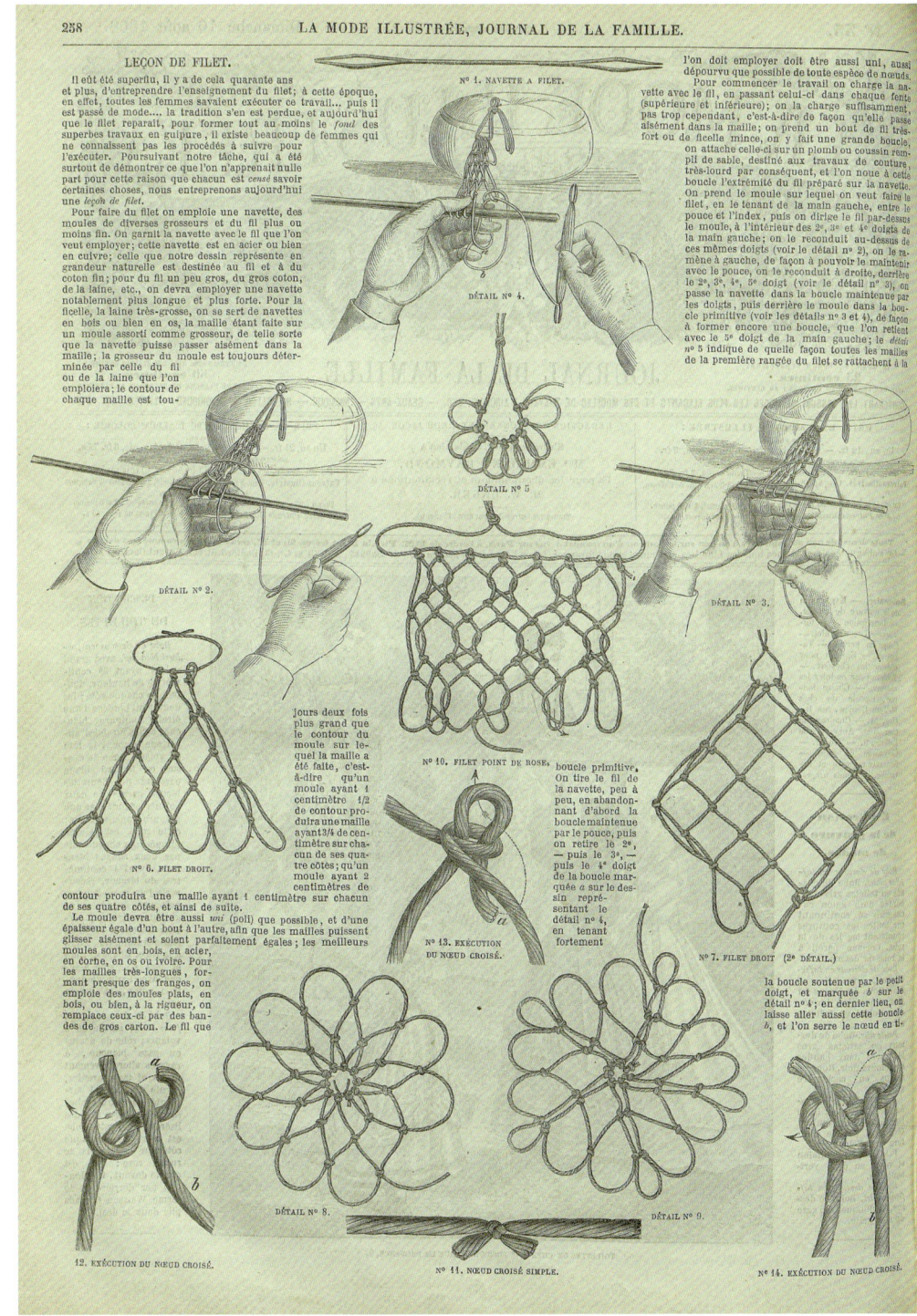

Figure 3.18 La Mode illustrée, *August 16, 1868, no. 33, p. 58. "Leçon de filet"* (netting lesson), Bibliothèque Forney Digital Collection, Ville de Paris/Bibliothèque Forney

LA MODE ILLUSTRÉE, JOURNAL DE LA FAMILLE.

Pour enjoliver ces *médaillons*, et pour les conserver sans inconvénient pendant la journée, on place sur l'un des cercles une rosette faite en ruban de même nuance que les cheveux. Le cercle à *bouclette* doit être le côté de dessus du médaillon. On roule les cheveux comme l'indiquent nos dessins, et on les renferme entre les deux cercles, que l'on ferme ensuite.

DESCRIPTION DE TOILETTES.

Toilette de mariée. Robe en poult-de-soie antique blanc, coupée à pointes, plate par devant; toute l'ampleur est rejetée par derrière et la jupe forme une longue queue; au-dessus de l'ourlet se trouve un bourrelet en poult-de-soie, surmonté d'un cordon en perles blanches, fixé de distance en distance par trois longues perles blanches en forme d'olives ; ce cordon de perles remonte sur toutes les coutures réunissant les lés. Corsage montant à pointes par devant, à trois basques par derrière ; les basques sont bordées avec une frange de perles blanches en forme d'olives; épaulettes assorties, boutons en perles. Bouquet de fleurs d'oranger placé au milieu du corsage. Couronne assortie. Voile de tulle blanc attaché sous le petit diadème de fleurs d'oranger.

Robe en poult-de-soie bleu clair, garnie avec un volant de dentelle blanche disposé en festons et surmonté d'une ruche coquillée en dentelle. Robe de dessus en tulle blanc, relevée par devant avec deux branches de clématite. Corselet bleu, draperie de gaze blanche avec branches de clématites par devant et sur l'épaulette bleue qui surmonte la manche courte bouillonnée. La coiffure se compose d'une natte-diadème ornée d'étoiles en diamants. Une branche de clématite est attachée sur le côté parmi les boucles du chignon.

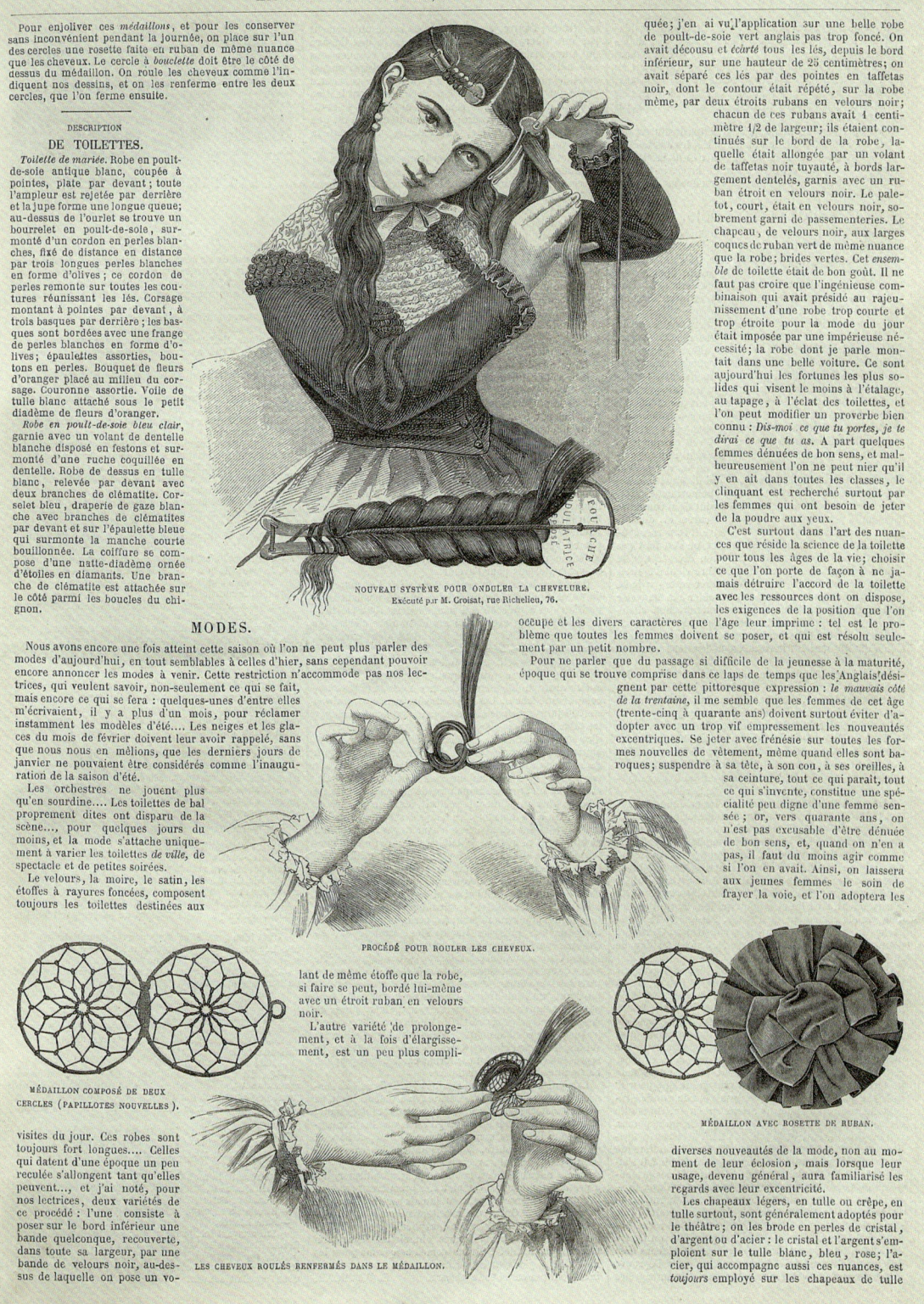

NOUVEAU SYSTÈME POUR ONDULER LA CHEVELURE.
Exécuté par M. Croisat, rue Richelieu, 76.

PROCÉDÉ POUR ROULER LES CHEVEUX.

MÉDAILLON COMPOSÉ DE DEUX CERCLES (PAPILLOTES NOUVELLES).

LES CHEVEUX ROULÉS RENFERMÉS DANS LE MÉDAILLON.

MÉDAILLON AVEC ROSETTE DE RUBAN.

MODES.

Nous avons encore une fois atteint cette saison où l'on ne peut plus parler des modes d'aujourd'hui, en tout semblables à celles d'hier, sans cependant pouvoir encore annoncer les modes à venir. Cette restriction n'accommode pas nos lectrices, qui veulent savoir, non-seulement ce qui se fait, mais encore ce qui se fera : quelques-unes d'entre elles m'écrivaient, il y a plus d'un mois, pour réclamer instamment les modèles d'été.... Les neiges et les glaces du mois de février doivent leur avoir rappelé, sans que nous nous en mêlions, que les derniers jours de janvier ne pouvaient être considérés comme l'inauguration de la saison d'été.

Les orchestres ne jouent plus qu'en sourdine.... Les toilettes de bal proprement dites ont disparu de la scène..., pour quelques jours du moins, et la mode s'attache uniquement à varier les toilettes *de ville*, de spectacle et de petites soirées.

Le velours, la moire, le satin, les étoffes à rayures foncées, composent toujours les toilettes destinées aux visites du jour. Ces robes sont toujours fort longues.... Celles qui datent d'une époque un peu reculée s'allongent tant qu'elles peuvent..., et j'ai noté, pour nos lectrices, deux variétés de ce procédé : l'une consiste à poser sur le bord inférieur une bande quelconque, recouverte, dans toute sa largeur, par une bande de velours noir, au-dessus de laquelle on pose un volant de même étoffe que la robe, si faire se peut, bordé lui-même avec un étroit ruban en velours noir.

L'autre variété de prolongement, et à fois d'élargissement, est un peu plus compliquée ; j'en ai vu l'application sur une belle robe de poult-de-soie vert anglais pas trop foncé. On avait décousu et *écarté* tous les lés, depuis le bord inférieur, sur une hauteur de 25 centimètres; on avait séparé ces lés par des pointes en taffetas noir, dont le contour était répété, sur la robe même, par deux étroits rubans en velours noir; chacun de ces rubans avait 1 centimètre 1/2 de largeur; ils étaient continués sur le bord de la robe, laquelle était allongée par un volant de taffetas noir tuyauté, à bords largement dentelés, garnis avec un ruban étroit en velours noir. Le paletot, court, était en velours noir, sobrement garni de passementeries. Le chapeau, de velours noir, aux larges coques de ruban vert de même nuance que la robe; brides vertes. Cet *ensemble* de toilette était de bon goût. Il ne faut pas croire que l'ingénieuse combinaison qui avait présidé au rajeunissement d'une robe trop courte et trop étroite pour la mode du jour était imposée par une impérieuse nécessité; la robe dont je parle montait dans une belle voiture. Ce sont aujourd'hui les fortunes les plus solides qui visent le moins à l'étalage, au tapage, à l'éclat des toilettes, et l'on peut modifier un proverbe bien connu : *Dis-moi ce que tu portes, je te dirai ce que tu as*. A part quelques femmes dénuées de bon sens, et malheureusement il n'en peut nier qu'il y en ait dans toutes les classes, le clinquant est recherché surtout par les femmes qui ont besoin de jeter de la poudre aux yeux.

C'est surtout dans l'art des nuances que réside la science de la toilette pour tous les âges de la vie; choisir ce que l'on porte de façon à ne jamais détruire l'accord de la toilette avec les ressources dont on dispose, les exigences de la position que l'on occupe et les divers caractères que l'âge leur imprime : tel est le problème que toutes les femmes doivent se poser, et qui est résolu seulement par un petit nombre.

Pour ne parler que du passage si difficile de la jeunesse à la maturité, époque qui se trouve comprise dans ce laps de temps que les Anglais désignent par cette pittoresque expression : *le mauvais côté de la trentaine*, il me semble que les femmes de cet âge (trente-cinq à quarante ans) doivent surtout éviter d'adopter avec un trop vif empressement les nouveautés excentriques. Se jeter avec frénésie sur toutes les formes nouvelles de vêtement, même quand elles sont baroques; suspendre à sa tête, à son cou, à ses oreilles, à sa ceinture, tout ce qui paraît, tout ce qui s'invente, constitue une spécialité peu digne d'une femme sensée ; or, vers quarante ans, on n'est pas excusable d'être dénuée de bon sens, et, quand on n'en a pas, il faut du moins agir comme si l'on en avait. Ainsi, on laissera aux jeunes femmes le soin de frayer la voie, et l'on adoptera les diverses nouveautés de la mode, non au moment de leur éclosion, mais lorsque leur usage, devenu général, aura familiarisé les regards avec leur excentricité.

Les chapeaux légers, en tulle ou crêpe, en tulle surtout, sont généralement adoptés pour le théâtre ; on les borde en perles de cristal, d'argent ou d'acier : le cristal et l'argent s'emploient sur le tulle blanc, bleu, rose; l'acier, qui accompagne aussi ces nuances, est *toujours* employé sur les chapeaux de tulle

Figure 3.19 *La Mode illustrée*, March 5, 1865, no. 10, p. 77. "Nouveau système pour onduler la chevelure" (New process for curling hair), Bibliothèque Forney Digital Collection, Ville de Paris/Bibliothèque Forney.

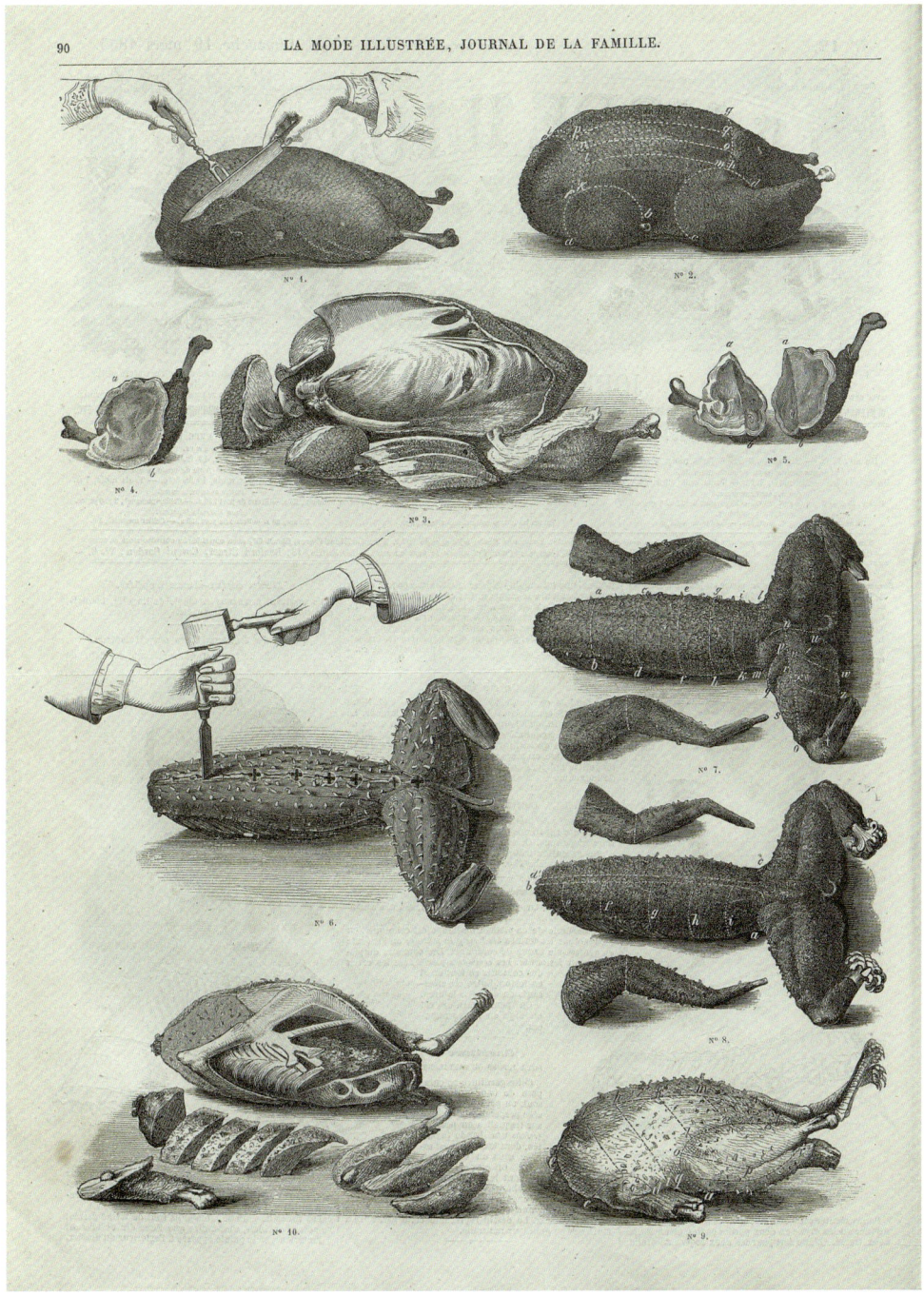

Figure 3.20 La Mode illustrée, *March 19, 1865, no. 12, p. 90. "L'art de découper" (the art of carving)*, *Bibliothèque Forney Digital Collection, Ville de Paris/Bibliothèque Forney.*

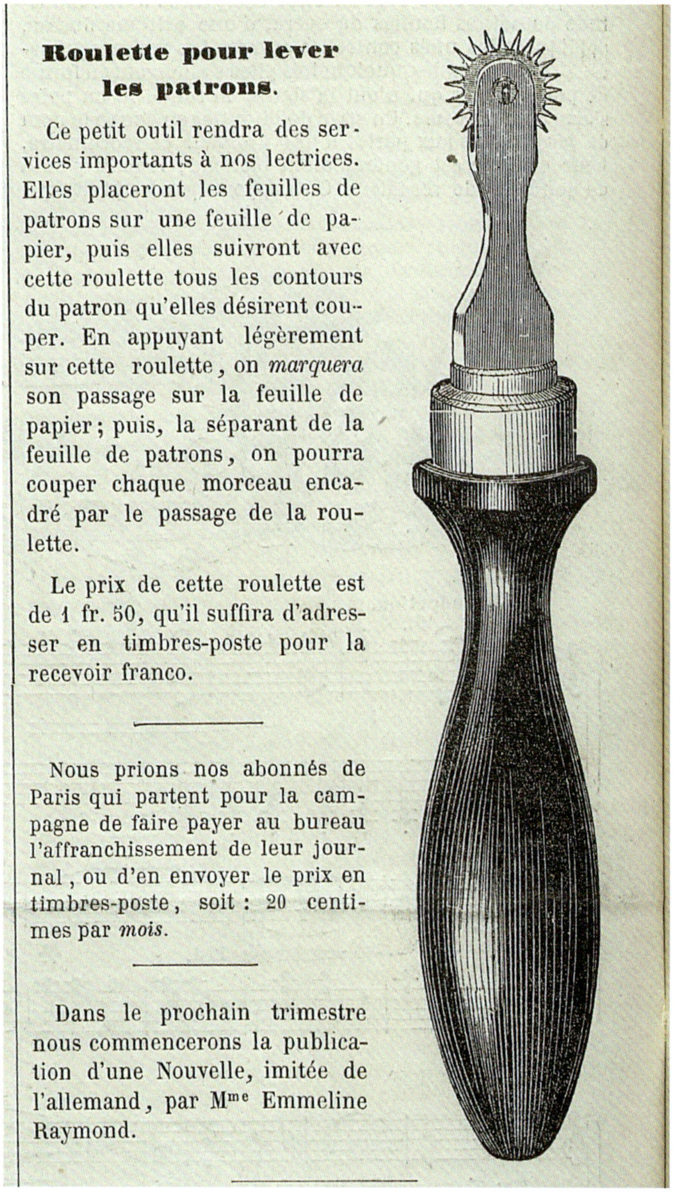

> **Roulette pour lever les patrons.**
>
> Ce petit outil rendra des services importants à nos lectrices. Elles placeront les feuilles de patrons sur une feuille de papier, puis elles suivront avec cette roulette tous les contours du patron qu'elles désirent couper. En appuyant légèrement sur cette roulette, on *marquera* son passage sur la feuille de papier; puis, la séparant de la feuille de patrons, on pourra couper chaque morceau encadré par le passage de la roulette.
>
> Le prix de cette roulette est de 1 fr. 50, qu'il suffira d'adresser en timbres-poste pour la recevoir franco.
>
> ---
>
> Nous prions nos abonnés de Paris qui partent pour la campagne de faire payer au bureau l'affranchissement de leur journal, ou d'en envoyer le prix en timbres-poste, soit : 20 centimes par *mois*.
>
> ---
>
> Dans le prochain trimestre nous commencerons la publication d'une Nouvelle, imitée de l'allemand, par Mme Emmeline Raymond.

Figure 3.21 La Mode illustrée, *July 6, 1863, no. 27, p. 216. "Roulette pour lever les patrons" (pattern cutter), Bibliothèque Forney Digital Collection, Ville de Paris/Bibliothèque Forney.*

productive household work, a virtuous pastime in its own right. Not only are fashion and homemaking equated through the similarity of the images' composition, but also the products of domestic activity—embellished and sewn goods, consumable meals—are made comparable to objectified young ladies themselves through the same process. Fashion was thus domesticated for a squarely middle-class readership; at the same time, domestic activities were aestheticized. In those eight very full pages, readers could also find short serialized fiction (often written or translated by Raymond herself); a social chronicle that recounted the various musical, theatrical, and social events of the capital each month; and, every week, one hand-painted color fashion plate.[121] The three regular organizational rubrics introduced above—*description des toilettes, modes, renseignements*—correspond roughly, in content, to the fashion columns we examined in the other two journals.

Descriptions of the outfits pictured in the color fashion plates were essential so that readers could attach names to objects: they provided something of a key to deciphering changing and newly introduced fashions. This decoding was particularly important given the expanded readership of *La Mode illustrée*. These descriptions also offered information as to where one might procure the garment in question, if the means were available, much like in *La Sylphide*. Although the magazine's editors claim not to print paid advertisements, product placement was nevertheless commonly practiced, and certain shops, such as that of the *modiste* Mme. Aubert, rue Neuve-des-Mathurins, and the *couturière* Mme. Castel-Bréant, 58 bis, rue Sainte Anne, receive frequent nods both in the *renseignements* column and in the form of captions under images.[122] It is worth noting that in figure 3.22, which dates from 1864, Mme. Castel-Bréant is referred to as Mlle. Castel. She must have later married and hyphenated her name, rather than taking her husband's name, in order not to confuse, or potentially lose, clients: in other words, her name was already her brand.

A fashion plate from an issue published in 1865 (figure 3.23) pictures two ladies in an outdoor setting appropriate to the social norm that dictated that bourgeois women remain protected or contained in the private sphere: one sits and the other stands in a garden-like space. Given the vibrant colors and exquisite detail of the clothing on display, a textual description might seem superfluous; and yet, week after week, we find a single, colored plate like this one—seemingly autonomous—with accompanying descriptions embedded on a different page. Why did Raymond need to include a detailed textual description of what was plain to see with one's own eyes? A quick examination of the description helps explain what the fashion plate alone fails to elucidate:

> Gray-lilac poplin skirt with very fine black stripes. The edge is cut into very pointy "teeth," edged in black taffeta, sewn with gray-lilac silk. Dress—the same as this skirt, cut in the same way, brought up, at regular intervals, with two interlocking rings of black taffeta, sewn with gray-lilac silk. Long lacy jacket like a dress; belt with very long rounded sections decorated with interlocking rings and falling to the back; black taffeta tie. Round, black straw hat, decorated with black feathers and a big black tulle veil.[123]

Fabric choices (poplin, taffeta, tulle); colors and materials for thread (gray-lilac silk); techniques of edging, shapes, and proportions of elements of the dress; details of accessories (feathers, veil, tie)—all come into focus in the description. In this and other examples, the vocabulary of both the *couturière* and the stylist is deployed, bringing readers (and quite plausibly, seamstresses) virtually into the

Figure 3.22 Anon. La Mode illustrée, July 24, 1864, no. 30. Fashion Plate, "Toilettes de Melle. Castel, 58 bis r. Ste. Anne, Coiffures de Mr. Croisat, r. De Richelieu. 76," Bibliothèque Forney Digital Collection, Ville de Paris/Bibliothèque Forney.

Figure 3.23 Anaïs Toudouze. La Mode illustrée, September 3, 1865, no. 36, Bibliothèque Forney Digital Collection, Ville de Paris/Bibliothèque Forney.

boutique and supplying them with the sensorial link to the absent material object through the imaginative space produced by the collusion of text and image.

Raymond's level of detail is far greater than what the vicomtesse de Renneville ever offered in her fashion columns because Raymond's reading public had expanded substantially. Her commentary schools the bourgeois (and frequently provincial) reader in the necessary lexicon of the stylish *Parisienne*—this is what poplin looks like; here is the sheen of black taffeta, the frothiness of tulle—thus providing her not only with the cultural capital of the *Parisienne* but also with a set of practical linguistic tools. For now she will know what to call the fabrics and notions she needs when she visits her local draper. Furthermore, while the plates typically announce the name and address of the shop where wealthy readers can order and purchase the illustrated dresses, hats, and hairstyles, the description offers the less affluent (and/or non-Parisian) reader the necessary information to approximate these looks herself should she decide to make them at home. Best asserts that "in fashion periodicals, one of the primary functions of textual discourse is to direct the reading of the image . . . On a basic level, the written text fills in the detail of what the fashion plate cannot show, such as the cut and the fabric."[124] If the *description de toilettes* section comprises empirical observations with factual details, the next section, which is almost always placed immediately following the *description de toilettes*, introduces elements of judgment that provide guidelines by which readers should adapt the models on display according to their individual circumstances.

Usually at least triple the length of the factual *description de toilettes*, the *modes* section is where Raymond pronounces on the more nuanced questions of fashion: Which trend to follow and when, at what age, in which circumstances? How to reconcile the bourgeois value of restraint with the changing demands of fashionability? How to assume appropriate styles without unwittingly slipping into absurdity? At times in this column, Raymond's voice seems to be at odds with that of the *description*, which touts new fashions simply by displaying and defining them. Her *modes* column offers keys to interpreting the unmediated fashions demonstrated by the description and plate, placing them in a social context inflected by bourgeois values. Again, here as elsewhere, Raymond remarks that her purpose is to be useful (*utile*)—that most bourgeois of qualities: "I must, above all, describe fashion as it is, in order to be useful to those of our readers who like to copy it precisely. After this first duty is filled, I look next to fashion, within fashion itself, for ingenious methods that might be useful to some other readers, those who want to follow fashion, but without imposing too great a burden on their budgets."[125] Usefulness and economy are thus emphasized as the guiding principles of Raymond's fashion column.

The supposed universality of the colored fashion plate and its description is moderated and mediated by the personal yet authoritative tone of the *modes* column: here, Raymond is intent on discouraging her readers from blindly following the trends on display; rather, each reader should study and modify these trends according to her budget, her age, her context. She quite regularly chastises her readers for not exercising choice and judgment in matters of fashion. To readers who resist changes in fashion, she admonishes: "My dear readers, you are not forced to adopt them, even if I am forced to point them out; I must note here the principal traits of fashion; but you are free to change them according to your whim, to adapt them to your own habits and relations, to take from it what you like, to reject what you don't like."[126] But while urging the importance of individual circumstances and the responsibility of personalized taste, she simultaneously reinforces the abstract moral/aesthetic categories of "good" and "bad" taste. As Raphaëlle Renken-Deshayes has noted in her study of *La Mode illustrée*, Raymond's discourse is frequently contradictory. She is, on the one hand, universalizing in her authoritative voice, but, on the other, she is deeply personal in many of her responses to individual readers; she overwhelmingly reinforces the conservative bourgeois values of a patriarchal society, rarely acknowledging working-class women and exhorting bourgeois women to put their industriousness to use in service of the family; and yet she takes bourgeois social prejudices to task with respect to women's education and even their potential to work.

Raymond's "*Modes*" column is characterized by a stern moralizing vocabulary that draws clear lines between good and bad taste, distinction and flamboyance, approbation and reprehensibility, thus emphasizing bourgeois appropriateness. Flashy clothes not only elicit disapproval but also *mésestime* (disdain), and *le mauvais goût* (bad taste) is deemed reprehensible—an aesthetic category, bad taste, is thus forcefully and rhetorically linked to disgrace, a moral one. Verbs such as *éviter* (avoid), *s'abstenir* (abstain), *écarter* (distance), and, of course, *devoir* (must) occur with great frequency and produce, even within the discourse of freedom of choice, an apparently rigid code of behavior that dictates in minute detail and thus undermines the very possibility of choice. "Any large face, or mature face, must carefully avoid [little hats] . . . a long face must abstain from hairstyles with ornamentation above the forehead . . . a too-thick waist will avoid adopting short corsets . . . and shun short or partly-fitted jackets."[127]

On the one hand, the injunctions directed at certain body parts and body types seem to work to limit choice and classify fashions, producing a normalizing discourse around female bodies that, in the end, repeats in textual form the universalizing structure and message of the reproducible and widely disseminated fashion plate. All fashion plate models are uniform, and uniformly idealized: they can thus model "appropriately" (because they are fictitious) any new fashion. On the other hand, however, Raymond's discourse also acknowledges the wide variety of her individualized readers, thus pushing back against the universalizing of the plate and its description and illustrating a tension between the perfect model and the limitations of real bodies belonging to real readers. This tension between description and counsel marks another key contradiction that underpins the journal. The range of available fashions, the choice and freedom that Raymond claims are available to all her readers, are nevertheless strictly circumscribed for them by the dictates of propriety that the fashion writer repeats on a weekly basis. Repetition is rhetorically powerful, and avid readers no doubt internalized the repeated admonitions, reproducing them on their bodies and in their behaviors.

An arbiter of trending fashions and chiding mistress of manners, Raymond also offered peculiarly personalized and often cryptic responses to the voluminous correspondence she received on a weekly basis. Her persona is primarily that of a domestic goddess, a particularly ironic identity for a woman living alone in no great splendor, who worked ceaselessly, writing columns, translating, writing edifying novels of her own; she even masqueraded in her journal as the male figure of a *vieux jardinier* (old gardener), in order to offer authentic gardening tips to her readers.[128] Her persona of domestic goddess, however, exaggerated though it may have been, is likely closer to Raymond's reality than that of her predecessors, as her readers seem to value direct information and pragmatic advice, and her success speaks to the evolution of the gradual acceptance that bourgeois women might openly work. As Fabienne Yvert has astutely remarked, the weekly "Renseignements" column represents the height of Raymond's "sharp wit and style … and echoes today, albeit involuntarily, with modernity."[129] Simultaneously highly intimate and yet anonymous, the "Renseignements" column includes weekly responses to queries about all matters pertaining to fashion and the domestic household; and, curiously, it is typically twice as long as the *modes* section, as much an indication of its importance to Raymond as of the enthusiastic engagement of her readers. The number of weekly responses varies but ranges from thirty to fifty, with each one introduced, after the first couple of years of the journal's circulation, by the reader's subscription account number and location. Readers would thus have had to scan through the tiny print of all the queries and numbers to find their personalized, anonymized response from the editor (figure 3.25). Questions from advice seekers were not published—only Raymond's responses, thus creating a secret, one-sided intimacy between individual reader and editor, as well as endowing her single voice with a high degree of authority.

With this innovative column Raymond thus makes a decidedly individualized and yet universal gesture to her readers. This paradoxical communicative process is illustrated even in the design surrounding the column's heading: the title *Renseignements* is flanked on both sides by a woman engaged in a specific activity: to the left, a seated woman writes, pen in hand; to the right, a seated woman reads what appears to be a letter; both are graphically linked by the illustration of a garland that sweeps between them (figure 3.24). Perhaps the two women represent two sides of Raymond herself, reader of queries and respondent; or, perhaps the illustration conjures the intimate, personal, yet opaque nature of the correspondence between editor and reader. In either case, female literacy and community are foregrounded.[130]

The content of the responses to queries is equally enigmatic, for in the absence of the grounding of a question, they often appear disjointed. In February 1869, for example, Raymond replies to a query from no. 111,067, living in the Dordogne, with a simple one-word response: *Probablement* (Probably). Immediately below this mysterious message, she then offers a concise but detailed message to a Belgian reader about the proper materials for a First Communion dress: "First Communion dresses are always made from white chiffon; bodices will be folded or crossed, like those in figure no. 10."[131] In the first response, her reply is deeply personal and reaches one reader alone, while in the second response, she offers information for any of her readers who may be wondering how to dress their daughters for the First Communion ritual. At once intimate and authoritative, Raymond's voice thus penetrates both to individual subscribers and to vast swaths of readers with similarly pertinent questions about dress etiquette. The disembodied and fragmented nature of Raymond's responses to reader queries repeats the visual fragmentation of the journal's many images, which, as we saw, are sized to fit like puzzle pieces with the columns and *descriptions*.

Like the *description* and fashion rubrics, the *renseignements* depended on the perceived need and sustained desire for instruction by its readership. These needs and desires were created by the serialized periodical itself, of course, just as the fashion economy continued to cycle through from season to season, perpetuating itself by introducing minor changes that reinforced the presumed subtlety of distinction. Raymond's sleight of hand in the queries section lies in her ability to foster intimacy with her many readers while keeping them dependent on her advice both by announcing her authority through her brief but potent dictums and by demonstrating the sheer volume of queries each week in this densely packed visual space (figure 3.25). Like the *Rébus*, the *Renseignements* rubric was a serializing strategy, but also one that exploited intimacy and personal connection.

Indeed, if we take even just the voluminous "Renseignements" column as a guide, published consistently over multiple decades and representing hours of silent communication with subscribers, we must conclude that the work of the journal was central to Raymond's life. While she was, in fact, more inclined to speak transparently about her work as a writer and editor than were her predecessors, she mostly tucks her comments away into her one-sided, secretive correspondence. In one of her many mysterious responses to a reader in Boulogne, for example, she writes: "I regret that the number of tasks I have completely prohibits me from taking the steps that would be indispensable to this subject."[132] She cannot reply in greater detail because of the presumably large number of tasks she has to perform; *mes travaux*, however, is rather elliptical, and the volume of columns, indefatigable responses, and detailed *descriptions* appear, seemingly effortlessly, each week.

Rules govern Raymond's replies: she will not respond to more than four questions per query, and no response will be offered to anyone who cannot prove subscription: this was, after all, a business venture.[133] These measures surely had to be put into place because of the volume of mail Raymond was receiving; indeed, she was something of a minor celebrity, and the journal made it possible to purchase a commemorative photograph of the fashion editor, demonstrating her popularity (figure 3.26).[134] Also attesting to the strength of her popularity with her fanbase, Raymond does not withhold her disapproval of certain subscribers, candidly expressing her exasperation with those who demand the impossible. To one such reader, for example, she writes, "It is absolutely impossible for me: (1) to repeat the explanations of projects, (2) to write them directly. Will our subscriber kindly ask herself how I could succeed in reconciling a direct correspondence with twenty-five thousand readers with the work required of editing a journal?"[135] And to another, who seems impatient to receive a rapid response

Figure 3.24 *"Renseignements" (details), header.* La Mode illustrée, *November 13, 1864, no. 46, p. 368, Bibliothèque Forney Digital Collection, Ville de Paris/Bibliothèque Forney.*

regarding a pattern or image, "Alas! How many times do I need to repeat that one cannot have a pattern, a drawing, even a response in the *next issue*? At the moment I receive this letter, we have been printing the issue in question for six days!"[136] These, and many other such comments, offer glimpses into the actual labor of the fashion journalist and editor, even as they bear witness to the resistance on the part of the reading public to recognize the time and attention it took to create these complex media objects.

Contrary to the image that emanates from the pages of the journal, as Montclair asserts, the fashion journalist was in fact a workhorse: "For more than twenty years, she [Emmeline Raymond] worked for ten hours a day."[137] But Raymond also worked to create a community of women, and this is perhaps the most lasting effect of the cryptic "*Renseignements*" page:

> Entirely devoted to her work, she liked solitude, going out very seldom, never to the theater, [she] compensated for this austerity by the superb results of her efforts. Moreover, the usual emptiness of solitude doesn't exist for such robustly tempered spirits. Her lovely salon on the rue de Clichy is always full of the gracious presence of her readers, an invisible presence, true, but one she conjures, knowing her correspondents through their letters better than she would know them from regular visits.[138]

As the journalist imagines it, in spite of a solitary life that did not conform to the domestic goddess persona she cultivated and projected for others to emulate, Raymond was never really alone. For she was in constant communication with her subscribers; they filled her mind's salon daily, and their concerns and interests occupied her time, leading to an industrious existence and a widely recognized professional career.[139]

By aestheticizing bourgeois moral principles such as economy, restraint, and sobriety, Emmeline Raymond successfully marketed the frivolities of fashion to a public whose identity was built on

RENSEIGNEMENTS

Madame Emmeline Raymond ne peut se charger d'aucune commission, ni répondre directement à aucune lettre.

S'adresser, pour tous les achats de toute nature, à Mme Page, boulevard Magenta, 129.

Pour tous les matériaux dont l'emploi est désigné dans les explications des divers travaux, s'adresser à la maison Sajou, rue Rambuteau, 52. On peut aussi y commander ces travaux, et les recevoir tout prêts.

N° 37,800. Mlle *de K...* a reçu une réponse dans les renseignements de l'un des précédents numéros; nous ne pouvons malheureusement nous conformer, pour le choix et la publication de nos dessins, aux modèles qui nous seraient envoyés par nos lectrices. J'ai déjà expliqué, dans la précédente réponse, qu'il nous est absolument impossible de faire tracer des lignes sur nos planches de patrons, pour marquer es mesures particulières de chaque abonnée. — N° 28,406, *Grenoble*. Les objets paraîtront, mais successivement, excepté les patrons de chapeau pour petit garçon et dame ; ces patrons n'existent pas; on fait les chapeaux sur des *formes* préparées dans des fabriques spéciales. — N° 40,823, *Marne*. Cette robe est tout à fait à la mode, mais je conseille un gilet brun ou noir, plutôt qu'un gilet blanc, pour toilette de ville, en hiver ; rien ne s'oppose à ce que l'on porte cette robe au théâtre. On ne porte jamais des chapeaux de crêpe en hiver, à moins que ce ne soit pour aller au théâtre. L'opticien est dans l'erreur; les femmes se servent des *jumelles* qu'elles préfèrent, et rien ne les oblige à employer les lorgnettes en voire. Les gants demi-clairs en peau de Suède se portent en hiver comme en été. La petite étoile qui figure dans les explications de travaux au crochet, ou tricot, marque le point à partir duquel on recommence les ndications qui viennent d'être données. — *A. M., Meuse*. On nous prépare une veste tricotée, et je crains qu'il ne soit difficile d'en publier une autre encore, au crochet; nous verrons. Merci pour cette excellente lettre. — *L. de V..., Saumur*. Au lieu de *donner* des primes, que les abonnés *payent* en fin de compte, nous préférons nous appliquer à perfectionner sans cesse l'utilité du journal; nous ne *donnons* par conséquent point de primes. On a reçu les patrons de manteaux, de pardessus pour enfant, de veste; la résille n'est nullement ridicule à 31 ans, et l'on se coiffe en cheveux, à cet âge, pour les réunions.

N° 37,842. Les petits garçons de trois ans et demi portent indifféremment des blouses ou des vestes; mais non plus des *jupes* qu'on leur met jusqu'à trois ans tout au plus. Merci pour l'approbation et la propagation. On recevra tôt ou tard le patron désiré. — Mme *F.... à la Mouche*. Pour l'hiver et *à la ville*, les jeunes filles de seize à dix-sept ans ne portent pas de chapeau rond. La forme Henri III, en velours noir, est la plus jolie. — N° 15,253, *Lot-et-Garonne*. Les jeunes filles ne portent aucun vêtement garni de guipure; leurs talmas sont bordés avec une frange, ou bien avec une ruche de ruban. Je conseille la forme du paletot Parisien, publié dans le n° 43; on le ferait de même étoffe que la robe. — N° 6,882, *Meuse*. La veste tricotée qui paraîtra dans le n° 47, avec son patron, peut très-aisément être faite au crochet. Pris note des autres demandes qui seront successivement satisfaites, et mille fois merci pour cette lettre. — *L. H.* On n'étale plus un mouchoir plus ou moins orné, c'est-à-dire qu'on ne le tient pas déplié à la main, à moins que l'on ne s'en soit déjà servi. Les jupons bordés en

Figure 3.25 *"Renseignements" (details).* La Mode illustrée, *November 13, 1864, no. 46, p. 368, Bibliothèque Forney Digital Collection, Ville de Paris/Bibliothèque Forney.*

Figure 3.26 *Jean-François Delintraz, "Portrait d'Emmeline Raymond, femme de lettres," 1860–90, Musée Carnavalet, CC0 Paris Musées/Carnavalet Museum—History of Paris.*

productivity within the domestic framework. She blurred the lines between fashion advice and *savoir-vivre*, and in so doing, Emmeline Raymond transformed fashion writing into ethical messaging over a forty-year period and energized vast audiences, educating a generation of readers. Hitching her utilitarian and family-focused ideology to one of the most powerful of popular cultural phenomena— the fashion periodical—she thus remade fashion as a moral imperative, expanding its empire and proselytizing bourgeois taste. Through the careful manipulation of word and image, she created the appearance of a reciprocal, intimate relationship, flattered her readers' intelligence, gave them things to do, and brought fashion down to earth for an emerging class of female consumers. Most important, however, and least acknowledged, Emmeline Raymond models a professional bourgeois woman whose career has supplanted marriage.[140]

Sometimes dissimulating her labor, and sometimes calling it out—in her responses to countless queries from readers, in her detailed written descriptions of fabrics, notions, and fashion items that could only have been examined in the shop itself, in her translations of various literary texts, and in the composition of her own works of *savoir-vivre*, good housekeeping, and serialized fiction— Raymond embodied the professional woman and helped expand the normalization of professional work for bourgeois women that emerged more fully in the later decades of the century.[141] In the occasional columns where she does address the question of bourgeois women working, she takes a pragmatic and, indeed, somewhat progressive position. "Sans dot" ("Without a Dowry"), a "Variétés" column from April 3, 1870, and "Le Travail des Femmes" ("Women's Work"), published December 5, 1869, exhort parents to educate their daughters in practical skills (needlework, of course), and a foreign language to work as a translator, if need be, but also in accounting, for example. In both columns, she appeals in particular to families of the lesser bourgeoisie, who could possibly slip into poverty, and expresses concern that women must be prepared to assume financial responsibility for the family in case of the death of a spouse or marriage to a poor man. Such women should have a practical skill and should not feel ashamed of working, she insists, objecting quite strongly to what she suggests is a "bourgeois prejudice" against the gainful employment of such women.[142]

Raymond repeatedly focuses on the need for women to be able to support the family and advocates for more practical education for women. She thus steps right up to the line of offering herself up as a model for such a progressive success story: never married, perhaps without a dowry herself, she mastered the journalist's pen as well as the marketer's rhetoric. Without more biographical information about Emmeline Raymond than what little is available to us, however, there is no knowing if, like so many middle-class girls, she did not marry for want of a dowry, or if it was, rather, a matter of choice. If the latter, then in choosing not to marry, Emmeline Raymond became a *femme majeure* who could more easily justify a professional career, one that she seems to have relished. Raymond thus points the way to contesting the veiling of women's work, thus showing the shifting of the tide.

Talking Commodities

The seemingly mercenary role of fashion writers notwithstanding, there is more depth to their columns at times than is usually acknowledged. For beneath an apparently descriptive prose solely intent on molding female consumers lay other ambitions and rhetorical moves. Their identities often shrouded in mystery and forged in the fantasy of the feminine, these writers, also savvy businesswomen, had a profound impact on nineteenth-century women readers and on the economies they helped to create and perpetuate. Despite their power to cultivate consumption, their columns sometimes reached well beyond the descriptive, betraying a duplicity, a performativity, or even an ironic positioning, that suggests tensions arising from the cultural production of fashion itself. These tensions emerged around frivolity and morality, narcissism and selflessness, ostentation and frugality, alienation and community.

If the peculiar—or "mystical," to return to Marx's terminology—quality of the commodity is that it exercises social power independently of its production and conceals the labor that created it, then the nineteenth-century fashion journal was certainly just such a phenomenon. The fashion journalist gives voice to that commodity—sometimes in the earnest declarations of a young lady, sometimes in the haughty tones of a high society lady, and sometimes in the firm, confident idiom of a bourgeois matron. These writers, each voguing in her own way, were also working to create a product to sell and create a community of women—writers, artisans, vendors, artists, and reader-consumers—who would fuel the fashion economy into the future.

"Tell me," mused Marie de l'Epinay, presciently, in 1840, "won't it be a great pleasure, in a distant future, to leaf through this panorama of behaviors, customs and fashions of today?"[143] Just as these journals were windows onto a fantasy of aspirational identity for so many nineteenth-century women, "talking commodities" instructing readers how to behave, how to dress, how to live, and where to shop, they also offered companionship, channeled frustrated energies, and allowed invisible presences to communicate over time and space. These journals serve now as telescopes into the early formation of the fashion system, a vast archive of women's fantasy and real lives in nineteenth-century France and beyond.

The *modistes des lettres* who crafted the journals worked both within and, sometimes, subtly against the context of bourgeois femininity in which they lived to create and grow a lucrative market, and to make their place within this economy, just as the *modistes* themselves worked to produce desirable commodities that would keep them employed from season to season. Both groups of women working in different contexts, they engaged in the new economy to forge career paths and make a space for themselves, a space that both endorsed and undercut the bourgeois fantasy of the feminine that dominated fashion culture in nineteenth-century France. We now turn to the women who visualized that fantasy world and reproduced it in living color for legions of eager readers and dazzled viewers. For they too were working within a dominant ideology that left few options for them outside of marriage and motherhood, and they too embraced that ideology to the extent that it allowed them to capitalize on their talents and forge careers when women were not supposed to work.

4

Fashion's Eyes: Painting in the Mirror

Mrs. Le Loir [sic], formerly Héloïse Colin, has but one preoccupation: to push watercolor to the meticulous precision of a miniature. We have explained ourselves on the confusion of these genres. Most female artists share this deplorable taste. We say to Mrs. Le Loir [sic], formerly Héloïse Colin (?), to Mrs. Bernard, formerly Anaïs Desgrange (??) and to Mrs. Toudouze, formerly Anaïs Colin (???): paint miniatures![1]

In his sardonic assessment of the watercolor submissions of several women artists included in the Paris Salon of 1857, the poet, journalist and, apparently, art critic, Alfred Busquet launches a brief but scathing critique of their entries to the preeminent art exhibition of the year. That Busquet misspells the name of Héloïse Leloir, who had consistently shown her work at the Paris Salon since 1835 and had even won a medal in 1844, and that he openly questions his own accuracy regarding the other women's maiden names (an impertinence signaled by his odd repetition of question marks after each surname) add further insult to his already quite dismissive remarks. Lurking in his explicit evaluation is a more generalized disdain for one of the "lesser" genres cultivated by many women artists in nineteenth-century France—namely, miniature painting.[2] Additionally, he denigrates the capacity of these artists to excel at watercolors, precisely *because* they are women, in spite of this medium's long association, like miniature painting, with the standard education of bourgeois members of the fair sex. For both watercolors and miniatures were feminized art forms, given their portability and decorative uses, and they were thus essential components of the *arts d'agréments*, or female accomplishment arts, in which all proper girls were typically schooled.[3] These same skills were fundamental to the artistic profession that, by the time of Busquet's writing, Héloïse Leloir (1819–73) and Anaïs Toudouze (1822–99) had come to dominate: fashion illustration.

Indeed, if Busquet had but glanced at the 1857 advertisements for *La France élégante: Journal des dames et des salons* that were regularly printed in multiple daily newspapers, he would not only have known the correct spelling of Héloïse's married name, but he would also have learned that she had quite a few preoccupations apart from the singular, ill-advised one of which he accuses her—that is, subjecting watercolors to the techniques of miniatures. Whether the poet-journalist *qua* art critic knew it or not, or whether he simply preferred to feign ignorance of these renowned fashion-plate artists, Héloïse Leloir and her sister Anaïs Toudouze—the "Colin sisters," as they have since come to be known—had by 1857 already made names for themselves as fashion illustrators in a commercial arts world that had been primarily occupied by men since the turn of the nineteenth century.[4] In fact, Héloïse's name was itself sufficiently commodified by the time of Busquet's writing to be a selling point for *La France élégante*, a high-end fashion periodical whose cachet is summed up in its title—and its endorsement by the socialite and author Madame la Comtesse Dash. Subscribers to this luxury publication would receive "24 colored fashion plates drawn by Mme. Héloïse Leloir."[5] Héloïse's younger sister's name was equally familiar and thus similarly touted to promote the sales of other fashion publications, such as *Le Conseiller des dames et des demoiselles*, which in 1853 advertised to readers of the popular daily paper *La Presse* that they would receive with their subscription "a delicious steel engraving" of "the portrait of H. R. H. Empress Eugénie in the exact costume she wore the day of her marriage, as drawn by Mlle. Anaïs Toudouze" (figure 4.1).[6] Even if it would appear that they were relatively unknown in the highly masculinist official art world, these women were clearly established, marketable artists in the domain of commercial graphic illustration. They put their finely tuned talents in the feminine *arts d'agréments* to productive, professional use, embracing fashion illustration both as art and as work.

In recent years, the Colin sisters have received some scholarly attention from fashion and cultural historians.[7] Yet over a century after they had saturated the fashion print market of the Second Empire, a glossy article published in 1974 for the arts and lifestyles magazine *Plaisir de France* still echoed Busquet's critique.[8] Without once identifying the Colin sisters accurately by name, the author, Robert Maury, describes the artistic value of fashion plates in a piece illustrated by the sisters' principal male competitors. He traces the history of the genre through those he considers its best practitioners—all artists, all male—from Louis-Marie Lanté and Horace Vernet in the period of the Restoration, to Gavarni in the July Monarchy, and on to François Claudius Compte-Calix and Jules David in the Second Empire.[9] Maury identifies fashion plates as "tableaux en miniature" and credits their creators with skill and innovation. Eager to rediscover this decorative genre in the late twentieth century, the author writes, "This entire era that elevated woman is truly a fantasy world of lines, colors, and styles illustrated by talented artists like the brothers Hippolyte and Polydor Pauquet, the Leloirs and, especially, the most talented of them all, Jules David."[10] Each of these fashion plate artists, or miniaturists, as Maury would have it, was also considered a painter in his own right, signing his works and exhibiting a finesse of line and a sense of color. Maury glibly inserts "les Leloir" in his retinue of great fashion painters, but, tellingly, he offers neither first names nor the historical detail provided for

Figure 4.1 *Anaïs Toudouze, "S.M. l'Impératrice Eugénie,"* Le Conseiller des Dames et des Demoiselles, *1853, Bibliothèque nationale de France.*

the other painters. It is hard not to surmise that "les Leloir" represent the (incorrectly identified) siblings Héloïse Colin Leloir and Anaïs Colin Toudouze; and though they, like David, signed most of their original fashion watercolors—as Héloïse Leloir and Anaïs Toudouze after their respective marriages—they could be admitted to the ranks of the creators of "authentiques petits chefs-d'œuvre" only if their gender, discernable in their first names, was obscured. The omission of the Colin sisters' names and, more importantly, the questions about identity and authority signaled by this omission suggest a difficulty in placing these women, and perhaps fashion-plate illustration more generally, in a graphic arts tradition. Whether the critic is contemporaneous (Busquet) or posthumous (Maury), the artistic identity of the Colin sisters has mostly been consigned to oblivion even as their fashion prints remain collectible and have recently made their way into several major art exhibitions.[11]

The paradoxes of invisibility and value that emerge in the juxtaposition of Busquet's denigration and the implicitly laudatory marketing strategies of popular publications point to a collision as well as an overlap of artworlds along the fault lines of gender. Busquet seems to have wished to impose an uncertainty, even an illegitimacy, upon these women artists as he generalizes about their "deplorable taste," enjoining them to stay in their highly gendered lane. His critique points to a general reluctance within nineteenth-century culture to acknowledge adequately the work of women artists, an omission that has been amply documented by scholars who have charted the marginalization of women artists from the official domain.[12] The gesture of gendered exclusion enacted by Busquet reflects in short form the historic reality for most female artists in mid-nineteenth-century France: women were not permitted to attend the prestigious École des Beaux-Arts; and with this exclusion followed others, such as the ineligibility to compete for some of the most important prizes and rewards.[13] After years of contentious debate, women were finally admitted to the École des Beaux-Arts in 1897, two years before the death of Anaïs Toudouze and twenty-four years after the death of Héloïse Leloir.[14] Official art, as acknowledged through institutional affiliation, master classes, and, eventually, signed works at the Salon and prizes, was thus primarily reserved for men, even if women artists like the Colin sisters did indeed repeatedly show their work at the Salon and occasionally won recognition.[15] More commonly, women artists were expected to serve a private, supportive role as they embellished their homes and transmitted their skills to their children: their engagement with the decorative arts primarily thus paralleled their own "decorative" status.[16]

This chapter argues that the Colin sisters both participated in and disrupted this narrative of invisibility. The production network to which they so voluminously contributed—the fashion magazine, instrumental to the roaring success of the fashion industry—gave them weekly visibility, and they signed their work products as though they were art, eschewing the anonymity of some who produced fashion plates;[17] well they should have, for while they were excluded from the official institutions of arts education—like other daughters, sisters, and wives of male painters—they were "able to acquire the studio training generally inaccessible to women" and could thus boast the skill that many of their male contemporaries were unquestionably accorded by their educations.[18] While they may have been visible and highly sought after as fashion illustrators, however, their artistic identities were obscured by multiple biases at work in the culture. For, alongside his gender bias, Busquet's critique also demonstrates a bias against art forms that were the object of female focus, which can be more broadly applied to fashion illustration itself, which was deemed a minor, commercial, feminized, and therefore negligible art form. The same ideologies surrounding bourgeois women that obscured the *chroniqueuses* discussed in chapter 3 confined the Colin sisters to the margins of the fine arts world. These omissions or mistakes should be interpreted as a relegation to a less important status, reinforced by the fact that their work was classed among the lesser arts at the Salon. They were thus kept figuratively, if not always literally, in the domestic sphere, as their art tended to be viewed as hobbyism, or amateur art, belonging on the continuum of the *arts d'agréments* practiced by bourgeois women.

That this media bias persisted even after death is aptly illustrated, for example, by Anaïs Toudouze's obituary, published in the "Chronique" column of *La Vie quotidienne* on September 9, 1899. The homage remembers the preeminent fashion illustrator primarily in the context of her familial relations to outstanding professional men—an architect, a novelist, and a painter: "It is with deep regret that we learn of the death, at 77 years, of Mme. Anaïs Toudouze, painter, widow of the architect Gabriel Toudouze, mother of the brilliant novelist Gustave Toudouze and the painter Édouard Toudouze, grandmother of our excellent Georges Toudouze."[19] While the tribute identifies her first as an "artiste peintre," thus acknowledging her vocation, it omits any details of her most important professional accomplishments—among them fashion illustration—casting her instead primarily as wife, mother, and grandmother to creative men. Significantly, the obituary omits her relationship to creative women, in spite of the fact that Anaïs's own daughter, Isabelle Desgrange (née Toudouze) went on to become a prolific fashion-plate artist herself. Oddly, there is no mention of Isabelle in this obituary—only of Anaïs's sons and grandson. By lingering with approbation on the roles of wife, mother, and grandmother, rather than elaborating on that of her vocation as "artiste peintre," the obituary—the epitaph of a life that would be reprinted and circulated widely in the French press—ignores the breadth of her professional achievements, ironically, in a subgenre of its own medium—fashion magazines—the professional domain where Anaïs Colin and her sister worked as prolific and successful artists for over fifty years.[20] Not only, then, were the artist's familial relations presented as the centerpiece of her identity, but when she was acknowledged as an "artiste peintre," the most significant work of her career—her fashion illustration—went unmentioned, sacrificed to a media bias that was also gendered.

The paradoxes of invisibility I have been tracing in this study through the complex and sometimes duplicitous work of women in the fashion industry take yet another form in the domain of fashion illustration, a key medium through which the material products of fashion were represented and disseminated. Enhancing interest in the garment or accessory by illustrating it in a context that envisioned what we might call bourgeois feminine genre scenes, fashion illustrations were powerful marketing tools and collectible commodities in and of themselves, as I showed in chapter 1. By the second half of the nineteenth century, fashion illustration would be dominated by the Colin sisters, who were, as I have just outlined, mostly invisible in the world of official art to which they aspired and yet ubiquitous in the fashion press and thus, by extension, influential in bourgeois households from Paris to Philadelphia and beyond. I do not wish to canonize the Colin sisters within the roster of overlooked women artists of the nineteenth century or to assert an equivalency between fine arts and fashion illustration. My concern in this chapter is rather to place the Colin sisters within the two artistic spheres they bridged and to explore their particular role as women illustrators in the nineteenth-century fashion industry in relation to the powerful commodity they produced: the fashion plate. For the fashion plate, especially as practiced by the Colin sisters, was not only an advertising tool designed to encourage consumption—it also both fetishized and fashioned the female community.

As Anne Higonnet and Kristen Ringelberg have argued, we have much to learn from considering women's artistic cultural production in terms of its difference from that of the official (male) art world.[21] The Colin sisters converted what was essentially an institutionalized and gendered exclusion from the so-called fine arts into profitable professional careers, making something meaningful of an art form that was deemed decorative at best and commercial at worst. In doing so, they offered a cheeky response to Busquet's rebuke that they stick to miniatures. Their fashion-plate illustration exploited to great effect the techniques of miniature painting, with its focus on detail and precision. Their skill with the challenging medium of watercolor is apparent in the preparatory work they did for the final commodified product—the hand-colored lithographic print—even if their watercolors and that preparatory work, i.e., the many studies and annotated sketches that comprised the process of creation, were and still are mostly unknown and unseen and were overshadowed by the reproducibility of the lithographic print. Furthermore, the female creative activities of amateur family portraiture and album-making, which so often presented women engaged in highly feminized domestic and leisure activities and which drew on the *arts d'agréments* tradition, are reflected in some of their early work, anticipating the feminine genre scenes of their fashion plates.[22] Perhaps the most ironic outcome was that the Colins channeled their talents, undervalued in one market, into a steady, remunerated career in another, remaking their limited artistic prospects as a feminine space and reaching a global public. This is surely not what Busquet had in mind when he consigned them to the obscurity of miniature painting.[23]

My analysis aims to recover the work of the Colin sisters not only as fashion illustrators but also as professional artists as they forged careers in spite of the cultural and social obstacles they encountered. Although reproductions of their work circulated widely, their original fashion art has been, with a few recent exceptions, housed in archival collections—unstudied, and certainly not celebrated as art. This is likely the case because the work was viewed (perhaps even by the artists themselves) as merely preparatory to the production of the commercial fashion plate.[24] While fashion plates certainly adhered to static conventions befitting a commercial enterprise, the Colin sisters also sometimes used them as vehicles for celebrating their sisterhood and asserting creative agency. Thus, unlike the work of their male counterparts, their fashion plate art was perhaps personal and even reflexive, as it was linked to the other so-called feminine arts they practiced throughout their lives. Capitalizing on the "lesser" genres open to women, such as miniatures and watercolor, to create their art, the Colin sisters regularly frequented some of the key spaces of modernity and interacted with the male worlds of lithography and publishing to accomplish their professional goals, contrary to social expectations for bourgeois women.[25] Upon a more careful consideration of the context of its production, then, fashion-plate art as practiced by the Colin sisters may also be read as the documentation of women's professional production as well as their social practices and consumption habits. Furthermore, this art became a pragmatic strategy through which these women artists managed to insert themselves, and art forms specific to women, into a masculine capitalist system from which bourgeois women, typically relegated to the class of consumers rather than producers, were largely excluded. By recognizing the artistic process of the Colin sisters, and by considering their works as aesthetic documents, my study makes visible a work process, laborious and complex, that remains hidden beneath the spectacular commodity of the fashion plate and beneath gendered assumptions about what counts as art and who makes it. Before turning to the work of the Colin sisters as fashion-plate artists, and my examination of their process of production through sketches and watercolors and the prints themselves, I will first consider the development of the Colins as artists in the heart of an artistic family. I will begin with an analysis of what I term their "mutual self-portrait," an early work that both inscribes them as artists and serves as a master lens through which to understand their fashion-plate art.

Family Histories of Art

Two figures, sisters and artists in training under their father's tutelage in the south of France, peer unabashedly from the foreground of a dark and mysterious landscape, one of them gripping her pencil and the other embracing her companion (figure 4.2). The artists and subjects of this double portrait are Héloïse Colin (Leloir) and her younger sister Adèle-Anaïs Colin (Toudouze), two daughters of the minor Romantic painter Alexandre Colin and Joséphine Colin, an accomplished miniaturist; as we know, the sisters would become two of the most successful fashion-plate artists of the second half of the nineteenth century.[26] Before they were commercial fashion illustrators, and before becoming accomplished miniaturists, watercolorists, and book illustrators, Héloïse and Anaïs Colin learned to paint in their parents' studio, a common practice for aspiring female artists who were not permitted access to the École des Beaux-Arts.[27] It was at around the time they began publishing their work in fashion magazines that they painted their 1836 "self-portrait," a picture that operates as a sort of precursor to their better known work—their fashion illustrations, which carry traces of this early painting's themes and compositional strategies. This painting, along with others that comprise a series of family portraits made by the Colins in their youth, relates to the tradition of feminine visual culture described by Higonnet, in which women artists typically took family members as subjects for

Figure 4.2 Adèle-Anaïs Colin, "Portraits d'Héloïse et Anaïs Colin par elles-mêmes," 1836, Musée Carnavalet, CC0 Paris Musées/Carnavalet Museum—History of Paris.

album-making or amateur painting, in large part because their sisters, mothers, and children, who inhabited the domestic space of the family home, presented the most readily available subjects.[28] Despite its attachment to a private, feminized tradition of amateur art, however, this canvas stands out for the ways in which it asserts the artistic identities, as well as the relationship, of the two sisters.

Many male artists, famous or not, practiced fashion-plate illustration from its earliest iterations at the end of the eighteenth century; but by the 1830s, female artists were increasingly entering this growing profession.[29] Héloïse and Anaïs's father—a painter and lithographer of the Romantic school, a student of Girodet and friend of Delacroix—focused primarily on historical and literary subjects. He was also a landscape artist and a portraitist, and, like many of his contemporaries in the art world, such as Gavarni, Vernet, and Devéria, he occasionally illustrated for the fashion press. Héloïse and Anaïs were trained by their father and their mother, who created fashion illustrations, along with miniatures.[30] By the 1840s, their signed work appeared regularly in the most popular and widely circulated women's magazines of the day. Indeed, from as early as 1839 and throughout the 1890s, their artwork was published in numerous journals, including *La Mode, Le Follet, Le Bon Ton, La Corbeille, La France élégante, Le Conseiller des demoiselles,* and *La Mode illustrée*.[31] Other European fashion magazines picked up and reproduced, with or without attribution, illustrations signed by the sisters, and they also could be found in the pages of *Harper's Bazaar* and *Godey's Lady's Book* in the United States.[32] Prints of the sisters' pictures were disseminated even as far away as South America.

The Colin sisters were omnipresent in the domain of fashion publication—sketching and painting on tight weekly deadlines to illustrate the latest fashions and to promote shops and styles. Anaïs's account book dating from March 1843 through October 1845, the very month in which she wed Gabriel Toudouze, shows steady productivity and remuneration for a range of artistic activities, the majority of which was related to the creation of fashion images, sometimes indicated as "costumes," "dessins de mode," or "têtes de femme," often with several delivered at a time. In addition to fashion work, the accounts indicate that Anaïs was paid for commissioned watercolors and other paintings and drawings, and, most interestingly, for lessons given to several young ladies.[33] The fact that Anaïs and no doubt Héloïse offered art lessons reinforces the ambiguity of their situation: on the one hand, by doing so, they follow in their father's and other male artists' tradition of instructing and inspiring younger generations of artists; more likely, however, they were being paid to participate in the transmission of the *arts d'agréments* to the young bourgeois girls of Paris—a Mademoiselle Byron and a Mademoiselle Michel in the case of Anaïs.

In spite of their engagement in varied art practices, the Colins were first and foremost commercial artists working in the sphere of fashion illustration, unlike most of their male counterparts: the account book shows that the vast majority of paid work was for fashion-related art.[34] For David, Gavarni, Vernet, Devéria, and their own father, fashion illustration was an income supplement rather than a principal occupation; for the sisters, their work in the fashion press largely consumed their artistic careers, and their livelihood depended upon this work.[35] Marie Bonin, who has also examined the existing accounts of Anaïs Colin, indicates that by 1843 the young artist was already receiving a fixed revenue stream for her fashion illustration and that she continued to create prints until her death in 1899. She extrapolates a similar model for Héloïse, for whom accounts do not exist, and informs that Anaïs was "under contract with the editor Jeannin, who paid her 125 francs monthly and bought the drawings she delivered to him at a cost of 30 francs per sketch. Fashion and other types of illustration afforded the young women a fixed and reliable income."[36] This would become particularly vital in the case of Anaïs, who was widowed in 1854 with three small children and thus very likely needed to support her family by the steady work associated with the endlessly regenerative fashion cycle.[37] Fashion illustration thus permitted the sisters professional art careers at a time when a successful career as a noncommercial artist was, for most women, out of reach.

The sisters' mutual self-portrait, which coincides with the first stages of these women's successful careers as fashion illustrators, is a curious and little-known artifact that raises questions about artistic identity, the female subject, and women's cultural production in nineteenth-century France. As noted above, it also serves as an important precursor of the sisters' later commercial work, which, when read in the light of this self-portrait, offers up new interpretive dimensions. The painting defines each sister in mutual relation with the other and subverts the prevailing model of artistic singularity, positing instead a collective model of creative production—as attached to the artisanal craft tradition that was intrinsic to the early fashion industry in which women were deeply implicated, if often invisible, as I have shown throughout this study.[38] Perhaps more important still, the painting depicts an embrace that becomes the unifying metaphor for female artistic creation, pointedly signaled by the image of hands on artistic tools. The sisters thus also figuratively embrace an artistic vocation that would lead them into the commercial art world of fashion-plate illustration, a highly collaborative process and vital component of the fashion system that would in turn allow them to represent and catalogue women's experience while they simultaneously fed the fashion industry, made art, and earned a living.

Their self-portrait is labeled, somewhat puzzlingly, "Portraits d'Héloïse et Anaïs Colin, par elles-mêmes."[39] It is not designated as a self-portrait, so we may assume that each sister painted the other; the plurals of the title indeed reinforce this idea. Yet it appears to be very much a shared self-portrait, with both sisters laying claim to the role of artist and celebrating what might be called, literalizing Tamar Garb's phrase, a "sisterhood of the brush."[40] For the sisters seem to support each other physically and, by extension, in their professional ambitions. The sisters' embrace points to a particular model of artistic creation, one that emphasizes solidarity and support over isolated achievement.[41] Indeed, in the Toudouze family papers, Anaïs's son, the writer Gustave, remarks that the sisters were *intime*, and their styles so similar that without signatures it would be difficult to tell their work apart. In Anaïs's ledger, one of the only remaining first-hand traces of the sisters in the archives apart from their artwork, we find a faint note penned on the back of a page that reads, "Returned 100 francs to Héloïse,

January 16, 1845"; likewise, in the columns of the ledger, another reads, "On October 7, received 50 francs for my fashion sketch for Héloïse."[42] These small traces of monetary and artistic exchange reflect the possibility that the sisters lent each other money, and either collaborated on projects or did work for each other, as well as painted side by side, as the self-portrait suggests. It thus illustrates the way they worked, perhaps in a kind of unofficial partnership, and offers a visual emblem of what remains only as faint archival tracings in Anaïs's account book.

With their self-portrait, the Colin sisters claim their artistic identities with vigor. Self-portraiture is a conscious act of self-identification and one that seems practically a rite of passage for artists. Yet the self-portrait genre held a special importance for women artists, who needed to picture themselves "performing art" to lay claim to the authority of the artist so often denied them.[43] As Mary-Jo Bonnet asserts in her historical study of the development of French self-portraiture by women, self-portraits of artists at work signify the accession to the designation of painter, an identity surpassing that of skilled artisan.[44] Though it is virtually unknown, their painting links the Colin sisters to other women artists, who, in spite of their marginalization from the institutionalized spaces of high art and the crises of self-confidence that we know many of them experienced, took themselves seriously as artists and recorded their artistic identities in self-portraits.[45] At the same time, this unusual painting also carries clues about the burgeoning careers of these young female artists and suggests a respect for the artisanal tradition in which they were steeped. Indeed, the assertions, perhaps aspirational, of the self-portrait invite viewers to approach the sisters' artistic products—the majority of which were fashion plates—as the work of self-avowed artists, and it serves as a visual intertext for their later art.

The Colins inscribed themselves within a tradition of reflexive self-portraiture, as evidenced by their insistence on signing their work and cultivating productive careers for themselves.[46] Charlotte Guichard explains that the artist's signature is a "highly complex sign, existing at the crossroads of several histories: that of the individual in European societies . . . of the subject with interiority, reflexivity, and agency . . . and of the self-affirming author in an artistic space structured by the market."[47] Attesting to their claim on professional artistic identity, then, and unlike many fashion-plate artists who remained anonymous, they signed their works, using first and last names, thus making their gender apparent and announcing the uniqueness of the image, even as it was reprinted through technologies of reproduction and widely disseminated.[48] However, the signature was also particularly fraught for women: because of their status as minors, they took their husbands' names, and with this, their husbands became legally entitled to take *their* profits. Furthermore, because many women artists were the "daughters, sisters or wives of painters," their works were suspected of having been retouched by their male relatives.[49] In spite of these challenges, the Colin sisters, first through their self-portrait and later with their repeated signing of their fashion-plate art, actively invested themselves with artistic authority.

The painting's connection to fashion is immediately apparent inasmuch as fashion helps establish the contemporaneity of the moment captured in the picture. Both women appear fashionably dressed

Figure 4.3 *"Walking Dress and Riding Dress,"* Modes de Paris, Petit Courrier des Dames, *1837, National Portrait Gallery, London.*

for 1836, the year of the painting's execution, with the trendy *gigot* sleeve of the 1830s and diaphanous *berthe* collar that remained popular throughout the century (figure 4.3).⁵⁰ Their fashionability also points to their belonging to the class of women who would have been versed in the kinds of cultural accomplishments—such as music, painting, drawing, embroidery—deemed appropriate for daughters of the middle classes. In the case of the Colin sisters, the specific training young women received in the *arts d'agréments* and the type of art production associated with women amateur artists influenced their later fashion art.

Along with generic differences between portraiture and fashion illustration, however, details of their self-presentation distinguish these subjects from the stylized femininity of fashion illustration. The visual codes of the fashion plate favored averted glances on regularized faces, interior or semi-urban settings, and ladies in richly detailed dresses engaged in appropriately feminine leisure activities. While their clothing and accessories are fashionable, they are also practical—in particular for women engaged in the potentially messy work of outdoor drawing or painting. Both figures sport accessories typically worn to keep hair out of the way while working: the sister on the left wears a red snood, a kind of hairnet attached to a headband, with long tassels, and her sister's headband is also visible.⁵¹ One wears a dark-colored apron over her creamy beige gown, similar to those worn by women working in the fashion trades, as described in chapter 2. The art of the Colin sisters, these details seem to imply, while linked to the accomplishment arts required of so many young ladies—leisurely pastimes laden with gendered social meanings—should also be understood as a serious occupation. These varied signals construct a symbolic system demanding that the viewer consider seriously not only the woman artist but also the actual work required to create art. With its mixed vestimentary clues and artistic props, the painting alludes at once to an artisanal tradition and to painting as work, thus suggesting a bridge between different statuses of artistic production. Female relationships, omnipresent in much of the fashion-plate art of the nineteenth century, are cast as the painting's thematic centerpiece, thus pointing to a continuum within the artistic œuvre of the Colin sisters. The slippage between fashionable objects and artistic subjects that characterizes this painting, and the ambiguity that slippage implies, demands a deeper reading of what might at first glance appear to be a typical family portrait, so commonly produced among amateur women painters in the nineteenth century.

To look more closely, then, at details of the composition: each woman's hands are visible, the pencil is firmly gripped, and on the open page of the sketchpad, we can make out the lines and the light color of a drawing still in progress. While one of the women's hands clasps her sister's wrist, her other hand appears on her sister's shoulder, as if together they form one unit. Whether foregrounded in the painting, wielding or in proximity to the tools of creative production, or resting on a shoulder in an enfolding gesture, these hands are powerfully communicative. The placement of hands at the center of their self-portrait further asserts a demystified conception of art and proclaims its reliance as much on manual labor—the so-called *petites mains*—as on artistic and intellectual vision, which was the supposedly more noble province of male designers and fine artists.

As I discussed in previous chapters, the term *petites mains* (literally, "little hands," figuratively "female workers") was, and remains, the euphemistic term used to designate the female manual laborers working in the garment industries.⁵² In the parlance of nineteenth-century garment and accessory workshops, the *petites mains* were the usually young manual workers who executed the menial tasks given to them by the *première main* (head worker). Reduced by metonymy to the body part that executed the vision of the designer, these women tended to be anonymous and occupied the lowest tier of the workshop hierarchy. Yet the dexterity required for the minute and painstaking labor of sewing, embroidery, beading, etc., required "small," nimble hands. The anonymous, laboring *petites mains* of the fashion industry are subtly acknowledged in some fashion plates as existing on a continuum with other women, including the skilled artists who created the prints, the less skilled colorists who hand-painted the reproductions, and even the bourgeois women who consumed them, often engaging in their own needlework, or *hand*work, as a respectable female pastime, one of the *arts d'agréments*.

The prominence of the sisters' hands in the self-portrait is significant, then, placing them as professional women in this broader context of women fashion workers whose skilled labor went largely unacknowledged. While the self-portrait is unsigned, the sisters' later work would consistently be signed; their prominent hands here look ahead, then, perhaps, to that distinguishing gesture. For the inscription of writing, in the form of the name, within the image itself calls attention to the painter's hand and thus points to the "materiality of artistic work," a key theme of the sisters' self-portrait, as we shall see.⁵³ Several other details further emphasize the sisters' identity as both creative artists and workers. The background, for instance, presents a brooding landscape that signals these artists' creative potential. This backdrop is incongruous with the conventional depiction of two fashionable young women sketching outdoors, whom one would expect to find situated in a more luminous and tranquil outdoor environment—and most likely a prescribed semi-urban one. The sisters stand out all the more against such a setting, which calls to mind the Romantic landscapes of their father's generation of painters. Indeed, they have boldly placed themselves within a traditionally masculine space of turbulent Romanticism.

The most striking feature of this painting, however, is the representation of the subjects' gazes. The sisters' frank and serious visual confrontation of the viewer offers a stark contrast to the demurely averted gaze typical of both fashion prints and contemporaneous portraits of women, such as the portrait of Héloïse Colin, entitled *Héloïse Colin dessinant dans la campagne nîmoise* (*Héloïse Colin Sketching in the Countryside near Nîmes*), executed by her father in the same year (1836) as the self-portrait (figure 4.4).⁵⁴ No matter how much he may have wished to celebrate his daughter's accomplishments as an artist here, Colin *père*, a representative of the gendered and exclusionary authority of fine art, depicts his artist-

Figure 4.4 *Alexandre-Marie Colin, "Héloïse Colin dessinant dans la campagne nîmoise," 1836, Musée Carnavalet, CC0 Paris Musées/Carnavalet Museum—History of Paris.*

daughter as an object to be looked at as much as an actively producing subject. In a sense, he portrays her as an amateur (read female) artist performing one of her very feminine accomplishments, similar to the portrait from 1830 that Achille Devéria created of his sister Laure, also an artist, for his very popular (and profitable) album of fashionable and leisurely *Parisiennes, Les Heures du jour*.[55] As in the representation of Héloïse in her father's painting, Laure Devéria's artistic accomplishments and professionalism are not foregrounded in her brother's representation. Instead of a "producer of art," Laure is presented rather as a "skillful consumer and product of art."[56] Similarly, Alexandre Colin's portrait of Héloïse exhibits multiple features one would find in a fashion plate from this year: from his daughter's unfocused gaze and her fashionable attire—including *gigot* sleeves and wide *pèlerine* collar classic for the period—to the single dainty foot peeping from beneath skirts and feminine accessories, poke bonnet and parasol, casually visible in the foreground (figure 4.5). Much more than the sisters' painting, this portrait introduces an ambiguity into Héloïse's role as artist, which is complicated by her gender. By removing the trappings of respectable femininity from her body—hats, shawls, parasols, gloves—but leaving them within the frame of the painting, Colin *père* indicates that the subject is nonetheless a lady even if she has momentarily set these accessories aside to have greater freedom of movement as she works. We find this trope in some fashion plates of the period that are set in the outdoors. In the sisters' painting, however, such accessories are nowhere visible, indicating that, for them, claims of feminine respectability are secondary to those of artistic identity. Taken together, the two paintings—by Alexandre Colin and his daughters—present two expressions of female identity and agency competing for interpretive purchase over the sisters' body of work.

While the father's work portrays his artist-daughter most clearly and perhaps unintentionally as a male artist's model, the daughters unambiguously seize the subject position by executing a painting that is both a self-portrait—the artistic genre through which artists traditionally lay claim to that role—and a double portrait of artistic solidarity.[57] Indeed, with its frank stare and turbulent setting, the painting seems to comment on the self-portrait genre that traditionally emphasizes solitary male creation.[58] For nineteenth-century women artists, of course, painting the self reflects the condition of the woman painter, who had little access to live models apart from herself and her family members. Each sister painted the other, then, but both seem to share the act of drawing represented: neither exclusively occupies subject or object position.[59] As Griselda Pollock contends in relation to Berthe Morisot's work, "One of the major means by which femininity is . . . reworked is by the rearticulation of traditional space so that it ceases to function primarily as the space of sight for a mastering gaze, but becomes the locus of relationships."[60] Héloïse and Anaïs mirror each other in physical appearance and in dress; they both look unflinchingly back at the viewer, sharing in the creative process and in the agency of looking. Asserting themselves as artists, they seem to say, "We, plural," are artists, thus destabilizing the prevailing ideology of the lone genius typical of self-portraiture of the era.[61] As budding fashion-plate artists already, perhaps they are also laying claim to fashion illustration as art.

Figure 4.5 *Louis-Marie Lanté,* La Mode, *August 31, 1833, Bibliothèque nationale de France.*

Figure 4.6 *Anaïs Colin, "Valse à Trois Temps"* Le Maître à danser, *1844, Jerome Robbins Dance Division, New York Public Library.*

Both Anaïs and Héloïse produced a variety of artworks in addition to fashion plates—from book illustrations for some of the most popular titles of the period, such as Eugène Sue's *Le Juif errant* and Dumas's *Le Comte de Monte Cristo*, to miniatures, portraits, and albums—although it should be noted that all of these genres remain within what has been classified as "minor" art. Anaïs collaborated, for example, with the engraver Frédéric Sourrieu on the 1844 illustrated series *Le Maître à danser* and was frequently commissioned for watercolors and portraits, as the account book shows (figure 4.6). She also collaborated with her architect husband, who died tragically in 1854, on a series of illustrations of edifices in Gabriel Toudouze's native Brittany.[62] Likewise, Héloïse was an accomplished miniaturist, book illustrator, and watercolorist, first exhibiting her watercolors at the Paris Salon of 1835 (figure 4.7).[63] Both sisters in fact earned spots to show at the Salon in multiple years between 1835 and 1850; Héloise exhibited twenty-six works and Anaïs exhibited thirty-three works over those fifteen years.[64] The "Œuvres des Femmes au Salon de 1835" exhibition was covered for *Le Journal des femmes* by the woman art critic Linna Jaunès in a clever review posing as a dialogue with her demanding editor.[65] This invented *directrice* insists that the critic write a short piece fitting her unimportant subject, a conceit that may be understood as illustrating the many biases in place against women artists, sometimes emanating from women themselves. Jaunès laments how little space her review is to be allotted: "But I would have liked to talk about all of our women painters who do good work, and, given the brevity of an article, this is impossible."[66] In spite of her limited space, the critic mentions first-time exhibitor Héloïse Colin twice, once to praise the "abandon and grace" of her watercolors, and again to note how well Héloïse chooses her subjects.[67] In 1842 both sisters' works were recognized by Wilhelm Ténint in his *Album du Salon de 1842* "for their distinction and grace."[68] Héloïse won a third-place medal in 1844 for the watercolor category; Anaïs also won a medal in that year, and both sisters continued to submit to the Salon well after 1850, as Busquet's critique of 1857 has affirmed.[69] The fine work of depicting graceful gesture and the drape and texture of fabric was apparent in these pieces—which were not commercialized fashion prints—to at least some critics. The skills and techniques required of watercolor and miniature painting, and the compositional content of the central self-portrait are all intertwined with the sisters' fashion-plate art, which was occurring simultaneously with their showings.

According to the documentation accompanying the sisters' self-portrait, it, too, was exhibited at the 1840 Salon under the name of Anaïs Colin and entitled *Portrait de Mlles C.*[70] Thus, a painting that no doubt began as a family portrait in the amateur tradition of album art ended up earning admission to the Salon four years after its creation. Much more than a private family commemoration, then, this painting also laid claim to artistic identities in addition to its sentimental, relational ones. We should view it, therefore, as a key link—among the feminine amateur tradition of family albums, the commercial profession of fashion-plate art, and the competitive fine arts world of the Salon. The

Figure 4.7 Héloïse Leloir, "Fillette en robe noire, assise et tenant des fleurs dans sa main droite," 1865–6, Fonds d'archives graphiques de Maurice Leloir, Palais Galliera, CC0 Paris Musées/Palais Galliera—musée de la Mode de la Ville de Paris.

mutual self-portrait can thus be interpreted as encapsulating the complexity of the Colin sisters' identities as artists.

Father and daughters engaged in much of the same kind of art production—genre painting, portraiture, book illustration and even fashion illustration.[71] Yet Colin *père*'s legacy is that of a history and genre painter, not a fashion illustrator, while for his daughters the latter is true. For although they were artists of considerable talent and capable of painting in genres outside of the fashion press, they are almost exclusively remembered today for their prolific work in the commercial sector of fashion illustration. In short, Alexandre (and his son Paul Colin, the sisters' half-brother) was an artist, if not a particularly memorable one, and his daughters were mere illustrators. In spite of the marked differences between father's and daughters' paintings, both family portraits, in different ways, express a deep ambivalence about the roles and possibilities of the female artist in nineteenth-century France. In the father's painting, we find a wistful representation of an artist nonetheless suffused with the gendered limitations on that role. In the daughters' painting, by contrast, we find a more assertive representation of women as artists inflected by an acknowledgment of their artisanal identities. Their art is thus complicated by the fact that they must always contend with conflicting identities: woman and artist. The family structure that can be gleaned through the comparison of the two paintings mirrors aspects of the gendered hierarchies of art in nineteenth-century France. The ambivalence of both paintings also highlights other hierarchical relationships as well, such as that of amateur, artisan, and artist, and commercial illustrator and academic painter.

In many ways, the work of the Colin sisters blurred these distinctions. Prohibited from studying the nude and from wandering unaccompanied in public spaces to paint landscapes or city scenes—both unacceptable activities for proper women—they ventured instead into fashion shops, milliners' ateliers, and, of course, publishing houses. They were thus ultimately negotiating and inhabiting the mixed spaces of urban modernity, even if what they depicted in their work was largely the visual fantasy of bourgeois women's restricted spheres. They had a rigorous training by an academic artist, the legitimacy of having competed and exhibited in the Paris Salons, and ancillary careers in book illustration and miniatures—all of which they brought to bear on what would become their most successful and widely disseminated artistic output. Ironically, the images they produced mostly celebrated traditional female roles of domesticity, leisure, and family life, reinforcing in a highly idealized format certain bourgeois norms of femininity. Yet, the Colin sisters were also simply women who worked, sketching and painting on exacting deadlines in much the same way that fashion writers like those I discussed in chapter 3 drafted their columns week after week for an eternal cycle of fashion publications.

While the obituary of Anaïs Colin Toudouze identified her as an "artiste peintre" and went on to enumerate her many familial relationships, her most important professional identity, that of the preeminent fashion illustrator of her day, went entirely unmentioned. Perhaps this is because, as I noted in chapter 1, the concept of a bourgeois working woman in the nineteenth century was incompatible with the ideal of wife and mother to which the hagiographic form of the obituary adheres.[72] Or perhaps it was because the work of a fashion illustrator was simply not viewed as compatible with that of an "artiste peintre." Both were likely true. In the next section of this chapter, I consider in greater depth the process behind the production of the fashion plate—the *work* of art—seeking to understand it both as a creative practice and as labor. By examining the ways in which the fashion print was created and the role the Colin sisters played in this process, we can reanimate the history behind the coveted commodity of the fashion plate and begin to see that, like the garments it depicted, it, too, was the product of a practice both laborious and aesthetic.

The Work of Art

Fashion illustration, like its object, is necessarily tied to the ephemeral: it projects or captures changing fashions, and it participates in the transient culture of the press.[73] In fashion as in journalism, this transience is itself a marketing tool and a means of commercial survival, but to produce the weekly illustrations that appeared in the fashion press consistently over decades, illustrators engaged in an even more ephemeral art form as they sketched models of hats, dresses, coats, and more, likely in close consultation with the designers and fabricators of these objects themselves. Similar to the preliminary sketches of any artist, these sketches, or *croquis*, were draft studies of incomplete or even fragmentary works, used to get the pose just right in order to show the correct angle of a garment, to understand how a fabric might drape on a body, to articulate a gesture in a way that suggested the activity depicted. The *croquis*, Patricia Mainardi contends, was considered "authentic, spontaneous, done from life, not labored, not artificial, and certainly not done from museum models."[74] Representing an authentic creative process, then, these sketches, presumably hastily drawn, offer clues that illuminate the method and preoccupations of the fashion illustrator, just as they incarnate an aspect of what Baudelaire famously termed "the painting of modern life." We may even regard the Colin sisters' drawings as helping to sketch the links between the aesthetic and the commercial.

A drawing by Héloïse Leloir made around 1869 depicts in very schematic terms four women and a little girl in a park (figure 4.8).[75] Typical of such sketches, the image is small, measuring approximately four by six inches, and has been drawn on cheap paper similar to newsprint. The women and little girl are represented from multiple angles, with frontal views, back views, and two side views, capturing different variations of dresses and outerwear. Diverse poses were typical of fashion-plate composition, which strove to best represent garments from multiple angles, even if such arrangements produced groupings that were sometimes unnatural or even awkward. For the aim was not veristic depictions of figures in a landscape but, rather, realistic depictions of fabrics, cuts, accessories, and combinations. In this case, however, we find a gestural harmony that underscores the artist's talent: the two women on the left attract the interest of the little girl placed squarely in the center of the drawing. The woman on the far right, who likely represents the child's mother, looks at and points to her, as if beckoning, even as she seems to be approaching a woman with a parasol, the sole accessory that helps us understand that we are viewing an outdoor park scene.

This sketch was never meant to be considered finished art and was perhaps not even meant to be seen by anyone other than the artist herself. Like so many others by Héloïse and Anaïs, it is a study in

Figure 4.8 *Héloïse Leloir. "Dessin préparatoire avec groupe de femmes en robes de sortie avec fillette au centre," 1869, Palais Galliera, CC0 Paris Musées/Palais Galliera—musée de la Mode de la Ville de Paris.*

speed as it maps the confident lines and the corrective erasures of the artist preparing a painting. Long strokes and jagged pencilings approximate the fold of fabric, the embellishment of a scarf; rapidly rendered draping and shading are marked out in a similar way with lines and hatch marks. Smudging creates the impression of shadow, and negative space is left open enough to envision a tree or building that would eventually be placed in the distance. The imprecision of facial features, while foretelling the substitutability of fashion-plate models, is here left in an extreme form of anonymity, and even the haziness with which hands are rendered implies that the artist needs to consider gestures and expressions at a later moment. What matters more than how the artist depicts the humans, evidently, is the symmetry of the composition and the angles she uses to maximize the display of fabrics and embellishments. Lines and erasures suggest that hairdos have been diminished, the parasol moved slightly, a shoulder tilted inward—all decisive choices to better express the details of dress: flounces and fringes, rosettes and tassels, buttons and lace, all indicated in the sketch.

Of course, fashion illustrators needed to pay attention to details of dress—the sheen and hues of ribbon and cloth, the texture of fabric or straw, the sweep and color of artificial flowers, feathers, or hair. It was crucial to take note of such minutiae in preliminary sketches, for one of the principal purposes of the fashion print was to render a specific style or the goods from a specific shop in such a way as to inspire consumption. As I elaborated in my discussion of fashion writers in chapter 3, the fashion plate was often used to entice readers to seek out the shop whose goods were being promoted; indeed, fashion plates were forms of publicity that often concealed their commercial motive.[76] As such, fashion illustration participated in a crucial way in the fashion industry more broadly.[77] The Colin sisters put their artistic pedigree and superior skills to work in the service of this industry, which offered an increasingly important way for women to practice an artistic *métier*. If they were two of the most highly desirable fashion illustrators for over a half a century, it is because of the quality of their work, which not only enticed shoppers to buy the goods portrayed but also even induced readers of the fashion press to dismantle their journals, separating the plate to be admired and collected.[78]

Other drawings combine the swift lines of a rapidly drafted sketch with hastily penciled notes, indicating either details that would need to be included in the final product or information about the authorship of the style (figure 4.9). A sketch by Anaïs Toudouze, executed sometime between 1864 and 1874, illustrates this process by rendering a detailed dress from the shop of Mme. Bréant Castel, a dressmaker whose garments were often illustrated and promoted in the pages of *La Mode illustrée*.[79] The dress itself appears completely dissociated from the body that wears it: the top edge of the drawing ends right at the neckline, effectively decapitating its wearer. Likewise, hands are absent; only dress sleeves and a fully formed seated female body are visible, further emphasizing the hierarchy of importance in fashion illustration: the dress must come first. And it appears to be quite a dress, even if quickly drawn, as the strong lines indicate. Like the dresses pictured in figure 4.8, here again we find penciled hatch work, suggesting sheen; darker-shaded shapes hinting at shadows and folds; symmetrically placed bows down the front, spaced to account for the seated position of the wearer; and parallel rows of frilly trim down the front of the skirt and on its hem, which is also embellished with a giant rosette. Diagonal spidery handwriting slopes upward from the right edge of the dress, "bleu clair, dentelles" (light blue, lace), reminding the artist of color and fabric choices that would need to be accurately rendered later with paint.

Close-up details, often of hats, illustrate the ways in which these fashion artists understood that forms, textures, patterns, and materials were both distinct and interactive (figures 4.10 and 4.11). Two "headshots," both by Anaïs Toudouze, one a frontal view and the other from behind, demonstrate a creative process that combines a deep knowledge of the materials of fashion (how they look and feel), the quick capturing of an object in motion (hat ribbon, sleeve fold), and a fluency with the vocabulary of fashion as it translates from word to a series of detailed patterns on the page—*tulle, ruban, fleur* (tulle, ribbon, flower), etc. The artist's rendering of a "chapeau de tulle vert" (hat of green tulle) is marked from left to right with notations surrounding the object: the ribbon hanging from the left is designated "rubans noirs" (black ribbons); atop the back portion of the hat, the word "dentelle"

Figure 4.9 Anaïs Toudouze. "Esquisse de figure assise en robe à nœuds et falbalas," 1864–74, Palais Galliera, CC0 Paris Musées/Palais Galliera—musée de la Mode de la Ville de Paris.

(lace) appears abbreviated, as does "perles" (pe) "de jaïs" (jet beads) that were to be placed along the top front portion of the hat. Framing the forehead, the leaf-like decorations are termed "feuillages" (foliage), and the hat ties are to be white ("liens blancs"). The specificity of the fabrics and colors implies collaboration with the *modiste* and is thus related to the commercial dimension of the art product, but it also indicates the skill of artists who manipulate paint to render a wide variety of materials, as we shall see below.

The second head view, sketched in 1860, focuses exclusively on the hat, as the drawing depicts the brim, crown, and embellishments only from behind. No face is visible—only the outline of sloping

Figure 4.10 Anaïs Toudouze, "Femme, en buste de trois-quarts, avec coiffe de dentelle," 1867, Palais Galliera, CC0 Paris Musées/Palais Galliera—musée de la Mode de la Ville de Paris.

shoulders and wispy ringlets minimally executed with two or three lines. By contrast, hatch work and shading give dimension and texture to the focal object, and, along with the detail expressed in the drawing itself, the artist has once again scribbled notes that emanate from various decorated elements of the hat, presumably so that when she turns to the watercolor production of this sketch, she will know precisely what color and texture to approximate. In this picture, the represented hat's brim will be colored to duplicate the look and sheen of cherry-colored ribbon ("ruban cerise"), likely coordinating with the long ribbon affixed to the feather at the back; the top portion of the crown will be painted to

Figure 4.11 Anaïs Toudouze, "Détail d'une coiffe vue de dos," 1860, Palais Galliera, CC0 Paris Musées/Palais Galliera—musée de la Mode de la Ville de Paris.

replicate the stiff yet sheer fabric of black tulle (" tulle noir"); a black feather ("plume noire") will be lightly painted with swishing brushstrokes and set against the dangling cherry-pink ribbon; and black lace, ("dentelle noire") executed with great care to reproduce lace's delicate filigree work, will appear to flutter from the back of the crown. An impressive range of painterly techniques is invoked simply by virtue of the wide variety of elements embodied in the material object represented. Color and brushstroke, as well as pen and ink work overlaying the watercolor, would build upon the artist's capturing of the object to produce a delicate miniature at once grounded in the material reality of commodities and in the utopia of desire—where the aspirational self resides.[80]

Sketches such as these illustrate both the commerciality and the aestheticization of the work of these fashion artists. Their skill is harnessed to the commercial eye, as deft drawing techniques combine with detailed annotations to create a working image that would be translated into a more refined form. These images aptly illustrate the ambiguity of art and commerce: the Colin sisters' early training in miniature painting now serves the commercial task of product rendering, which required exactitude of color, texture, draping, etc. These preliminary, annotated sketches and the signed watercolors to which I shall next turn reveal that the steps in the production of the fashion plate demanded concentrated attention, specific sets of knowledge, and multiple skills—drawing, color nuancing, and particularly the fine precision of miniature painting.

After completing sketches in the boutique or atelier of a *couturière* or *modiste*, the artist then returned to her home studio to produce a watercolor, which would subsequently be sent to a lithographer, then a printer, and finally to a team of colorists, "who applied the color to each individual print, one at a time."[81] There would have been little time to linger over an image since the journal had to go to press on time, and an entire production team was waiting. Watercolor, or *aquarelle*, was an appropriate medium for quickly executing a colored model because it was associated, like the *croquis*, with rapidity of production. It also required a high level of skill. As Nicolas-Toussaint Charlet—a watercolorist, lithographer, and professor of drawing at the École Polytechnique in the 1840s—explains in his "Technique de l'aquarelle,"

> Watercolor painting done in the studio can, *when done by a skilled man,* compete with oil painting, and even be superior to it in terms of finesse of tone in light; but the pitfall is in the shadows and the chiaroscuro. By absorbing the tone and forming a light white fuzz on its surface, the paper sometimes forces a further blurring, and from then on, it is very difficult to correct one's work.[82]

In spite of Charlet's dismissal of women from the ranks of fine artists, his observations about the immediacy of watercolor and its capacity to render effects of light are astute. Unlike the pencil sketch (or even oil painting, for that matter), a watercolor painting could not be retouched. This fact of the technique suggests that the skilled watercolorist (male or female) would need confidence and experience to execute the image quickly and without error. Indeed, according to François Daulte, in his study of the watercolor tradition in nineteenth-century France, the genre demands "an acuity of the eye, a sureness of the hand, a quasi-daily practice of 'overcolor' and especially a speedy execution, of which only great artists are capable."[83]

Notwithstanding Daulte's favorable judgment, no doubt intended for "grands artistes" such as Delacroix and Manet, watercolor had long been considered a minor art form, one that was tied to the tradition of the *arts d'agréments* for young ladies.[84] The medium began to enjoy a new popularity in France during the 1830s—precisely when Alexandre Colin was coming of age as an artist and beginning to instruct his daughters. A close friend of Richard Parkes Bonington, a renowned English watercolorist with whom he worked and traveled, Alexandre Colin was part of a generation of artists, along with Delacroix, who practiced and valued watercolor painting, largely under the influence of Great Britain and, in particular, Turner.[85] In spite of the increasing valorization of the medium, however, watercolors nonetheless functioned primarily as studies for oils; and even later in the century, "the state continues to consider watercolor as an 'elegant and frivolous' genre, and on the whole negligible," relegating these Salon entries to "obscure rooms."[86] Apart from their self-portrait, which was done in oil, the Colin sisters usually entered watercolors into the Paris Salons, and their works were displayed in such "obscure rooms" alongside those of other women painters.[87]

It is no small wonder that the Colin sisters should have been well instructed in the art of watercolor; first, because for bourgeois young ladies, it would have been a natural part of their education, the "elegant and frivolous" form of art deemed appropriate for women; and second, because as young ladies growing up in the Romantic era with artist parents interested in training all of their progeny for a professional life in the arts, mastering watercolor was an essential element of an *artistic* education, regardless of gender.[88] It was a step in the production of "high" art, but it was also a means to financial security, as illustrators were needed for a wide variety of industries. As seems frequently to have been the case with the Colin sisters, their artistic careers were thus marked by paradox: watercolor was considered both frivolous and essential; and, although they were master technicians of the medium, as we shall see, they produced original works that reside in fashion archives rather than in art museums. Straddling art and commerce, their fashion watercolors bear witness to their formidable talent both as *aquarellistes* and as entrepreneurs, who regularly churned out their work product to meet the expanding demands of the fashion press.

Like the rapidly executed preliminary sketches, the watercolor renderings illuminate the work process that lay behind the more public product. They also reveal the translation into color and composition of what began, in the sketchbook, as lines and notes, experiments and ideas. These works were signed, one-of-a-kind pictures, not yet produced in multiple copies through the process of engraving or lithography but, rather, existing as unique works of art in the miniaturist tradition in which Héloïse and Anaïs Colin had been trained by their mother Joséphine Colin.[89] Their watercolors help to flesh out a creative activity that has been obscured by the widely disseminated final product—the commercial fashion plate. As we have seen, in the hierarchy of art, watercolor, like miniature painting, was feminized and thus deemed less valuable than oil painting. For practical reasons too, such as the fact that watercolor was less expensive to produce and less time-consuming than oil painting, this medium was better suited for a commercial venture that demanded speedy turnaround by female artists who may have had fewer resources and less time to devote solely to their art.

The watercolors were the aesthetic development of the more schematic *croquis*, which were done on site in a shop and mostly focused on objective particulars of pattern, fabric, line, and color. These sketches not surprisingly lacked details of setting and composition, for they served as the annotated model on which the watercolor rendering, which was created in the artist's studio, would be based. The watercolor, as Bonin notes, was the more imaginative step, in which the artist's vision of composition and setting as well as her skill with color and form could be showcased.[90]

Figure 4.12 portrays the watercolor version of the rough sketch pictured in figure 4.8, and a comparison of the two reveals the extent to which the artist develops in the watercolor the setting and composition absent in the *croquis*. This sketch is not annotated, so we must assume that Héloïse Leloir kept separate notes for some drawings. It is as if the *croquis* has been "accessorized" in the watercolor. For here, all the figures now wear hats adorned with feathers, flowers, or ribbons; two of the ladies carry parasols; and details such as fringes, pleats, scalloping, lacework, veils, hairstyles, and jewelry, either only schematically rendered or nonexistent in the sketch, are now painted in exquisitely detailed color.

Figure 4.12 *Héloïse Leloir, "Figure vue de trois quarts face en robe gris bleu et mante noire bordée de franges, figure vue de profil en robe verte à bords dentelés, fillette en robe blanche à galons bleus, figure vue de trois quarts dos en robe violette garnie de dentelle noire, . . ."* c. 1869, Palais Galliera, CC0 Paris Musées/Palais Galliera - musée de la Mode de la Ville de Paris.

The watercolor expands the vignette that was only suggested in the *croquis*. The two ladies on the left gaze off into the distance, but hold hands—one gloved, one naked—as if upon greeting each other, they were distracted by something outside of the picture's frame. The lady on the far right who seems in the sketch to beckon to the little girl in the watercolor now offers her a sprig of lilac, whose colors resonate with the purple and green silk taffetas of the two gowns in the center of the image. The skill of the flower artist—Héloïse Leloir's *La Corbeille de Flore* was published as a lithographic album in 1852—is apparent not only in the tiny delicate petals of the lilac sprig but also in the pink and red roses and what I take to be violets on the headpieces of three of the women.[91] Flower painting, like miniatures and watercolors, was a feminized genre, and fashion art merged this genre with that of the miniature in Héloïse's practice. Writing about the English artist Mary Gartside, Ann Bermingham notes that "women could develop their intellectual interests and artistic ambitions within the confines of flower painting. . . . Rather than a confinement, flower painting was a liberation . . . an opportunity, even an excuse, to explore color and color theory."[92] Similarly, we find the Colin sisters making productive use of the skills they were allowed as women to develop. Like the English Gartside, the Colin sisters pursued artistic ambitions under cover of the so-called feminine arts—flower painting, miniature portrait painting, watercolor, and, ultimately, commercial fashion art.

The speed of execution demanded by watercolor made it a medium well suited to capturing the fleeting shifts in tone and shade of the satin and silk fabrics popular for nineteenth-century women's clothing. As I mentioned before, however, women were typically trained in watercolor primarily because of its portability and relatively low cost, and thus the level of skill their work achieves, given the challenges of the medium, is all the more remarkable. The sheen of the dresses in figure 4.12 is produced through the interplay of greater or lesser applications of paint and water, producing subtle and realistic reflective light as the dresses seem to move and undulate as the women walk in the park. The watery, faded blues, grays, and greens of the background represent the trees, bushes, and plants of this outdoor setting and contrast with the beiges and browns that approximate the park's dusty pathways. On the far left, what appears to be a lilac bush offers an echo of the sprig in the figure's hand and visually rhymes with the purple gown of the lady viewed from behind whose head is turned. The oversized urn at the far right lends solidity to an otherwise ethereal background, anchoring the scene in a park and helping the viewer visualize the probability of such a composition: ladies of leisure in an 1860s Paris springtime might indeed stroll in the city's parks dressed in the latest fashions. Aspirational readers of the fashion press would certainly be attracted to the prospect of such an outing.

The background is stylized and unfocused, perhaps resulting from the application of the painterly advice acquired from Héloïse's parents, or from a treatise on watercolor like the one authored by Armand Chassagne, who instructed that for nature paintings, useless details are distracting, and so one should only paint the principal elements, "Otherwise, the ensemble would disappear there."[93] By contrast, the five foregrounded figures are represented with a stunning precision that serves both the commercial and aesthetic motivations of the painting: commercial, to offer a clear example of the quality of goods readers might acquire at a given dress or *modiste* shop; and aesthetic, because the depiction of fabrics and accessories demands of the artist a wide variety of techniques. Filmy white ties keep the headpiece of the woman on the far left in place, their transparency indicated by their transformation to gray as they lie upon her black silk *pelisse*. Each pleat of her light gray taffeta dress is marked out in different shades of white, gray, light blue, and black, approximating the effect of light and shadow that pleated silk in *plein air* (outside) would create. Likewise, the pale pink skirt with horizontal striping in light beige expresses both movement and luminosity as five or six variants on the pale pink interact in the bottom right quadrant of the painting. The two figures on the right are resplendent in a coat with black lace embellishments, headpieces, dresses, and parasol. The lacework was likely created with pen and ink after the watercolor was completed, and the precision is all the more astonishing when we consider that these works were used as models for lithographs that would in turn be printed; thus, they had to be produced speedily and consistently.

Contemporary treatises on watercolor, such as that of Chassagne, associate the medium primarily with *plein air* painting, for, with watercolors, the artist could quickly capture nature's rapid changeability. In the case of the Colin sisters, as we have seen, the rapid depiction of an image was dictated primarily by the commercial imperative to produce multiple models at a steady pace for the press, and, as women, they would most likely not have been painting out of doors. Their "landscapes" were thus predominantly urban, occasionally referencing the Paris of the mid-century onward through telltale signs of Haussmannization, such as parks and gardens, occasionally shops and museums, and even travel—the spaces of urban leisure. Of course, many fashion plates pictured indoor scenes, staging domestic and social activities like sewing, visiting, clothing selection, or outings such as balls. Drawing in part on their own experience as middle-class nineteenth-century women, steeped in the traditions of bourgeois domesticity and the centrality of family, the Colin sisters thus created a visual fantasy that may have referenced a world with which they were familiar but that quite probably had little to do with what they actually saw as they worked and interacted with other women, some no doubt working-class, in the shops, or the male artisans they must have encountered in the lithography studio or at the publisher, or the teams of anonymous women colorists who hand-painted the printed image. This demonstrates one of the ways in which their occupations enabled them to cross class boundaries.

Their images succeed at representing a luminosity and shadow in fabrics. Technically, the immediacy of their watercolor technique was thus attached less to the content of their images and more to their style and form, which is visible in the representation of fabric or flowers and in the gestural sweep of a line as a dress moves, folds, pleats. Indeed, one can almost see the variations of light and shadow of an entire sky in the blue silk skirt pictured in figure 4.13. A detail of the skirt showcases the watercolorist's technique of rapidly applying paint and water in layers to produce a wide range of shades of blue, white, gray, and black that represent the folds, sheen, and voluminous expanse of this stiff taffeta skirt, whose rustle we can just about hear (figure 4.14).

Figure 4.13 Colin, Héloïse, "Femme en robe grise et femme en robe bleue dans un jardin," 1863, Palais Galliera, CC0 Paris Musées/Palais Galliera—musée de la Mode de la Ville de Paris.

Figure 4.14 *Detail of Héloïse Colin, "Femme en robe grise et femme en robe bleue . . .," Palais Galliera, CC0 Paris Musées/Palais Galliera—musée de la Mode de la Ville de Paris.*

Explaining effects of shadow and light when depicting skies, Chassagne might as well be describing Héloïse Leloir's approach to painting this skirt: "Shadows, which, in the foreground, engage clearly for the eye the tones of nature, tend to become gray in the background, and the more distant the shadows are, the more they engage the tones of the sky, which makes them bluish if the sky is blue and gray-blue if the sky is gray."[94] The technical skill, choice of color and contrast, and variation of methods used to render in very short order different objects, materials, and effects of light and shadow in this and many other such watercolors illustrate the artistic virtuosity of these artists. These watercolors, which required so much skill and effort and yet were seen by so few, and when seen, were understood as only preparatory work for the more widely viewed (and collected) reproductions, serve nonetheless as important archival evidence of the Colin sisters' artistic ambition. As for Mary Gartside, the painter described by Bermingham, the luminous preparatory watercolors of the Colin sisters' fashion plates gave them "the freedom to embrace the dominant cultural stereotypes of femininity"—here flowers, fashion, fabrics—while pursuing "art in a professional way."[95]

This virtuosity was put to commercial use, for, as we know, the Colin sisters entered the commercial system of fashion illustration, their sketches and watercolors serving as the basis for thousands of reproduced prints that were distributed globally over a fifty-year period in the heyday of the lithograph and that remain highly collectible today both for their beauty and for their historic value. Other archival material, such as Anaïs's account ledger from early in her career, helps us uncover the day-to-day pacing of their artistic output and offers insight into the *work* of art. Although we only have accounts for a short period, and for but one of the two sisters, Bonin concludes, "It seems logical, given the number of published prints of the two sisters, that they had the same type of revenue."[96] Based on these accounts, it would appear that Anaïs Colin was steadily producing at least one watercolor per week in the fall of 1843 along with multiple drawings.[97] This production would include the site visits to shops where the *croquis* were made and the notes were taken, as well as studio time at home and the calculation that the illustration would need to be ready a month in advance of its printing to allow time for the lithograph to be created, printed, and hand-colored.[98]

Other archival material that is available to us—the preserved watercolors, which are far more delicate and artistic than the final lithographed reproductions—offer insight into the sisters' sense of their own self-worth as artists. It seems clear that Héloïse Leloir's and Anaïs Toudouze's watercolors were not created with only their reproduction and dissemination in mind. Given the technical quality of the watercolors and the attention to details that these artists must have known would be diminished in the final printed product, they may have considered the watercolors to be works of art that could *also* serve the purpose of a commercial endeavor. Indeed, it was only after the watercolor left the artists' studios that the commercial information contained in captions beneath the images would be inserted. It is clear, however, that the work products of the Colin sisters—whether fashion illustrations, book illustrations, or miniature portraits—were made to be sold and disseminated, but they were also painstakingly crafted as works of art—and these are not incompatible, despite cultural biases that presented them as such. As entrepreneurial artists and freelancers, the Colin sisters recognized that art was also labor, a realization that was already inscribed in their self-portrait of 1836 and reiterated in the account ledger; and they put their considerable talents to work as much for their own financial stability as for the pleasure of aesthetic creation.

The Stealthy Work of the Fashion Plate

In their most obvious function, fashion plates celebrated and constructed women as spectacular objects to be consumed.[99] Their contents repeat familiar scenarios: idealized women are posed in various spaces of nineteenth-century bourgeois leisure—parks, shops, museums, opera houses, balls, drawing rooms—dressed to evoke an activity, a season, or an event, and almost always in the company of other women (although most likely, there was a single model posing for all of the women pictured).[100] They stage social negotiation in the various vignettes they portray—conversing, going on outings, visiting, reading, child-rearing, ball-going—and they serve as social negotiators themselves between consumers, merchants, and producers (of both plates and products). As noted above, plates usually depict multiple views of dresses to display the design skill of the creators and to show the front, back, and side of the dress. Through color and detail, artists attempted to recreate the sensuous quality of fabrics—velvets, silks, laces, feathers, and so on—thus increasing the desirability of garments that conferred status and beauty on their wearer. As aspirational images, then, fashion plates (re)produced beauty and behavioral ideals for a consuming public anxious to emulate those in higher classes. The conventions of fashion-plate illustration within which the Colin sisters worked include the typical number of figures (two or three) per plate; a standard distance between figures allowing for garments and accessories to be as fully visible as possible, with poses showcasing the dress silhouette and novel elements; and figures typically shown in domestic interiors or outside in prescribed settings engaging in leisure activities.[101]

Some recent scholarship pushes beyond the traditional reading of a fashion plate as pure advertisement, spectacle, or commodity and introduces vital social and cultural dimensions to it as an ideological product—an analysis of which opens up new areas of inquiry and invites fresh perspectives on images that read primarily as flat and static idealizations. Some scholars have focused on the fashion plate as a useful artifact for understanding the social experience of women in the nineteenth century. Heidi Brevik-Zender, for example, argues that fashion plates "depict the very spaces of bourgeois feminine modernity" and analyzes the fashion plate's participation in the development of female subjectivities in particular in relation to space.[102] In her astute contention that the fashion plate is doing work far more complicated than has usually been assumed, she follows Sharon Marcus's important contributions establishing the fundamental feminocentrism and homosociability implicit in fashion plates.[103] Indeed, Marcus proposes a reading hyper-attentive to the surface of the images and reveals what is perfectly visible if largely unseen: women in fashion plates are depicted as desiring, gazing agents. Perhaps more significant to the present study, she also discovers in the nineteenth-century fashion plate "a female world of love and ritual" and "a female universe saturated by a tactile sensuality."[104] Within the body of work inaugurated by the self-portrait, the Colin sisters' fashion plates were also archives of female community and occasionally of messages, perhaps even to each other, about their own sisterhood and their place in the world of art and fashion in nineteenth-century Paris.

Building on this scholarship, in this final section of the chapter, I consider what I term the stealthy work of the fashion plate, which operates on multiple levels simultaneously in the artistic production of the Colin sisters.[105] First, and most obviously, the phrase refers to the plate's function as a somewhat covert advertising tool, thinly veiling this purpose under an idealized fantasy of the feminine. While fashion plates were most certainly spectacular commodities and guides, they can also be understood as signposts for women who had little control over their social roles and activities, sometimes evoking experiences that were becoming increasingly possible for women, such as shopping and traveling, in the modern city.[106] We may thus complicate the conventional understanding of fashion plates as purely objectifying and commodifying women's bodies by considering them also as documents demonstrating aspects of female community and activity. Even as they mimicked shop windows, displaying luxurious commodities and fashionable products framed in a rectangular view, they could also present narrative possibilities and spaces for projection.

As both advertisements and aesthetic objects, fashion plates were communicative, commodified, and collected. In their function as advertisements, they transmitted practical information, which is evinced by the descriptive captions typically found in the lower frame of the images. The spatial conventions of the fashion plate remained static for two centuries, with the textual description—the factual information that would provide the basis for either the procurement or re-creation of the pictured garment—at the margins of the image, thus ceding priority to the visually arresting colored image and understating the commercial aim of the picture. But the inclusion of the textual description is crucial, and in the space between image and word, aspiration could be transformed into reality.[107] In the example of figure 4.15, created by Anaïs Toudouze in 1853 for *Le Follet*, viewers learn that children's clothing can be procured from a shop called Le Zéphyr on the boulevard des Capucines; likewise, addresses for shops selling hair ornaments and perfumes are listed.

Pictorial details of illustrated clothing served not only to impart veracity in a fabric's sheen or a lace's delicacy: they also offered information for home sewers or for women who might take the image to be copied by their local dressmaker.[108] In figure 4.15, for example, there is an imaginative correlation between the content, which pictures a woman with three young girls picking and arranging roses and other flowers in a vase and a basket, and the objects advertised. Since perfume cannot be represented visually in the same way a dress or hat could be, the artist has instead evoked the olfactory sense of fragrance through a visual abundance of flowers. The fashion plate is thus engaged in multi-sensory fantasy work, conjuring various sensual effects through visual techniques and spectacularizing, whether as a window, a mirror, or even a portal, the desires of its consuming public.

Plates such as this one transmit more than merely commercial information about the goods on display: they simultaneously reinforce gender limitations and expand possibilities within certain constraints. Along with exercising its function as an advertisement of goods, this image, like so many others, enacts the ideological work of female inculcation into the socially appropriate behaviors and self-fashioning for women in nineteenth-century France. In this sense, the fashion plate has a norming function and serves even as a surrogate mother, illustrating respectable femininity for spectator-readers and showcasing what appears to be a mother's modeling of feminine behavior and dress for her own daughters.[109] It is certainly true that motherhood is a frequent theme of the plates, as illustrated

Figure 4.15 *Anonymous, after Anaïs Colin-Toudouze,* Le Follet, *1853, No. 1816: "Toilettes d'enfants (…)," 1853, Rijksmuseum, Amsterdam.

in the many images that feature women with children, along with other socially sanctioned roles for women, such as visiting friends, attending church, offering charity, and the like. The plates thus often reinforce a domestic ideology restricting bourgeois women to limited roles, but they also convey detailed information that could be freely adopted and used to understand and order bourgeois female existence in a society in which prevailing ideologies presented women as exercising little control over their scripted roles and performances. The plates thus suggest a kind of principle of improvisation within certain bounds.

While I am not suggesting that developed narratives can be gleaned from these images, it would also be inaccurate to deny their potential narrative structure, as some critics have done.[110] Figure 4.16, for example, pictures a trio—two adult women and a sleeping baby—settled in an outdoor park. A woman (mother, sister, friend?) in a pink and white crinoline skirt and black *pelisse* and hat with red trim gazes on as a young mother, hatless and dressed in a yellow gown with black embroidery, uses her handkerchief to shoo an insect from the head of her sleeping baby. She holds an open book, maybe a fashion magazine, in her other hand and is perhaps reading from it to her companion. The young mother's eyes are focused in particular on the black insect—drawn with the same pen and ink as the

Figure 4.16 *Anonymous, after Héloïse Leloir-Colin,* La Gazette Rose, *1 juin 1865, No. 650: "Etoffes et confections (...),"* 1865, Rijksmuseum, Amsterdam.

wheat designs on her dress—which threatens to alight on and wake the baby. How should we interpret the visual parallel the artist establishes between the dress's black ornamentation and the distracting and potentially vexing black insect hovering over the baby's head?

The insect certainly draws attention to one of the key commodities pictured in the plate: handkerchiefs from the shop of Chapron—thus accomplishing the plate's commercial aim. The large black insect also pushes against the presumed boundaries of the fashion plate, however, by introducing erratic movement, potential ugliness, or simply realistic detail into this utopian scene of balanced natural harmony. Insect illustration was common among naturalists and book illustrators of the nineteenth century.[111] One of the best known illustrators and caricaturists, J. J. Grandville, a contemporary of the Colin sisters, famously sent up flower and fashion illustration—quintessentially feminized art forms—in his 1847 *Les Fleurs animées*, by pointedly including anthropomorphized (male) bugs feasting on the clothing of lady-flowers.[112] But the bug also evokes the improvisational quality of the Impressionist masters, contemporaneous with the Colin sisters, who were painting outside and capturing fleeting impressions. Indeed, although the dragonfly was drafted nearly a decade earlier, it bears a marked resemblance to the *eau-forte* illustration by Manet, "La Libellule" ("The Dragonfly"), gracing the cover of Charles Cros's long poem of 1874, *Le Fleuve* (figure 4.17).

It is an unexpected motif in the fashion-plate genre, which typically repeats a limited range of predictable scenes. Scholars have discussed the influence of fashion plates on Impressionist art, but not the inclusion of a highly aesthetic and nonstatic detail such as Héloïse Leloir's dragonfly within the conventional zone of the fashion plate.[113] Might it be read as a self-conscious reference to the artistry of the fashion plate itself and, in this sense, as an echo of the frank stare from the canvas of the sisters' shared self-portrait proclaiming their artistic identity? As an aesthetic detail having nothing to do with the conventions of the fashion plate, the bug asserts itself as a disruption of the inert tranquility of idealized femininity that the plates tend to represent, and it thus opens the image up for speculation.

The visual homology between the black lines of the bug and the black embroidered designs on the young mother's yellow dress is also significant, for embroidery work (*broderie*) would be included in the category of *passementerie*, stitched ornamentation for women's clothing as well as military uniforms, here advertised as having been fabricated by "La Glaneuse" in the print's caption. Painstakingly sewn into the heavy fabric of a silk dress, the embroidery details of this dress represent hours of labor by the *petites mains* of the workshop. Likewise, their representation by the fashion-plate artist also exacted time and labor with fine pen and ink drawn by the artist's hand over the just dried watercolor image. By accentuating this detail in such a whimsical way, Leloir establishes parallels between the skilled labor of the fashion worker and that of the fashion illustrator.[114] The black lines of the insect seem almost to escape from the field of the dress, with its wisps of black wheat—renegade embroidery come to life as a startling interruption in an otherwise predictable domestic idyll—or an artistic whim reinforcing the skill and imagination of the fashion-plate artist.[115]

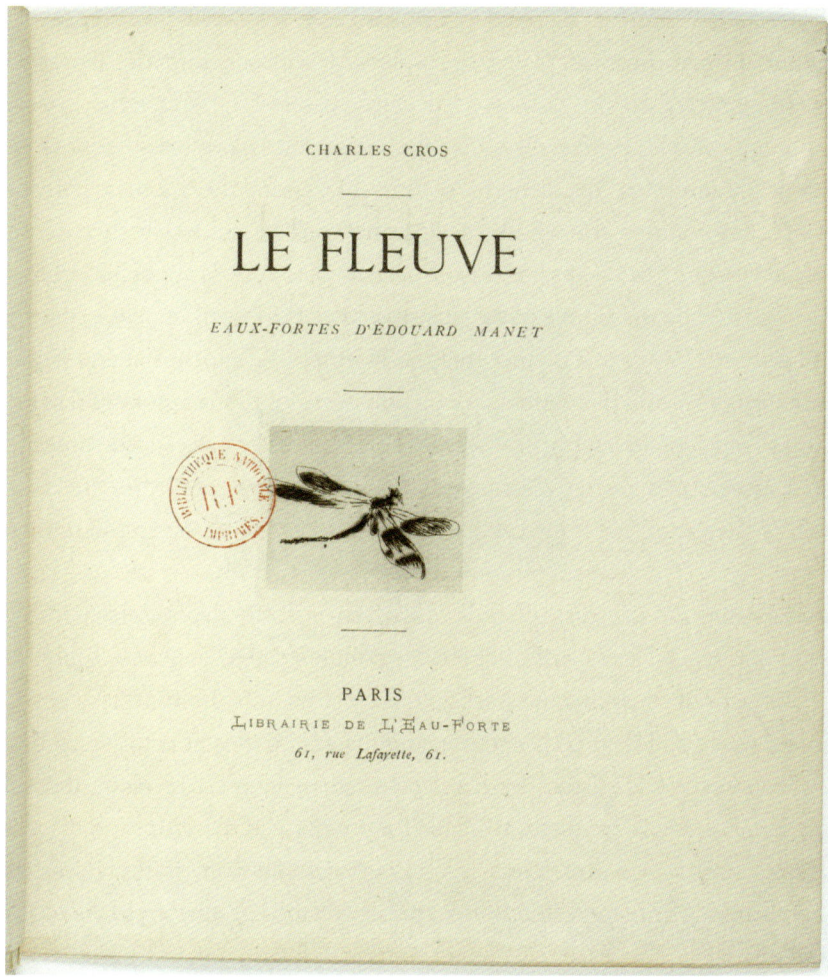

Figure 4.17 *Édouard Manet, "La Libellule," Le Fleuve, Charles Cros, Paris, 1874, Bibliothèque nationale de France.*

This insect and other details of the image trouble the commercial messaging of the plate and introduce a narrative interest that might even override its commercial intent. Indeed, it is a cue to look differently, a signifier of alterity that potentially prompts a short-circuiting of the normative codes of reading fashion plates. The other woman looks on at this scene but focuses principally on the young mother, as if approving of her protective gesture. The grouping of women, smartly dressed, is presented in the foreground in great detail—so that viewers will know what to shop for—while the pastoral background with trees and a faint church steeple fill in the scene beyond. At a short distance behind the group, however, perhaps to complete the composition by filling in the negative space created by the slope of figures, we see the casually discarded blue parasol and yellow and white trimmed hat belonging to the young mother. These abandoned accessories recall Alexandre Colin's portrait of his daughter

Héloïse (figure 4.4), in which her hat and parasol occupy the front left corner of the painting. Here, however, unlike in most such plates, the accessories recede into the background and thus are hardly actively marketed by the fashion-plate artist to serve a commercial imperative—despite what the caption indicates.[116] Rather, like the black bug, the accessories serve a narrative, even affective, function, accentuating the heat of a June afternoon, the moment of repose, and the insouciance of a young woman for whom fashion may be less central to her existence than her child's well-being. Discarding her accessories frees her hands to care for her child or to read to herself or to a friend. Ever so slightly disruptive of the seamlessness of the fashion plate's commercial mission, these details add aesthetic depth to a picture that might otherwise appear flat and commonplace, and they tell a story that goes beyond that of female consumption alone. It is a story of female relationships, feminine identities, and female support networks. For here, as in other such images, relationships are foregrounded rather than merely clothing, and the protective gesture of the young mother as well as the attentive interest of her companion echo the master theme expressed in the sisters' shared self-portrait.

Both the embrace and the expressive hands of the self-portrait also regularly find their way into prints executed by the sisters, as we see in another example created by Anaïs Toudouze in the early 1850s (figure 4.18). Set out of doors, the backdrop resembles an exhibition space; with its hanging banners, scaffolded wood and iron construction, and distant crowds, it could even be a reference to the recent 1851 London World's Fair. The print pictured in figure 4.18 ostensibly advertises hats, dresses, lace, and handkerchiefs, products available for purchase at the shops indicated in the caption. Like so many others, this print is quite conventional, showcasing women interacting in conversation and gesture. Their arms are entwined, and their expressive hands gesture, hold an accessory, touch an intimate companion, or point to a scene beyond the frame of the print, indicating at once familiarity, mobility, and possibility. These are the types of gestures that animate otherwise static plates in which faces are often identical and glances sometimes miss their mark.[117] While these gestures are typical of all fashion plates of the period, when we view them through the prism of the sisters' early work, where creative and caring hands were so central, they acquire a dimension that reinforces the value and perhaps the necessity of female community.

In his study on the importance of hands in Victorian literature, Peter Capuano argues that their startling, if previously unrecognized, ubiquity is a response to "questions about creation, about labor, about mechanization, about gender, about class and racial categorization."[118] While his context is British literary studies, Capuano's recognition of the highly visible yet unacknowledged presence of hands in cultural production of the nineteenth century is pertinent to a genre such as the fashion plate, in which hands are featured in nearly every image. Indeed, in fashion plates, hands are the only body part that regularly show skin, except for the face. Hands engage in a wide variety of gestures in these prints, becoming the silent communicators of intention, desire, care, or even action. Like many

Figure 4.18 *Anonymous, after Anaïs Colin-Toudouze,* Le Follet, *1852, No. 1687: "Chapeaux de la maison (…),"1852, Rijksmuseum, Amsterdam.*

fashion-plate artists, the Colin sisters often project into their fashion illustration pictures of women performing what might be considered unessential labor—activities that pass the time but are not remunerated.[119] Given what we know of the Colin sisters' own biographies, however, this labor potentially takes on a deeper resonance. Herein lies the stealthy work of the plate: when these hands are represented working—at embroidery, sewing, or even painting—they reflect in a bourgeois consumer mirror the real labor that created the very garments they display as well as the plates themselves.

Read in relation to the early self-portrait, the communicative, caring, or active hands of many such plates produced by the Colin sisters thus become tantalizingly self-referential. For the hands at the center of the shared self-portrait tell a layered story about art and craft. The artist's hand, symbol of creation, extends to the instrument it will activate. In a parallel manner, the metonymized *petites mains* of the fashion industry signify the literalization of the creative artisanal work of (mostly) women who, working in teams in workshops, stitched the garments, embroidered embellishments, glued and sewed feathers and flowers, and performed all manner of other detailed manual labor. Likewise, once a fashion plate was printed and reproduced, teams of anonymous women colorists, each tasked with painting a unique color, would hand-paint the black-and-white print produced through the printing process from the original watercolor created by the fashion-plate artist.[120] If the stylized hands of the fashion plates are hardly intended to represent the labor of women working behind the scenes in the workshops of fashion and its illustration, in the work of the Colin sisters they nevertheless express a trace of the woman artist's hand and, by extension, affirm the networks of women artisans and laborers who produced the commodities pictured and the commodified and disseminated fashion plate itself. They also echo the leisurely needlework of bourgeois women and thus suggest gendered links between radically different classes of women, summoning overlaps between consumption and production. It is the spectral presence of the self-portrait that helps us perceive these links.

The self-referentiality evoked in certain fashion plates produced by the Colin sisters is particularly discernible in plates featuring women engaged in painting. The 1871 print created by Héloïse Leloir featured in figure 4.19 illustrates the ways in which the Colin sisters played with and referred to female artistic and artisanal production. In an image that repeats many of the familiar tropes of fashion plates—a grouping of two women and a girl, an outdoor setting combining natural and human-made elements, a parasol and shawl lying negligently in the grass in the foreground—this print also, potentially, stages the work of the fashion plate artist herself. While the artist may be self-reflexively staging the amateur at work in a family portrait that will ultimately make its way into the private family album—a typical leisure activity of the female bourgeois subjects who consumed both fashions and fashion journals—we may also be witnessing a deeper self-referentiality. Perhaps the standing woman represents a fashion model: smartly hatted, gloved, and striking a pose that offers a view of the

Figure 4.19 *Huard, after Héloïse Leloir-Colin,* La Mode Illustrée, *1871, No. 24: "Toilettes de Mme Fladry (…),"* 1871, Rijksmuseum, Amsterdam.

Figure 4.20 *Héloïse Leloir, née Colin (1820–73), "Portrait d'une petite fille," provenant de la famille de l'artiste, vers 1850, courtesy of Galerie Jaegy-Théolyre.*

dress's bustle and pleat details as well as the ornamentation on the top of her hat. The seated woman, ungloved and also fashionably attired, is sketching in her open book, pencil in hand, her sketchbook upright in her other hand as she looks intently at her subject. The young girl standing between them studies the sketch and gestures with her open hand at its subject, the fashionable standing lady. Is she being educated in fashion, or in painting, or both? Like Héloïse, portrayed by her father as sketching in the countryside near Nîmes some four decades earlier (figure 4.4), the artist depicted here has cast aside her protective outdoor wear, a sign that she allows herself the freedom of movement necessary to work.

Unlike her father's sketch artist, however, who is not captured in the process of sketching, here Héloïse's artist uses her pencil, hands engaged, and looks with great concentration at her subject. She is an artist at work, which suggests that this print might even be staging a second veiled self-portrait, or perhaps a portrait of her sister, Anaïs, busy at work, with her daughter Isabelle Toudouze, the future fashion artist, at her side. In turn, her artistic production is the focus of the girl's gaze, thus further suggesting tutelage and its implied level of achievement as well as intersubjective agency between generations of women. Perhaps this young woman, peer to the daughters arranging roses with their mother in figure 4.15, will aspire to a career in fashion illustration or some other form of skilled, compensated work inspired by possibilities created within the community of women.

We might be tempted to see a similar self-referentiality in a miniature painted by Héloïse in the 1850s, depicting a fair-haired baby girl rather improbably leafing through an album of watercolors (figure 4.20). Though large for a miniature, it is nonetheless an exquisitely detailed piece, measuring 9 by 7.5 centimeters, and painted on ivory with watercolor and gouache, a typical technique for miniature paintings.[121] Above the child's left hand, faintly emanating from the foliage on the rounded edge of the painting—Héloïse has signed her work, hiding in plain sight her creative gesture. Her sister Anaïs's third child, Isabelle, who ably and prolifically followed in her mother's and aunt's footsteps—even if the obituary published to commemorate Anaïs's death ignored her existence—was born in 1850. Might this miniature, also self-referential with its incorporation of the watercolor album, reminiscent of the "amateur" works of the young Colin sisters, represent the female family tradition of artistry inculcated by Isabelle's grandmother, Joséphine, the aspiration to art that was indeed fulfilled in Isabelle?

Feminized Commodities, Female Communities

In 1879, five years after the death of Héloïse Leloir but still twenty years before the death of Anaïs Toudouze in 1899, Anaïs's son, Gustave Toudouze, published a novel entitled *Madame Lambelle*, based on his mother's life, marked as it was by the tragic death of her husband Gabriel. Dedicated to the memory of Gustave's "cher père," who had died suddenly of cerebral apoplexy in 1854 at the age of forty-three, and to his "bien-aimée mère," the book was praised by a sentimental Gustave Flaubert, just months before his own death, for its sensitivity and attention to the details of the artistic milieu: "It is clear that you love your mother—this is deeply felt. Keep her for as long as possible. I envy you!" (figure 4.21).[122] Toudouze, writing to a friend after his novel had been awarded a prize from the Académie Française, explains that *Madame Lambelle* is very much his mother's life story: "All the

Figure 4.21 *Portrait d'Anaïs Toudouze*, anon. n.d., Bibliothèque nationale de France.

characters exist, I know them, I see them often and love them. I changed only the names, the professions and the circumstances in which the events occurred, and only a little; it is thus a sincere work, lived and suffered."[123] In the fictionalized world recreated by Gustave Toudouze, his two siblings do not exist, his father, an architect, is recast as a self-sacrificing doctor who dies in the service of a patient, Héloïse Leloir is long dead and barely mentioned, and his mother, Anaïs, or "Jeanne Lambelle," whose passion for art was nourished in the heart of her artistic family, is forced to turn to a commercial occupation to support her family as a widow of little means.

While the novel is mostly concerned with plot twists and character development and portrays Jeanne as a venerated, self-abnegating, idealized mother, it also offers, perhaps unintentionally, revelatory insights into what must have been a shocking turn of events for a young artist who, recently married, was collaborating with her architect husband and producing Salon-quality art as well as working commercially for fashion magazines. Like Anaïs, Jeanne was full of artistic ambition, "having always lived since childhood in an artists' milieu … under the intelligent direction of her father, she quickly acquired a great talent," and, the author continues, "her watercolors were beginning to be noticed": she had won a third-place medal at the Salon.[124] The death of her husband derails her artistic path, and, like her model Anaïs, Jeanne sells the family home in l'Haÿ-les-Roses in the southern suburbs of Paris, moves back to the city, and concentrates on earning a living. In the family papers, written by a grateful Gustave, we read that with her husband's death and three children to raise on scant resources, Anaïs had to "renounce exhibitions and those works that could have given some glory to her name"; she never ceased "to work up until practically her final hour, painting watercolors in 1898–9, bought by some Austrians."[125] However, unlike Anaïs, who focused her artistic attentions more fully on the commercial fashion illustration she had always been practicing in addition to her other art work, the fictional Jeanne purchases a fashion business and becomes a "modiste-couturière" on the rue Saint-Honoré. The novelist presents this career move as an unfortunate, even tragic, step down: "She would be a merchant, she, who, like most artists, had a profound, unconscious horror of commerce. A seamstress-*modiste* and menial laborer, she scratched her name forever from the book of artists, with a simple and great abnegation."[126]

Although the author-son leans into his mother's sacrifice of the artistic for the commercial, repeating a cultural bias that is undercut by Anaïs's and Héloïse's fashion watercolors, a close reading of his novel reveals that, thanks to her hard work, Jeanne grows her small establishment into a bustling and successful *atelier* and shop and that she channels her artistic talent for design and painting to produce the trendiest new fashions. Although the fictional Jeanne feels her heart constrict every year at the opening of the Paris Salon, the novel presents us, perhaps in spite of itself, with a successful businesswoman who had the perspicacity to transfer her skills in a most modern fashion. Never fully comfortable with the commercial world she inhabits, the fictionalized Anaïs Toudouze nevertheless manages to make her name there and achieve professional success. Gustave Toudouze, son and nephew of the Colin sisters, likely did not intend with this biographical novel to plead the case of bourgeois women achieving commercial artistic success, but the novel obliquely illustrates precisely this.

The Colin sisters likewise may not have intended to achieve name-recognition or establish professional careers through fashion-plate art, but they adapted to the circumstances of their historical moment, and in the early flourishing of the French fashion industry their work sheds light on women's shifting trajectories in the nineteenth century. Through their subtle interruptions of the visual vocabulary of the fashion plate, images such as those I have examined here offer commentaries on fashion, leisure, or women's roles that are slightly at odds with the explicit commercial aim of the print. Perhaps they even propose a widening of options, predicated on female community, within the apparently static and unyielding code of the fashion plate and, in this sense, offer a counterpoint to the standard presentation of the idealized woman. Contesting the limits placed upon their own professional ambitions, the Colin sisters engaged in the production of desire, visual and material, and not only deployed their painterly skills for maximum effect, channeling their talent into a lucrative market, but also explored, reproduced, and exploited the circuit of desire of consumer culture best expressed in fashion's endless cycle. Less leisured than their imagined subjects, or presumably their purchasing public, these female artists who produced fashion plates were actively involved in commerce. By projecting scenes of female sociability, their illustrations end up both representing female relationships and reproducing them in their viewership, which had reached more than a million women by 1899, the year of Anaïs Colin's death.[127]

The bourgeois ladies of leisure pictured in fashion plates were decidedly not mirror images of the Colin sisters, who worked all their lives. Given the rate of production and the volume of plates they produced, it is hard to imagine that the Colin sisters had much leisure time for garden parties, visits, or crocheting. Unlike the idealized women of the plates, who traverse the modern city in the company of equally respectable companions, always wearing the appropriate garment and accessory for the outing or event being showcased, the Colin sisters would have busily crisscrossed Paris from home to shop, shop to studio, studio to lithographer's, and even to the press. Commercial fashion-plate art, like fashion journalism and the needle trades, was a sanctioned way for women to move about the city and work, and in this regard, fashion illustration, and the fashion system more broadly, opened pathways to professionalization for women that their institutionalized exclusion from the world of high art prohibited. They would thus have been well acquainted with the many layers of mostly invisible labor attending the production of fashion; indeed, they participated in that layered process. They would also have been in regular communication with shop owners, dressmakers, and milliners about how best to market goods and also with fashion writers, who offered lengthy explanations to accompany their plates. Theirs was a professional, social, and spatial mobility, for they were bourgeois women working in the urban center of the fashion industry.

The exquisite fantasy of the fashion plate elides the intense and accelerated labor of its own production. This fantasy, grounded in bourgeois values of leisure, also relegates the finely detailed work of small, dexterous hands required for both needlework and fashion illustration or miniatures to a female pastime, even as it relies on both for its reproduction through fashion. The hours spent sketching, the detailed notes indicating color and fabric, the composition work and expert watercoloring—are all sublimated into the final printed and reproduced image: the fashion plate, widely disseminated, gazed upon, collected, and cherished. Like the products it advertises, the commodity hides the labor required to create it; but for the fact that—trained artists that they were—

the Colin sisters signed their work, they might also be consigned to the invisibility and anonymity of the many *petites mains* of the fashion industry, and because of their specific context, their plates also carry traces of their family history of art.

In the fashion plates produced by the Colin sisters, commodity and community coexist in a distinctly feminized form of cultural production. Paradoxically, its status as a commodity also allows the fashion plate, like the products it advertises, to function as a screen hiding the labor of its creation, also enacted in large part by communities of women. It is a screen at once for projection—of desires, aspirations, and relationships—and a screen for concealing. The fashion plate is thus a key visual document not only for understanding women's place and role in nineteenth-century French culture and its cultural production, but also for grasping how women's work was hidden behind a cultural fantasy of the feminine. Ironically, the spectacularization of one community of women—bourgeois, leisured, idealized—fed a narrative that rendered invisible other communities of women—those working behind the scenes to make the very commodities on display. This was an effacement of female labor endemic to the nineteenth-century fashion industry. Nevertheless, the Colin sisters, in seeming defiance of this effacement, boldly claimed their artistic agency in their early self-portrait and reiterated it consistently by signing their work. Through their stealthy artistic interventions within the commercial print, the sisters shrewdly painted their way to professional careers and left traces of their artistic gifts, along with their occasional subtle challenges to the limits of their gender, in the "minor genre" of the fashion plate, an invaluable catalyst of both consumer desire and employment for hosts of women to come.

Epilogue: Midinettes *in Motion*

Figure 5.1 Grey, "Monoplan de Course pour Midinettes," c. 1900 [carte postale], Bibliothèque Marguerite Durand, Paris.

The woman pictured in this early twentieth-century postcard (figure 5.1), flying high above a French countryside, is at once fashion creator, fashion disseminator, and fashion icon. Soaring over this landscape dotted with villages and trees, the smartly dressed *midinette* steers her monoplane as she smiles triumphantly out at the viewer, her hat ribbons, scarf, and lacy petticoat flapping behind her, signaling both her mobility and velocity. Although the image certainly reproduces the familiar visual rhetoric of the *modiste* and her many alluring sisters, we can also see in it a new version of Gavarni's fleeing *trottin* (figure 2.10), who seems to have come into her own in this fantasy of female ascendancy, talent, and momentum. With her dainty hands on the wheel, this *midinette* has a new agency that recalls a *modiste* at the helm of her workshop. Mistress of her modern machine, loaded up with hatboxes for deliveries far and wide, she embodies both fashion production and fashion consumption. In her wake, she leaves a clownish old suitor who is attempting to steer his own outdated biplane with levers rather than a wheel, his mouth lasciviously agape and his cramped body seemingly frozen in the frustration of his inability to keep up.[1] However, he will certainly never catch her, for he will remain in the nineteenth century as she zooms into the twentieth! This, at least, is the narrative the image promises.

Printed in the first decade of the twentieth century, the postcard undeniably reproduces many clichés of the century it claims to be leaving behind, yet the image also attests to the new visibility and, indeed, modernity of working women, especially those in the fashion industry at the turn of the century. The medium upon which it appears—a postcard—itself conveys this modernity, as postcards were, after all, among the popular fruits of new technologies, whose immediacy and legibility, coupled with their mass reproducibility and circulation, made them powerful modes of visual communication.[2] The topicality of the medium is echoed in the postcard's title, "Monoplan de course pour Midinettes" ("Monoplane for the race of the *midinettes*"), which links new forms of transport to a recent event, the *course des midinettes* (race of the *midinettes*). Organized by the journal *Le Monde sportif* in 1903, the race was a competitive twelve-kilometer walk from the Jardin des Tuileries to Nanterre featuring the "young, joyous, fresh" fashion workers of Paris.[3] As the illustration from *Le Petit Journal* suggests (figure 5.2), the event quickly devolved into chaos, as many more women turned up than anticipated for the race, and male "onlookers became so unruly in their pursuit of the racing garment workers that the police had to intervene."[4] For all of its apparent celebration of the woman fashion worker, the representation of the race of the *midinettes* merely repeated the familiar trope that had for decades been attached to many working women—that their visible presence in the street signified an invitation to an erotic encounter and often elicited social disorder.

In contrast, the postcard reimagines the plight of the racing *midinettes*, and indeed the plight of the victimized woman fashion worker more generally, in a technological dream of speed, skill, and success. While the image serves as an allegorical fantasy, I linger on it because, for all its absurdity, this flying *modiste* captures the central paradoxes I have explored in this book: the ubiquity of women working in fashion even as their labor was cloaked in erotic tropes, good housekeeping tips, or pretty pictures of dresses; the economic necessity of women's labor to the foundation and growth of the French fashion industry even as that labor hid in plain sight; the unprecedented circulation and dissemination of texts and images promoting fashion, and ultimately of garments themselves, even as the processes of their construction remained concealed. In short, the gendering of fashion work veiled its own identity as work.

Figure 5.2 *"La Course des Midinettes,"* Le Petit Journal. Supplément du dimanche, *November 8, 1903, Bibliothèque nationale de France (RetroNews).*

Fashion indisputably continues to exploit workers, mostly women, and today, as before, as Dana Thomas elucidates in her study of contemporary fast fashion, "Because pay is egregiously low, workers are forced to find less reputable ways to make ends meet."[5] *Plus ça change, plus c'est la même chose.* Yet while this exploitation was certainly a tragic reality for many in nineteenth-century France, fashion could also provide a means through which some women could convert the skills they had been perfecting in the home for centuries—decorative or utilitarian sewing, tasteful and economical homemaking, miniature painting celebrating family—into paid employment.

It was not until the *midinette* strike of 1917, when the seamstresses of the Jenny fashion house took to the streets to protest unfair working hours and low pay, that the women fashion workers of Paris would become a visible presence on the street in ways other than as eroticized playthings.[6] Ironically, however, the strike—which rewarded the seamstresses with a pay increase and a reduction in working hours—succeeded in part because of the workers' own skill at harnessing both an eroticizing mythology and the benign feminized qualities generally attributed to women working in fashion. Like the strategies I explored in preceding chapters that allowed women entrepreneurs, journalists, and painters to achieve the freedom to escape the exaggerated femininity much of their labor encouraged, here again *fashion* itself provided cover for activities that might otherwise be deemed threatening. While the strike was termed *la grève joyeuse* and, according to reports and images, featured neatly dressed *midinettes* smiling and singing in the streets, their demands were serious and eventually paved the way for more equitable work conditions for women across all sectors.[7]

By peering behind the seams of fashion's glamorous garments, we find that in nineteenth-century France, fashion work was the principal pathway for both working and middle-class women to enter the workforce, replacing certain service or agricultural jobs, prostitution, and even marriage as legitimate occupations for women, and opening doorways to entrepreneurship, the professional worlds of publication and the graphic arts, as well as other commercial and office work. Fluent in the same mythologies that had kept them in their place, the *modistes, chroniqueuses,* and *dessinatrices de mode* also deployed their skills—with needle, pen, and brush—to shape the French fashion economy and to change women's work. They did so not by ripping the seams but by subtly cutting "along" the bias, we might say, anticipating on a grand scale fashion designer's Madeleine Vionnet's innovative bias-cut, which gave women a certain freedom of movement by eliminating unnecessary seams.[8] Working both with and against the bias, the "little hands" of the nineteenth century produced complex networks among women and created new silhouettes that would empower them as they moved into the twentieth.

Notes

Introduction

1 Honoré de Balzac, "The Proper Woman," in *Popular Literature from Nineteenth-Century France: English Translation*, trans. and ed. Masha Belenky and Anne O'Neil-Henry (New York: MLA of America, 2021), 164. The text, "La Femme comme il faut," was first published in 1840 as part of the vast luxury volume *Les Français peints par eux-mêmes* and was subsequently published in 1842 as part of a short novel entitled *Autre Étude de femme*, in which Balzac places these comments in the mouth of his recurring narrator, the journalist Émile Blondet.

2 Balzac, "The Proper Woman," 168.

3 Susan Hiner, *Accessories to Modernity: Fashion and the Feminine in Nineteenth-Century France* (Philadelphia: University of Pennsylvania Press, 2010).

4 Key exceptions exist, of course. In the scholarly field of nineteenth-century French women's labor, the classic historical studies remain: Louise A. Tilly and Joan W. Scott, *Women, Work, and Family* (New York: Holt, Rinehart and Winston, 1978); Joan W. Scott, *Gender and the Politics of History* (1988; New York: Columbia University Press, 2018); and Judith G. Coffin, *The Politics of Women's Work: The Paris Garment Trades, 1750–1915* (Princeton, NJ: Princeton University Press, 2014). More recent studies include Maria Tamboukou, *Gendering the Memory of Work: Women Workers' Narratives* (Abingdon, UK: Routledge, 2016) and Patricia A. Tilburg, *Working Girls: Sex, Taste, and Reform in the Parisian Garment Trades, 1880–1919* (Oxford: Oxford University Press, 2019).

5 It is important to distinguish between the *couturière* (seamstress or dressmaker), which designated a strictly female profession with its own guild, established in 1675, and the *couturier*, a male high-fashion designer, who entered the professional sphere in the mid-nineteenth century, most notably in the person of Charles Frederick Worth. The word *couture* meant sewing long before it was associated with high fashion, and a *couture* is also a seam or a stitch.

6 See Clare Haru Crowston, *Fabricating Women: The Seamstresses of Old Regime France, 1675–1791* (Durham, NC: Duke University Press, 2001).

7 The term "panoramic literature" was coined by Walter Benjamin in *The Arcades Project* to refer to the proliferation of urban literature from the 1830s and 1840s that encompassed "physiologies" of social types and guidebooks such as the one referred to in the epigraph. Walter Benjamin, *The Arcades Project* (Cambridge, MA: Harvard University Press, 1999), 5. See Aimée Boutin, "Rethinking the Flâneur: Flânerie and the Senses," *Dix-Neuf: Journal of the Society of Dix-Neuviémistes* 16, no. 2 (2012): 127.

8 On the *grisette*, see especially Alain Lescart, *Splendeurs et misères de la grisette: Évolution d'une figure emblématique* (Paris: Champion, 2008); Jennifer Jones, *Sexing La Mode* (Oxford: Berg, 2004); Nathalie Preiss and Claire Scamaroni, *Elle coud, elle court, la grisette!* (Paris: Paris Musées, 2011); and Tilburg, *Working Girls*.

9   See Marni Reva Kessler, *Sheer Presence: The Veil in Manet's Paris* (Minneapolis: University of Minnesota Press, 2006) for a rich analysis of both the object and the metaphor of the veil in nineteenth-century France. My use of this metaphor also builds on historian Béatrice Craig's use of the term "discursive veil" in her *Female Enterprise behind the Discursive Veil in Nineteenth-Century Northern France* (London: Palgrave Macmillan, 2017).

10 I will use the standard term "fashion plate" to refer to these images. The fashion plate differs from the watercolor illustrations that the Colin sisters and others produced, which were transformed through the engraving or lithography process (hence the use of the term plate) into reproduced and colored prints. See April Calahan, *Fashion Plates: 150 Years of Style*, ed. Karen Trivette Cannell (New Haven: Yale University Press, 2015), 1.

11 Marie-Ève Thérenty, *Femmes de presse, femmes de lettres: De Delphine Girardin à Florence Aubenas* (Paris: CNRS, 2019), 40.

12 Jillian Lerner, *Graphic Culture: Illustration and Artistic Enterprise in Paris, 1830–1848* (Montreal: McGill-Queen's University Press, 2018). See especially ch. 4.

13 Alexandre Colin (1798–1875) studied with Girodet and was a close friend of Delacroix. He achieved professional success as a history painter in the Romantic tradition and served as director of the École de Dessin de Nîmes from 1834 to 1838. His son from his second marriage, Paul-Alfred Colin (1838–1916), became a landscape painter.

14 See especially Françoise Tétart-Vittu, "Who Creates Fashion?" in *Impressionism, Fashion, and Modernity*, ed. Gloria Groom (New Haven: Yale University Press, 2012); and André Dombrowski, *Cézanne, Murder, and Modern Life* (Berkeley: University of California Press, 2012).

15 Working-class women working in textile and other factories did not benefit from the strategies deployed by these women, but many working-class women working in small *ateliers*, in publishing houses, or in the world of print and art reproduction did find increased forms of employment. Some, like Coco Chanel (1873–1971) and Madeleine Vionnet (1876–1975), who both began as impoverished apprentices to seamstresses, rose to the top of their fields. See Rhonda K. Garelick, *Mademoiselle: Coco Chanel and the Pulse of History* (New York: Random House, 2014); and Mary Lynn Stewart, *Dressing Modern Frenchwomen: Marketing Haute Couture, 1919–1939* (Baltimore: Johns Hopkins University Press, 2008). Likewise, the *midinettes* of Paris in the Belle Époque and the colorists of the fashion-plate industry, who with the advent of cinema became colorists for the early film industry, often chose, through opportunities in fashion, forms of employment that were alternatives to domestic work or to marriage and a life spent in the provinces.

16 For the cultural history of the *catherinette*, see the work of Anne Monjaret, especially *La Sainte-Catherine: Culture festive dans l'entreprise* (Paris: CTHS, 1997).

17 On the history of the figure of the *midinette*, see especially Tilburg, *Working Girls*. See also Maude Bass-Krueger, "From the '*union parfaite*' to the '*union brisée*': The French Couture Industry and the *midinettes* during the Great War," *Costume* 47, no. 1 (Jan. 2013): 28–44.

Chapter 1

1   Antoine Fontaney, "Un Magasin des modes: Histoire d'une capote," *Paris, ou Le Livre des cent-et-un*, 1; accessed July 5, 2022, http://www.bmlisieux.com/curiosa/fontan01.htm. Antoine Fontaney (1803–37) was a "diplomat, writer, poet, and journalist who signed his name as either 'Lord Feeling' or 'O'Donnoz,' and wrote for various magazines, notably *La Revue des deux mondes*." *Le Bouquin de la mode*, ed. Olivier Saillard (Paris: Laffont, 2019),

964. This story was reprinted in 1852 by Edmond Texier, editor of the renowned weekly *L'Illustration,* in his *Tableau de Paris,* with no mention of its authorship. The fact that this *atelier* tale remained a credibly realistic portrayal of the work of the *modiste* attests to the unchanging nature of perceptions of this work environment. Portions of the present discussion were first developed in an earlier essay. See Susan Hiner, "Fashion Animation: Heads, Hats, and the Uncanny Work of Fashion," in *Fashion, Modernity, and Materiality in France: From Rousseau to Art Deco,* ed. Heidi Brevik-Zender (Albany: SUNY Press, 2018). A note on vocabulary: in French, *bonnet* refers to a soft cloth head-covering, often lacy, that is worn indoors—the equivalent, in English, of a "mobcap." A "bonnet" in English is a firmer headpiece, with a structure and embellishments. On the other hand, the *capote* was the most popular form of outdoor hat for European and American women for most of the nineteenth century. Its wide brim, or hood, protected the eyes and allowed for decorative flourishes, and it was attached with ribbon ties, or *brides,* under the chin.

2   For a discussion and contextualization of so-called panoramic literature, see Belenky and O'Neil-Henry, introduction to *Popular Literature from Nineteenth-Century France: English Translation,* xxiii–xxiv. See also 17n7.

3   Marx first used the term "fetishism" in an essay of 1842, but did not use the expression "commodity fetish" until *Das Kapital,* published in 1867. Karl Marx, "The Fetishism of Commodities and the Secret Thereof," in *The Marx-Engels Reader,* ed. Robert C. Tucker, 2nd ed. (New York: W. W. Norton, 1978). See also Alfonso Maurizio Iacono, "Marx's Theory of Fetishism," ch. 4 in *The History and Theory of Fetishism,* trans. and ed. Viktoria Tchernichova and Monica Boria (Houndmills, U.K.: Palgrave Macmillan, 2016). Fontaney's narrator describes the hats in the shop window in a way that personifies them: "As soon as they are finished, they are taken down to the store below, which has a shop on the street; then they are exhibited in the window display, placed on top of long mahogany poles, which resemble fairly closely, wearing these hats, certain Englishwomen of our counties, who arrive in Paris around the month of October." Fontaney, "Histoire d'une capote," 2. It is critical to note that Fontaney uses Marx's key descriptor "magical" to describe the commodity. I would like to be clear that while the present work is certainly informed by Marxist scholarship, I situate my intervention as a work of interdisciplinary cultural studies.

4   Ibid., 3.

5   Ibid.

6   In theory, any of the fashion workers in the *atelier* could be elevated to the rank of *première* through talent and seniority. These workers could, presumably, eventually take the place of the *maîtresse* and thus enter the *petite-bourgeoisie.* In this sense, then, the profession of *modiste* offered a distinct pathway towards upward social mobility, and for this reason among others, *modistes* were considered the "aristocracy" of fashion workers. See Crowston, *Fabricating Women.*

7   Fontaney, "Histoire d'une capote," 4.

8   This is of course a rhetorical question, since the phrase "women have always worked" is used to rebut the notion that domestic work and other forms of unremunerated labor associated with women are not actually "work." It was adopted by Kessler-Harris as the title of her analysis of American working-class women, first published in 1981. Alice Kessler-Harris, *Women Have Always Worked: A Concise History,* 2nd ed. (Urbana: University of Illinois Press, 2018). It is also the title (in French) of Sylvie Schweitzer's exploration of working women in nineteenth- and twentieth-century France, focusing mainly on working-class women. Unlike Kessler-Harris, Schweitzer does begin to consider middle-class women as well. Sylvie Schweitzer, *Les Femmes ont toujours travaillé: Une Histoire de leurs métiers, XIXe et XXe siècle* (Paris: Odile Jacob, 2002). Anna Bellavitis pursues these questions in her *Women's Work and Rights in Early Modern Europe* (Cham, Switzerland: Palgrave Macmillan, 2018).

9   See Craig, *Female Enterprise.*

10 See Schweitzer, *Les Femmes ont toujours travaillé*; and Craig, *Female Enterprise*, among others, for the legal restrictions on married women in nineteenth-century France.

11 On the figure of the *grisette*, the generic term for a working girl, particularly in the fashion sector, see especially Lescart, *Splendeurs et misères de la grisette*; Preiss and Scamaroni, *Elle coud, elle court, la grisette!* and Tilburg, *Working Girls*, 16–58. For a treatment of this topic in the art of the latter third of the nineteenth century, see especially Hollis Clayson, "Suspicious Professions," ch. 4 in *Painted Love: Prostitution in French Art of the Impressionist Era* (New Haven: Yale University Press, 1991).

12 Among many others, the most wide-ranging and influential studies of women's work in nineteenth-century France, paving the way for subsequent studies, are Tilly and Scott, *Women, Work and Family*; and Coffin, *The Politics of Women's Work*.

13 Hence, my suggestion that Fontaney, in a move that presages Marx, appears to disenchant the commodity; we shall see, however, that Fontaney's text quickly re-enchants it. Marx, "Fetishism of Commodities," 319.

14 The key passage from Marx is the following: "A commodity is therefore a mysterious thing, simply because in it the social character of men's labour appears to them as an objective character stamped upon the product of that labour; because the relation of the producers to the sum total of their own labour is presented to them as a social relation, existing not between themselves, but between the products of their labour. This is the reason why the products of labour become commodities, social things whose qualities are at the same time perceptible and imperceptible by the senses." Marx, "Fetishism of Commodities," 320–1. Of course, Marx was interested in the commodity under industrialization and was describing the factory setting. He also paid little attention to women workers, other than to acknowledge and lament their commodification.

15 Andrew Smith, *The Ghost Story 1840–1920: A Cultural History* (Manchester: Manchester University Press, 2010), 11.

16 Roland Barthes, *Système de la mode* (Paris: Éditions du Seuil, 1967). For Barthes, the fashion system is foremost, like language, a system of signs. His study establishes the abstraction of fashion, but later interpretations have understood it as a "concept that embraces not only the business of fashion but also the art and craft of fashion, and not only production but also consumption." J. S. Major and Valerie Steele, "Fashion industry," *Encyclopedia Britannica*, August 21, 2022, https://www.britannica.com/art/fashion-industry.

17 Craig, *Female Enterprise*.

18 One important exception, studied by Tamboukou, is the autodidact seamstress Jeanne Bouvier, who left not only a memoir, but also a social history of the industry of the *lingère* (needleworker/linen maker). Tamboukou's work on the working-class women of Paris, in particular, seamstresses, is a key resource for any study of French working women. My work is primarily concerned with bourgeois women and those who, like many *modistes*, strove to enter the middle classes through work that they sometimes concealed as such. See Tamboukou, *Gendering the Memory of Work*; and Jeanne Bouvier, Daniel Armogathe, and Maïté Albistur, *Mes Mémoires: ou, 59 années d'activité industrielle, sociale et intellectuelle d'une ouvrière: 1876–1935* (Paris: La Découverte/Maspero, 1983). See also Jeanne Bouvier, *La Lingerie et les lingères* (Paris: Gaston Doin, 1928).

19 See Tamboukou, *Gendering the Memory of Work,* 16, 32–3, where the author builds on Janet Zandy's idea of "class amnesia."

20 Hazel V. Carby, foreword to *Silencing the Past: Power and the Production of History* by Michel-Rolph Trouillot, rev. ed. (New York: Beacon Press, 2015), xiii. Saidiya Hartman similarly addresses the historian's challenge in the context of Black women at the turn of the twentieth century, writing: "Every historian of the multitude, the dispossessed, the subaltern, and the enslaved is forced to grapple with the power and authority of the archive and the limits it sets on what can be known, whose perspective matters, and who is endowed with the gravity and

authority of historical actor." Saidiya Hartman, *Wayward Lives, Beautiful Experiments: Intimate Histories of Riotous Black Girls, Troublesome Women, and Queer Radicals* (New York: W. W. Norton, 2019), xv. Likewise, in a nineteenth-century Francophone context, Robin Mitchell's *Vénus Noire: Black Women and Colonial Fantasies in Nineteenth-Century France* (Athens: University of Georgia Press, 2020) confronts a missing history by reading "the document[s] and interpret[ing] the silences" (xv). Craig's intervention into the women entrepreneurs of Northern France in her *Female Enterprise* is another such attempt to offer a more complete analysis of the historical record. Gary Cohen, author of the foreword to Julie M. Johnson's *The Memory Factory: The Forgotten Women Artists of Vienna 1900* (West Lafayette, IN: Purdue University Press, 2012) writes that Johnson's work reveals "vividly how the gender politics of producing art criticism and eventually writing art history worked to denigrate the work of the women artists and eventually to erase much of their contributions from memory" (xvii).

21 Arlette Farge, *Vies oubliées, au cœur du xviiie siècle* (Paris: La Découverte, 2019), 7–12.

22 Two examples are telling in this instance. While researching this book, I looked in vain for a text mentioned by Tamboukou, an autobiographical study of the lives of *modistes* listed in the same series as Bouvier's work on *lingères*. This work, supposedly written by a former *modiste* named Marguerite Boural, and entitled "Fleurs, Plumes, Modes," presumably appeared in Georges Renard's series "La Bibliothèque sociale des métiers." But despite the help of research librarians, no trace of the book could be found. Perhaps its publication was only projected. See Tamboukou, *Gendering the Memory of Work*, 46. There is the additional problem of false autobiographies, such as the tantalizingly titled *Mémoires d'une modiste écrits par elle-même* (1866), a lurid tale of seduction and romance that repeats many of the tropes of the mythology surrounding this figure but offers little in the way of actual memoir. *Mémoires d'une modiste écrits par elle-même* (Paris: F. Cournol, 1866), accessed July 10, 2022, https://gallica.bnf.fr/ark:/12148/bpt6k5838886h.

23 Craig's analysis (2017) focuses on the bourgeois women of northern France in the late nineteenth century. She asserts that there was a generalized resistance to acknowledging that bourgeois and elite women sometimes worked for money. Craig nuances the argument made by Bonnie Smith in her influential *Ladies of the Leisure Class: The Bourgeoises of Northern France in the Nineteenth Century* (Princeton, NJ: Princeton University Press, 1981). Craig pushes back on the driving presupposition of Smith's argument, the separate spheres ideology, and mines different archives for findings that reveal that bourgeois women were more deeply implicated in business than previously understood. I am not using the term "discursive veil" in precisely the same way Craig does, however, as she is interested in applying the notion to historiography. I am interested in the discursive veils created by literary and other texts of popular culture, and the visual culture (representational veils) that supplemented and reinforced those discourses.

24 Craig, *Female Enterprise*, 207.

25 Ibid., 17.

26 Ibid., 210.

27 Tilburg, *Working Girls*, 5. *Midinette* was the term given to the large number of trendy Parisian female fashion workers of the Belle Époque. Focusing on this era, Tilburg asserts that the *midinettes* were the descendants of the *grisette*, the generalized term for working-class women fashion workers earlier in the century. *Modistes* were key figures in the broad landscape of women fashion workers in nineteenth-century France, particularly well known for their ability to straddle working- and middle-class experience.

28 At the beginning of Coffin's comprehensive study of nineteenth-century women's work, she writes, "Even the driest technical or economic studies seemed compelled to address larger social and gender issues, drawing lessons about female labor and poverty, pronouncing on women's fitness for work in industry and their duties as guardians of the hearth, and speculating about the origins and future of the gender division of labor." *Politics of Women's Work*, 3.

29 There is a substantial body of scholarly work on this topic. See especially Leonore Davidoff and Catherine Hall, *Family Fortunes: Men and Women of the English Middle Class, 1780–1850*, 2nd ed. (Abingdon, UK: Routledge, 2002); Wendelin Guentner, ed., *Women Art Critics in Nineteenth-Century France: Vanishing Acts* (Newark: University of Delaware Press, 2013); Monica F. Cohen, *Professional Domesticity in the Victorian Novel: Women, Work and Home* (Cambridge: Cambridge University Press, 1998); Linda K. Kerber, *Toward an Intellectual History of Women: Essays* (Chapel Hill: University of North Carolina Press, 1997); Ellen Bayuk Rosenman and Claudia C. Klaver, eds., *Other Mothers: Beyond the Maternal Ideal* (Columbus: Ohio State University, 2008); Dorothy O. Helly and Susan M. Reverby, eds., *Gendered Domains: Rethinking Public and Private in Women's History* (Ithaca, NY: Cornell University Press, 1992); Kirstin Ringelberg, *Redefining Gender in American Impressionist Studio Paintings: Work Place/Domestic Space* (Farnham, UK: Ashgate, 2010); and Kirstin Ringelberg, "The Court of Lilacs, the Studio of Roses, the Garden at Réveillon: Madeleine Lemaire's Empire of Flowers," *Marcel Proust Aujourd'hui* 14 (2018): 178–88.

30 See especially James F. McMillan, *France and Women, 1789–1914: Gender, Society, and Politics* (London: Routledge, 2000).

31 Ibid., 43.

32 We know, of course, that many of them did work, but this reality does not loosen the grip exerted by the ideology, both at the time and in subsequent understandings of the period. That very ideology helped hide the reality of work. See Craig, *Female Enterprise*.

33 Louis-Marie Lanté (1789–1871), was an illustrator and lithographer; Achille Devéria was an illustrator, lithographer, and director of the Bibliothèque Nationale's *département des estampes*; Numa (Pierre Numa-Bassaget, 1840–85) was an illustrator and caricaturist; and Paul Gavarni (Sulpice Guillaume Chevalier, 1804–66) was one of the most celebrated illustrators and lithographers of the Romantic period through the July Monarchy, known especially for his satirical work for *Le Charivari*. See Lerner, *Graphic Culture*; especially chs. 4 and 5. See also H. Hazel Hahn, *Scenes of Parisian Modernity: Culture and Consumption in the Nineteenth Century* (New York: Palgrave Macmillan, 2009).

34 See especially Kessler, *Sheer Presence*. See also Claire d'Harcourt, *Les Habits: Histoire des choses* (Paris: Éditions du Seuil, 2001), 62; and Susan Hiner, "The *Modiste*'s Palette and the Artist's Hat," in *Degas, Impressionism, and the Paris Millinery Trade*, ed. Simon Kelly and Esther Bell (San Francisco: Fine Arts Museums/Legion of Honor, 2017).

35 See ch. 1, n. 1 above.

36 Hats provide a particularly eloquent example of Thorstein Veblen's classic theory of "conspicuous consumption." See Thorstein Veblen, *Conspicuous Consumption* (New York: Penguin Books, 2006).

37 See Tilly and Scott, *Women, Work and Family*.

38 Coffin, *Politics of Women's Work*. See also Scott, *Gender and the Politics of History*.

39 Jules Simon, preface to *L'Ouvrière*, 6th ed. (Paris: Hachette, 1867), 4–5. Also quoted in Coffin, *Politics of Women's Work*, 69. Scott also analyzes Simon's work in detail, and explains that his book was the culmination of decades of debate on the problem of women working. Scott, *Gender and the Politics of History*; see especially ch. 7.

40 Scott explains this slippage as, among other things, one of terminology. "In the regime of the policing of prostitution, *femmes isolées* referred to clandestine prostitutes who were not registered . . . In 1848, *femmes isolées* denoted women wage-earners (usually seamstresses or dressmakers), living alone in furnished rooms where they sewed garments at piece rates for the ready-made clothing trades. The fact that the term was the same was not coincidental. Ever since Parent-Duchâtelet's massive inquiry into prostitution in 1836 it was generally recognized

that casual prostitutes came from the ranks of working girls." Scott, *Gender and the Politics of History,* 142. In her analysis of contemporary sources, Scott emphasizes that the principal concern was with single women living and working alone in urban centers like Paris. She explains that *ateliers* were viewed as more orderly and thus acceptable workspaces for women. But as we shall see in ch. 2, the iconography of the *atelier* often repeated the tropes of sexual license associated with the *femme isolée*.

41 L.-Charles Desmaisons, *"Tu seras ouvrière," simple histoire: Livre de lecture courante à l'usage des écoles de filles* (Paris: A. Colin, 1892), accessed July 11, 2022, https://gallica.bnf.fr/ark:/12148/bpt6k3149840.

42 Ibid., viii.

43 The story echoes that of Zola's fictional department store employee, Denise Baudu, heroine of his *Au Bonheur des Dames* (1883). Like Jeanne, Denise is rewarded for her hard work and uncompromising morality with both marriage and business success, and with children on the horizon, she has discovered the so-called formula for "having it all." In both cases, the fictional stories that end with a married woman entrepreneur reflect a reality for a certain configuration that permitted married women to work. For both Denise and Jeanne were business partners with their husbands, and thus by default, had his permission to work. See Craig, *Female Enterprise*; Tilly and Scott, *Women, Work and Family*.

44 Craig writes, "Lower- and middle-class widows and single women were most often free agents, working towards their own goals. They emerge from the sources as entrepreneurs in their own right, and we find them doing business like men—when not doing 'men's business.' The economic expansion engendered by industrialization and urbanization created opportunities for women." *Female Enterprise*, 153.

45 Ibid., 161.

46 Schweitzer suggests as much, explaining: "Without a husband, the mature woman and the childless widow are the most independent. But, while nineteenth-century law is based on the free will of the individual, married women are in a position of total subordination to their husbands." *Les Femmes ont toujours travaillé*, 18. Further, on the relative autonomy of single women and childless widows vis à vis married women: "Single women and widows without children manage their fortune and their income, including that of work. For the married woman, the husband's authorization is obligatory to accept an inheritance, make a gift *inter vivos*, acquire, sell or mortgage property and, in any case, to take legal action" (20). "All of these arrangements obviously make us pause to reflect on the high rate of celibacy among women, especially those who work" (20).

47 It is important to note that the writer who was divorced, J. J., born to an aristocratic family based in the region of the Loiret, did so before 1816, when divorce was outlawed. It would not be reinstated until 1884. See Schweitzer, *Les Femmes ont toujours travaillé*.

48 Desmaisons, *"Tu seras ouvrière,"* 56.

49 Ibid., iii.

50 Ibid., 50.

51 Ibid., 185–6.

52 Ibid., 236.

53 The possession of a cashmere shawl indicated a respectable marriage, or the promise of marriage, so we may assume that this *ex-modiste* is hoping to be well on her way to a suitable marriage, if she is not already there. See Hiner, *Accessories to Modernity*; especially ch. 3. It is also notable that the officer's helmet is festooned with a large feather, as is his lady-friend's hat. In an 1855 account of Parisian feather workers, we learn that "Feather making, done in bulk by twenty companies and by some fifty home workers, is subdivided into two branches: fine feathers

for fashion and tufted pieces for military officers." "Paris illustré" (Paris: Hachette, 1855), quoted in Saillard, *Le Bouquin de la mode*, 1032.

54 Helen Chenut explains that in the garment-making industry, "manual tasks were assigned to women who became known as 'petites mains.'" Helen Harden Chenut, *The Fabric of Gender: Working-Class Culture in Third Republic France* (University Park: Pennsylvania State University Press, 2005), 176. As couture houses developed, the somewhat dismissive term continued to be used even as these female workers gained visibility and importance. Today their couture handiwork is sometimes recognized as highly skilled, although the original notion of *petites mains* persists in the sweatshop sector.

55 Fontaney, "Histoire d'une capote," 6.

56 Ibid.

57 Ibid.

58 These, too, would have been produced by specialist artisans—*fleuristes* and *fabricants de rubans*—often women. See *Artisans de l'élégance*, exhibition catalogue (Paris: Réunion des musées nationaux, 1993); and Alison Matthews-David, *Fashion Victims: The Dangers of Dress Past and Present* (London: Bloomsbury Visual Arts, 2015).

59 Fontaney, "Histoire d'une capote," 9.

60 Ibid. The *poupées*, or dolls, refer to the empty cardboard head-forms, also called *marottes*, that *modistes* used to simulate ladies' heads while fabricating hats. For more on the *marotte*, see Hiner, "Fashion Animation."

61 Fontaney, "Histoire d'une capote," 12.

62 Ibid, 14.

63 Ibid., 3.

64 The *calicot*, a term applied in the first quarter of the century to foppish salesclerks, usually working in drapers' shops (hence *calicot,* from the cloth), was typified by certain physical characteristics: bushy sideburns and large spurs. The figure was popularized and caricatured in vaudeville theater and in print culture of the period and was usually cast as the suitor of a fashion worker such as a *modiste*. Fontaney's passing description of the *première*'s companion calls to mind this figure and thus conjures a narrative of social climbing. See Susan Hiner, "Monsieur Calicot: French Masculinity between Commerce and Honor," *West 86th* 19, no. 1 (2012): 32–60.

65 Indeed, as Tilburg and others have pointed out, unlike the Victorian seamstress, who was a "figure of pure tragedy," in the French tradition, while similar "melodramatic danger" is certainly present, "the female garment worker's sexuality also was heralded as part of the aesthetic and physical pleasure of Paris, and crucial to the French cultural and industrial *patrimoine*, even as she was perceived as vulnerable in many of the same ways as her laboring sisters in London and New York." *Working Girls*, 3.

66 Fontaney, "Histoire d'une capote," 9.

67 Smith, *Ghost Story 1840–1920*, 11.

68 See Veblen, *Conspicuous Consumption*. On this subject, see also Philippe Perrot, *Fashioning the Bourgeoisie: A History of Clothing in the Nineteenth Century* (Princeton, NJ: Princeton University Press, 1994); Barbara Vinken, *Fashion Zeitgeist: Trends and Cycles in the Fashion System*, trans. Mark Hewson (Oxford: Berg, 2005); Valerie Steele, *Paris Fashion: A Cultural History* (New York: Oxford University Press, 1988); and Hiner, *Accessories to Modernity*.

69 Eliane Bolomier, *Le Chapeau: Grand art et savoir-faire* (Paris: Somogy, 1996), 70; Florence Müller and Lydia Kamitsis, *Les Chapeaux: Une Histoire de tête* (Paris: Syros Alternative, 1993), 36. I have discussed elsewhere the

importance of the notion of "seamlessness" to the construction of proper bourgeois femininity with respect to fashion more broadly. See Hiner, *Accessories to Modernity*; and "The *Modiste*'s Palette."

70 Desmaisons, "*Tu seras ouvrière*," 182. This text was published in 1892, six decades after Fontaney's imagined *atelier* scene, but the labor of the *modiste*, as well as the highly hierarchized ecosystem of the *atelier*, persisted throughout the nineteenth century. *Modistes*, unlike most fashion workers, had opportunities for social advancement: they occupied a liminal social space, but their potential entry into the middle class depended more on their talent and interest in work than on their skill in seducing potential bourgeois husbands.

71 As Matthews-David documents about the dangers faced by flower-makers, for example, "the scale and nature of professional flower-making exposed workers who assembled craft kits and dusted foliage to potentially lethal quantities of arsenic." *Fashion Victims*, 92. See also *Artisans de l'élégance*.

72 The claiming of authorship and creative autonomy is an important counterpoint to the story of invisible female labor.

73 See P. Bourdieu and Y. Delsaut, "Le Couturier et sa griffe: Contribution à une théorie de la magie," *Actes de la Recherche en Sciences Sociales* 1 (1975): 7–36.

74 Katherine Withy, *Heidegger on Being Uncanny* (Cambridge, MA: Harvard University Press, 2015), 19.

75 See Dana Thomas, *Fashionopolis: The Price of Fast Fashion and the Future of Clothes* (London: Head of Zeus, 2019); and Susan B. Kaiser, *Fashion and Cultural Studies* (Oxford: Berg, 2012; London: Bloomsbury Academic, 2013). Today's fast fashion dehumanizes sweatshop workers, rendering them both anonymous and substitutable; likewise, shoppers of fast fashion are equally replaceable to the corporate companies that "serve" them. The seeds for this familiar structure were sown in the nineteenth century.

76 For a fascinating history of the *mannequin* or fashion model and its connection to the "mannequin" or inanimate dummy, see Caroline Evans, *The Mechanical Smile: Modernism and the First Fashion Shows in France and America, 1900–1929* (New Haven: Yale University Press, 2013). See also Jane Munro, *Mannequin d'artiste, mannequin fétiche*, exhibition catalogue (Paris: Paris Musées, 2015).

77 See Valerie Steele, "Paris, 'Capital of Fashion,'" ch. 1 in *Paris, Capital of Fashion*, ed. Valerie Steele (London: Bloomsbury Visual Arts, 2019).

78 Sharon Marcus, "Reflections on Victorian Fashion Plates," *differences: A Journal of Feminist Cultural Studies*, 14:3 (2005), 14.

79 *Paris Fashion* details the conventions of fashion-plate illustration within which fashion-plate artists like the Colin sisters worked. Such conventions include the typical number of figures (two to three) per plate, a standard distance between figures allowing for garments and accessories to be as fully visible as possible and poses showcasing the silhouette and novel elements of dress. Figures are typically shown in domestic interiors or engaging in leisure activities outside. Steele, "Fashioning the *Parisienne*," (2017), 100–2; she also offers pertinent biographical information about the Colin sisters. See also Anne Higonnet, *Berthe Morisot's Images of Women* (Cambridge, MA: Harvard University Press, 1992), 96–9.

80 Doris Langley Moore, *Fashion through Fashion Plates, 1770–1970* (New York: Clarkson N. Potter, 1971), 10; Calahan, *Fashion Plates*, 1.

81 See Kate Nelson Best, *The History of Fashion Journalism* (London: Bloomsbury Academic, 2017); Annemarie Kleinert, *Le "Journal des dames et des modes", ou, La Conquête de l'Europe féminin, 1797–1839* (Stuttgart: Jan Thorbecke Verlag, 2001); and Évelyne Sullerot, *La Presse féminine*, 2nd ed. (Paris: A. Colin, 1966). See ch. 3.

82 In many library collections the colored images (fashion plates) of fashion journals have been removed.

83 Marie Bonin, "Les Sœurs Colin: Héloïse et Anaïs, femmes artistes dans la seconde moitié du XIXe siècle" (master's thesis, Université de Paris-Sorbonne, 2013), 80. This unpublished master's thesis is the only full-length study of the Colin sisters, to my knowledge.

84 For more on the practice of embellished plates, which was a practice that predated the nineteenth century, see Alice Dolan, "An Adorned Print: Print Culture, Female Leisure and the Dissemination of Fashion in France and England, around 1660–1779," *V&A Online Journal*, no. 3, (Spring 2011), accessed August 27, 2022, http://www.vam.ac.uk/content/journals/research-journal/issue-03/an-adorned-print-print-culture,-female-leisure-and-the-dissemination-of-fashion-in-france-and-england,-c.-1660-1779/; John L. Nevinson, "Origin and Early History of the Fashion Plate," *United States National Museum Bulletin*, 250, paper 60 (Washington, DC: Smithsonian Institution Press, 1967): 67–92; Kathryn Norberg and Sandra L. Rosenbaum, eds. *Fashion Prints in the Age of Louis XIV: Interpreting the Art of Elegance*, Costume Society of America Series (Lubbock, TX: Texas Tech University Press, 2014); Lise Schreier, "Setting the Tone: Commodified Black Children and Slave Imagery in the Eighteenth- and Nineteenth-Century French Fashion Press," *H-France Salon*, Volume 14, Issue 8, no. 6 (2022); https://h-france.net/Salon/SalonVol14no08.6.Schreier.pdf, accessed November 15, 2022.

85 Marie de l'Epinay, "Modes," *La Sylphide* (December 5, 1840), 3; accessed August 21, 2022, https://gallica.bnf.fr/ark:/12148/bpt6k6144375j/f20.item.

86 Calahan, *Fashion Plates*, 6.

87 For a curated collection of Emmeline Raymond's curious "Renseignements" column, discussed below in ch. 3, see Fabienne Yvert, *L'Endiguement des renseignements* (Bouches-du-Rhône: Attila, 2012).

88 In Raymond's "Renseignements," we find many queries from Paris and the provinces, and from many distant locations, such as St Petersburg, Algiers, Valladolid, Palermo, Vienna, Warsaw, Alexandria, and Baltimore—to name but a few.

89 One of Tilburg's principal arguments regarding Belle Époque *midinettes* is that they harnessed their endearingly frivolous, sexy media image in order to make more palatable their demands regarding work rights, pay, and hours. Because Tilburg focuses on the last two decades of the nineteenth century, she locates the political engagement of the *midinette* as a strategy that manipulates the nostalgia industry around the earlier figure of the *grisette*. I argue that, earlier in the century, before nostalgia converted the picturesque *grisette* into a rhetorical tool of labor activists, some of these figures, in particular, *modistes*, were already aware of the power of their image and used it to penetrate the new capitalist economy.

90 Tilburg explores how the *midinette* manipulated the very mythology that presented her as an eroticized object to enhance the value of her products and carve out a professional living in an environment resistant to working women.

Chapter 2

1 Garien, "La Modiste—Air: De la grisette," in *La Gaudriole de 1835: Recueil des meilleures chansons* […], ed. Béranger, Désaugiers, Debraux […] (Paris, 1835); accessed July 21, 2022, http://catalogue.bnf.fr/ark:/12148/cb334003140.

2 Portions of this discussion appear in Hiner, "The *Modiste*'s Palette."

3 See Lipton's groundbreaking study of the representation of the milliner as well as other women workers in nineteenth-century France. Speaking of frequent subjects for nineteenth-century illustration, she asserts:

"Unbeknownst to later, twentieth-century eyes, the milliner was considered a 'tart' and the naked woman with the basin, a prostitute." Eunice Lipton, *Looking into Degas: Uneasy Images of Women and Modern Life* (Berkeley: University of California Press, 1986), 152.

4   See Preiss and Scamaroni, *Elle coud, elle court, la grisette!*

5   Daniel Roche analyzes a similar print from Diderot's *Encyclopédie* in *The Culture of Clothing: Dress and Fashion in the Ancien Régime*, trans. Jean Birrell (Cambridge: Cambridge University Press, 1994), 320.

6   See Hollis Clayson, *Painted Love*; and Ruth E. Iskin, *Modern Women and Parisian Consumer Culture in Impressionist Painting* (Cambridge: Cambridge University Press, 2007). I wish to acknowledge here the important scholarship of feminist art historians who have worked on the representation of women, most notably, Norma Broude, Carol Duncan, Beatrice Farwell, Mary Garrard, Abigail Solomon-Godeau, Linda Nochlin, and Griselda Pollock, among others.

7   The grisette is understood here as a fashion worker of loose morals and a stock character of nineteenth-century literature and visual culture. See Ernest Desprez, "Les Grisettes à Paris," in *Paris, ou le livre des cent-et-un* (Paris: Librairie Ladvocat, 1832), 211–37 and Jules Janin, "La Grisette," in *Les Français peints par eux-mêmes: Encyclopédie morale du XIXe siècle*, ed. Pierre Bouttier (1840–42; repr., Paris: Omnibus, 2003), 1: 35–44; see also Denise Z. Davidson, "Making Society 'Legible'" People-Watching in Paris after the Revolution," *French Historical Studies* 28, no 2 (Spring 2005): 265–96. Jones, *Sexing* La Mode; Lescart, *Splendeurs et misères de la grisette*; and Preiss and Scaramoni, *Elle coud, elle court, la grisette!* See also ch. 1, nn. 11, 27, 92.

8   Illustrations of the *lever* and the *coucher* of female fashion workers were plentiful in nineteenth-century popular visual culture. Milliners, *lingères* (linen maids), and dressmakers, and more generically *les ouvrières en mode* (female fashion workers) had been portrayed in such voyeuristic scenes since the eighteenth century. The Maciet collection of the Bibliothèque des arts décoratifs in Paris contains numerous examples of prints in this genre. For a partial list of prints of the eighteenth century, see Gustave Bourcard, *Les Estampes du XVIIIe siècle* (Paris, 1885).

9   "It was not at all uncommon to find visibly upper-class men visiting and lounging in *ateliers* in which specifically feminine activities like dress- and hat-making were taking place, as both nineteenth-century prints and early twentieth-century plays (such as Alfred Desfossez's *Les Midinettes* of 1904 or Artus's *Les Midinettes*) show. We also know, for example, that Manet and Mallarmé passed many an afternoon in couturier salons with Méry Laurent." Lipton, *Looking into Degas*, 213n7.

10 Writing about the profession in the latter part of the nineteenth century, Lipton says, "There were three categories of milliners: apprentices, finishers, and trimmers. All three, according to Benoist, were privileged workers, and the most fortunate could ultimately go into partnership with the owner of a shop." Ibid., 160.

11 See Clayson, *Painted Love*.

12 Roland Barthes, *Mythologies,* trans. Annette Lavers (New York: Hill and Wang, 1972), 11.

13 The association between needleworkers and prostitutes has been well established in nineteenth-century France. Parent-Duchâtelet specifically calls out the needle-trades and blames insufficient salaries for working women's descent into prostitution. See also Rachel G. Fuchs, *Poor and Pregnant in Paris: Strategies for Survival in the Nineteenth Century* (New Brunswick, NJ: Rutgers University Press, 1992); Victoria Thompson, *The Virtuous Marketplace: Women and Men, Money and Politics in Paris, 1830–1870* (Baltimore: Johns Hopkins University Press, 2000). See also Bouvier, Armogathe, and Albistur, *Mes Mémoires*.

14 See Jean-Marie Querard, *Les Supercheries littéraires dévoilées*: *Galerie des auteurs apocryphes, supposes . . . de la littérature française pendant les quatre derniers siècles (etc.)*, vol. 1 (Paris: L'Éditeur, 1847), https://www.google.com/books/edition/Les_supercheries_litteraires_devoilees_G/OuxOAAAAcAAJ. The entry for Maria d'Anspach

indicates that her name is the pseudonym for "Miss Julie Bordier, formerly a *modiste*, now Mrs. Delacroix" (1:48). She was the author of three entries in the volume *Les Français peints par eux-mêmes*, and of several other works of fiction.

15 Maria d'Anspach, "La Modiste," in *Les Français peints par eux-mêmes*, 3: 110; accessed August 28, 2022, https://gallica.bnf.fr/ark:/12148/bpt6k2079830. The 1866 "autobiographical" work entitled *Mémoires d'une modiste*, most likely a false autobiography, written by a certain "Gabrielle," expresses the lure of the *métier* of *modiste* for young girls of little means: "When they begin to work in a shop, it is rare that girls are not overcome with an ardent love for their profession, some because it raises them up, and born for humble housework, they prefer spending their days fiddling with ribbons and lace, others like me, because the profession doesn't lower them too much and has an aura of the luxury to which they aspire" (14). While Gabrielle's portrayal of the typical *modiste* is sympathetic, her story is nonetheless one of moral lapse, and the social-commercial space of the *atelier* is instrumental to her demise. It is impossible to know to what extent this "mémoire" is authentic and not fictional.

16 D'Anspach, "La Modiste," 3:107.

17 Thompson's *Virtuous Marketplace* offers a thorough historical overview of the evolution of the elision between *ouvrière* and prostitute; she places the onset at mid-century, arguing that the *grisette* had incarnated self-sufficiency prior to 1848, and that her work was not threatening.

18 See Alain Corbin, *Les Filles de noce: Misère sexuelle et prostitution (19ᵉ et 20ᵉ siècles)* (Paris: Flammarion, 2015).

19 "She was endowed by her myth with a precarious, unstable, and possibly venal sexuality that, according to the legend, equipped her with an unstable purchase on her own subjectivity." Clayson, *Painted Love*, 131. Clayson's analysis, as well as fellow art historian Ruth Iskin's later intervention, nuances the reception and application of the myth of the *modiste* in paintings of the 1870s and 1880s. Clayson acknowledges that "the low pay and unstable conditions of the garment industry and domestic service, which were the trades of most poor women in Paris, caused many to turn to prostitution" (116), and she convincingly argues that the popular 1870s–1880s visual representation of the milliner works to separate cause from effect: the *modiste* is either impoverished or sexy, never both at once. In Impressionist paintings of the same period, however, the *modiste* and her workspace are ambiguous. According to Clayson, this ambiguity does not challenge the myth but, rather, is the result of its internalization—or naturalization: that is, by this time, the *modiste*'s sexual instability was so commonly presumed that it no longer needed to be overtly signaled. She was "an ideal example of the commodified, modern lower-class woman, and thus an ideal trope of modernity . . . supposed to sell hats to women, she allegedly sold herself to men" (131).

20 See Nicole Le Maux, *Histoire du chapeau féminin* (Paris: Charles Massin, 2000).

21 Contributions to scholarship on French *vaudeville* theater include Lise Schreier, *Gens de couleur dans trois vaudevilles du XIXᵉ siècle* (Paris: L'Harmattan, 2017); and Jennifer Terni, "A Genre for Early Mass Culture: French Vaudeville and the City, 1830–1848," *Theatre Journal* 58, no. 2 (2006): 221–48. See also Henry Gidel, *Le Vaudeville* (Paris: Presses universitaires de France, 1986) for an earlier study of the genre. Vaudeville theater's ephemeral nature links it clearly to fashion.

22 The *fait divers* is a sensationalized news story. The genre gained in popularity during the nineteenth century, often involving crime and/or violence.

23 Crowston explains, "One hundred years after their guild was established, with only limited rights to clothe women in competition with the tailors, the seamstresses had succeeded in eliminating men from the production of made-to-measure female clothing." *Fabricating Women,* 66.

24 See Colette Cosnier, *Le Silence des filles: De L'Aiguille à la plume* (Paris: Fayard, 2001).

25 Crowston, *Fabricating Women*, 67.

26 As Jones rightly points out, ultimately, the artist would be gendered male: "If for a brief moment in the eighteenth century it was possible for a woman like Rose Bertin to climb up from her humble origins to reign as queen of fashion, new gendered hierarchies of skill and genius would crown men like Charles-Frédéric Worth emperor of *la mode* in the nineteenth century." Jones, *Sexing* La Mode, 103.

27 The evolution of the term "modiste" is instructive. In French, *modiste* signified a worker who did much more than fashion hats, whereas in English, "milliner" was the term for hatmaker. By the nineteenth century, the purview of the French *modiste* was becoming more limited (to hat-making). This is why the word *modiste* and milliner can become interchangeable. Jones writes: "The confusion over the origins of the *marchandes de modes* is telling. These women, who became the principal fashion merchants of their day, had risen, so to speak, from within the cracks in the corporate system." Ibid., 95. See also Roche, *Culture of Clothing*; and Crowston, *Fabricating Women*.

28 Roche uses the terms *marchandes de modes* and *modistes* interchangeably, although he acknowledges that the latter term entered the lexicon only in the nineteenth century. "Central to the speeding up in clothing consumption . . . the *modiste* incarnated both the frivolous manners of the last days of the *ancien régime* and the new dynamism of a luxury economy based on the professional skills of its artisans and the more rapid change to manners and things." *Culture of Clothing*, 307. See also Kimberly Chrisman-Campbell, *Fashion Victims: Dress at the Court of Louis XVI and Marie-Antoinette* (New Haven: Yale University Press, 2015).

29 Georg Simmel famously articulated this paradoxical structure of fashion in his essay "On Fashion," *International Quarterly* 10 (1904), 130–55; accessed August 20, 2022, http://www.modetheorie.de/fileadmin/Texte/s/Simmel-Fashion_1904.pdf.

30 Roche, *Culture of Clothing*, 309.

31 Artifice was of course also a key identifying feature of prostitutes. As Nead has pointed out in her analysis of the visual culture surrounding prostitution in Victorian Britain: "Sexual ideologies defined the prostitute as an unnatural woman and this was reflected in her physical condition: Surface decoration, showy pattern, elaborate textures, jewellery, cosmetics—all these elements connoted that the prostitute had transgressed the laws of God, nature, and respectable society." Lynda Nead, *Myths of Sexuality: Representations of Women in Victorian Britain* (New York: Basil Blackwell, 1988), 175.

32 Carol Rifelj confirms: "By 1827, the word *modiste* referred in particular to those who made and designed hats and other head coverings for women. When journalists wrote about 'modes,' they might be referring either to fashion in general or just to millinery. Hats were an indispensable category in a woman's vestimentary repertoire." Carol Rifelj, *Coiffures: Hair in Nineteenth-Century French Literature and Culture* (Newark: University of Delaware Press, 2010), 67. A successful *modiste*, however, might still be engaged in fashion design/styling more broadly and would also have been a skilled seamstress.

33 According to Rifelj, they were "thought to have loose morals or even to engage in clandestine prostitution to supplement their miserable wages," even more so than the *grisettes*, the larger group of female garment workers with whom they were associated. Ibid., 71. Rifelj also clarifies that, by 1827, the term *modiste* referred exclusively to hat-maker, or milliner. See 256n65. See also Roche, *Culture of Clothing*. "The 'modistes'—the word only appeared with its final meaning in nineteenth-century dictionaries—emerged at a point where the needs of court society in this sphere had become more demanding. They were not directly involved in the manufacture of articles, which continued to be made by other bodies of artisans such as the ribbon-weavers, trimmings-makers (*passementiers*), braiders, linen-drapers, dressmakers and tailors, but they embellished them, and it was this further process which developed into a veritable industry" (307).

34 *Agaçante* is the feminine form of *agaçant*, an adjective that normally follows the noun it modifies, but which, in the feminine form, can precede it. The *Dictionnaire de l'Académie française* (1835) defines the adjective as something like "provocative" and links it to the eyes: "AGAÇANT, ANTE. adj. Qui agace, qui excite. *Des regards, des propos agaçants. Des manières agaçantes. Une fille agaçante.*" Dictionnaire de l'Académie française, 6th ed. (1835); accessed August 28, 2022, https://www.dictionnaire-academie.fr/article/A6A0561.

35 "In a general fashion, and almost throughout Europe, yellow is a color more or less closely associated with all those who find themselves on the margins of the social order. That was the case with the mentally ill, sometimes dressed in yellow camisoles or tunics, like the fools and clowns of medieval iconography . . . That was the case again with prostitutes, who were certainly not still required in the nineteenth century to wear an item of brightly colored clothing to distinguish themselves from honest women, but who, in big cities, willingly donned yellow clothing, hats, ribbons, or gold-colored accessories in order to be spotted by possible clients in the dim light of street lamps . . . it was quite often a yellow shawl, imitating those worn in the winter by upper-middle-class women." Michel Pastoureau, *Yellow: The History of a Color*, trans. Jody Gladding (Princeton, NJ: Princeton University Press, 2019), 189–90.

36 See Carl Goldstein, *Print Culture in Early Modern France: Abraham Bosse and the Purposes of Print* (New York: Cambridge University Press, 2012). See also Susan Hiner, "Picturing Work," in *A Cultural History of Work in the Age of Empire*, ed. Victoria E. Thompson (London: Bloomsbury Academic, 2020).

37 See Lerner, *Graphic Culture*, for a discussion of the most prolific male graphic artists of nineteenth-century France, particularly during the July Monarchy (1830–48).

38 Again, the color yellow seems significant as it was the color associated with cuckoldry. See Pastoureau, *Yellow*. In a vaudeville song about the *modiste*, analyzed below, the *modiste* sings that she'll create white crowns for the wedding day and yellow hats for the day after. The significance of yellow in this print may well be to solidify the man's (rather than the woman's) infidelity, which is already insinuated in his gaze.

39 Abigail Solomon-Godeau, "The Other Side of Venus: The Visual Economy of Feminine Display," in *The Sex of Things: Gender and Consumption in Historical Perspective*, ed. Victoria de Grazia (Berkeley: University of California Press, 1996), 113.

40 The caption of this caricature reads: "Let me introduce my friend, Jules Fremichon . . . he's the life of the party in Chaumont!" which translates to "Je vous présente mon ami, Jules Frémichon . . . il est le boule [*sic*] en train de la ville . . . de Chaumont!" The word should be *boute*. My thanks to Lise Schreier for pointing this out. *Boute-en-train* refers to an excitable male animal used to detect when a female was in heat. The crude sexual overtones are thus obvious.

41 Michelle Sapori, *Rose Bertin: Ministre des modes de Marie-Antoinette* (Paris: Éd. de l'Inst. Français de la Mode, 2003), 63.

42 Anne Higonnet, "Real Fashion: Clothes Unmake the Working Woman," in *Spectacles of Realism: Gender, Body, Genre*, eds. Margaret Cohen and Christopher Prendergast (Minneapolis: University of Minnesota, 1995), 145.

43 The *coiffe à la Titus*, sported by most of the women in this image, was prevalent enough to authorize women going hatless. It was a hairstyle particularly popular in the first decade of the nineteenth century. See Rifelj, *Coiffures*.

44 See Higonnet, "Real Fashion." Higonnet asserts that these types of images, fabricated "before 1820 did not gender labor" (147). Later, however, "once out on the streets, women workers became the sexual objects of a middle-class masculine gaze. Images of laundresses, milliners, and seamstresses proliferated during the Restoration and July Monarchy, precisely because the fact that these tradeswomen did not actually make or sell anything on the street allowed interpretation of their presence there the scope of fantasy" (147). This dating is perhaps not entirely accurate, as the print I am analyzing dates from before 1820 and is highly eroticized. See also Vincent Milliot, *Les*

"Cris de Paris," ou Le Peuple travesti: Les Représentations des petits métiers parisiens (XVIe –XVIIIe siècles) (Paris: Éditions de la Sorbonne, 2014).

45 See Lerner, *Graphic Culture*.

46 The *trottin* would typically be the lowest on the totem pole of the hierarchy in a *modiste*'s shop. She would learn the trade in the *atelier*.

47 I am grateful to Kalbryn McLean for offering this incisive analysis of the voyeur's presence.

48 The theme of tricking the mistress (often constructed as an antagonist) for a night out with a boyfriend is common in theatrical representations of the *modiste*. In the *Mémoires d'une modiste* (1866), the protagonist Gabrielle lies to her *maîtresse* after spending a night out with a suitor (28).

49 For a more complete discussion of the *marotte* in relation to the *modiste*, see Hiner, "Fashion Animation."

50 This print is one of a series featuring foldable "doors and windows," which, when opened, reveal pornographic scenes. Marie-Françoise Quignard and Raymond Josué Seckel, eds., *L'Enfer de la bibliothèque: Éros au secret* (Paris: Bibliothèque nationale de France, 2007), 234. See also Patricia Mainardi, *Husbands, Wives, and Lovers: Marriage and Its Discontents in Nineteenth-Century France* (New Haven: Yale University Press, 2003) for insightful discussions of pornographic imagery.

51 It is remarkable how often the grammar and poses of nineteenth-century fashion plates were repeated in nineteenth-century pornographic prints; clothing was essential to both.

52 Terni writes, "The rise of spectacle thus helped to blur the boundaries between different orders of urban space, as theaters, shops, dance halls, and restaurants began to seem more like each other—thereby overshadowing any local and historical associations they may once have carried." Terni, "Genre for Early Mass Culture," 232.

53 Bouvier, Armogathe, and Albistur, *Mes mémoires*, 92. In addition to a long career as a worker in the garment trades, Bouvier also became an amateur historian and author as well as a union activist.

54 Schreier has articulated the immense value of vaudeville as primary source material in that it most often represents real events and packages this information for a popular audience. See also Masha Belenky, *Engine of Modernity: The Omnibus and Urban Culture in Nineteenth-Century Paris* (Manchester: Manchester University Press, 2019).

55 For the present work, I have studied approximately twenty such plays and located many more on the BnF Gallica site; selected titles may be found in my bibliography. See Mary Gluck, *Popular Bohemia: Modernism and Urban Culture in Nineteenth-Century Paris* (Cambridge, Mass: Harvard University Press, 2005).

56 In addition to the reference cited earlier from Jeanne Bouvier, in the *Mémoires d'une modiste* (1866), Gabrielle's "autobiography" frequently mentions evenings at the Gymnase or the Ambigu, two prominent vaudeville theatres, indicating the regularity of vaudeville theater as a common pastime for *modistes*. *Mémoires d'une modiste*, 23.

57 Gidel marvels at the exclusion of vaudeville from formal academic analysis, given its wide influence and popularity. *Le Vaudeville*, 3–5. Gluck and Terni have resituated the analysis of vaudeville in social and historical criticism rather than literary analysis. Recent interventions by Schreier and Belenky, as well as O'Neil-Henry and Belenky's anthology of popular nineteenth-century French literature, which includes a vaudeville play, and the digitization of many vaudeville plays on Gallica, have made this genre more accessible to scholars. See also my "Fashion Animation" for analysis of some vaudeville plays featuring *modistes*. As with nineteenth-century print culture surrounding *modistes*, which was voluminous, I also selected plays representing key repeated elements of a mythology that spanned the century. My examples are largely from the first half of the century; print and vaudeville theater continued to reinforce the image/myth into the second half of the century.

58 It is tempting to see a connection here to the "cris de Paris," made popular by Sébastien Mercier in the eighteenth century in his *Tableau de Paris*. Gidel also explains an etymology anterior to the *voix de villes*, attributing the origin of vaudeville to "vau-de-Vire," or the "vallée de la Vire," a place name in Normandy where the first of these songs supposedly emerged. *Le Vaudeville*, 7–13.

59 Garien, "La Modiste—Air: De la grisette."

60 Terni, "Genre for Early Mass Culture," 237.

61 Desmaisons's primer from the *fin de siècle*, discussed in chapter 1, tells a similar moralizing tale.

62 Valory and Cogniard frères, *La Révolte des modistes: Vaudeville en 3 actes* (Paris: Vollet, 1834), I: vii, 15.

63 This prefigures the *midinette* strike of the early twentieth century. See Tilburg, *Working Girls*.

64 Eugène Labiche, *Un Chapeau de paille d'Italie*, ed. Olivier Balazuc and Stavroula Kefallonitis (Paris: Larousse, 2000), II: i, 84.

65 Ibid., II: i, 87.

66 Like most vaudeville plays, this one's plot is complex. A *modiste* marries her ne'er-do-well boyfriend, with whom she had clandestinely had a baby; her father disapproves. Her friend, Aphanasie, the main protagonist of the play and *première modiste* of the shop where they work, tries to help her by concealing a baby's layette in a hatbox, which is transported by her ignorant *trottin*, Loriot, about town. At one point the baby itself is concealed in the box. Eventually, all is resolved and Aphanasie is rewarded for her smarts and generosity by learning that she will inherit the shop of Madame Batavia, who turns out to be her long-lost mother. Loriot, who is secretly in love with Aphanasie, discovers that he will inherit his former boss's tailor's shop and will be rich: he can now marry Aphanasie.

67 M. Clairville, *Le Trottin de la modiste: Vaudeville en deux acte*s (n.p., 1848), I: viii, 15; accessed August 28, 2022, https://gallica.bnf.fr/ark:/12148/bpt6k9809217h.

68 See Schreier, *Gens de couleur dans trois vaudevilles*. Although the news item is dated sixteen years after the performance of the play, its tragic plot was commonplace, given the lack of social support for unwed poor mothers in nineteenth-century Paris. See also Fuchs, *Poor and Pregnant*. On the *fait divers*, see Roland Barthes, "Structure du fait divers," in *Essais critiques* (Paris: Seuil, 1964); Michelle Perrot, "Fait divers et histoire au XIXe siècle," in *Annales: Economies, sociétés, civilisations* 38 no. 4, 1983, 911–19; Sylvie Dion, "Fait Divers (Human Interest Stories) as a Narrative Genre," *Sociocriticism* 7, no. 2 (1992), 79–88; Lionel Gossman, "Anecdote and History," *History and Theory* 42, no. 2 (2003): 143–68; and Dominique Jullien, "Anecdotes, *Faits Divers*, and the Literary," *SubStance* 38, no. 1 (2009): 66–76.

69 *Le Petit Journal* (November 12, 1866); accessed August 28, 2022, https://gallica.bnf.fr/ark:/12148/bpt6k589462g/f2.item. This incident anticipates Zola's recounting in his 1882 novel *Pot-Bouille*, the unfortunate destiny of the infant of the anonymous *piqueuse de bottines*, who ends up dead in a "bonnet box." See Sara Phenix, "*Le Corset Expérimental*: Fashion, Fertility, and Fiction in Zola's *Pot-Bouille* and *Au Bonheur des dames*." *Dix-Neuf*, 2022, vol. 26, no. 4, 243–62.

70 Gossman, "Anecdote and History," 168.

71 See Saillard, *Le Bouquin de la mode*, 1021–33.

72 Before the 1860s, Michelle Perrot tells us, *faits divers* were mostly an oral affair, or sensational anecdotes published on single sheets as *canards*. It was with the founding of *Le Petit Journal* in 1863, that the term *fait divers* came into popular usage and was given a prominent place in the daily paper. Perrot, "Fait divers et histoire au XIXe siècle," 912. For a historical overview of the *fait divers*, see also Sylvie Dion, "*Fait Divers* (Human Interest Stories) as a

Narrative Genre." For this study, I consulted items from newspapers available on Gallica's digitized news site, Retronews. Titles include those focused on judicial news, such as *Le Droit* and *Le Constitutionnel*, political papers such as *Le Journal des débats, La République française* and *La Gazette nationale*, and more general interest papers like *Le Figaro, Le Siècle*, and *Le Petit Journal*.

73 The examples proliferate in a wide range of newspapers and across the century. These examples are a sampling from one year, 1852, from the daily paper covering mostly political and legal news, *Le Journal des débats* (March 4, 1852, July 20, 21, 22, 1852), accessed on Gallica.

74 Perrot, "Fait divers et histoire au XIXe siècle," 914.

75 *Le Figaro* (November 14, 1869), 3; via Retronews.

76 *L'Echo de l'arrondissement de Bar sur Aube* (August 24, 1899), 3; via Retronews.

77 Ibid.

78 *La Liberté* (September 29, 1876), 3; via Retronews.

79 *Le Parti ouvrier* (December 20, 1889), 3; via Retronews.

80 *Le Petit Moniteur* (June 3, 1893), 3; via Retronews.

81 In her *Mémoires*, Bouvier describes the young female workers sharing her apartment floor in the lean days of her career, who, out of distress and hopelessness, "descended" to the street, either literally, by throwing themselves from windows, or figuratively, by turning to prostitution.

82 See ibid.

83 *La République française* (April 26, 1889), 3; via Retronews.

84 *Le Siècle* (January 6, 1857), 3; via Retronews.

85 Perrot, "Fait divers et histoire au XIXe siècle," 915. *Canard* is a term used to describe what we would call today "fake news"; see Jean-Yves Chevalier, "La mare aux canards," *Médium* 3–4, no. 52–3 (2017): 149–57.

86 *Gazette nationale ou le moniteur universel* (August 12, 1868), 4; via Retronews.

87 *Le Droit* (April 10, 1863), 3; via Retronews.

88 Ibid.

89 I discovered thousands of such records from 1800 to 1899 in the bankruptcy files spanning the city, housed at the City of Paris Archives at the Mairie des Lilas. These records are organized in the catalogue of "Actes des Faillites" by profession (*modiste*) and by year. Most records contain legal documents, and some contain inventories, which offer a glimpse into the lives of these working women.

90 "Gobley Dossier," 1854, inventory no. 11,437, Archives de Paris.

91 https://data.bnf.fr/fr/12215239/maison_d_education_de_la_legion_d_honneur_saint-denis__seine-saint-denis/.

92 See Desbordes dossier, 1873, inventory no. 17074, Archives de Paris.

93 "Literary Milliners." I borrow this phrase from Marie-Ève Thérenty, *Femmes de presse, femmes de lettres*, 41. She is citing, in turn, Jacques Sydra, writing a short story in *Messidor: Information du monde entire*, dir. Gérault-Richard (April 29, 1907), and using a term that was no doubt in common usage to refer to women fashion writers; accessed August 28, 2022, https://gallica.bnf.fr/ark:/12148/bpt6k7643636k/f5.item.r="modistes des lettres".

Chapter 3

1. Gustave Flaubert, *Madame Bovary: Mœurs de province*, vol. 1 (Paris: Michel Lévy frères, 1858), 83; accessed August 29, 2022, https://gallica.bnf.fr/ark:/12148/bpt6k1518572b. In his history of the *presse féminine*, Vincent Soulier repeats the observation that Emma Bovary's fate was the result of her reading habits, and in particular, "la presse féminine de modes et de frivolités" and concludes his remarks with this well-known passage from Flaubert's novel. Vincent Soulier, *Presse féminine: La Puissance frivole* (Paris: L'Archipel, 2008), 146.

2. As H. Hazel Hahn has detailed, by the time of the July Monarchy (1830–48), "Fashion columns—much of which were paid advertisements—promoted shops, dressmakers, manufacturers and specific streets, and Paris as the fashion capital." Hahn, *Scenes of Parisian Modernity*, 63. See especially chapter 3. Although the scholarship devoted to the fashion press of the nineteenth century in France is not extensive, there are several key texts that deserve note alongside Hahn's. See, in particular, Annemarie Kleinert, *Le "Journal des dames et des modes"*; Évelyne Sullerot, *La Presse féminine*; Dean de la Motte and Jeannene M. Przyblyski, *Making the News: Modernity and the Mass Press in Nineteenth-Century France* (Amherst: University of Massachusetts Press, 1999); Rosemonde Sanson, "La Presse féminine," in *La Civilisation du journal: Histoire culturelle et littéraire de la presse française au dix-neuvième siècle*, eds. Dominique Kalifa, Philippe Régnier, Marie-Ève Thérenty, Alain Vaillant (Paris: Nouveau Monde, 2011); and Kate Nelson Best, *History of Fashion Journalism* (London: Bloomsbury Academic, 2017).

3. By the mid-nineteenth century, writes Best, "Different publications posited competing versions of the 'ideal' woman, highlighting types such as *La Parisienne*, The Mother, and The Young Lady, or *Jeune Fille*." Ibid., 9.

4. Jennifer Smith Maguire and Julian Matthews, *The Cultural Intermediaries Reader* (London: SAGE, 2014). In a contemporary update, they define the concept as: "the taste makers defining what counts as good taste and cool culture in today's marketplace" (1). Pierre Bourdieu coined the term in his *Distinction: A Social Critique of the Judgement of Taste*, trans. Richard Nice (Cambridge, MA: Harvard University Press, 1984), and although primarily concerned with new cultural and economic practices of the French petite-bourgeoisie and bourgeoisie of the mid-twentieth century, his term and the concept it embodies are productive for thinking about the female fashion writers of the previous century.

5. Smith Maguire and Matthews, "Bourdieu on Cultural Intermediaries," in *Cultural Intermediaries Reader*, 21.

6. "In the context of nineteenth-century France, a long ribbon cordoned off the *roman de femme* and then the *press* [sic] *féminine* from the larger print culture. Tied into a fashion knot, this ribbon strained to check the frivolous and nefarious effects of commodification by fashion taken in its least playful sense. Such marginalization has resulted in the exclusion of the *presse féminine* from scholarship on nineteenth-century French print culture in general, and more particularly, on the status of French female authorship in that culture." Cheryl A. Morgan, "Unfashionable Feminism? Designing Women Writers in the *Journal Des Femmes* (1832–1836)," in de la Motte and Przyblyski, *Making the News*, 208. The "rhetoric of the *chiffon*" was, for Morgan, who uses the example of the short-lived *Journal des femmes*, a strategy to co-opt a burgeoning women's press in the early July Monarchy by the emerging fashion press and its powerful advertisers.

7. Here I borrow the apt title of a study of the American *Ladies' Home Journal* by Jennifer Scanlon, *Inarticulate Longings: The 'Ladies' Home Journal,' Gender, and the Promises of Consumer Culture* (New York: Routledge, 1995). In her preface, Scanlon attributes the phrase to a 1924 article by an ad woman, Lois Ardery, who "argued that the modern woman 'wants it but she doesn't know it—yet!'" (10). The techniques of the twentieth-century American women's press were pioneered in the nineteenth century by the French fashion columnists I treat in this chapter.

8. The encyclopedic *La Civilisation du journal* offers the beginnings of a remedy to this oversight. Other notable exceptions include Morgan, who argues that this journal is "an important example of writing women's

entanglements with the rhetoric of the *chiffon*." "Unfashionable Feminism?" 208. See also Sullerot, whose brief study, *La Presse féminine*, makes clear that the female fashion press was infinitely more popular and lucrative than the "feminist" press in the nineteenth century; it is, ironically, the fashion press, though, that has received the least critical attention in recent times. See also Rachel Mesch, *Having It All in the Belle Epoque: How French Women's Magazines Invented the Modern Woman* (Stanford: Stanford University Press, 2013) for an inquiry into the *fin-de-siècle* women's press. Finally, and most recently, Thérenty's *Femmes de presse, femmes de lettres* offers a brief but enlightening discussion of some of the nineteenth-century's most prolific fashion writers.

9 According to Keith Negus, when social hierarchies are more fluid, as they were in nineteenth-century France, cultural intermediaries enter and fill a vacuum that has opened up. They "become ever more significant in contributing to social change . . . [when] 'cultural hierarchies are much more fragmented and plural,'" citing Justin O'Connor. Keith Negus, "The Work of Cultural Intermediaries and the Enduring Distance between Production and Consumption," *Cultural Studies* 16, no. 4 (2002): 511.

10 Marianne Van Remoortel discusses this gender divide in "Women Editors and the Rise of the Illustrated Fashion Press in the Nineteenth Century," *Nineteenth-Century Contexts* 39, no. 4 (2017): 269–95. I will return to this article throughout this chapter, but particularly with respect to *La Mode illustrée*, as Van Remoortel's research offers important new information about this period.

11 Renneville worked for several journals. In addition to *La Sylphide*, she also wrote for *La Gazette rose* (which she founded, with Villemessant's patronage), *Le Moniteur de la mode*, and *Le Journal de la mode*, among others. See Thérenty, *Femmes de presse, femmes de lettres*, 42. Fouqueau de Pussy and Raymond were more tied to the single journal they directed, *Le Journal des demoiselles* and *La Mode illustrée*, respectively, although Raymond had worked under the tutelage of J. J. early in her career.

12 See Samra-Martine Bonvoisin and Michèle Maignien, *La Presse féminine* (Paris: Presses universitaires de France, 1986); and Sullerot, *La Presse féminine*. These studies focus primarily on the feminist press, which comprised a number of journals founded and written by women, beginning with *L'Athénée des dames*; they tended to be short-lived, for reasons of censorship and/or financial viability.

13 Bonvoisin and Maignien, *La Presse féminine*, 13.

14 Sanson tells us that the journal was originally founded "under the Direction of Mme. Clement, née Hémery, authoress and wife of a printer, and by a former professor of rhetoric, Sellèque." Sanson, "La Presse féminine," 524. For an exhaustive history of this journal, see Kleinert, *Le "Journal des dames et des modes"*, which is devoted entirely to this journal.

15 Soulier, *Presse féminine*, 36.

16 Kleinert, *Le "Journal des dames et des modes"*, 17. This phrase is the subtitle to Kleinert's book.

17 Ibid., 22.

18 Ibid., 19.

19 See Van Remoortel, "Women Editors," 277.

20 Margaret Waller, "Disembodiment as Masquerade: Fashion Journalists and Other 'Realist' Observers in Directory Paris," *L'Esprit Créateur* 37, no. 1 (1997): 46.

21 Sanson distinguishes the "presse féminine" from the "presse féministe," stating: "The women's press, which was considered a 'specialized press,' must be distinguished from the feminist press even if, in France, the separation is not absolute. Nevertheless, the former targets essentially the readership of women whose tastes and morals it tries to guide, attempting to entertain them in both senses of the term, but also to inform and instruct them. The other

takes a militant position—to express the demands of the *deuxième sexe* confronted with male domination." Sanson, "La Presse féminine," 523.

22 From 1836 to 1848, Delphine de Girardin used the pseudonym Charles, vicomte de Launay, to write a weekly fashion and society column entitled "Courrier de Paris" for Emile de Girardin's *La Presse*. It was reprinted in a volume entitled *Lettres parisiennes* after her death. Kleinert, *Le "Journal des dames et des modes"*, 9. See Alison Finch, "The Journalist: Delphine de Girardin," chapter 14 in *Women's Writing in Nineteenth-Century France* (Cambridge: Cambridge University Press, 2000); and Cheryl A. Morgan, "Les chiffons de la M(éd)use: Delphine Gay de Girardin, journaliste," *Romantisme* 85 (1994): 57–66. See also Thérenty, *Femmes de presse, femmes de lettres*.

23 See Kleinert, *Le "Journal des dames et des modes"*.

24 Thérenty, *Femmes de presse, femmes de lettres*, 45.

25 See Montclair, "Silhouettes féminines: Mme Emmeline Raymond," *Le Figaro: Supplément littéraire du dimanche* (February 1, 1890), 18; accessed July 31, 2022, https://gallica.bnf.fr/ark:/12148/bpt6k2725298.

26 Nicole Le Maux, *Histoire du chapeau féminin*, 26. The only extended study of the *Journal des demoiselles* remains an unpublished dissertation. Christine Léger-Paturneau, *Le "Journal des demoiselles" et l'éducation des filles sous la Monarchie de Juillet (1833–1848)* (diss., Université de Paris VII, 1988).

27 Sarah Mombert, "L'Aiguille moderne: Les Ouvrages de dames dans la petite presse du XIXe siècle" (unpublished conference presentation, Congrès Médias 19, Paris, June 12, 2015). Columns by Emmeline Raymond appear already in the *Journal des demoiselles*. Emmeline Raymond was a "journaliste d'origine moldave," according to Sanson; "La Presse féminine," 529. There are two excellent studies dedicated to Raymond. One is scholarly: Raphaëlle Renken-Deshayes, "*Miroir mon beau miroir . . .: L'Identité féminine définie par un journal de mode 'La Mode illustrée: Journal de la famille*'" (Neuchâtel: Alphil, 2004). The other is an entertaining collection drawn from Raymond's advice column. See Yvert, *L'Endiguement des renseignements*.

28 See Guillaume Pinson, *L'Imaginaire médiatique: Histoire et fiction du journal au XIXe siècle* (Paris: Classiques Garnier, 2012); and Cary Hollinshead-Strick, *The Fourth Estate at the Fourth Wall: Newspapers on Stage in July Monarchy France* (Evanston, IL: Northwestern University Press, 2019).

29 Renneville wrote for *La Sylphide* for just several years in the 1850s, but her imprint was important; the columns she wrote for *La Gazette rose* appeared in a few other journals, including *Le Figaro*, *Le Moniteur de la mode*, and *La Sylphide*.

30 I do not cover entire runs of these journals exhaustively, but rather focus on J. J. in the 1830s and 1840s, Renneville in the 1850s, and Raymond in the 1860s and 1870s.

31 Kate Nelson Best, "Text and Image in Fashion Periodicals of the Second French Empire," in *Text and Image in Modern European Culture*, eds. Natasha Grigorian, Thomas Baldwin, and Margaret Rigaud-Drayton (West Lafayette, IN: Purdue University Press, 2012), 111.

32 For valuable biographical information, see Léger-Paturneau, '*Le Journal des demoiselles*' *et l'éducation des filles sous la Monarchie de Juillet (1833–1848)*.

33 See Lucie Roussel-Richard, "A City for Young Ladies: The Parisian *Flâneuse* of the *Journal des Demoiselles*," in *Women and the City in French Literature and Culture: Reconfiguring the Feminine in the Urban Environment*, eds. Siobhán McIlvanney and Gillian Ni Cheallaigh (Cardiff: University of Wales Press, 2019).

34 Léger-Paturneau, '*Le Journal des demoiselles*' *et l'éducation des filles sous la Monarchie de Juillet (1833–1848)*, 712.

35 This column is introduced in the journal's fourth issue (May 15, 1833), and is unsigned until June of the following year, when the fashion writer begins to use the initials "J. J."

36 Léger-Paturneau, *'Le Journal des demoiselles' et l'éducation des filles sous la Monarchie de Juillet (1833–1848)*, 748.

37 An earlier version of this material appears in my article "Becoming (M)other: Reflectivity in *Le Journal des Demoiselles*," 84–100.

38 Sanson, "La Presse féminine," 535.

39 See Anne-Marie Sohn, *Chrysalides: Femmes dans la vie privée (XIXe–XXe siècles)* (Paris: Publications de la Sorbonne, 1996).

40 Jeanne-Justine Fouqueau de Pussy, "La Robe de bal," *Journal des demoiselles* (February 1833), digital archive, Gerritsen Collection, Vassar College, Poughkeepsie, NY.

41 See Joy Spanabel Emery, *A History of the Paper Pattern Industry: The Home Dressmaking Fashion Revolution* (London: Bloomsbury Academic, 2014). "The French publication *Journal des Demoiselles*, issued in 1833, was especially for the home sewer. In its early years it had scaled proportional pattern drafts with sufficient measurements to produce a good pattern. It continued to publish scaled patterns throughout the 1840s and by 1845 was beginning to include a few full-sized patterns, mostly for baby clothes and caps, as pullout inserts in the periodical . . . the patterns were a boon to the home seamstress of the time, but to modern eyes they present a number of problems. They come in only one medium size, leaving the customer to adjust them to fit a particular body. The pattern pieces are still the basic body and sleeve shapes. There are minimal, if any, instructions" (21–22).

42 Fouqueau de Pussy, "La Robe de bal."

43 Fashion plates did not, at first, accompany every issue of *Le Journal des demoiselles*, and the number per year varied, but generally corresponded to winter and summer fashions (thus two or three plates) per year in the journal's first decade. J. J. sometimes referred readers to plates in previous issues. By the mid-1840s, however, plates became more frequent, appearing almost monthly.

44 Sharon Marcus, *Between Women: Friendship, Desire, and Marriage in Victorian England* (Princeton, NJ: Princeton University Press, 2007), 114.

45 Marcus describes this practice in the British context, explaining that "voluminous sales of dolls and fashion plates in the Victorian era, for instance, prove that women responded eagerly to their presentation of femininity as a voluptuous, pliable spectacle." Ibid., 114.

46 See also Sharon Marcus, "Reflections on Victorian Fashion Plates," *differences* 14: 4–33.

47 Fouqueau de Pussy, *Journal des demoiselles* (1835), 381. The epistolary trope is reminiscent of Balzac's 1842 *Mémoires de deux jeunes mariées*, which recounts the lives over twelve years of two brides who had met in boarding school.

48 Ibid. (1835), 355.

49 Ibid. (1833), 158.

50 Ibid. (1833), 318.

51 Ibid. (1833), 222.

52 Ibid. (1836), 190.

53 Léger-Paturneau's primary focus is the theme of girls' education running through the journal.

54 See Fouqueau de Pussy, *Journal des demoiselles* (1836), 222, for a good example.

55 Ibid. (1852), 374.

56 Ibid.

57 Ibid. (1852), 80.

58 See Archives de Paris, accessed August 20, 2022, https://bit.ly/3KgiNmr.

59 Léger-Paturneau, 'Le Journal des demoiselles' et l'éducation des filles sous la Monarchie de Juillet (1833–1848), 719.

60 Fouqueau de Pussy, *Journal des demoiselles* (1852), 380.

61 According to the Comtesse Dash, who discusses Renneville in her memoirs, she called herself, no doubt ironically, "la reine des chiffons." See Comtesse Dash, *Mémoires des autres: Souvenirs anecdotiques sur mes contemporains* (Paris: Librairie illustrée, 1896–1898), 6:85; accessed August 28, 2022, ark:/12148/bpt6k9601294b.

62 Hippolyte de Villemessant, *Mémoires d'un journaliste*, rev. ed. (Paris: E. Dentu, 1867), 1:89.

63 As it has been noted, *berthe* has an important fashion significance as well: it was the term given to a kind of lacy collar worn to cover a low-necked dress.

64 Others, such as Juliette Lormeaux (wife of journalist Jules Janin), Mme. la vicomtesse de Senneville, and the baronne de Martigny, also wrote for the journal.

65 Literally, "for the sake of the cause." De Villemessant, *Mémoires*, 1:106.

66 Dash, *Mémoires des autres*, 6:83–84.

67 See Schweitzer, *Les Femmes ont toujours travaillé*, 18–19.

68 Dash, *Mémoires des autres*, 6:84.

69 De Villemessant, *Mémoires*, 1:106.

70 Félix Ribeyre, Jules Brisson, and Firmin Maillard, *Les Grands Journaux de France* (Paris: Jouast Père et Fils, 1862), 93.

71 The *particule* in French, usually a variation on the preposition *de*, or "of," is an indication of place, and thus of aristocratic landholding. It is true, however, that after Napoléon I, it was possible to acquire a *particule* through means other than heredity.

72 Best, *History of Fashion Journalism*, 6. Best uses this term in reference to the eighteenth-century fashion press, defining it as "advertising masquerading as editorial." While introduced in the eighteenth century, this and other persuasive methods of advancing a business agenda were refined and multiplied in the nineteenth century. See also Jean Morienval, "Villemessant, l'inventeur," in *Les Créateurs de la grande presse en France: Emile de Girardin, H. de Villemessant, Moïse Millaud* (Paris: SPES, 1934).

73 De Villemessant, *Mémoires*, 84. Thérenty, *Femmes de presse, femmes de lettres*, 44.

74 When in 1857 Renneville started *La Gazette rose*, she took pains in the first issue to claim that this journal, unlike all those that had come before, would offer something for all classes: "Bourgeois fashion will be analyzed and discussed with as much attention and discernment as the fashion of the *grande dame*. Every fashion will be considered." *La Gazette rose* (January 1, 1857), 4. However, this formulation recreates the same hierarchies that marked the previous journals she wrote for, and it should be noted that, at least in this first issue, the *chroniqueuse* devotes her time and space primarily to the discussion of the fashions of the *grande dame*.

75 Patterns for sewing and embroidery were also included in this journal, but the *chroniqueuse* very rarely talks about these items, and when she does, it is primarily to plug the haberdashery Sajou. Instead, her primary focus is the glittering scene of the world of consumable fashion.

76 Vicomtesse de Renneville, *La Sylphide* (December 30, 1854), 284; accessed August 20, 2022, https://gallica.bnf.fr/ark:/12148/bpt6k58649495/f12.item.

77 Best astutely pursues this connection: "Seduced by the fantasy of *la Parisienne*, she is nevertheless required to behave as the wife of a physician in the province. The two periodicals to which she subscribes were publications promoting the lifestyle of Parisian society ladies. Emma's choice of the magazines is arguably misguided: as a country doctor's wife, she would do better with *Le Conseiller des dames et des demoiselles*, which targeted the lower echelons of the bourgeoisie. However, this would not serve her identificatory fantasy of superiority." Best, "Text and Image," 111. Flaubert, who began composing his novel in 1850, may well have been perusing the pages of *La Sylphide* when seeking inspiration for his fictional reader of fashion journals.

78 Vicomtesse de Renneville, "Causeries sur la mode," *La Sylphide* (January 18, 1850), 27; accessed August 20, 2020, https://gallica.bnf.fr/ark:/12148/bpt6k6125272q/f11.item.

79 *La Sylphide* (March 30, 1850), 140; accessed August 20, 2022, https://gallica.bnf.fr/ark:/12148/bpt6k6125279m/f11.item.

80 *La Sylphide* (October 30, 1850), 186; accessed August 20, 2022, https://gallica.bnf.fr/ark:/12148/bpt6k61277455/f12.item.

81 Vicomtesse de Renneville, "De l'influence de la mode," *La Sylphide* (May 10, 1850), 202; accessed August 20, 2022, https://gallica.bnf.fr/ark:/12148/bpt6k6125283h/f10.item.

82 Ibid.

83 Ibid.

84 Renneville, "Où en est le plaisir," *La Sylphide* (December 20, 1850), 266; accessed August 20, 2022, https://gallica.bnf.fr/ark:/12148/bpt6k6127751w/f10.item.

85 Vicomtesse de Renneville, "Pendant le Carême," *La Sylphide* (February 18, 1850), 73; accessed August 20, 2022, https://gallica.bnf.fr/ark:/12148/bpt6k6125275z/f9.item.

86 Vicomtesse de Renneville, "La Saison des Concerts," *La Sylphide* (February 28, 1853), 92; accessed August 20, 2022, https://gallica.bnf.fr/ark:/12148/bpt6k6109755m/f12.item.

87 Ibid.

88 Vicomtesse de Renneville, "Le Printemps et le Giboulées," *La Sylphide* (April 10, 1850), 153; accessed August 20, 2022, https://gallica.bnf.fr/ark:/12148/bpt6k61252808/f9.item.

89 Vicomtesse de Renneville, "La Nouvelle Année," *La Sylphide* (January 10, 1857), 11; accessed August 20, 2022, https://gallica.bnf.fr/ark:/12148/bpt6k146594z/f10.item.

90 Vicomtesse de Renneville, "Comment employer sa journée," *La Sylphide* (October 10, 1850), 170; accessed August 20, 2022, https://gallica.bnf.fr/ark:/12148/bpt6k6127743b/f10.item.

91 Ibid.

92 By contrast, as I discussed in chapter 1, consumer desire among working women is perceived as a threat to social stability because of what it implies.

93 Vicomtesse de Renneville, "Passe-temps de la mode," *La Sylphide* (November 30, 1850), 236; accessed August 20, 2022, https://gallica.bnf.fr/ark:/12148/bpt6k6127749t/f11.item.

94 Ibid., 237.

95 I focus on columns from *La Sylphide* instead of *La Gazette rose* in part because of chronology—Renneville's stint at *La Sylphide* coincided with the first glory days of the Second Empire, and it was here that she invented her *chroniqueuse* persona—but also, and perhaps coincidentally, because the seven years Renneville spent writing columns for *La Sylphide*, 1850–7, correspond exactly to the period Flaubert spent drafting *Madame Bovary*.

96 Let us not forget that Emma swallowed vinegar to slim her silhouette.

97 Vicomtesse de Renneville, *La Gazette rose* (January 1, 1857, 1); see also Morienval, "Villemessant, l'inventeur," 141, for an account of the founding of this journal.

98 This was an adjustable, personalized mannequin that would reside with one's dressmaker, who could thus tailor clothes specifically for the customer without requiring fittings.

99 Vicomtesse de Renneville, *La Sylphide* (March 20, 1856), 124; accessed August 20, 2022, https://gallica.bnf.fr/ark:/12148/bpt6k6109730s/f12.item.

100 Ibid.

101 Dash, *Mémoires des autres*, 6: 84.

102 La Marquise Athénie de la Sainte-Colombe, "Renneville (Madame la vicomtesse de): La verité sur le cas de Madame la vicomtesse de Renneville," *Le Figaro* (August 29, 1858), 5.

103 Ibid.

104 *Le Figaro* (January 18, 1890), 2; accessed August 20, 2022, https://gallica.bnf.fr/ark:/12148/bpt6k2810090/f2.item.

105 Ibid.

106 Ibid.

107 Note that "La Bonne Ménagère" was the title of Raymond's 1867 book, published by Firmin-Didot frères.

108 Montclair, "Silhouettes féminines," 18.

109 "Subscription rates for *La Mode illustrée* in 1866, for example, ranged from four francs a year for illustrated patterns only, through to twenty-four francs a year for the deluxe 'album colorié ('full-color edition'), complete with fifty color plates." Best, "Text and Image," 105.

110 Van Remoortel, "Women Editors," 292.

111 See Renken-Deshayes for an analysis of the journal in its first decade. The author raises many themes that are of interest to my argument and suggests the value that future studies could offer in comparing this journal to others. Noting the journal's contradictory nature, she likewise proposes that future studies consider the following question: "What silences has Emmeline Raymond dared to break?" Renken-Deshayes, *"Miroir mon beau miroir"*, 203.

112 See Hiner, "Fashion Animation"; see also Anne Friedberg, *The Virtual Window: From Alberti to Microsoft* (Cambridge, MA: MIT Press, 2006).

113 Van Remoortel, "Women Editors"; see especially 278–9, 288. In Raymond's "Prospectus," published in the first issue, she hints at borrowings from other nationalities, but does not admit to the wholesale lifting of images and text: "Reserving the better part for France, the birthplace, so to speak, of elegance and taste, still we will not show ourselves to be too exclusive—borrowing with discernment from neighboring peoples that which will seem to suit our country. Thus, we will ask them to share a number of treatises and formulas of domestic chemistry that show how to prevent accidents and how to fix them. We shall also ask them about their secrets for caring for and preserving these collections of flowers." Emmeline Raymond, "Prospectus de *La Mode illustrée*," *La Mode illustrée*, no. 1 (January 1, 1860), 8.

114 "The colored plates aimed at the elite focused on social settings such as Longchamp, while the black and white lithographs of more mainstream magazines showed women in more domestic situations . . . Certain magazines, such as *La Mode illustrée*, also included ideas for handicrafts, recipes, and dinner table plans, thus articulating femininity around domesticated fashionable display." Best, "Text and Image," 109. I will discuss the fashion plate in greater detail in ch. 4.

115 For a thorough discussion of the intersection of fashion and Haussmann's Paris renovations, see Kessler, *Sheer Presence*.

116 See Susan Hiner, "When Fashion Stood Still: From *La Mode Assiégée* to *La Mode Durable*," *Nineteenth-Century French Studies* 49, no. 3–4 (2021): 549–66.

117 Raymond, "Prospectus," 8.

118 Emmeline Raymond, "La Rédaction de *La Mode illustrée* à ses lectrices," *La Mode illustrée*, no. 53 (December 30, 1866), 433; accessed August 20, 2022, https://bit.ly/3AvrRj5.

119 Le Bon Marché, considered the first modern department store, was renovated by Aristide Boucicaut in 1852. See Geoffrey Crossick and Serge Jaumain, *Cathedrals of Consumption: The European Department Store, 1850–1939* (Aldershot, UK: Ashgate, 1999).

120 See Emery, *History of the Paper Pattern Industry*.

121 The author's data on the Bibliothèque Nationale de France website indicate the extent of Raymond's authorship and translation work, accessed July 31, 2022, https://data.bnf.fr/fr/documents-by-rdt/12996905/te/page1. Van Remoortel also discusses Raymond's multilingual gifts and accomplishments as translator, not only of German language literary pieces included in *La Mode illustrée*, but also of unattributed descriptions of black and white images in the journal. "Women Editors," 288.

122 Raymond explains to her readers her objection to *réclames* or advertisements and promotions: "'Recommend this store.' 'Bring work to a worthy mother.' 'Call the public's attention to this worker who lacks bread.' This part of my correspondence is completely heartbreaking for me . . . and to continue it would be unnecessarily heartbreaking. Yes, I confess, I have yielded to some of these requests; but their very number forbids me to satisfy them from now on, because, having no reason to welcome some more than others, *La Mode illustrée* would be transformed little by little into an address book and would lose some of the usefulness that it owes its subscribers. And it would lose more than this. The public, which does not read the letters that are written to us, could confuse us, to our extreme prejudice, with the publications that subsist on advertisements, and we cannot consent to a comparison that would be unfair and offensive. We cannot refrain from publishing the sources from which we draw our models, any more than a bookseller could refuse to list the names of the authors whose works he publishes . . . But we urge our readers not to request that we recommend their protégés, because we could not be useful to a few people, without harming our publication. . . . I will go further . . . I will beg our subscribers not to demand of me the addresses of all the businesses they may need." Raymond, "La Rédaction de *La Mode illustrée* à ses lectrices," 434.

123 Emmeline Raymond, "Description des toilettes," *La Mode illustrée*, no. 36 (September 3, 1865), 285; accessed August 29, 2022, https://bit.ly/3CGIOte.

124 Best, "Text and Image," 107.

125 Emmeline Raymond, "Modes," *La Mode illustrée*, no. 22 (May 28, 1865), 171; accessed August 20, 2022, https://bit.ly/3QLfJRW.

126 Emmeline Raymond, "Modes," *La Mode illustrée*, no. 46 (November 11, 1866), 382; accessed August 20, 2022, https://bit.ly/3T2VK2p.

127 Emmeline Raymond, "Esthétique de la mode," *La Mode illustrée*, no. 2 (January 7, 1866), 14; accessed August 20, 2022, https://bit.ly/3PE2vVq.

128 Emmeline Raymond was the author of the eponymous column "Conseils d'un vieux jardinier" ("Advice from an old gardener").

129 See Yvert, *Endiguement des renseignements*.

130 The details of the design shift through the decades, but the key element of women reading and writing remain constant.

131 Emmeline Raymond, "Renseignements," *La Mode illustrée*, no. 9 (February 28, 1869), 72; accessed August 20, 2022, https://bit.ly/3AaYGBA.

132 Emmeline Raymond, *La Mode illustrée*, no. 19 (May 11, 1863), 152; accessed August 20, 2022, https://bit.ly/3QZG3Ho.

133 See "Renseignements," *La Mode illustrée,* no. 15 (April 13, 1863), 120; accessed August 20, 2022, https://bit.ly/3A7TkXP. Notice from W. Unger to subscribers: "The ever-increasing number of letters we receive that are addressed to Mme. E. Raymond obliges us to attempt to contain the correspondence within more reasonable limits. The *Renseignements* feature cannot invade all the columns of the newspaper—and Mme. Raymond's entire existence will soon no longer suffice to unravel this correspondence. Many people contact Mme. Raymond about matters that may not be handled in the newspaper, since it is sometimes impossible to reply in a public forum. Others consult the newspaper for their friends and relatives who are not subscribers; and others address questions that are answered in the features "Modes," "La Bonne Ménagère," and "La Civilité." Some letters contain up to sixteen exacting questions, the answers to which alone would occupy a quarter of a column. As of today, *only those letters will be answered that are accompanied by a strip of the newspaper bearing the name of the subscriber.* [. . .] We beg our subscribers . . . to make their questions as brief as possible, not deviating from the limitations of space and subject matter as prescribed by the newspaper." See also Yvert, *Endiguement des renseignements*.

134 One reference to the sale of Raymond's photograph to subscribers occurs in "Renseignements," *La Mode illustrée*, no. 6 (February 9, 1863), 48; accessed August 20, 2022, https://bit.ly/3PxkXPG.

135 Raymond, "Renseignements," *La Mode illustrée*, no. 9 (March 2, 1863), 72; accessed August 20, 2022, https://bit.ly/3QVOhjU.

136 Raymond, "Renseignements," *La Mode illustrée*, no. 30 (July 27, 1863), 240; accessed August 20, 2022, https://bit.ly/3K7w14M.

137 Montclair, "Silhouettes féminines," 18. Quoted also in Van Remoortel, "Women Editors."

138 Montclair, "Silhouettes féminines," 18.

139 See Van Remoortel, "Women Editors." She also insists upon the industriousness, skill, and professionalism of women fashion editors in the nineteenth century.

140 As Van Remoortel observes, for all of Raymond's determination to direct her gender in appropriately domestic behaviors, she "herself in many ways embodied the emerging female professional, quickly rising to become a star of French fashion journalism and beyond." "Women Editors," 287. Renken-Deshayes also notes that "Emmeline Raymond is the very embodiment of the advice she dispenses, but she neglects to mention, among the prescribed feminine activities, the role of journalist, which does not enter into the definition of femininity. Similarly, one might wonder how Emmeline Raymond reconciles the submissive position of women and the position of mastery obtained by possessing the knowledge and power implied by writing a fashion periodical in a didactic

tone. What else should we think of an editor who participates in the world of print culture, while the representative practices of this same culture lock women into the private sphere?" *"Miroir mon beau miroir"*, 200.

141 See Mesch, *Having It All in the Belle Epoque*.

142 See Emmeline Raymond, "Le Travail des Femmes," *La Mode illustrée*, no. 49 (December 5, 1869), 390–1; accessed August 20, 2022, https://bit.ly/3T5kmaJ; and "Sans Dot," *La Mode illustrée*, no. 14 (April 3, 1870), 108–9; accessed August 20, 2022, https://bit.ly/3Ciix4v. Renken-Deshayes cites these important columns as well.

143 *La Sylphide* (December 5, 1840), 3; accessed August 20, 2022, https://gallica.bnf.fr/ark:/12148/bpt6k6144375j/f20.item.

Chapter 4

1 Alfred Busquet, "Salon de 1857: Dessins et Aquarelles," *Le Portefeuille de l'amateur: Journal artistique contenant un cours de dessin gradué*, vol. 1, no. 4 (September 15, 1857), 13–15; accessed August 21, 2022, https://gallica.bnf.fr/ark:/12148/bpt6k9819212q/f5.item. Héloïse Leloir and Anaïs Toudouze are the primary subjects of my analysis. Anaïs Bernard, née Desgranges, was their contemporary and also a watercolorist, specializing in flower painting.

2 Miniature painting, the origins of which in France date to illuminated manuscripts, had its heyday in the eighteenth century and had, by the nineteenth century, become associated with "feminine" art practice. It was thus a less highly regarded art form. Some have argued that the miniature was displaced by photography in the nineteenth century, which led to its demise. See Henri Bouchot, *La Miniature française, 1750–1825* (Paris: Émile-Paul, 1910); accessed August 18, 2022, https://gallica.bnf.fr/ark:/12148/bpt6k12687822.

3 The *arts d'agréments* were the cultural accomplishments in which young bourgeois and upper-class girls were trained to become cultivated wives and mothers and to provide appropriate leisure activities and the social entertainment (music, art, languages) for a properly ornamented household. "A pedagogic curriculum emphasizing the fine arts gave women basic expressive means. Most middle- and upper-class girls were taught at an early age, and for some years, the rudimentary techniques of drawing and painting. Visual literacy was considered a feminine accomplishment that brought out a girl's best qualities and enabled her to find a suitable husband." Anne Higonnet, "Secluded Vision: Images of Feminine Experience in Nineteenth-Century Europe," *Radical History Review* 38 (1987), 19. See also Ann Bermingham's study of drawing as an important signifying social practice, *Learning to Draw: Studies in the Cultural History of a Polite and Useful Art* (New Haven: Yale University Press, 2000); and Guentner, *Women Art Critics*.

4 There were in fact four sisters: Héloïse (1819–73), who married painter Auguste Leloir; Adèle Anaïs (1822–99), who married architect Gabriel Toudouze; Laure (1828–78), who married painter Gustave Noël, and Isabelle, who married engineer Hippolyte Malibran and, unique among the girls, did not pursue an artistic career. Anaïs's daughter, Isabelle Toudouze Desgrange, continued the family tradition as a fashion illustrator. Isabelle's daughter, Jeanne, married the painter Paul Signac. The sisters had a half-brother, Paul Colin, who became a genre painter like his father and married Sarah Devéria, the daughter of Achille Devéria. See Valerie Steele, *Paris Fashion: A Cultural History*, 2nd ed. (Oxford: Peter Berg, 1999), 99–132. See also Madeleine Ginsburg, *An Introduction to Fashion Illustration* (London: HMSO, 1980), 10; and Bonin, "Les Sœurs Colin." In her excellent study of the graphic arts tradition in nineteenth-century France, Jillian Lerner traces the history and the primary players of the world of early fashion illustration. See Lerner, "The Hours of Her Day: Fashion Prints, Feminine Ideals, and the Circle of Achille Devéria," chapter 4 in *Graphic Culture*.

5 *Le Journal du Cher* (January 29, 1857), 5.

6   *La Presse* (February 14, 1853), 4; accessed August 15, 2022, https://gallica.bnf.fr/ark:/12148/btv1b53020119n.

7   See Steele, *Paris Fashion*, 2nd ed. (1999); Heidi Brevik-Zender, "Interstitial Narratives: Rethinking Feminine Spaces of Modernity in Nineteenth-Century French Fashion Plates," *Nineteenth-Century Contexts* 36, no. 2 (2014): 91–123; Françoise Tétart-Vittu, "Colin, les Sœurs," in *Encyclopædia Universalis*, accessed August 19, 2022, https://www.universalis.fr/encyclopedie/les-soeurs-colin/; and Bonin, "Les Sœurs Colin."

8   Robert Maury, "Quand les aquarellistes créaient la haute couture," *Plaisir de France* 40, no. 422 (September 1974): 30–5. Cited also in Bonin, "Les Sœurs Colin."

9   Louis-Marie Lanté (1789–1871), an illustrator and lithographer, and his contemporary Horace Vernet (1789–1863), an academic painter as well as an illustrator, were both creators of illustrations for *Le Bon Genre*; Paul Gavarni (Sulpice Guillaume Chevalier, 1804–66) was one of the most celebrated illustrators and lithographers of the Romantic period throughout the July Monarchy, known especially for his satirical work for *Le Charivari*; François Claudius Compte-Calix (1813–80) was a genre painter and the primary fashion illustrator for *Les Modes parisiennes*; and Jules (Jean-Baptiste) David (1808–92), also a painter and lithographer, became the primary fashion illustrator for *Le Moniteur de la mode*. See Gaudriault, *La Gravure de mode feminine en France*; and Lerner, *Graphic Culture*.

10 Robert Maury, "Quand les aquarellistes créaient la haute couture," 34.

11 I am thinking, for example, of the exhibit shown in Paris, New York, and Chicago "Impressionism, Fashion, and Modernity," associated with the printed catalogue, *Impressionism, Fashion, and Modernity*, ed. Gloria Groom (New Haven: Yale University Press, 2012).

12 See especially Linda Nochlin, *Women, Art, and Power: And Other Essays* (New York: Harper & Row, 1988) and *Representing Women* (New York: Thames and Hudson, 1999); Griselda Pollock, *Vision and Difference: Femininity, Feminism and the Histories of Art* (Abingdon, UK: Routledge, 1988); Higonnet, *Berthe Morisot's Images of Women*; Tamar Garb, *Sisters of the Brush: Women's Artistic Culture in Late Nineteenth-Century Paris* (New Haven: Yale University Press, 1994); Gabriel P. Weisberg and Jane R. Becker, eds., *Overcoming All Obstacles: The Women of the Académie Julian* (New York: Dahesh Museum; New Brunswick, NJ: Rutgers University Press, 1999). In the last several years, two exhibitions have attempted to bring to light some of the many women painters of the era whom history has mostly overlooked. See *Women Artists in Paris, 1850–1900* (New Haven: Yale University Press, 2017), curated by Laurence Madeline, and held at the Clark in 2017; and *Les Peintres Femmes, 1780–1830: Naissance d'un combat* (Paris: Découvertes Gallimard, 2021), curated by Martine Lacas, and held at the Musée du Luxembourg, Paris, in 2021.

13 Garb has detailed that art schools for women emerged during this period, showing that there was significant activity, as a result of their exclusion from the official venue.

14 This history has been amply charted by Nochlin and Garb, among others. While women had been permitted entry prior to the nineteenth century (four women were admitted in 1783 per Marie-Antoinette's order . . . Labille-Guiard and Vallayer-Coster, etc.), Napoléon ended that practice. Garb follows the history of the women of the Union des Femmes Peintres et Sculpteurs in their struggle to be officially recognized by institutions such as the Prix de Rome. See Garb, *Sisters of the Brush*, 70–104. See also James Kearns and Alister Mill, eds., *The Paris Fine Art Salon/Le Salon, 1791–1881* (Oxford: Peter Lang, 2015), for a history and analysis of the Salon and the place of women artists.

15 See the database produced by the University of Exeter in collaboration with the Archives des Musées Nationaux, which lists all artists and works submitted to and accepted by the Paris Salon from 1835 through 1850. The database also compiles information about medals. Harriet Griffiths and Alister Mill, "Database of Salon Artists," accessed August 19, 2022, http://humanities-research.exeter.ac.uk/salonartists/artist/id/8493. Women were

allowed to exhibit in the Salon even if they were not allowed in the official institutions, and while their work was often consigned to rooms housing works from the so-called "lesser" category of "dessin" (drawing), which also comprised watercolor and miniature, we should not underestimate how important it was for women to be able to exhibit at the Salon. See Debra J. Dewitte, "The Exhibition of Drawings, Pastels and Watercolours in the French Salon, 1863–1881," in Kearns and Mill, *The Paris Fine Art Salon/Le Salon*.

16 As Alexandra Wettlaufer has detailed in her study of women painters and authors in nineteenth-century Britain and France, women artists were primarily considered amateurs, their work undertaken for personal pleasure rather than professional accomplishment. *Portraits of the Artist as a Young Woman: Painting and the Novel in France and Britain, 1800–1860* (Columbus: Ohio State University Press, 2011), 31.

17 See Gaudriault, who lists a number of illustrators—some well-known and others not; included are a number of feminine names. Overwhelmingly, however, even if they were working in the industry, women did not sign their fashion-plate art. Gaudriault, *La Gravure de mode feminine*, 204–9.

18 Wettlaufer, *Portraits of the Artist*, 32.

19 Anaïs Toudouze, obituary, *La Vie quotidienne*, no. 35 (September 9, 1899), 274; accessed August 19, 2022, https://gallica.bnf.fr/ark:/12148/bpt6k6343499g. By contrast, the death notice of her contemporary Jules David, also a fashion illustrator, reads as follows: "Well-known painter Mr. Jules David, member of the Committee of the Association of Artists, knight of the Legion of Honor, died yesterday. The funeral will take place tomorrow at ten o'clock, at Saint-Sulpice; burial at Montparnasse cemetery," *Le Figaro* (October 21, 1892).

20 Anaïs Colin's obituary affirms a guiding principle of Wettlaufer's study, which, building on Nochlin and Garb, asserts that "only the male artist (author, painter) was constructed as visible within the structures of the social edifice, while women's identities were constructed primarily in terms of marriage, maternity, and domesticity." Wettlaufer, *Portraits of the Artist*, 13. While much about the obituary reinforces this principle, I would like to spotlight instead the first, unelaborated identifier used to describe Anaïs Toudouze: *artiste-peintre*. Bonin also tells us that immediately after Anaïs's death in 1899, she was officially determined to have no profession, although we know from her son's private papers that she was busy working up until her death. "The declaration of succession, finalized some months after Anaïs's death, stated that she had no profession. Yet it was in the last years of her life that Anaïs worked the most." Bonin, "Les Sœurs Colin," 13.

21 Both scholars propose that the presumed lesser women's arts, such as album-making, amateur art, and flower painting were deemed inferior because of an entrenched gendered standard that also excluded women from the institutions of official art. See Higonnet, "Secluded Vision"; and Ringelberg, "The Court of Lilacs, the Studio of Roses, the Garden at Réveillon." Their work is key to my understanding of the Colin sisters in their particular context.

22 "Women's album pictures accept the domain allotted to them—indeed, they insist on it . . . At home, in twos or threes, women most often read, play the piano, sew or embroider, perhaps pose or draw." Higonnet, "Secluded Vision," 23.

23 Busquet is of course repeating a cliché of the gendered hierarchy in western aesthetics. As Naomi Schor explains, "To focus on the detail and more particularly on the *detail as negativity* is to become aware . . . of its participation in a larger semantic network, bounded on the one side by the *ornamental*, with its traditional connotations of effeminacy and decadence, and on the other, by the *everyday*, whose 'prosiness' is rooted in the domestic sphere of social life presided over by women . . . the detail is gendered and doubly gendered as feminine." Naomi Schor, *Reading in Detail: Aesthetics and the Feminine* (New York: Routledge, 1989), 4.

24 "Feminine picture-makers tended to work with delicate, evanescent materials like paper, pencil and watercolor; high art painters made their finished works in oil and canvas and framed them with carved wood." Higonnet,

"Secluded Vision," 32. As works on paper, too, these original pieces, whether watercolors or sketches, are fragile and delicate, and their ephemeral nature makes it difficult perhaps to display them.

25 Higonnet's "Secluded Vision" offers an early, but still highly relevant contribution to questions of women's art and, in particular, to the place of private feminine cultural production such as albums, and she briefly discusses the Colin sisters. She makes the important connection between feminine picture-making, in particular the creation of albums featuring portraits of family members, and fashion illustration, which took off in the 1840s, a connection on which my own discussion builds. She states, however, that fashion illustration "would exhaust feminine visual culture's energies by the end of the century" (28) through its exploitation of the themes and techniques of the private world of feminine art forms. While I am indebted to this richly researched piece, I wish to draw a slightly different conclusion. For in my view, rather than falling victim to the perils of the commodification of art imposed by the fashion industry and their exclusion from the institutions of high art, the Colin sisters negotiated a pragmatic and professionalizing pathway through their "feminine" talent, seizing on the popularity of the private album—its immense powers of communication between women, its capacity to celebrate female sociability—precisely to insert themselves into a capitalist system as artists.

26 Unfortunately, little is known about the girls' mother, Joséphine Colin, née Marie-Josèphe Juhel (1796–1837). She did show at the Paris Salon, however, under the name of Mme. Colin, and Bonin believes "she played an essential role in the artistic training of her daughters." Bonin, "Les Sœurs Colin," 35.

27 See, among others, Charlotte Guichard, *La Griffe du peintre: La Valeur de l'art, 1730–1820* (Paris: Seuil, 2018); Garb, *Sisters of the Brush*; and Pollock, *Vision and Difference*.

28 Higonnet, "Secluded Vision," 17.

29 See Vyvyan Holland, *Hand Coloured Fashion Plates: 1770 to 1899* (London: B. T. Batsford, 1955); and Higonnet, *Berthe Morisot's Images of Women*.

30 Bonin contends that their mother Joséphine viewed fashion illustration, which she also practiced, as a "a safe bet as a source of income for a nineteenth-century woman." Bonin, "Les Sœurs Colin," 45.

31 Tétart-Vittu, "Colin, les Sœurs," 67. See also Gaudriault, *La Gravure de mode féminine en France*, for a complete list of journals in which their work appeared (207–9). Gustave Toudouze writes that his mother was already employed at the age of 16. "Une Famille d'artistes," MS 15011 (1–2), Bibliothèque de l'Arsenal.

32 Regarding the illustrations of Laure Noël, who published in a dozen fashion publications, Steele notes that *Godey's* (among others) actually "stole her images"—which was possible because of the absence of copyright laws at the time. Valerie Steele, "Fashioning the *Parisienne*," in *Paris Fashion: A Cultural History*, 3rd ed. (New York: Bloomsbury USA, 2017), 109. See also Brevik-Zender, "Interstitial Narratives."

33 The account book, comprising ten small pages organized like a ledger and about the size of a postcard, is held as "Carnet des comptes d'Anaïs Colin" ("Account book of Anaïs Colin"), MS 15011 (1–2), Bibliothèque de l'Arsenal.

34 See B. S. Wright, "'That Other Historian, the Illustrator': Voices and Vignettes in Mid-Nineteenth Century France." *Oxford Art Journal* 23, no. 1 (2000): 113–36.

35 For excellent discussions of the careers and graphic art of Gavarni and Devéria, among other male printmakers of the period, see Lerner, *Graphic Culture*. See ch. 4, n. 8, for more information about these artists. Jules David would become primarily a fashion illustrator later in his career, but he began as a graphic artist and painter.

36 Bonin, "Les Sœurs Colin," 48.

37 See Higonnet, *Berthe Morisot's Images of Women*, 96–9; and Brevik-Zender, "Interstitial Narratives," 99.

38 See Mary Lynn McDougall for a discussion of artisanal and industrial labor of women in nineteenth-century France and England. "Working-Class Women during the Industrial Revolution, 1780–1914," in *Becoming Visible: Women in European History*, ed. Renate Bridenthal (Boston: Houghton Mifflin, 1977). See also Leora Auslander, *Taste and Power: Furnishing Modern France* (Berkeley: University of California Press, 1998), for a thorough exploration of the changing world of artisanal furniture production in eighteenth- and nineteenth-century France.

39 "Inscription concerning the date and the author—inscription on the reverse, on the stretcher: 'Héloïse Colin (Mme. Leloir) et Anaïs Colin (Mme G. Toudouze) / par elles-mêmes 1836'" (by themselves). Also included with the inscription is the following information: "Each of the two sisters is the author of the portrait of the other. No doubt the painting was shown at the Salon of 1840 (no. 282, "Portraits of Mlles. C."), under the name of Anaïs Colin." Although it could certainly be called a double portrait, I refer to this painting as a "self-portrait" in order to emphasize the portrayal of a shared identity.

40 Garb refers specifically to the tenacious group of women artists who struggled to form the Union of Women Painters and Sculptors in nineteenth-century Paris, but I use her phrase to evoke quite literally the sisterhood and the art that is celebrated in the painting. Tamar Garb, "Vision and Division in the Sisterhood of Artists," chapter 1 in *Sisters of the Brush*.

41 Siân Reynolds, "Mistresses of Creation: Women and Producers and Consumers of Art since 1700." In *The Routledge History of Women in Europe since 1700*, ed. Deborah Simonton (Abingdon, UK: Routledge, 2006). See also John Hope Mason, *The Value of Creativity: The Origins and Emergence of a Modern Belief* (Abingdon, UK: Routledge, 2017); and Laura Auricchio, "Self-Promotion in Adélaïde Labille-Guiard's 1785 'Self-Portrait with Two Students,'" *Art Bulletin* 89, no. 1 (March 2007): 45–62.

42 "Carnet des comptes d'Anaïs Colin."

43 Guichard, *La Griffe du peintre*, 196. See also Auricchio, "Self-Promotion."

44 Marie-Jo Bonnet, "Femmes peintres à leur travail: De L'Autoportrait comme manifeste politique (XVIIIe–XIXe siècles)," *Revue d'histoire modern et contemporaine* 49, no. 3 (2002): 140.

45 See especially, on Vigée-Lebrun, Mary D. Sheriff, *The Exceptional Woman: Elisabeth Vigée-Lebrun and the Cultural Politics of Art* (Chicago: University of Chicago Press, 1996); on Morisot, Kessler, *Sheer Presence*, 62–93, and Higonnet, *Berthe Morisot's Images of Women*; on Cassatt, Nancy M. Mathews, *Cassatt and Her Circle: Selected Letters* (New York: Abbeville Press, 1984); and Nochlin, *Representing Women*.

46 See Auricchio, "Self-Promotion."

47 "To write the history of the signature in the painting is to write the history of a sign dense with meaning, formed at the crossroads of several stories: that of the individual in European societies with the invention of the onomastic system and the functions assigned to the signature; and that of the subject, carrying an interiority, a reflexivity and a capacity for singular action within a social group. It is also to write the history of the figure of the author who asserts himself in an artistic space structured by the market, by institutional and scholarly recognition." Guichard, *La Griffe du peintre*, 13.

48 The meaning of the artist's signature, according to Guichard, relates to artistic authority as well as to the increasing commodification of art; and the practice of signing the work of art had gained traction, argues Guichard, in the late eighteenth and early nineteenth centuries, precisely when "techniques of reproduction—such as lithography and later photography—were becoming more efficient." While Guichard is primarily concerned with the generation of women artists preceding the Colin sisters, many of her observations remain pertinent to this discussion.

49 "Women painters were often the daughters, sisters or wives of painters. They were therefore suspected of having their canvases retouched by men who were often more professionally advanced than they were." Ibid., 196.

50 *Gigot* sleeves were so named because of their size and shape, which resembled a leg of lamb; the *berthe* collar was a collar made of lace or otherwise of thin fabric used to cover the neck and bosom of a woman wearing a low-cut dress. Higonnet has argued that feminine forms of art such as the album and amateur art indeed provided the blueprint for the fashion plates of the 1840s and beyond: "In the 1840s feminine imagery developed a public and professional avatar in the form of fashion illustration." Higonnet, "Secluded Vision," 28. See also Auricchio, "Self-Promotion."

51 A snood is a kind of hair net, particularly fashionable in the Middle Ages and again in the nineteenth century. It was both fashionable and practical, as it kept long hair out of the way, thus reinforcing the identity of worker.

52 See Chenut, who explains that in the garment-making industry "manual tasks were assigned to women who became known as 'petites mains,'" *Fabric of Gender*, 176. As couture houses developed, the somewhat dismissive term continued to be used even as these female workers gained visibility and importance. Today their couture handwork is sometimes recognized as highly skilled, although the original notion of *petites mains* persists in the sweatshop sector. See Laurence Marti, "Singes, ours, géants, petites mains et pauvres diables: Le Corps dans le travail ouvrier au XIXe siècle," in *Faire corps: Temps, lieu et gens,* ed. Monica Aceti, Christophe Jaccoud, and Laurent Tissot (Neuchâtel: Alphil, 2018); and Leon Roger-Milès, *Les Créateurs de la mode* (Paris: Ch. Eggimann, 1964).

53 "The hand is no longer just the metaphor of the creative spirit; it also designates the materiality of the pictorial work." Guichard, *La Griffe du peintre*, 129.

54 The nineteenth-century aesthetic taboo on a frank and outward-looking stare of a woman is perhaps best encapsulated in the vehement response to Manet's *Olympia* (1865). See George Heard Hamilton, *Manet and his Critics* (New Haven: Yale University Press, 1954); and T. J. Clark, *The Painting of Modern Life*: Paris in the Art of Manet and His Followers, rev. ed. (Princeton, N.J: Princeton University Press, 1999). For a more recent exploration of female vision, the gaze and its representation, see Kessler, *Sheer Presence*. Higonnet makes the case that the image of a young lady sketching was a trope of nineteenth-century art that made its way into fashion plate art as well, writing, "Over and over again the motif of a woman sketching appears in contemporary painting and in fashion illustration especially." "Secluded Vision," 18.

55 Jillian Lerner sees a similarly gendered relationship in her treatment of the graphic arts world in the France of the July Monarchy, in an informative discussion of the life and work of Laure Devéria, sister of Achille, who famously created the 1830 fashion-inspired series *Les Heures du jour*. In this series, Devéria pictures Laure, an accomplished flower painter who, like the Colin sisters, was trained by a male artist relation (her brother), as both an artist captured in the act of sketching and as a fashionably aesthetic object. Lerner, *Graphic Culture*, 122–3.

56 Ibid., 123.

57 See Shearer West, *Portraiture* (Oxford: Oxford University Press, 2004), 163–285; and Richard Brilliant, *Portraiture* (London: Reaktion Books, 1991), 45–77.

58 Marsha Meskimmon, *The Art of Reflection: Women Artists' Self-Portraiture in the Twentieth Century* (New York: Columbia University Press, 1996), 15. See also Auricchio, "Self-Promotion"; and Wettlaufer, *Portraits of the Artist*.

59 Taken together, the two paintings also suggest a variation on the "feminist dilemma" Pollock describes in *Vision and Difference* "wherein the woman who is an artist sees her experience in terms of the feminine position, that is as object of the look, while she must also account for the feeling she experiences as an artist occupying the masculine position as subject of the look," 86.

60 Ibid., 87.

61 For a discussion of the complexity of feminine self-portrait in nineteenth-century France, see especially Anne Higonnet, "The Other Side of the Mirror," chapter 4 in *Perspectives on Morisot*, ed. T. J. Edelstein (New York: Hudson Hills Press, 1992).

62 Gustave Toudouze explains that after their marriage, Anaïs and Gabriel relocated to Toudouze's native Brittany in 1845–6, during which time she collaborated with him on a commissioned project—an *eaux-fortes* collection of the edifices of Breton churches. According to Gustave, his father Gabriel rendered the architecture and his mother Anaïs rendered the characters in costume. It was Anaïs who completed this work after the death of Gabriel. The architect had begun a new project of restoring the Sainte-Chapelle and was commuting regularly into Paris from their suburban home in l'Haÿ-les-Roses. He died of cerebral apoplexy in his garden on May 25, 1854. "Une Famille d'artistes."

63 In the catalogue of the 1835 Salon, we find seven paintings by Alexandre Colin, ranging from historical studies to landscapes and character studies like "Un duel dans une grotte." Following his listing we find watercolors painted by Madame J. Colin on subjects such as "baptism" and "marriage," executed in Nîmes like those of her husband. Finally, two watercolors by Mademoiselle H. Colin, "Une prise de voile" and "Une religieuse morte, avec la cérémonie de funérailles" are listed after her parents' works. See Pierre Sanchez and Xavier Seydoux, *Les Catalogues des Salons* (Paris: Échelle de Jacob, 1835–40), 3: 44. On miniature arts, see *Moniteur des arts* (Dec. 24, 1886), 3; accessed August 19, 2022, https://www.retronews.fr/embed-journal/moniteur-des-arts/24-decembre-1886/3328/5029990/3.

64 See Griffiths and Mill, "Database of Salon Artists." Unfortunately, as the database extends only to 1850, it does not track their works exhibited after that date, although both sisters certainly exhibited beyond 1850.

65 For more on Lina Jaunès and the importance and ubiquity of women art critics in nineteenth-century France, see Guentner, *Women Art Critics in Nineteenth-Century France*.

66 Linna Jaunès, "Œuvres des Femmes au Salon de 1835," *Journal des femmes: Gymnase littéraire*, ed. Louis Janet (March 15, 1835), 18: 137.

67 Ibid., 18: 138, 140.

68 Ténint goes on to wish for "a little more truth in the color, and also in the light." Wilhelm Ténint, *Album du Salon de 1842: Collection des principaux ouvrages exposé au Louvre* (Paris, 1842), 54; accessed August 20, 2022, https://gallica.bnf.fr/ark:/12148/bpt6k63221829.

69 The letter from the Maison du Roi, Direction des Musées Royaux, addressed to Mlle. A. Colin on May 26, 1844, announcing Anaïs's third-place medal for the 1844 Salon is located among the family papers at the Bibliothèque de l'Arsenal, Paris.

70 Exeter's "Database of Salon Artists" does not list a title for the single portrait that was accepted to the Salon under the name of Adèle-Anaïs Colin, but the Musée Carnavalet's records indicate that in the materials associated with the painting, the donor indicated that this was the title submitted to the Salon.

71 Bonin asserts that critics have misattributed a number of Alexandre Colin's works to his daughter, given that they share the initial "A." "Les Sœurs Colin," 47–8.

72 See chapter 1. See also Guentner, "The Ideology of the Two Spheres," in *Women Art Critics* for further discussion of this topic.

73 For the seminal text, see Charles Baudelaire's widely cited essay, "Le Peintre de la vie moderne," *Œuvres completes* (Paris: Laffont, 1980), 790–815. Many fashion historians have cited and elaborated on Baudelaire's essay in great

74 Patricia Mainardi, *Another World: Nineteenth-Century Illustrated Print Culture* (New Haven: Yale University Press, 2017), 31.

75 The title likely given by Maurice Leloir, as noted in the archives of the musée Galliera, was "4 Femmes et une fillette dans un parc, esquisse." It was drawn *c*. 1869.

76 Calahan, *Fashion Plates*, 1. See also Hahn, *Scenes of Parisian Modernity*, for the importance of the fashion plate to advertisements.

77 Ginsburg, *Introduction to Fashion Illustration*, 3.

78 Bonin observes that items in the fashion-plate archives in Rouen show signs of having been tacked to walls, and my own personal experience reinforces this assumption: I was given a plate by a former teacher who told me that she discovered it hanging on the wall of her family's country home—it had been there ever since she could remember, and as we saw in chapter 1, plates were enhanced materially with bits of fabric and lace in a gesture of fetishistic embellishment.

79 The name of the dressmaker is penciled in at the top right corner of the sketch. No. KD3955, musée Galliera.

80 "Fashion photography is therefore located in two places. Its data are taken from the world, but it is not that world. Its locus is always elsewhere, *hors champ*, a threshold ideality of desiring, that need not discriminate between beauty or its degradation." Adam Geczy and Vicki Karaminas, *Fashion's Double: Representations of Fashion in Painting, Photography and Film* (London: Bloomsbury Academic, 2016), 18.

81 Calahan, *Fashion Plates*, 236. See also Moore, *Fashion through Fashion Plates*, 14–15, and Steele, *Paris Fashion*, 2nd ed. (Oxford: Berg, 1999), 112. It is also likely that in some cases, garments were sent to their homes to be drawn. In the case of Héloïse Leloir in the 1860s, her studio was located at 3 rue d'Erfurth, in Paris's sixth arrondissement near the Jardin du Luxembourg. Paul Lacroix, *Annuaire des artistes et des amateurs* (Paris: P. L. Jacob, 1861), https://books.google.com/books?id=yF0oAAAAYAAJ&hl=fr&pg=PA1#v=onepage&q&f=false. Héloïse's death notice indicates that she died at her home, also in the sixth arrondissement, at 8 rue Furstemberg, in 1874. It is likely that both women worked in home studios, but Héloïse, whose husband was also an artist, may have had access to his studio space.

82 My emphasis. Quoted in François Daulte, *L'Aquarelle française au XIXe siècle* (Paris: Bibliothèque des arts, 1969), 118.

83 Ibid., 10.

84 Brettell writes, "Although the medium [watercolor] had existed in art since medieval times, it did not attain widespread use (and specialized markets and societies) until the nineteenth century, when it was taken up by non-professionals or 'amateur' middle-class artists, particularly women, and non-art professionals like archaeologists, travelers, historians, geographers, botanists, and so on." Richard R. R. Brettell, "The Paper Century: French Painting in the 1800s," *Color, Line, Light: French Drawings, Watercolors, and Pastels from Delacroix to Signac*, ed. Margaret Morgan Grasselli and Andrew Robison (New York: Prestel Publishing, 2012), 10.

85 Daulte, *L'Aquarelle française*, 12.

86 Ibid., 16.

87 See, for example, the review of Linna Jaunès, "Œuvres de femmes au Salon de 1835." See also Dewitte, who writes: "In nineteenth-century France, the category of drawing (*dessin*) was widely understood to comprise

watercolour, pastel, gouache and charcoal in addition to pen and pencil. The French sometimes call this grouping 'the graphic arts', a term the English language uses to denote the inclusion of prints. Within Salon catalogues, drawings were usually grouped alongside 'lesser' decorative arts, such as enamels, porcelain and stained glass, as well as with miniature paintings, which were considered to be a different and lesser practice than larger paintings." Debra J. Dewitte, "Exhibition of Drawings, Pastels and Watercolors in the French Salon: 1863–1881," in Kearns and Mill, *Paris Fine Art Salon/Le Salon*, 371.

88   Bonin rightly asserts that the Colin girls were trained with practical, professional goals in mind, given that, in spite of Alexandre Colin's relative success as an artist, it was never terribly lucrative, and artistic talent could be put to profit in book and fashion illustration, as both parents did. "Les Sœurs Colin," 47–8.

89   The watercolor pictured in figure 4.12 has not been located as a fashion plate, or in any lithographic form, which begs the question if, in some cases, the watercolor itself is the finished product.

90   Bonin, "Les Sœurs Colin," 62–3.

91   See Gallica link for a reference to the publication of this lithographic work, accessed August 20, 2022, https://gallica.bnf.fr/ark:/12148/bpt6k62028269/f472.image.r="la corbeille de flore"?rk=171674;4.

92   Bermingham, *Learning to Draw*, 223–4. See also Ringelberg for a discussion of renowned flower painter Madeleine Lemaire and the ways in which "a recontextualization of Lemaire's association with flowers not only allows us to see her own work in a less anachronistically negative light, but it also opens up important heterotopic possibilities for non-normative identification and engagement as opposed to association with mere superficial 'feminine' (and effeminate) vapidity." Ringelberg, "The Court of Lilacs, the Studio of Roses, the Garden at Réveillon," 179.

93   Armand Chassagne, *Traité d'aquarelle* (Paris: C. Fouraut et fils, 1875), 105; accessed August 17, 2022, https://gallica.bnf.fr/ark:/12148/bpt6k62078011. It should be noted that Chassagne addresses himself to a male audience.

94   Ibid., 100.

95   Bermingham, *Learning to Draw*, 224.

96   Bonin, "Les Sœurs Colin," 48.

97   "If Anaïs is more famous than Héloïse," Steele explains, "it is partly because she lived longer and had a larger *œuvre* than her elder sister." Her husband died in 1854, "leaving Anaïs with three small children to support. It was therefore largely economic necessity that made the young widow the most industrious of the Colin sisters, working nonstop through the 1870s, sometimes collaborating with Héloïse, and continuing regularly to produce fashion plates up to the time of her death." Steele, *Paris Fashion*, 2nd ed. (Oxford: Berg, 1999), 105–6.

98   Bonin, "Les Sœurs Colin," 62–3.

99   As stated earlier, I use the standard term "fashion plate" to refer to these images. The fashion plate differs from the watercolor illustrations that the Colin sisters and others produced and that were transformed through the engraving or lithography process (hence, plate) into reproduced and colored prints. See Calahan, *Fashion Plates*, 1.

100 Steele, "Fashioning the *Parisienne*," in *Paris Fashion*, 3rd ed. (2017), 101.

101 Ibid., 100–2; and Higonnet, *Berthe Morisot's Images of Women*, 96–9.

102 Brevik-Zender, "Interstitial Narratives," 95.

103 See Marcus, "Reflections on Victorian Fashion Plates."

104 Ibid., 8, 17. See also Lynda Nead, "The Layering of Pleasure: Women, Fashionable Dress and Visual Culture in the Mid-Nineteenth Century," *Nineteenth-Century Contexts* 35, no. 5 (2013): 489–509.

105 An earlier version of some of this material appears in the form of an article, "Feminized Commodities, Female Communities: The Colin Sisters and the Stealthy Work of the Fashion Plate," *French Historical Studies* 43, no. 2 (2020): 223–52.

106 Justine De Young, "Representing the Modern Woman: The Fashion Plate Reconsidered (1865–1875)," in *Women, Femininity, and Public Space in European Visual Culture, 1789–1914*, ed. Temma Balducci and Heather Belnap Jensen (Farnham, UK: Ashgate, 2014), 103.

107 Calahan, *Fashion Plates*, 6.

108 Coffin, *Politics of Women's Work*, 116.

109 See chapter 3.

110 Marcus repeats the characteristic judgment that fashion plates lack narrative, citing Moore, *Fashion through Fashion Plates*, and Vanda Foster, *A Visual History of Costume: The Nineteenth Century* (London: B.T. Batsford, 1984), 24. Sharon Marcus, "Reflection on Victorian Fashion Plates" *differences: A Journal of Feminist Cultural Studies*, 14 no. 3 (2003): 4–33.

111 See J. F. M. Clark, *Bugs and the Victorians* (New Haven: Yale University Press, 2009); and Eric Baratay, *Portraits d'animaux: Les Planches du Dictionnaire universel d'histoire naturelle de Charles d'Orbigny (1841–1849)* (Lyon: Fage Éditions, 2007).

112 See also J. J. Grandville's 1847, *Les Fleurs animées*, for a sardonic take on the tradition of the "language of flowers" and women's association with flowers, and my analysis of this work. Susan Hiner, "From Pudeur to Plaisir: Grandville's Flowers in the Kingdom of Fashion," *Dix-Neuf: Journal of the Society of Dix-Neuviémistes* 18, no. 1 (2014): 45–68.

113 See Dombrowski, *Cézanne, Murder, and Modern Life*; Higonnet, *Berthe Morisot's Images of Women*; and Justine De Young, "Fashion and the Press," in Groom, *Impressionism, Fashion, and Modernity*.

114 The question of skill is important here. Many would classify female fashion workers as "unskilled," but as Nina Lerman points out, this is a coarse classification that does not account for the nuances of skill required for certain types of labor. Labor history, she suggests, typically cast female workers (including housewives) as unskilled as the result of a masculine bias in the discipline, which looks only within parameters defined by itself for proof of its claims. Nina Lerman, "Problems with 'Skill,'" in *Major Problems in the History of American Technology*, ed. Merritt Roe Smith and Gregory Clancy (New York: Houghton Mifflin, 1997), 15–17.

115 See Rozsika Parker, *The Subversive Stitch: Embroidery and the Making of the Feminine* (London: Women's Press, 1984), for a history of the gendering of embroidery and its place on the arts/crafts divide.

116 The caption reads "Chapeaux de Mad. Herst," thus indicating by the plural that the *modiste* being advertised created both hats.

117 See Marcus, "Reflections on Victorian Fashion Plates" and *Between Women*. Marcus discusses at length the strangeness of the gaze in many plates.

118 Peter J. Capuano, *Changing Hands: Industry, Evolution, and the Reconfiguration of the Victorian Body* (Ann Arbor: University of Michigan Press, 2015), 2.

119 See Wettlaufer, *Portraits of the Artist*, 31. It has been amply demonstrated that bourgeois women's more substantial "occupation" may well have been to signify and telegraph through their appearance the social status, wealth, and respectability of their husbands and family. See also Hiner, *Accessories to Modernity*.

120 Gaudriault quotes from Paul Prouté's *souvenirs* entitled *Un Vieux Marchand de gravures raconte*, in which he describes the manual labor of fashion-plate colorists. *La Gravure de mode feminine*, 130. By 1899, the mass production of fashion plates eliminated the need for hand-coloring; these teams of female colorists moved into the sector of early cinema, becoming the first film colorists. See John Hadfield, *Victorian Delights: Reflections of Taste in the Nineteenth Century* (London: New Amsterdam Press, 1987), 33; and Joshua Yumibe, "French Film Colorists," on website "Women Film Pioneers Project" (New York: Columbia University Libraries, 2013), accessed August 20, 2022, https://wfpp.columbia.edu/essay/french-film-colorists/. See also Bonin, "Les Sœurs Colin," who describes the gradual mechanization of the colorizing of fashion plates.

121 See the Galerie Jaegy-Theoleyre's website for identifying information, accessed August 20, 2022, https://www.jaegy-theoleyre.fr/produit/1573.

122 Gustave Flaubert to Gustave Toudouze, June 2, 1879, MS 15077 (1), Bibliothèque de l'Arsenal.

123 Gustave Toudouze to Paul Eudel, 1898, MS 15077 (1), Bibliothèque de l'Arsenal.

124 Gustave Toudouze, *Madame Lambelle* (Paris: E. Dentu, 1880), 84–5; accessed August 18, 2022, https://gallica.bnf.fr/ark:/12148/bpt6k65418188. Like her sister Héloïse, Anaïs Colin also won a third-place medal at the Salon, in 1844.

125 Gustave Toudouze, "Une Famille d'artistes."

126 Gustave Toudouze, *Madame Lambelle*, 87.

127 Higonnet, *Berthe Morisot's Images of Women*, 91. See also Brevik-Zender, "Interstitial Narratives."

Epilogue

1 With a focus on the Belle Epoque, Tilburg offers a rich discussion of *midinette* imagery in her excellent history of the figure in *Working Girls*. See also Anne Monjaret and Michela Niccolai, "Elle trotte, danse et chante, la midinette! Univers sonore des couturières parisiennes dans les chansons (XIXe–XXe siècles)," *L'Homme: Revue française d'anthropologie*, no. 215/216, special issue, "Connaît-on la chanson?" (July/December 2015), 47–79.

2 See Susan Hiner, "Picturing the Catherinette: Reinventing Tradition for the Postcard Age," in *French Cultural Studies for the Twenty-First Century*, ed. Masha Belenky, Kathryn Kleppinger, and Anne O'Neil-Henry (Newark: University of Delaware Press, 2017); Naomi Schor, "*Cartes Postales*: Representing Paris 1900," *Critical Inquiry* 18, no. 2 (1992): 188–244; and Lynda Klitch and Benjamin Weiss, *The Postcard Age* (Boston: MFA, 2012).

3 *Le Petit Journal: Supplément du dimanche* (November 8, 1903), 2; accessed August 20, 2022, https://bit.ly/3QYkK9j, RetroNews.

4 Tilburg, *Working Girls*, 46.

5 Thomas, *Fashionopolis*, 7.

6 See especially Bass-Krueger, "From the '*union parfaite*' to the '*union brisée*.'" See also Tilburg, *Working Girls*; and Sophie Kurkdjian and Sandrine Tinturier, *Au Cœur des maisons de couture: Une Histoire sociale des ouvrières de la mode (1880–1950)* (Ivry-sur-Seine: Les Editions de l'Atelier, 2021).

7 See Tilburg, *Working Girls*, 156–96; and Bass-Krueger, "From the '*union parfaite*' to the '*union brisée*.'"

8 Vionnet famously said that "Women's bodies had no seams," and strove with her bias-cut to drape fabric in order to fit clothes more naturally to women's bodies. Madeleine Chapsal, *Madeleine Vionnet, Ma mère et moi: L'Éblouissement de la haute couture* (Paris: Editions de la Loupe, 2010), 127.

Works Consulted

Archives Consulted

Archives de Paris, France
    Actes d'état civil
    Actes des faillites
Beinecke Library, Yale University, New Haven, CT
    Le Journal des demoiselles
Bibliothèque de L'Arsenal, Paris, France
    MS 15011 (1–2)
Bibliothèque de la Sorbonne, Paris, France
    Bonin, Marie. "Les Sœurs Colin: Héloïse et Anaïs: Femmes artistes dans la seconde moitié du XIXe siècle." (mémoire de master 2)
Bibliothèque Forney, Paris, France
    La Mode illustrée (digital archive)
Bibliothèque Historique de la ville de Paris, Paris, France (visual materials)
Bilbliothèque Marguerite Durand, Paris, France
    Léger-Paturneau, Christine, *Le "Journal des demoiselles" et l'éducation des filles sous la Monarchie de Juillet (1833–1848)*. Dissertation, Université de Paris VII, 1988.
Bibliothèque Nationale de France, Gallica
    La Sylphide, journal de modes
Bibliothèque Nationale de France; vaudeville plays consulted (some available on Gallica online):
    La Nina de la rue Vivienne, Francis, Dartois, et Gabriel, 1821
    Les Modistes, Villeneuve et Dupeuty, 1824
    Les Visites au Louvre, Philadephe (Alhoy) et Ludwig (Isnère de Sainte-Lorette), 1823
    La Fiancée, Scribe et Auber, 1829
    L'Art de ne pas monter sa garde, Barthélemy et Lhérie, 1832
    La Révolte des modistes, Valory et Cogniard frères, 1834
    Le Commis et la grisette, de Kock et Labie, 1834
    Femme et maîtresse, Guillard, 1837
    Rose et Blanche, Anvers, 1837
    Une Vengeance de modistes, Lubize et Brisebarre, 1838
    Le Bonheur sous les toits, Burat et Didier, 1839
    Les Belles Femmes de Paris, Angel et Vanel, 1839
    C'est ma chambre, Pierron et D'Almbert, 1841
    L'Omelette fantastique, Duvert et Boyer, 1842
    L'Art de tirer des carottes, Jaime et Marc-Michel, 1843

Le Trottin de la modiste, Clairville, 1847

L'Atelier des demoiselles, de Kock, 1848

Un Chapeau de paille d'Italie, Marc-Michel et Labiche, 1851

Les Débuts de la modiste, Jouhaud, 1855

Deux Veillées d'un pensionnat, Lejeune, 1860

Modiste et modeste, Jallais et Prével, 1860

Tête de Linotte, Barrière et Gondinet, 1886

L'Anglais et la modiste, Deschamps et Berge, n.d.

Bibliothèque Nationale de France, RetroNews (online)

Musée Carnavalet, Le Cabinet des arts graphiques (visual materials)

Musée Galliera, Paris, France (archives des Sœurs Colin)

Gerritsen Collection, Vassar College, Poughkeepsie, NY

Le Journal des demoiselles (digital archive)

Books and Articles

D'Anspach, Maria. "La Modiste." In Bouttier, *Les Français peints par eux-mêmes*, 3: 105–12.

Artisans de l'élégance. Catalogue for an exhibition of the same name at the Musée national des arts et traditions populaires (ATP), November 17, 1993–May 15, 1994. Paris: Réunion des musées nationaux, 1993.

Auricchio, Laura. "Self-Promotion in Adélaïde Labille-Guiard's 1785 'Self-Portrait with Two Students.'" *The Art Bulletin* 89, no. 1 (March 2007): 45–62.

Auslander, Leora. *Taste and Power: Furnishing Modern France*. Berkeley: University of California Press, 1998.

Balzac, Honoré de. "The Proper Woman." In *Popular Literature from Nineteenth-Century France: English Translation*. Translated and edited by Masha Belenky and Anne O'Neil-Henry, 162–84. New York: MLA of America, 2021.

Baratay, Eric. *Portraits d'animaux: Les Planches du Dictionnaire universel d'histoire naturelle de Charles d'Orbigny (1841–1849)*. Lyon: Fage Éditions, 2007.

Barthes, Roland. "Structure du fait divers." In *Essais critiques*, 188–97. Paris: Seuil, 1964.

Barthes, Roland. *Système de la mode*. Paris: Seuil, 1967.

Barthes, Roland. *Mythologies*, translated by Annette Lavers. New York: Hill and Wang, 1972.

Bass-Krueger, Maude. "From the '*union parfaite*' to the '*union brisée*': The French Couture Industry and the *midinettes* during the Great War." *Costume* 47, no. 1 (Jan. 2013): 28–44.

Baudelaire, Charles. "Le Peintre de la vie moderne." *Œuvres completes*. Paris: Laffont, 1980.

Belenky, Masha. *Engine of Modernity: The Omnibus and Urban Culture in Nineteenth-Century Paris*. Interventions: Rethinking the Nineteenth Century. Manchester: Manchester University Press, 2019.

Belenky, Masha, and Anne O'Neil-Henry, trans and eds. *Popular Literature from Nineteenth-Century France: English Translation*. New York: MLA of America, 2021.

Bellavitis, Anna. *Women's Work and Rights in Early Modern Urban Europe*. Cham, Switzerland: Palgrave Macmillan, 2018.

Benjamin, Walter. *The Arcades Project*. Cambridge, MA: Harvard University Press, 1999.

Bermingham, Ann. *Learning to Draw: Studies in the Cultural History of a Polite and Useful Art*. New Haven: Yale University Press, 2000.

Best, Kate Nelson. "Text and Image in Fashion Periodicals of the Second French Empire." In *Text and Image in Modern European Culture*. Edited by Natasha Grigorian, Thomas Baldwin, and Margaret Rigaud-Drayton, 101–14. West Lafayette, IN: Purdue University Press, 2012.

Best, Kate Nelson. *The History of Fashion Journalism*. London: Bloomsbury Academic, 2017.

Bolomier, Eliane. *Le Chapeau: Grand art et savoir-faire.* Paris: Somogy, 1996.

Bonin, Marie. "Les Sœurs Colin: Héloïse et Anaïs, femmes artistes dans la seconde moitié du XIXᵉ siècle." Unpublished master's thesis. Université de Paris, Sorbonne, 2013.

Bonnet, Marie-Jo. "Femmes peintres à leur travail: De L'Autoportrait comme manifeste politique (XVIIIᵉ–XIXᵉ siècles)." *Revue d'histoire modern et contemporaine* 49, no. 3 (2002): 140–67.

Bonvoisin, Samra-Martine, and Michèle Maignien. *La Presse féminine.* Paris: Presses universitaires de France, 1986.

Bouchot, Henri. *La Miniature française, 1750–1825.* Paris: Émile-Paul, 1910. Accessed August 29, 2022. https://gallica.bnf.fr/ark:/12148/bpt6k12687822.

Bourcard, Gustave. *Les Estampes du XVIIIᵉ siècle*. With a preface by Paul Eudel. Paris: E. Dentu, 1885.

Bourdieu, Pierre. *Distinction: A Social Critique of the Judgement of Taste*, translated by Richard Nice. Cambridge, MA: Harvard University Press, 1984.

Bourdieu, P., and Y. Delsaut. "Le Couturier et sa griffe: Contribution à une théorie de la magie." *Actes de la Recherche en Sciences Sociales* 1 (1975): 7–36.

Boutin, Aimée. "Rethinking the Flâneur: Flânerie and the Senses." Special issue, *Dix-Neuf: Journal of the Society of Dix-Neuviémistes* 16, no. 2 (2012): 124–32.

Bouttier, Pierre, ed. *Les Français peints par eux-mêmes: Encyclopédie morale du XIXᵉ siècle*. 1840–42. Accessed August 28, 2022. https://gallica.bnf.fr/ark:/12148/bpt6k2079830.

Bouvier, Jeanne. *La Lingerie et les lingères*. Paris: Gaston Doin, 1928.

Bouvier, Jeanne, Daniel Armogathe, and Maïté Albistur. *Mes mémoires, ou, 59 années d'activité industrielle, sociale et intellectuelle d'une ouvrière: 1876–1935*. Paris: La Découverte/Maspero, 1983.

Brettell, Richard R. "The Paper Century: French Drawing in the 1800s." *Color, Line, Light: French Drawings, Watercolors, and Pastels from Delacroix to Signac*. Edited by Margaret Morgan Grasselli and Andrew Robison. New York: Prestel Publishing, 2012. Exhibition catalogue, 2–15.

Brevik-Zender, Heidi. "Interstitial Narratives: Rethinking Feminine Spaces of Modernity in Nineteenth-Century French Fashion Plates." *Nineteenth-Century Contexts* 36, no. 2 (2014): 91–123.

Brevik-Zender, Heidi. *Fashioning Spaces: Mode and Modernity in Late-Nineteenth-Century Paris*. Toronto: University of Toronto Press, 2015.

Brilliant, Richard. *Portraiture*. London: Reaktion Books, 1991.

Busquet, Alfred. "Salon de 1857: Dessins et Aquarelles." *Le Portefeuille de l'amateur: Journal artistique contenant un cours de dessin gradué*, vol. 1, no. 4 (Sept. 15, 1857), 13–15. Accessed August 21, 2022. https://gallica.bnf.fr/ark:/12148/bpt6k9819212q/f5.item.

Calahan, April. *Fashion Plates: 150 Years of Style*. Edited by Karen Trivette Cannell, with a foreword by Anna Sui. New Haven: Yale University Press, 2015.

Capuano, Peter J. *Changing Hands: Industry, Evolution, and the Reconfiguration of the Victorian Body*. Ann Arbor: University of Michigan Press, 2015.

Carby, Hazel V. Foreword to *Silencing the Past: Power and the Production of History* by Michel-Rolph Trouillot, xi–xiii. Rev. ed. New York: Beacon Press, 2015.

Cassatt, Mary, and Nancy M. Mathews. *Cassatt and Her Circle: Selected Letters*. New York: Abbeville Press, 1984.

Chapsal, Madeleine. *Madeleine Vionnet, Ma mère et moi: L'Éblouissement de la haute couture*. Paris: Editions de la Loupe, 2010.

Chassagne, Armand. *Traité de aquarelle*. Paris: C. Fouraut et fils, 1875. Accessed August 17, 2022. http://catalogue.bnf.fr/ark:/12148/cb302028770.

Chenut, Helen Harden. *The Fabric of Gender: Working-Class Culture in Third Republic France*. University Park: Pennsylvania State University Press, 2005.

Chevalier, Jean-Yves. "La mare aux canards." *Médium* 3–4, no. 52–3 (2017): 149–57.

Chrisman-Campbell, Kimberly. *Fashion Victims: Dress at the Court of Louis XVI and Marie-Antoinette*. New Haven: Yale University Press, 2015.

Clairville, M. *Le Trottin de la modiste: Vaudeville en deux acte*s. N.p., 1848. Accessed August 28, 2022. https://gallica.bnf.fr/ark:/12148/bpt6k9809217h.

Clark, J. F. M. *Bugs and the Victorians*. New Haven: Yale University Press, 2009.
Clark, T. J. *The Painting of Modern Life: Paris in the Art of Manet and His Followers.* Rev. ed. Princeton, NJ: Princeton University Press, 1999.
Clayson, Hollis. *Painted Love: Prostitution in French Art of the Impressionist Era*. New Haven: Yale University Press, 1991.
Coffin, Judith G. *The Politics of Women's Work: The Paris Garment Trades, 1750–1915*. Princeton, NJ: Princeton University Press, 2014.
Cohen, Gary B. Foreword to *The Memory Factory: The Forgotten Women Artists of Vienna 1900*, by Julie M. Johnson, xvii–xviii. West Lafayette, IN: Purdue University Press, 2012.
Cohen, Monica F. *Professional Domesticity in the Victorian Novel: Women, Work and Home*. Cambridge Studies in Nineteenth-Century Literature and Culture, vol. 14. Cambridge: Cambridge University Press, 1998.
Corbin, Alain. *Les Filles de noce: Misère sexuelle et prostitution (19e et 20e siècles)*. Paris: Flammarion, 2015.
Cosnier, Colette. *Le Silence des filles: De L'Aiguille à la plume.* Paris: Fayard, 2001.
Craig, Béatrice. *Female Enterprise behind the Discursive Veil in Nineteenth-Century Northern France.* London: Palgrave Macmillan, 2017.
Crossick, Geoffrey, and Serge Jaumain. *Cathedrals of Consumption: The European Department Store, 1850–1939*. Aldershot, UK: Ashgate, 1999.
Crowston, Clare Haru. *Fabricating Women: The Seamstresses of Old Regime France, 1675–1791*. Durham, NC: Duke University Press, 2001.
Dash, Comtesse. *Mémoires des autres: Souvenirs anecdotiques sur mes contemporains*, 6:85. Paris: Librairie illustrée, 1896–8. Accessed August 28, 2022. ark:/12148/bpt6k9601294b.
Daulte, François. *L'Aquarelle française au XIXe siècle*. Paris: Bibliothèque des arts, 1969.
Davidoff, Leonore, and Catherine Hall. *Family Fortunes: Men and Women of the English Middle Class, 1780–1850*. 2nd ed. Abingdon, UK: Routledge, 2002.
Davidson, Denise Z. "Making Society 'Legible'" People-Watching in Paris after the Revolution." *French Historical Studies* 28, no. 2 (2005): 265–96
De la Motte, Dean, and Jeannene M. Przyblyski. *Making the News: Modernity and the Mass Press in Nineteenth-Century France*. Studies in Print Culture and the History of the Book. Amherst: University of Massachusetts Press, 1999.
De Young, Justine. "Fashion and the Press." In Groom, *Fashion, Impressionism, and Modernity*, 235–43.
De Young, Justine. "Representing the Modern Woman: The Fashion Plate Reconsidered (1865–1875)." In *Women, Femininity, and Public Space in European Visual Culture, 1789–1914*. Edited by Temma Balducci and Heather Belnap Jensen, 97–114. Farnham, UK: Ashgate, 2014.
Desmaisons, L.-Ch. *"Tu seras ouvrière," simple histoire: Livre de lecture courante à l'usage des écoles de filles*. Preface by Jules Simon. Paris: A. Colin, 1892. Accessed July 11, 2022. https://gallica.bnf.fr/ark:/12148/bpt6k3149840.
Desprez, Ernest. "Les Grisettes à Paris." In *Paris, ou le livre des cent-et-un*, 211–37. Paris: Librairie Ladvocat, 1832.
Dewitte, Debra J. "The Exhibition of Drawings, Pastels and Watercolors in the French Salon: 1863–1881." In Kearns and Mill, *Paris Fine Art Salon/Le Salon*, 371–84.
Dictionnaire de l'Académie française. 6th ed. Paris, 1835. Accessed August 28, 2022. https://www.dictionnaire-academie.fr.
Dion, Sylvie. "Fait Divers (Human Interest Stories) as a Narrative Genre." *Sociocriticism* 7:2 (1992): 79–88.
Dolan, Alice. "An Adorned Print: Print Culture, Female Leisure and the Dissemination of Fashion in France and England, around 1660–1779." *V&A Online Journal*, no. 3 (Spring 2011). Accessed August 27, 2022. http://www.vam.ac.uk/content/journals/research-journal/issue-03/an-adorned-print-print-culture,-female-leisure-and-the-dissemination-of-fashion-in-france-and-england,-c.-1660-1779/.
Dombrowski, André. *Cézanne, Murder, and Modern Life*. Phillips Collection Book Prize Series, vol. 3. Berkeley: University of California Press, 2012.
Edelstein, T. J., ed. *Perspectives on Morisot*. New York: Hudson Hills Press, 1992.

Emery, Joy Spanabel. *A History of the Paper Pattern Industry: The Home Dressmaking Fashion Revolution*. London: Bloomsbury Academic, 2014.

Evans, Caroline. *The Mechanical Smile: Modernism and the First Fashion Shows in France and America, 1900–1929*. New Haven: Yale University Press, 2013.

Farge, Arlette. *Vies oubliées, au cœur du xviiie siècle*. Paris: La Découverte, 2019.

Farwell, Beatrice. *The Charged Image: French Lithographic Caricature, 1816–1848*. Santa Barbara: Santa Barbara Museum of Art, 1989.

Finch, Alison. "The Journalist: Delphine de Girardin." In *Women's Writing in Nineteenth-Century France*, 130–38. Cambridge: Cambridge University Press, 2000.

Flaubert, Gustave. *Madame Bovary: Mœurs de province*. 2 vols. Paris: Michel Lévy frères, 1858. Accessed August 29, 2022. https://gallica.bnf.fr/ark:/12148/bpt6k1518572b.

Fontaney, Antoine. "Un Magasin des modes: Histoire d'une capote." *Paris, ou Le Livre des cent-et-un*. Accessed July 5, 2022. http://www.bmlisieux.com/curiosa/fontan01.htm.

Foster, Vanda. *A Visual History of Costume: The Nineteenth Century*. London: B.T. Batsford, 1984.

Friedberg, Anne. *The Virtual Window: From Alberti to Microsoft*. Cambridge, MA: MIT Press, 2006.

Fuchs, Rachel G. *Poor and Pregnant in Paris: Strategies for Survival in the Nineteenth Century*. New Brunswick, NJ: Rutgers University Press, 1992.

Garb, Tamar. *Sisters of the Brush: Women's Artistic Culture in Late Nineteenth-Century Paris*. New Haven: Yale University Press, 1994.

Garelick, Rhonda K. *Mademoiselle: Coco Chanel and the Pulse of History*. New York: Random House, 2014.

Garien. "La Modiste—Air: De la grisette." In *La Gaudriole de 1835: Recueil des meilleures chansons* [...]. Edited by Béranger, Désaugiers, Debraux [...]. Paris, 1835. Accessed July 21, 2022. http://catalogue.bnf.fr/ark:/12148/cb334003140.

Gaudriault, Raymond. *La Gravure de mode feminine en France*. Paris: Editions de l'amateur, 1983.

Geczy, Adam, and Vicki Karaminas. *Fashion's Double: Representations of Fashion in Painting, Photography and Film*. London: Bloomsbury Academic, 2016.

Gidel, Henry. *Le Vaudeville*. Paris: Presses universitaires de France, 1986.

Ginsburg, Madeleine. *An Introduction to Fashion Illustration*. London: HMSO, 1980.

Gluck, Mary. *Popular Bohemia: Modernism and Urban Culture in Nineteenth-Century Paris*. Cambridge, MA: Harvard University Press, 2005.

Goldstein, Carl. *Print Culture in Early Modern France: Abraham Bosse and the Purposes of Print*. New York: Cambridge University Press, 2012.

Gossman, Lionel. "Anecdote and History." *History and Theory* 42, no. 2 (2003): 143–68.

Groom, Gloria, ed. *Impressionism, Fashion, and Modernity*. New Haven: Yale University Press, 2012. Exhibition catalogue.

Guentner, Wendelin, ed. *Women Art Critics in Nineteenth-Century France: Vanishing Acts*. Newark: University of Delaware Press, 2013.

Guichard, Charlotte. *La Griffe du peintre: La Valeur de l'art, 1730–1820*. Paris: Seuil, 2018.

Hadfield, John. *Victorian Delights: Reflections of Taste in the Nineteenth Century*. London: New Amsterdam Press, 1987.

Hahn, H. Hazel. *Scenes of Parisian Modernity: Culture and Consumption in the Nineteenth Century*. New York: Palgrave Macmillan, 2009.

Hamilton, George Heard. *Manet and His Critics*. Yale Publications in the History of Art, vol. 7. New Haven: Yale University Press, 1954.

D'Harcourt, Claire. *Les Habits: Histoire des choses*. Paris: Seuil, 2001.

Hartman, Saidiya V. *Wayward Lives, Beautiful Experiments: Intimate Histories of Riotous Black Girls, Troublesome Women, and Queer Radicals*. New York: W. W. Norton, 2019.

Helly, Dorothy O., and Susan M. Reverby, eds. *Gendered Domains: Rethinking Public and Private in Women's History*. Essays from the Seventh Berkshire Conference on the History of Women. Ithaca, NY: Cornell University Press, 1992.

Higonnet, Anne. *Berthe Morisot's Images of Women*. Cambridge, MA: Harvard University Press, 1992.

Higonnet, Anne. "The Other Side of the Mirror." In Edelstein, *Perspectives on Morisot*, 67–78.

Higonnet, Anne. "Real Fashion: Clothes Unmake the Working Woman." In *Spectacles of Realism: Gender, Body, Genre*. Edited by Margaret Cohen and Christopher Prendergast, 137–62. Minneapolis: University of Minnesota, 1995.

Higonnet, Anne. "Secluded Vision: Images of Feminine Experience in Nineteenth-Century Europe." *Radical History Review* 38 (1987): 16–36.

Hiner, Susan. *Accessories to Modernity: Fashion and the Feminine in Nineteenth-Century France*. Philadelphia: University of Pennsylvania Press, 2010.

Hiner, Susan. "Monsieur Calicot: French Masculinity between Commerce and Honor." *West 86th* 19, no. 1 (2012): 32–60.

Hiner, Susan. "Becoming (M)other: Reflectivity in *Le Journal des Demoiselles*," *Romance Studies* 31, no. 2 (2013): 84–100.

Hiner, Susan. "From Pudeur to Plaisir: Grandville's Flowers in the Kingdom of Fashion." *Dix-Neuf: Journal of the Society of Dix-Neuviémistes* 18, no. 1 (2014): 45–68.

Hiner, Susan. "The *Modiste*'s Palette and the Artist's Hat." In *Degas, Impressionism, and the Paris Millinery Trade*. Edited by Simon Kelly and Esther Bell, 67–81. San Francisco: Fine Arts Museums–Legion of Honor, 2017. Exhibition catalogue.

Hiner, Susan. "Picturing the Catherinette: Reinventing Tradition for the Postcard Age." In *French Cultural Studies for the Twenty-First Century*, edited by Masha Belenky, Kathryn Kleppinger, and Anne O'Neil-Henry, 119–52. Newark: University of Delaware Press, 2017.

Hiner, Susan. "Fashion Animation: Heads, Hats, and the Uncanny Work of Fashion." In *Fashion, Modernity, and Materiality in France: From Rousseau to Art Deco*. Edited by Heidi Brevik-Zender, 33–56. Albany: SUNY Press, 2018.

Hiner, Susan. "Feminized Commodities, Female Communities: The Colin Sisters and the Stealthy Work of the Fashion Plate." *French Historical Studies* 43, no. 2 (2020): 223–52.

Hiner, Susan. "Picturing Work," in *Cultural History of Work in the Age of Empire*. Vol. 5. Edited by Victorian Thompson, 31–50. London: Bloomsbury Academic, 2019.

Hiner, Susan. "When Fashion Stood Still: From *La Mode Assiégée* to *La Mode Durable*." *Nineteenth-Century French Studies* 49, no. 3–4 (2021): 549–66.

Holland, Vyvyan. *Hand Coloured Fashion Plates 1770 to 1899*. London: B. T. Batsford, 1955.

Hollinshead-Strick, Cary. *The Fourth Estate at the Fourth Wall: Newspapers on Stage in July Monarchy France*. Evanston, IL: Northwestern University Press, 2019.

Iacono, Alfonso Maurizio. *The History and Theory of Fetishism*. Marx, Engels, and Fetishisms. Translated and edited by Viktoria Tchernichova and Monica Boria, with the collaboration of Elizabeth MacDonald. Houndmills, UK: Palgrave Macmillan, 2016.

Iskin, Ruth E. *Modern Women and Parisian Consumer Culture in Impressionist Painting*. Cambridge: Cambridge University Press, 2007.

Janin, Jules. "La Grisette." In Bouttier, *Les Français peints par eux-mêmes*, Vol. 1, 35–44.

Jaunès, Linna. "Œuvres des Femmes au Salon de 1835," *Journal des femmes: Gymnase littéraire*, ed. Louis Janet (March 15, 1835), 18: 137.

Johnson, Julie M. *The Memory Factory: The Forgotten Women Artists of Vienna 1900*. West Lafayette, IN: Purdue University Press, 2012.

Jones, Jennifer M. *Sexing* La Mode: *Gender, Fashion and Commercial Culture in Old Regime France*. Oxford: Berg, 2004.

Jullien, Dominique. "Anecdotes, *Faits Divers*, and the Literary." *SubStance* 38, no. 1 (2009): 66–76.

Kaiser, Susan B. *Fashion and Cultural Studies*. Oxford: Berg, 2012; London: Bloomsbury Academic, 2013.

Kearns, James, and Alister Mill, eds., *The Paris Fine Art Salon/Le Salon, 1791–1881*. French Studies of the Eighteenth and Nineteenth Centuries, vol. 33. Oxford: Peter Lang, 2015.

Kerber, Linda K. *Toward an Intellectual History of Women: Essays*. Chapel Hill: University of North Carolina Press, 1997.

Kessler, Marni Reva. *Sheer Presence: The Veil in Manet's Paris*. Minneapolis: University of Minnesota Press, 2006.

Kessler-Harris, Alice. *Women Have Always Worked: A Concise History*. 2nd ed. The Working Class in American History. Urbana: University of Illinois Press, 2018.

Kleinert, Annemarie. *Le "Journal des dames et des modes": ou, La Conquête de l'Europe féminin, 1797–1839*. Stuttgart: Jan Thorbecke Verlag, 2001.

Klitch, Lynda, and Benjamin Weiss, *The Postcard Age*. Boston: MFA, 2012.

Kurkdjian, Sophie, and Sandrine Tinturier. *Au Cœur des maisons de couture: Une Histoire sociale des ouvrières de la mode (1880–1950)*. Ivry-sur-Seine: Les Editions de l'Atelier, 2021.

Labiche, Eugène. *Un Chapeau de paille d'Italie*. Edited by Olivier Balazuc and Stavroula Kefallonitis. Paris: Larousse, 2000.

Lacas, Martine. *Les Peintres Femmes, 1780–1830: Naissance d'un combat*. Paris: Découvertes Gallimard, 2021. Exhibition catalogue.

Lacroix, Paul. *Annuaire des artistes et des amateurs*. Paris: P. L. Jacob, 1861. https://books.google.com/books?id=yF0oAAAAYAAJ&hl=fr&pg=PA1#v=onepage&q&f=false

Léger-Paturneau, Christine. *Le "Journal des demoiselles" et l'éducation des filles sous la Monarchie de Juillet (1833–1848)*. Dissertation, Université de Paris VII, 1988.

Lehmann, Ulrich. *Tigersprung: Fashion in Modernity*. Cambridge, MA: MIT Press, 2000.

Le Maux, Nicole. *Histoire du chapeau féminin*. Series "Modes de Paris." Paris: Charles Massin, 2000.

Lerman, Nina. "Problems with 'Skill.'" In *Major Problems in the History of American Technology*. Edited by Merritt Roe Smith and Gregory Clancy, 15–17. New York: Houghton Mifflin, 1997.

Lerner, Jillian. *Graphic Culture: Illustration and Artistic Enterprise in Paris, 1830–1848*. Montreal: McGill-Queen's University Press, 2018.

Lescart, Alain. *Splendeurs et misères de la grisette: Évolution d'une figure emblématique*. Paris: Champion, 2008.

Lipton, Eunice. *Looking into Degas: Uneasy Images of Women and Modern Life*. Berkeley: University of California Press, 1986.

Madeline, Laurence, Bridget Alsdorf, Richard Kendall, Jane R. Becker, Vibeke Waallann Hansen, and Joëlle Bolloch. *Women Artists in Paris, 1850–1900*. With a foreword by Pauline Willis. New York: American Federation of Arts; New Haven: Yale University Press, 2017. Exhibition catalogue.

Mainardi, Patricia. *Husbands, Wives, and Lovers: Marriage and Its Discontents in Nineteenth-Century France*. New Haven: Yale University Press, 2003.

Mainardi, Patricia. *Another World: Nineteenth-Century Illustrated Print Culture*. New Haven: Yale University Press, 2017.

Major, J. S., and Valerie Steele. "Fashion industry." *Encyclopedia Britannica*. August 21, 2022. https://www.britannica.com/art/fashion-industry.

Marcus, Sharon. *Between Women: Friendship, Desire, and Marriage in Victorian England*. Princeton, NJ: Princeton University Press, 2007.

Marcus, Sharon. "Reflections on Victorian Fashion Plates." *differences: A Journal of Feminist Cultural Studies*, 14, no. 3 (2003): 4–33.

Marti, Laurence. "Singes, ours, géants, petites mains et pauvres diables: Le Corps dans le travail ouvrier au XIXe siècle." In *Faire corps: Temps, lieu et gens,* edited by Monica Aceti, Christophe Jaccoud, and Laurent Tissot, 217–32. Neuchâtel: Alphil, 2018.

Marx, Karl. "The Fetishism of Commodities and the Secret Thereof." In *The Marx-Engels Reader*. Edited by Robert C. Tucker, 319–29. New York: W. W. Norton, 1978.

Mason, John Hope. *The Value of Creativity: The Origins and Emergence of a Modern Belief*. Abingdon, UK: Routledge, 2017.

Matthews David, Alison. *Fashion Victims: The Dangers of Dress Past and Present*. London: Bloomsbury Visual Arts, 2015.

Maury, Robert. "Quand les Aquarellistes créaient la haute couture." *Plaisir de France* 40, no. 422 (September 1974): 30–5.

McDougall, Mary Lynn. "Working-Class Women during the Industrial Revolution, 1780–1914." In *Becoming Visible: Women in European History*. Edited by Renate Bridenthal, 255–79. Boston: Houghton Mifflin, 1977.

McMillan, James F. *France and Women, 1789–1914: Gender, Society and Politics*. London: Routledge, 2000.

Mémoires d'une modiste écrits par elle-même. Paris: F. Cournol, 1866. Accessed July 10, 2022. https://gallica.bnf.fr/ark:/12148/bpt6k5838886h.

Mesch, Rachel. *Having It All in the Belle Epoque: How French Women's Magazines Invented the Modern Woman*. Stanford: Stanford University Press, 2013.

Meskimmon, Marsha. *The Art of Reflection: Women Artists' Self-Portraiture in the Twentieth Century*. New York: Columbia University Press, 1996.

Milliot, Vincent. *Les "Cris de Paris," ou Le Peuple travesti: Les Représentations des petits métiers parisiens (XVIe–XVIIIe siècles)*. With a preface by Daniel Roche. Paris: Éditions de la Sorbonne, 2014.

Mitchell, Robin. *Vénus Noire: Black Women and Colonial Fantasies in Nineteenth-Century France*. Athens: University of Georgia Press, 2020.

Mombert, Sarah. "L'Aiguille moderne: Les Ouvrages de dames dans la petite presse du XIXe siècle." Unpublished paper presented at the Congrès Médias 19, Paris, June 12, 2015.

Montclair. "Silhouettes féminines: Mme Emmeline Raymond," *Le Figaro: Supplément littéraire du dimanche* (February 1, 1890): 18; accessed July 31, 2022, https://gallica.bnf.fr/ark:/12148/bpt6k2725298.

Monjaret, Anne. *La Sainte-Catherine: Culture festive dans l'entreprise*. Series "Le Regard de l'ethnologie," no. 8. Paris: CTHS, 1997.

Moore, Doris Langley. *Fashion through Fashion Plates, 1770–1970*. New York: Clarkson N. Potter, 1971.

Morgan, Cheryl A. "Unfashionable Feminism? Designing Women Writers in the Journal Des Femmes (1832–1836)." In de la Motte and Przyblyski. *Making the News*, 207–32.

Morgan, Cheryl A. "Les chiffons de la M(éd)use: Delphine Gay de Girardin, journaliste." In "Pouvoirs, puissances: qu'en pensent les femmes?" Special issue, *Romantisme* no. 85 (1994), 57–66.

Morienval, Jean. "Villemessant, l'inventeur." In *Les Créateurs de la grande presse en France: Emile de Girardin, H. de Villemessant, Moïse Millaud*, 119–64. Paris: SPES, 1934.

Müller, Florence, and Lydia Kamitsis. *Les Chapeaux: Une Histoire de tête*. Paris: Syros Alternative, 1993.

Munro, Jane. *Mannequin d'artiste, mannequin fétiche*. Catalogue for an exhibition of the same name at the Musée Bourdelle, April 1–July 12, 2015. Paris: Paris Musées, 2015.

Nead, Lynda. "The Layering of Pleasure: Women, Fashionable Dress and Visual Culture in the Mid-Nineteenth Century." *Nineteenth-Century Contexts* 35, no. 5 (2013): 489–509.

Nead, Lynda. *Myths of Sexuality: Representations of Women in Victorian Britain*. New York: Basil Blackwell, 1988.

Negus, Keith. "The Work of Cultural Intermediaries and the Enduring Distance between Production and Consumption." *Cultural Studies* 16, no. 4 (2002): 501–15.

Nevinson, John L. "Origin and Early History of the Fashion Plate," *United States National Museum Bulletin,* 250, paper 60, 67–92 (Washington, DC: Smithsonian Institution Press, 1967).

Niccolai, Michela. "Elle trotte, danse et chante, la midinette! Univers sonore des couturières parisiennes dans les chansons (XIXe–XXe siècles)." *L'Homme: Revue française d'anthropologie*, no. 215/216. Special issue, "Connaît-on la chanson?" (July/December 2015): 47–79.

Nochlin, Linda. *Women, Art, and Power: And Other Essays*. New York: Harper & Row, 1988.

Nochlin, Linda. *Representing Women*. New York: Thames and Hudson, 1999.

Norberg, Kathryn and Sandra L. Rosenbaum, eds. *Fashion Prints in the Age of Louis XIV: Interpreting the Art of Elegance*. Costume Society of America Series, Lubbock, TX: Texas Tech University Press, 2014.

Paris illustré. Paris: Hachette, 1855.

Parker, Rozsika. *The Subversive Stitch: Embroidery and the Making of the Feminine*. London: Women's Press, 1984.

Pastoureau, Michel. *Yellow: The History of a Color*. Translated by Jody Gladding. Princeton, NJ: Princeton University Press, 2019.

Perrot, Michelle. "Fait divers et histoire au XIXe siècle." *Annales: Economies, sociétés, civilisations* 38, no. 4 (1983): 911–19.

Perrot, Philippe. *Fashioning the Bourgeoisie: A History of Clothing in the Nineteenth Century*. Princeton, NJ: Princeton University Press, 1994.

Phenix, Sara. "*Le Corset Expérimental*: Fashion, Fertility, and Fiction in Zola's *Pot-Bouille* and *Au Bonheur des dames*." *Dix-Neuf* (2022), vol. 26, no. 4: 243–62.

Pinson, Guillaume. *L'Imaginaire médiatique: Histoire et fiction du journal au XIXe siècle*. Paris: Classiques Garnier, 2012.

Pollock, Griselda. *Vision and Difference: Femininity, Feminism, and Histories of Art*. Abingdon, UK: Routledge, 1988.

Preiss, Nathalie, and Claire Scamaroni, *Elle coud, elle court, la grisette!* Paris: Paris Musées, 2011.

Querard, Jean-Marie. *Les Supercheries littéraires dévoilées: Galerie des auteurs apocryphes, supposés . . . de la littérature française pendant les quatre derniers siècles (etc.)*. Vol. 1. Paris: L'Éditeur, 1847. https://www.google.com/books/edition/Les_supercheries_litteraires_devoilees_G/OuxOAAAAcAAJ.

Quignard, Marie-Françoise, and Raymond Josué Seckel. *L'Enfer de la bibliothèque: Éros au secret*. Paris: Bibliothèque nationale de France, 2007.

Renken-Deshayes, Raphaëlle. *"Miroir mon beau miroir . . . : L'Identité féminine définie par un journal de mode 'La Mode illustrée: Journal de la famille.'* Neuchâtel: Alphil, 2004.

Reynolds, Siân. "Mistresses of Creation: Women and Producers and Consumers of Art since 1700." In *The Routledge History of Women in Europe since 1700*. Edited by Deborah Simonton, 341–79. Abingdon, UK: Routledge, 2006.

Ribeyre, Félix, Jules Brisson, and Firmin Maillard. *Les Grands Journaux de France*. Paris: Jouaust père et fils, 1862.

Rifelj, Carol. *Coiffures: Hair in Nineteenth-Century French Literature and Culture*. Newark: University of Delaware Press, 2010.

Ringelberg, Kirstin. "The Court of Lilacs, the Studio of Roses, the Garden at Réveillon: Madeleine Lemaire's Empire of Flowers." *Marcel Proust Aujourd'hui* 14 (2018): 178–88.

Ringelberg, Kirstin. *Redefining Gender in American Impressionist Studio Paintings: Work Place/Domestic Space*. Farnham, UK: Ashgate, 2010.

Roche, Daniel. *The Culture of Clothing: Dress and Fashion in the Ancien Régime*. Translated by Jean Birrell. Cambridge: Cambridge University Press, 1994.

Roger-Milès, Léon. *Les Créateurs de la mode*. Paris: Ch. Eggimann, 1964.

Rosenman, Ellen Bayuk, and Claudia C. Klaver, eds. *Other Mothers: Beyond the Maternal Ideal*. Columbus: Ohio State University, 2008.

Roussel-Richard, Lucie. "A City for Young Ladies: The Parisian *Flâneuse* of the *Journal des Demoiselles*." In *Women and the City in French Literature and Culture, Reconfiguring the Feminine in the Urban Environment*. Edited by Siobhán McIlvanney and Gillian Ni Cheallaigh, 25–46. Cardiff: University of Wales Press, 2019.

Saillard, Olivier, ed. *Le Bouquin de la mode*. Paris: Laffont, 2019.

Sanchez, Pierre, and Xavier Seydoux. *Les Catalogues des Salons*, vol. 3. Paris: l'Echelle de Jacob, 1835–40.

Sanson, Rosemonde. "La Presse féminine." In *La Civilisation du journal: Histoire culturelle et littéraire de la presse française au dix-neuvième siècle*. Edited by Dominique Kalifa, Philippe Régnier, Marie-Ève Thérenty, Alain Vaillant, 523–42. Paris: Nouveau Monde, 2011.

Sapori, Michelle. *Rose Bertin: Ministre des modes de Marie-Antoinette*. Paris: Éd. de l'Inst. Français de la Mode, 2003.

Scanlon, Jennifer. *Inarticulate Longings: The 'Ladies' Home Journal,' Gender, and the Promises of Consumer Culture*. New York: Routledge, 1995.

Schor, Naomi. *Reading in Detail: Aesthetics and the Feminine*. New York: Routledge, 1989.

Schor, Naomi. "*Cartes Postales*: Representing Paris 1900." *Critical Inquiry* 18, no. 2 (1992): 188–244.

Schreier, Lise. *Gens de couleur dans trois vaudevilles du XIXe siècle*. Autrement Mêmes. Paris: L'Harmattan, 2017.

Schreier, Lise. "Setting the Tone: Commodified Black Children and Slave Imagery in the Eighteenth- and Nineteenth-Century French Fashion Press," *H-France Salon*. Vol. 14, Issue 8, no. 6 (2022).

Schweitzer, Sylvie. *Les Femmes ont toujours travaillé: Une Histoire de leurs métiers, XIXe et XXe siècle*. Paris: Odile Jacob, 2002.

Scott, Joan W. *Gender and the Politics of History*. 30th anniversary edition. New York: Columbia University Press, 2018.

Sheriff, Mary D. *The Exceptional Woman: Elisabeth Vigée-Lebrun and the Cultural Politics of Art*. Chicago: University of Chicago Press, 1996.

Simmel, Georg. "On Fashion." *International Quarterly* 10 (1904), 130–55. Accessed August 20, 2022. http://www.modetheorie.de/fileadmin/Texte/s/Simmel-Fashion_1904.pdf.

Simon, Jules. *L'Ouvrière*. 8th ed. Paris: Hachette, 1876.

Smith, Andrew. *The Ghost Story 1840–1920: A Cultural History*. Manchester: Manchester University Press, 2010.

Smith, Bonnie G. *Ladies of the Leisure Class: The Bourgeoises of Northern France in the Nineteenth Century*. Princeton, NJ: Princeton University Press, 1981.

Smith Maguire, Jennifer, and Julian Matthews. *The Cultural Intermediaries Reader*. London: SAGE, 2014.

Sohn, Anne-Marie. *Chrysalides: Femmes dans la vie privée (XIXe–XXe siècles)*. Paris: Publications de la Sorbonne, 1996.

Solomon-Godeau, Abigail. "The Other Side of Venus: The Visual Economy of Feminine Display." In *The Sex of Things: Gender and Consumption in Historical Perspective*. Edited by Victoria de Grazia, 113–50. Berkeley: University of California Press, 1996.

Solomon-Godeau, Abigail with Beatrice Farwell, *The Image of Desire; Femininity, Modernity, and the Birth of Mass Culture in Nineteenth-Century France*. Santa Barbara: University Art Museum, University of California, 1994.

Soulier, Vincent. *Presse féminine: la puissance frivole*. Paris: L'Archipel, 2008.

Steele, Valerie, ed. *Paris Fashion: A Cultural History*. New York: Oxford University Press, 1988.

Steele, Valerie, *Paris Fashion: A Cultural History*. 3rd ed. New York: Bloomsbury USA, 2017.

Steele, Valerie, ed. *Paris, Capital of Fashion*. London: Bloomsbury Visual Arts, 2019.

Stewart, Mary Lynn. *Dressing Modern Frenchwomen: Marketing Haute Couture, 1919–1939*. Baltimore: Johns Hopkins University Press, 2008.

Sullerot, Évelyne. *La Presse féminine*. 2nd ed. Paris: A. Colin, 1966.

Tamboukou, Maria. *Gendering the Memory of Work: Women Workers' Narratives*. Abingdon, UK: Routledge, 2016.

Ténint, Wilhelm. *Album du Salon de 1842: Collection des principaux ouvrages exposé au Louvre*. Paris, 1842. Accessed August 20, 2022. https://gallica.bnf.fr/ark:/12148/bpt6k63221829

Terni, Jennifer. "A Genre for Early Mass Culture: French Vaudeville and the City, 1830–1848." *Theatre Journal* 58, no. 2 (2006): 221–48.

Tétart-Vittu, Françoise. "Who Creates Fashion?" In Groom, *Impressionism, Fashion, and Modernity*, 63–83.

Tétart-Vittu, Françoise. "Colin, les Sœurs." In *Encyclopædia Universalis*. Accessed August 21, 2021. https://www.universalis.fr/encyclopedie/les-soeurs-colin/.

Thérenty, Marie-Ève. *Femmes de presse, femmes de lettres: De Delphine de Girardin à Florence Aubenas*. Paris: CNRS, 2019.

Thomas, Dana. *Fashionopolis: The Price of Fast Fashion and the Future of Clothes*. London: Head of Zeus, 2019.

Thompson, Victoria. *The Virtuous Marketplace: Women and Men, Money and Politics in Paris, 1830–1870*. Baltimore: Johns Hopkins University Press, 2000.

Tilburg, Patricia A. *Working Girls: Sex, Taste, and Reform in the Parisian Garment Trades, 1880–1919*. Oxford: Oxford University Press, 2019.

Tilly, Louise A., and Joan W. Scott. *Women, Work and Family*. New York: Holt, Rinehart and Winston, 1978.

Toudouze, Gustave. *Madame Lambelle*. Paris: E. Dentu, 1880, 84–5. Accessed August 18, 2022, https://gallica.bnf.fr/ark:/12148/bpt6k65418188.

Trouillot, Michel-Rolph. *Silencing the Past: Power and the Production of History*. Boston, Mass: Beacon Press, 1995.

Van Remoortel, Marianne. "Women Editors and the Rise of the Illustrated Fashion Press in the Nineteenth Century." *Nineteenth-Century Contexts* 39, no. 4 (2017): 269–95.

Veblen, Thorstein. *Conspicuous Consumption*. New York: Penguin Books, 2006.

de Villemessant, Hippolyte. *Mémoires d'un journaliste*. 6 vols. Rev. ed. Paris: E. Dentu, 1884.

Vinken, Barbara. *Fashion Zeitgeist: Trends and Cycles in the Fashion System*. Translated by Mark Hewson. Oxford: Berg, 2005.

Valory and Cogniard frères. *La Révolte des modistes: Vaudeville en 3 actes*. Paris: Vollet, 1834.

Waller, Margaret. "Disembodiment as Masquerade: Fashion Journalists and Other 'Realist' Observers in Directory Paris." *L'Esprit Créateur* 37, no. 1 (1997): 31–60.

Weisberg, Gabriel P., and Jane R. Becker, eds. *Overcoming All Obstacles: The Women of the Académie Julian*. New York: Dahesh Museum; New Brunswick, NJ: Rutgers University Press, 1999.

West, Shearer. *Portraiture*. Oxford: Oxford University Press, 2004.

Wettlaufer, Alexandra. *Portraits of the Artist as a Young Woman: Painting and the Novel in France and Britain, 1800–1860*. Columbus: Ohio State University Press, 2011.

Withy, Katherine. *Heidegger on Being Uncanny*. Cambridge, MA: Harvard University Press, 2015.

Wright, B. S. "'That Other Historian, the Illustrator': Voices and Vignettes in Mid-Nineteenth Century France." *Oxford Art Journal* 23, no. 1 (2000): 113–36.

Yumibe, Joshua. "French Film Colorists." On website "Women Film Pioneers Project." New York: Columbia University Libraries, 2013. Accessed August 20, 2022. https://wfpp.columbia.edu/essay/french-film-colorists/.

Yvert, Fabienne. *L'Endiguement des renseignements*. Bouches-du-Rhône: Attila, 2012.

Illustrations

1.1	Anaïs Toudouze, *Le Follet*, Paris, 1856–7	15
1.2	Héloïse Leloir, *La Mode illustrée*, 1870	17
1.3	Anon. "La Voix de la foule," n.d.	19
1.4	S. Paul, "Ex-modiste," *Scène Parisienne*, no. 2. Paris, 1826	23
1.5	Numa (Pierre Numa Bassaget), "Phénomène vivant," 1832	28
1.6	"Costumes Parisiens," May 30, 1832	31
1.7	Jeanne. Embellished fashion plate by Anaïs Toudouze, *Magasin des demoiselles*, Laura Gail Diamond and Judith Lipnick, private collection	36
2.1	"Atelier de modistes," *Le Bon Genre*, 1802–14	42
2.2	"Les Marchandes de modes," n.d.	43
2.3	Charles Philipon, "L'Agaçante Modiste," No. 3 *Têtes de femmes*, 1828–9	45
2.4	Louis-Marie Lanté. "Modiste," *Costumes d'ouvrières parisiennes*, 1824	49
2.5	"Les Garnitures," *Le Bon Genre*, Paris, 1812	51
2.6	J. J. Chalon, "La Marchande de Modes," 1822	55
2.7	Charles Vernier, "Les Grisettes," 1846–7	56
2.8	"Rencontres des petites ouvrières," *Le Bon Genre*, 1814	57
2.9	Paul Gavarni, "Porteuse de modes," 1856	59
2.10	Paul Gavarni, "La Chasse au trottin," *Baliverneries Parisiennes*, 1804–66	60
2.11	Dequevauviller, "Le Lever des ouvrières en modes," 1784	62
2.12	"Dortoir de Modistes," anon., 1830s, Musée Carnavalet, CCØ Paris Musées/Carnavalet Museum—History of Paris	63
2.13	A. de Valmont, "Si Madame vient la Poupée fera son jeu," n.d.	64
2.14	"Luxe et Indigence." *Le Bon Genre*, 1827 (1817)	66
2.15	"Modiste de la rue Vivienne," *Portes et fenêtres, les Douze arrondissements de Paris*, 1840	67
3.1	Jules David, "Les devoirs, le bonheur, l'amour et le respect," *Journal des Demoiselles*, 1834	98
3.2	"Modèle de Robe à la Sévigné," *Journal des Demoiselles*, 1833	100
3.3	"La robe de bal." *Journal des Demoiselles*, 1833	102

3.4	"Planche VI," *Journal des Demoiselles*, 1836	104
3.5	"Modes de Paris," *Journal des Demoiselles*, 1849	106
3.6	"Modes d'automne," *Journal des Demoiselles*, 1844	107
3.7	"Acte de Décès: Fouqueau de Pussy" 1863	108
3.8	Nadar, "Vicomtesse de Renneville, Journaliste de Modes"	111
3.9	Héloïse Leloir, Gravure de Mode, "Chapeau de Mlle Soller," *La Sylphide*, 1855	118
3.10	*La Sylphide*, December 1850	119
3.11	*La Mode illustrée*, price scales, November 5, 1871	123
3.12	*La Mode illustrée*, October 27, 1872	124
3.13	*La Mode illustrée*, November 26, 1865, no. 48, p. 381. "Presse-papier" (paperweight)	125
3.14	*La Mode illustrée*, December 16, 1866, no. 51. Toothpick and match holders made from lobster shells	125
3.15	"Rébus," *La Mode illustrée*, February 28 and March 7, 1869	126
3.16	"Rébus," *La Mode illustrée*, February 28 and March 7, 1869	126
3.17	*La Mode illustrée*, March 7, 1869	128
3.18	*La Mode illustrée*, August 16, 1868, no. 33, p. 58. "Leçon de filet" (netting lesson)	131
3.19	*La Mode illustrée*, March 5, 1865, no. 10, p. 77. "Nouveau système pour onduler la chevelure" (New process for curling hair)	132
3.20	*La Mode illustrée*, March 19, 1865, no. 12, p. 90. "L'art de découper" (the art of carving)	133
3.21	*La Mode illustrée*, July 6, 1863, no. 27, p. 216. "Roulette pour lever les patrons" (pattern cutter)	134
3.22	Anon. *La Mode illustrée*, July 24, 1864, no. 30. Fashion Plate, "Toilettes de Melle. Castel, 58 bis r. Ste. Anne, Coiffures de Mr. Croisat, r. De Richelieu. 76"	136
3.23	Anaïs Toudouze. *La Mode illustrée*, September 3, 1865	137
3.24	"Renseignements" (details), header. *La Mode illustrée*, November 13, 1864	142
3.25	"Renseignements" (details). *La Mode illustrée*, November 13, 1864	143
3.26	Jean-François Delintraz, "Portrait d'Emmeline Raymond, femme de lettres," 1860–90	144
4.1	Anaïs Toudouze, "S.M. l'Impératrice Eugénie," *Le Conseiller des Dames et des Demoiselles*, 1853	149
4.2	Adèle-Anaïs Colin, "Portraits d'Héloïse et Anaïs Colin par elles-mêmes," 1836	154
4.3	"Walking Dress and Riding Dress," Modes de Paris, *Petit Courrier des Dames*, 1837	158
4.4	Alexandre-Marie Colin, "Héloïse Colin dessinant dans la campagne nîmoise," 1836	161
4.5	Louis-Marie Lanté, *La Mode*, August 31, 1833	163
4.6	Anaïs Colin, "Valse à Trois Temps" *Le Maître à danser*, 1844	164
4.7	Héloïse Leloir, "Fillette en robe noire, assise et tenant des fleurs dans sa main droite," 1865–6	166

4.8	Héloïse Leloir. "Dessin préparatoire avec groupe de femmes en robes de sortie avec fillette au centre," 1869	169
4.9	Anaïs Toudouze. "Esquisse de figure assise en robe à nœuds et falbalas," 1864–74	171
4.10	Anaïs Toudouze, "Femme, en buste de trois-quarts, avec coiffe de dentelle," 1867	172
4.11	Anaïs Toudouze, "Détail d'une coiffe vue de dos," 1860	173
4.12	Héloïse Leloir, "Figure vue de trois quarts face en robe gris bleu et mante noire bordée de franges, figure vue de profil en robe verte à bords dentelés, fillette en robe blanche à galons bleus, figure vue de trois quarts dos en robe violette garnie de dentelle noire,…"c. 1869	176
4.13	Héloïse Colin, "Femme en robe grise et femme en robe bleue dans un jardin," 1863	179
4.14	Detail of Héloïse Colin, "Femme en robe grise et femme en robe bleue…"	180
4.15	Anonymous, after Anaïs Colin-Toudouze, *Le Follet*, 1853, No. 1816: "Toilettes d'enfants (…),". 1853	184
4.16	Anonymous, after Héloïse Leloir-Colin, *La Gazette Rose*, 1 juin 1865, No. 650: "Etoffes et confections (…)," 1865	185
4.17	Édouard Manet, "La Libellule," *Le Fleuve*, Charles Cros, Paris, 1874	187
4.18	Anonymous, after Anaïs Colin-Toudouze, *Le Follet*, 1852, No. 1687: "Chapeaux de la maison (…),"1852	189
4.19	Huard, after Héloïse Leloir-Colin, *La Mode Illustrée*, 1871, No. 24: "Toilettes de Mme Fladry (…)," 1871	191
4.20	Héloïse Leloir, née Colin (1820–73), "Portrait d'une petite fille," provenant de la famille de l'artiste, vers 1850	192
4.21	Portrait d'Anaïs Toudouze, anon. n.d.	194
5.1	Grey, "Monoplan de Course pour Midinettes," *c*. 1900 [carte postale]	199
5.2	"La Course des Midinettes," *Le Petit Journal. Supplément du dimanche*, November 8, 1903	201

Index

Page numbers in *italics* refer to illustrations.

Abrantès, Amet-Junot d' 110
adultery 63, 73, 216 n.38
agaçante modiste 53, 54, 56–7, 58, 216 n.34
"L'Agaçante Modiste" (Philipon) *45*, 48, 53, 56, 216 n.35
album-making
    Colin sisters and 165, 232 n.25
    fashion plates and 232 n.25, 234 n.50
    female art form 152, 155, 190, 231 nn.21–2, 232 n.25, 234 n.50
amateur art 151, 155, 231 n.21, 234 n.50
Anspach, Maria d' 213–14 n.14
    "La Modiste" 46–7
archive 12–13, 206–7 n.20
    fashion plate as 7, 146
aristocracy
    domesticity 14
    Emma Bovary's fascination with 110
    fashion as frivolous aristocrat 127
    fashion journals as window onto 110
    J. J.'s aristocratic origins 209 n.47
    modistes as "aristocracy" of fashion workers 4, 205 n.6
    particule 111, 224 n.71
    readers of fashion journals 92
    Renneville's invented title 94, 110–11, 120–1
artifice
    modistes and 52–3, 54, 70, 74, 87
    prostitutes and 215 n.31
    vaudeville and 69
artist's signature 157, 233 n.48, 241 nn.47–8
    Colin sisters 7, 149–50, 155, 157, 160, 174, 175, 197
    fashion-plate artists 35, 39, 148, 157
    maîtresse-modiste 32
arts d'agréments, 160, 229 n.3

    Colin sisters and 147, 148, 152, 155, 159
    watercolor and 147, 174
Artus, Louis
    Les Midinettes 213
atelier
    apprenticeship 5, 20, 21, 71, 79, 204 n.15
    doubling as shop 52, 54, 56
    female community 8, 54, 61
    hierarchy, 5 10, 44, 70–1, 73, 76, 82, 83, 160, 205 n.6, 211 n.70, 217 n.46
    rue Vivienne 9
    space of licentious behavior 43, 56–7, 65–6, 209 n.40
    vaudeville setting 68–9, 70–3
    visual tropes 55–6
    see also "Story of a Bonnet"
"Atelier de modistes" (Mésangère) 41–2, *42*, 44, 54

Balzac, Honoré de 93
    "La Femme comme il faut" 1, 2, 203 n.1
    Mémoires de deux jeunes mariées 233 n.47
Barthes, Roland
    fashion system 3, 11, 206 n.16
    Mythologies 46
Baudelaire, Charles
    "Le Peintre de la vie moderne" 168, 235–6 n.73
Der Bazar 127
Belle Époque 14, 92
    midinettes 204 n.15, 207 n.27, 212 n.89, 239 n.1
Benjamin, Walter
    The Arcades Project 54, 203 n.7
Bermingham, Ann 177, 180
berthe collar 159, 224 n.63, 234 n.50
Bertin, Rose 48, 50–2, 215 n.26

Best, Kate Nelson 95, 112, 138, 220 n.3, 224 n.72, 225 n.77
bias-cut 202, 239 n.8
Le Bon Genre 61, 230 n.9
    "Atelier de modistes" 41–2, *42*, 44, 54
    "Les Garnitures" 50, *51*
    "Luxe et indigence" 65, *66*
    "Rencontre des petites ouvrières" 57–8, *57*
Bonin, Marie 35, 156, 176, 181, 231 n.20, 232 n.26, n.30, 235 n.71, 236 n.78, 237 n.88
Bonington, Richard Parkes 175
Bonnet, Mary-Jo 157
Le Bon Ton 155
book illustration
    Colin sisters and 153, 165, 166, 167, 181
    insect illustration 186
Boucicaut, Aristide 227 n.119
Boural, Marguerite
    "Fleurs, Plumes, Modes" 207 n.22
Bourdieu, Pierre 90, 220 n.4
bourgeois femininity 6, 33, 39, 92, 109, 146
    fashion plates 14–16, 24, 38, 39, 101, 151, 182
    "seamlessness" 211 n.69
    social valorization of 14
bourgeois motherhood 89, 95, 97
Bouvier, Jeanne 68, 217 n.53
    La Lingerie et les lingères 206 n.18, 207 n.22
    Mémoires 68, 81–2, 206 n.18, 219 n.81
Brevik-Zender, Heidi 182
Buisson, Jules 111
Busquet, Alfred
    "Salon de 1857" 147–8, 150, 152, 165, 231 n.23
buste mécanique 120, 226 n.98

calicot 27, 210 n.64
calotte 29, 30, 32
capote 9, 18, 25–6, 29–30, 42, 205 n.1
Capuano, Peter 188
Carby, Hazel 12
caricature and satire 14, 72, 208 n.33, 210 n.64, 230 n.9
    "Atelier de modistes" 41–2, *42*, 44, 54
    "Ex-Modiste" 22, *23*, 27, 209–10 n.53
    Les Fleurs animées 186, 238 n.112
    "Les Garnitures" 50, *51*
    "Les Grisettes" 55–7, *56*, 216 n.40
    "Phénomène vivant" 27–30, *28*
    see also "Story of a Bonnet"; vaudeville

cashmere shawl 22, 50, 109, 209 n.53
Castel-Bréant, Mme. 135, 170
    "Toilettes de Melle. Castel…" 135, *136*
catherinette 8
Chalon, John James
    "La Marchande de Modes" 54–5, *55*, 216 n.38
Chanel, Coco 204 n.15
"Chapeau de Mlle Soller" (Héloïse Colin) *118*
chapeau de paille (straw hat) 16–18, 25, 26, 43, 135
Un chapeau de paille d'Italie (play) 73–4
"Chapeaux de la maison (…)" (Anaïs Colin) 188, *189*
Le Charivari 208 n.33, 230 n.9
Charlet, Nicolas-Toussaint
    "Technique l'aquarelle" 174
Chassagne, Armand
    Traité d'aquarelle 177, 178, 180, 237 n.93
"La Chausse au trottin" (Gavarni) *60*, 61, 82, 200
Chenut, Helen 210 n.54, 234 n.52
chroniqueuse de mode 4, 5–6, 88, 90–2, 202
    cultural intermediary 6, 90–1, 92, 220 n.4, 221 n.9
    see also Fouqueau de Pussy, Jeanne-Jacqueline; Raymond, Emmeline; Renneville, vicomtesse de
chrysalide 97
Clayson, Hollis 42, 214 n.19
Clément-Hémery Albertine, 93, 221 n.14
Code Civil 14, 20–1
Coffin, Judith G. 18, 207 n.28
coiffe à la Titus 42, 216 n.43
coiffer sainte Catherine 8
Colin, Alexandre 153, 166–7, 174–5, 204 n.13, 237 n.88
    artistic instructor to Anaïs and Héloïse 174–5, 237 n.88
    "Héloïse Colin dessinant dans la campagne nîmoise" 160–2, *161*, 187–8, 192
    Salon of 1835, 235 n.63
    works by, misattributed to Anaïs 235 n.71
Colin, Anaïs (Anaïs Toudouze)
    account book/ledger 43, 155, 156–7, 165, 181, 232 n.33
    fashion plates and *croquis*
        "Détail d'une coiffe vue de dos" 170, *173*
        "Esquisse de figure assise en robe à noeuds et falbalas" 170, *171*
        "Femme, en buste de trois-quarts, avec coiffe de dentelle" 170–4, *172*
        Le Follet 184, 188, *189*, 193

Magasin des demoiselles 35, *36*
"Toilettes d'enfants (...)" *184*
Le Maître à danser 164, 165
obituary 151, 167, 193, 231 nn.19–20
portrait of *194*
Salon 165, 167, 175, 235 n.64, 239 n.124
  medal 165, 195, 235 n.69
"S.M. l'Impératrice Eugénie" 148, *149*
Gabriel Toudouze, husband of
  collaboration with 165, 235 n.62
  marriage to 151, 155, 229 n.4, 235 n.62
Gustave Toudouze, son of 151, 156, 195, 232 n.31, 235 n.62
  Mademoiselle Lambelle 193–5
Isabelle Toudouze, daughter of 151, 193, 229 n.4
watercolor 155, 165
widow 21, 151, 156, 194, 237 n.97
works by Alexandre misattributed to 235 n.71
Colin, Anaïs and Héloïse
  arts d'agréments 147, 148, 152, 155, 159
  book illustration 153, 165, 166, 167, 181
  miniature painting 147, 148, 152, 165, 167, 174, 177
  parents' artistic training of 174–5, 232 n.26, 237 n.88
  "Portraits d'Héloïse et Anaïs Colin par elles-mêmes"
    (shared self-portrait) 153–68, *154*, 186, 188
    gazes 160–2
    hands 156, 159–60, 188, 190
    Salon of 1840 165, 233 n.39, 235 n.70
    snood 159, 234 n.51
  signing of their works 7, 149–50, 155, 157, 160, 174, 175, 197
  watercolors 147, 149–50, 152–3, 180–1, 195, 237 n.99
Colin, Héloïse (Héloïse Leloir)
  Alexandre's portrait of 160–2, *161*, 187–8, 192
  La Corbeille de fleur 177
  fashion plates and *croquis*
    "Chapeau de Mlle Soller" *118*
    "Dessin préparatoire avec groupe de femmes en robes de sortie avec fillette au centre" 168–9, *169*, 170, 176
    "Etoffes et confections..." 184–8, *185*
    La France élégante 147–8
    La Gazette rose 184–8, *185*
    La Mode illustrée 16, *17*, 35, 190–2, *191*
    "Toilettes de Mme Fladry..." 190–3, *191*
  obituary 236 n.81
  "Portrait d'une petite fille" *192*, 193

Salon 147, 165, 167, 175, 235 n.64, 239 n.124
studio 236 n.81
watercolors 165
  "Femme en robe grise et femme en robe bleue dans un jardin" 178, *179*, 180
  "Figure vue de trois quarts en robe gris bleu..." 176–7, *176*, 237 n.89
  "Fillette en robe noire, assise et tenant des fleurs dans sa main droite" 165, *166*
Colin, Isabelle 229 n.4
Colin, Joséphine 153, 175, 193, 232 n.26, n.30
Colin, Laure 229 n.4, 232 n.32
Colin, Paul 167, 204 n.13, 229 n.4
Colin sisters, *see* Colin, Anaïs and Héloïse
Compte-Calix, François Claudius 148, 230 n.9
Le Conseiller des dames et des demoiselles 155, 225 n.77
  "S.M. l'Impératrice Eugénie" 148, *149*
La Corbeille 89, 155
Corbin, Alain 47
"Costumes Parisiens" *31*, 32, 35
coup d'état 112
"La Course des Midinettes" 200, *201*
couture houses 21, 210 n.54, 234 n.52
couturier 203 n.5
couturier, *see* seamstresses
Craig, Béatrice 4, 12, 13, 20, 204 n.9, 207 n.20, n.23, 209 n.44
Cros, Charles
  Le Fleuve 186, *187*
Crowston, Claire 50, 214 n.23

Dash, Comtesse
  Mémoires des autres 110–11, 120, 148, 244 n.61
Daulte, François 174
David, Jacques-Louis
  "The Oath of the Horatii" 72
David, Jules 148, 149, 155, 230 n.9, 232 n.35
  "Les devoirs, le bonheur, l'amour et le respect" 97, *98*
  Le Moniteur de la mode 230 n.9
  obituary 231 n.19
décolletage 42, 53
Delacroix, Eugène 155, 174–5, 204 n.13
Delintraz, Jean-François
  "Portrait d'Emmeline Raymond, femme de lettres" 141, *144*
department stores 37, 117, 129, 209 n.43, 227 n.119
Dequevuaviller

"Le Lever des ouvrières en modes" 61–3, *62*
Desbordes, Lucie 84–5
Desfossez, Alfred
   Les Midinettes 213 n.9
Desgrange, Isabelle Toudouze, *see* Toudouze, Isabelle
Desmaisons, L.-Ch.
   "*Tu seras ouvrière*" 20–2, 24, 30, 32, 38, 73, 211 n.70, 218 n.61
dessinatrice de mode 88, 201
"Dessin préparatoire avec groupe de femmes en robes de sortie avec fillette au centre" (Héloïse Colin) 168–9, *169*, 170, 176
"Détail d'une coiffe vue de dos" (Anaïs Colin) 170, *173*
Devéria, Achille 14, 155, 208 n.33, 229 n.4
   Les Heures du jour 162, 234 n.55
Devéria, Laure 162, 234 n.55
Devéria, Sarah 229 n.4
"Les devoirs, le bonheur, l'amour et le respect" (Jules David) 97, *98*
Didot *frères* 37, 94, 122, 226 n.107
Directory 93
"discursive veil" 4, 6, 13, 38, 207 n.23
divorce
   J. J. as divorcée 21, 92, 95, 105, 108, 109, 209 n.47
   outlawing of 95, 209 n.47
   Renneville's separation from husband 92, 110, 112
"Dortoir de Modistes" (anon.) 62–3, *63*
drawing 231 n.15, 236–7 n.87
Dumas, Alexandre
   Le Comte de Monte Cristo 165

École des Beaux-Arts 7, 150, 153
engraving 2, 175, 204 n.10, 237 n.99
   steel 127, 148
   wood 127
Epinay, Marie de l' 35–7, 94, 110, 146
"Esquisse de figure assise en robe à noeuds et falbalas" (Anaïs Colin) 170, *171*
etiquette manuals 14
"Etoffes et confections…" (Héloïse Colin) 184–8, *185*
Eugénie (empress of France) 112
   "S.M. l'Impératrice Eugénie" 148, *149*
"Ex-Modiste" (Paul) 22, *23*, 27, 209–10 n.5

fait divers 75–6, 78–83, 214 n.22, 218 nn.68–9
   canards and 83, 218 n.72, 219 n.85
   "Drame d'amour" 79–80
   "Drame de la misère" 82
   Le Petit Journal 75–6, 218 n.69, n.72
   "Une nouvelle Dalila" 80
family portraiture 152, 153, 159, 165, 167, 190
Farge, Arlette 12–13
fashion
   cyclicality 5, 122, 141, 156, 167, 196
   fast 202, 211 n.75
   frivolity 99, 127–9, 130, 146, 220 n.6
   Paris as capital of 3, 108, 220 n.2
   photography 236 n.80
   a virtuous pastime 127, 134
   see also fashion economy; fashion system
fashion economy 33, 52
   cyclicality of 141
   fashion journals and plates as central to 37, 91, 202
   growth of 2, 88
   Renneville on 114
   women's role in 1–2, 27, 50, 88, 146
fashion illustrators 2, 3, 6–7, 33, 34, 39, 88
   see also Colin, Anaïs; Colin, Anaïs and Héloïse; Colin, Héloïse
fashion plates
   advertising tool 34–5, 112, 152, 182–3, 186, 188, 196–7
   aspirational images 2, 11, 33, 34–5, 99, 182
   bourgeois femininity 14–16, 24, 38, 39, 101, 151, 182
   collecting of, 7, 35, 170, 180, 183, 196
   conventions 182, 183, 186, 211 n.79
   croquis 168, 174–7, 181
   embellishment of 35, *36*, 236 n.78
   framing and display of 35, 101, 183, 238 n.78
   hand coloring of 1, 101, 127, 130, 152, 181, 239 n.120
   Impressionism and 7, 186
   mass production of 239 n.120
   motherhood 183–4
   signing of 35, 39, 148, 157
   text and image 34, 88, 183
fashion press (*presse féminine*, women's press) 3, 94, 220 n.1, 220 nn.6–7, 221 n.8, n.21
   July Monarchy 90, 92–3, 94, 220 n.2, n.6
   see also Le Bon Genre; Le Bon Ton; Le Conseiller des demoiselles; fashion plates; *Le Follet;* Fouqueau de Pussy, Jeanne-Jacqueline; *La Gazette rose; Le Journal des demoiselles; La Mode; La Mode illustrée;* Raymond, Emmeline; Renneville, vicomtesse de; *La Sylphide*

fashion system 32, 38, 196
    Barthes and 3, 11, 206 n.16
    cyclicality 122
    economy of exclusivity 120
    fashion press in 6, 11, 33, 38, 146, 156
    women's role in 3, 33
fashion workers, *see modiste*; needleworkers and needlework; seamstresses
fashion writers, see *chroniqueuse de mode*
fast fashion 202, 211 n.75
feathers
    feather workers 32, 209–10 n.53
    marabout 70
    plume d'autruche 29
feminist press 91, 221–2 n.21, 221 n.8, n.12
"Femme, en buste de trois-quarts, avec coiffe de dentelle" (Anaïs Colin) 170–4, *172*
femme comme il faut 1
"Femme en robe grise et femme en robe bleue dans un Jardin" (Héloïse Colin) 178, *179*, *180*
femme isolée 208–9 n.40
femme majeure 21, 145
Le Figaro 37, 78–9, 94, 120, 121, 122, 222 n.29
"Figure vue de trois quarts en robe gris bleu …" (Héloïse Colin) 176–7, *176*, 237 n.89
"Fillette en robe noire, assise et tenant des fleurs dans sa main droite" (Héloïse Colin) 165, *166*
fine arts 39, 152, 165, 174, 229 n.3
    artist's signature 35, 157, 233 n.48, 241 nn.47–8
    women's institutionalized exclusion from 7, 151, 152, 160
flâneur 9, 26, 61, 82
Flaubert, Gustave 193
    Madame Bovary 89, 90, 93, 116–17, 220 n.1
        Emma as aspiring *Parisienne* 89, 113, 116, 225 n.77
        Emma's fascination with the aristocracy 110
        Emma's suicide 94
        La Sylphide and 89, 117, 225 n.77, 226 nn.95–6
flower-makers 22, 32, 211 n.71
flower painting 177, 231 n.21, 234 n.55, 237 n.92
    Colin sisters and 177, 229 n.1
Le Follet 15, 155
    "Chapeaux de la maison (…)" 188, *189*
    "Toilettes d'enfants (…)" 183, *184*, 193
Fontaney, Antoine 204 n.1

"Story of a Bonnet" 9–10, 22, 25–30, 43, 68, 211 n.70
    calicot 210 n.64
    hat as commodity fetish 9–10, 24–6, 27, 29, 38, 205 n.3, 206 n.13
    modiste as object of voyeurism 9, 27
Fouqueau de Pussy, Jeanne-Jacqueline (J. J.) 6, 37
    aristocratic origins 209 n.47
    childless 92
    divorcée 21, 92, 95, 105, 108, 109, 209 n.47
    Journal des demoiselles 91, 94–109, 130
        bonne amie 95, 96, 109
        epistolary conceit 95, 96, 103, 105, 223 n.47
        jeune fille 95, 96–7
        obituary 108, *108*
        parting letter 105
        retirement from 96, 108
        "Robe de Bal" 97–101, 104
        signing as "J. J." 94
        successor to 96
Les Français peints par eux-mêmes 214 n.14
    "La Femme comme il faut" 203 n.1
    "La Modiste" 46–7
La France élégante 147–8, 155
Franco-Prussian War 129

Garb, Tamar 156, 230 nn.13–14, 231 n.20, 233 n.40
"Les Garnitures" 50, *51*
Gartside, Mary 177, 180–1
Gavarni, Paul 14, 148, 155, 208 n.33, 230 n.9
    "La Chausse au trottin" *60*, 61, 82, 200
    "Porteuse de modes" 58–61, *59*, 82
La Gazette rose 94, 117–20, 121, 221 n.11, 222 n.29
    fashion plate 184–8, *185*
    first issue 117–20, 224 n.74
genre painting 166, 229 n.4, 230 n.9
Gidel, Henri 70, 217 n.57, 218 n.58
gigot sleeves 53, 159, 162, 234 n.50
Girardin, Delphine de 94, 222 n.22
Girardin, Emile de 94, 222 n.22
Girodet, Anne-Louis 204 n.13, 155
Gluck, Mary 69, 217 n.57
Gobley, Clothilde Augustine 84–5, *86*
Gobley Élisa Anastasie 84–5, *86*
Godey's Lady's Book 155, 232 n.32
Gossman, Lionel 76
Grandville, J. J.
    Les Fleurs animées 186, 238 n.112

Grey
    "Monoplan de course pour Midinettes" 199–200, *199*
griffe de mode 32
grisette 61, 206 n.11
    "air de la grisette" 70
    loose morals and carefree sexuality 4, 42, 213 n.7, 215 n.33
    midinette as descendant to 207 n.27, 212 n.89
    self-sufficiency 214 n.17
"Les Grisettes" (Vernier) 55–7, *56*, 216 n.40
Guerlain 112
Guichard, Charlotte 157, 233 n.48
guilds 50, 52, 203 n.5, 214 n.23

Hahn, H. Hazel 220 n.2
Harper's Bazaar 122, 155
Hartman, Saidiya 206–7 n.20
hats
    calotte 29, 30, 32
    capote 9, 18, 25–6, 29–30, 42, 205 n.1
    chapeau de paille (straw hat) 16–18, 25, 26, 43, 135
    concealment of fabrication of, 9, 11, 24, 29, 30–2
    "conspicuous consumption" 208 n.36
    embellishments and trimmings, 18, 25, 29, 41, 53, 171, 205 n.1
    hat form 41, 43, 52, 56
    hatbox 55, 87
        emblem of *modiste* 46, 54, 56–8, 61, 62–3, 65, 70, 72, 75, 80, 200
        locus of desire 58, 75
        means of concealment 53, 58, 66, 218 n.66
        slapstick device 70, 72, 75, 218 n.66
    hatpin 72, 75, 79, 80
    marotte (head-form, *poupée*) 26, 32, 43, 56, 70, 210 n.60
        "Si Madame vient la Poupée fera son jeu" 63–5, *64*
        suggestive placements of 53, 54, 72
        vaudeville 72, 73, 75
    stand 55, 63, 72
    top hat 18
    toque 22, 53
    see also milliners and millinery
Haussmann, Georges-Eugène (Baron) 129, 178
head-form, *see* marotte
"Héloïse Colin dessinant dans la campagne nîmoise" (Alexandre Colin) 160–2, *161*, 187–8, 192

high art 7, 39, 175, 231 n.24
    women's institutionalized exclusion from 157, 196, 232 n.25
Higonnet, Anne 57, 152, 153–5, 216 n.44, 232 n.25, 234 n.50, n.54
home economics 121, 129
Huard *191*

L'Illustration 205 n.1
Impressionism 7, 186, 214 n.19

Janin, Jules 224 n.64
Jaunès, Linna 165
jeune fille 89, 95–7
J. J., *see* Fouqueau de Pussy, Jeanne-Jacqueline
Jones, Jennifer 50–2, 215 nn.26–7
Le Journal de la mode 221 n.11
Le Journal des dames et des modes 93–4
Le Journal des débats 77
Le Journal des demoiselles 89, 92, 130
    "Les devoirs, le bonheur, l'amour et le respect" 97, *98*
    fashion plates 101, 104–5, 223 n.54
        "Modes d'automne" 105, *107*
        "Modes de Paris" *106*
        "La robe de bal" 101, *102*
    J. J. (Fouqueau de Pussy), editor-in-chief and columnist 91, 94–109, 130
        bonne amie 95, 96, 109
        epistolary conceit 95, 96, 103, 105, 223 n.47
        jeune fille 95, 96–7
        obituary 108, *108*
        parting letter 105
        Raymond and 122, 221 n.11, 222 n.37
        retirement from 96, 108
        "Robe de Bal" 97–101, 104
        signing as "J. J." 94
        successor to 96
    readership 113
    run 95
    sewing instructions and patterns 99–101, 103–5, 223 n.41
        "Modèle de Robe à la Sévigné" 99–101, *100*
        "Planche VI" 103, *104*
Le Journal des femmes 165, 220 n.6
July Monarchy 148, 208 n.33, 216 n.44, 230 n.9, 234 n.55
    fashion press during 90, 92–3, 94, 220 n.2, n.6

Girardin, leading journalist of 94
J. J.'s career as corresponding to 91, 94, 95
Juno, Jean-Andoche 110
Junot, Laure, duchesse d'Abrantès 110

Kessler, Marni Reva 4
Kessler-Harris, Alice 10, 205 n.8
Kirchleim, Madame 85, 86
Kleinert, Annemarie 93

Labiche, Eugène
    Un Chapeau de paille d'Italie 73–4
Lanté, Louis-Marie 14, 148, 208 n.33, 230 n.9
    La Mode fashion plate 162, *162*
    "Modiste" 48, *49*
Lascaux, Paul Descubes de 110
Laurent, Méry 213 n.9
Léger-Paturneau, Christine 96, 109, 233 n.53
Leloir, Héloïse Colin, *see* Colin, Héloïse
Lemaire, Madeleine 237 n.92
Lerat, Pierre 105, 108
Lerman, Nina 238 n.114
Lerner, Jillian 229 n.4, 234 n.55
Les Midinettes (Desfossez) 213 n.9
"lesser" or "minor" arts 147, 151, 153, 165, 174, 197
"Le Lever des ouvrières en modes" (Dequevuaviller) 61–3, *62*
lingère, *see* needleworkers and needlework
Lipton, Eunice 212–13 n.3, 213 nn.9–10
lithography 153, 175, 178, 181, 233 n.48
    creation of fashion plates 204 n.10, 237 n.99
    heyday of 181
Longchamps 113, 114
Lormeaux, Juliette 224 n.64
"Luxe et indigence" 65, *66*

McMillan, James F. 14
Le Magasin des demoiselles 35, *36*
magasins de modes 65, 68–9, 84
Mainardi, Patricia 168
maîtresse-modiste 13, 43, 44, 68, 70–2, 76, 205 n.6
    première as successor to 10
    signature of 32
    tricking the mistress 65, 217 n.48
Malibran, Hippolyte 229 n.4
Mallarmé, Stéphane 213 n.9
Manet, Édouard 174, 213 n.9
    "La Libellule" 186, *187*
    Olympia 234 n.54
"La Marchande de Modes" (Chalon) 54–5, *55*, 216 n.38
marchandes de modes 50–2, 84, 93, 215 nn.27–8
    Gobley sisters 84–5
"Les Marchandes de modes" 41–4, *43*
Marcus, Sharon 101, 182, 223 n.45, 238 n.110, 238 n.117
Marie-Antoinette 48, 50, 230 n.14
marotte (head-form, *poupée*) 26, 32, 43, 56, 70, 210 n.60
    "Si Madame vient la Poupée fera son jeu" 63–5, *64*
    suggestive placements of 53, 54, 72
    vaudeville 72, 73, 75
marriage
    career as alternative to 38, 74, 145
    cashmere shawl as sign of 209 n.53
    J. J.'s promotion of 91, 96–7, 108
    legal restrictions on married women 20–1
    wedding announcements 48, 76–8, 83
    see also divorce
Martigny, baronne de 224 n.64
Marx, Karl
    commodity fetish 3, 9, 11, 146, 205 n.3, 206 nn.13–14
Maury, Robert
    "Quand les aquarellistes créaient la haute couture" 148–50
Mercier, Sébastien
    Tableau de Paris 218 n.58
Mésangère, Pierre de la 92–3, 95
    "Atelier de modistes" 41–2, *42*, 44, 54
    Le Bon Genre 57
    Le Journal et des dames et des modes 93, 110
midinette 8, 13, 199–202, 204 n.15, 207 n.27, 212 nn.89–90
    descendant of *grisette* 207 n.27, 212 n.89
    plays 213 n.9
    strike 8, 202, 218 n.63
Les Midinettes (Artus) 213 n.9
Les Midinettes (Desfossez) 213 n.9
milliners and millinery 8, 13, 26, 44, 58, 70, 214 n.19, 216 n.44
    Bertin as 50–2
    categories of 213 n.10
    lever and *coucher* 213 n.8
    modiste as associated or interchangeable with 52, 215 n.27, 215 nn.32–3
    "tart" 213 n.3
    see also hats

miniature painting
    Joséphine Colin and 155
    Colin sisters and 147, 148, 152, 165, 167, 174, 177
    fashion plates and 152, 165, 167, 174, 177, 196
    female art form 147, 148, 153, 177, 202, 229 n.2
    "lesser" genre 147, 153, 175, 229 n.2, 237 n.87
    origins and heyday of 229 n.2
    "Portrait d'une jeune fille" *192*, 193
La Mode 155
La Mode illustrée 89, 94, 122–45
    Raymond, editor-in-chief 37, 91, 94, 95, 121, 122–45, 221 n.11, 226 n.111, 228–9 n.140
        Der Bazar and 127
        bonne ménagère (good housewife) 92, 95, 140, 142
        craft projects, sewing patterns, and household tips 122, *125*, 130–4, *131*, *132*, *133*, *134*
        description de toilettes 130, 135, 138
        fashion plates 16, *17*, 35, 127, 130, 135, *137*, 138–9; "Toilettes de Melle. Castel . . ." 135, *136*
        frugality 126, 130, 138, 146
        large format 122–3
        modes 130, 135, 138–9, 140
        morality 127–9, 139, 142–4, 146
        objection to advertisements 135, 227 n.122
        price points 122, *123*, 226 n.109
        prospectus 129, 226 n.113
        readership 122
        rébus 123, *126*, 141
        renseignements 130, 135, 140–2, *142*, *143*, 212 n.88, 228 n.133
        sale of Raymond's portrait to subscribers 141, *144*
        La Sylphide and 122
        usefulness 129–34, 138
"Modes d'automne" 105, *107*
"Modes de Paris" *106*
Les Modes parisiennes 230 n.9
modiste
    agaçante modiste 53, 54, 56–7, 58, 216 n.34
    artifice 52–3, 54, 70, 74, 87
    "autobiography" 214 n.15, 217 n.56
    bankruptcies 5, 76, 77, 84–6
    commodification of 27, 33, 57
    concealing of labor of 1–2, 13, 24, 30, 32, 88
    coquettishness 22, 38, 53, 69, 87
    dormitory 61–5, 66

    fashionable attire 22, 25, 38, 44, 46, 53
    hatbox as emblem of 46, 54, 56–8, 61, 62–3, 65, 70, 72, 75, 80
    lever and *coucher* 43, 61, 213 n.8
    liminality 44, 46, 50–3, 54, 65, 78, 87, 211 n.70
    living and working conditions of 46, 72, 82–3
    loose morals and sexual promiscuity 8, 14, 22, 46, 63, 69, 213 n.7, 215 n.33
    marchandes de modes as forerunner to 50
    sexual prey and object of voyeurism 9–10, 27, 61–3, 65, 79, 82, 86, 213 n.8
    skilled seamstress 4, 215 n.32
    social advancement and social mobility 4, 24, 46, 68, 86, 205 n.6, 211 n.70
    solitary travels and spatial mobility 46, 58, 61
    term 215 n.27, 215 nn.32–3
    venality 14, 47, 54, 65, 214 n.19
    wages 46, 72, 215 n.33
    work apron 22, 53, 54, 56
    see also atelier; *maîtresse-modiste*; needleworkers and needlework; *petites mains*; *première modiste*; print culture; prostitutes and prostitution; seamstresses; *trottin*; vaudeville
"La Modiste" (Anspach) 46–7
"La Modiste" (Lanté) 48, *49*
La Modiste au camp (play) 72–3
Modiste et modeste (play) 74
Les Modistes (play) 70–1, 78
Le Monde sportif 200
Le Moniteur de la mode 221 n.11, 222 n.29, 230 n.9
"Monoplan de course pour Midinettes" (Grey) 199–200, *199*
Morgan, Cheryl 90, 92, 220 n.6, 221–1 n.8
Morisot, Berthe 162
motherhood
    bourgeois 89, 95, 97
    fashion plates 183–4
    Le Journal des demoiselles 95–7, 99–105, 108
    unwed mothers 75, 77–8, 218 n.68

Nadar
    "Vicomtesse de Renneville, Journaliste de Modes" 111, *111*
Napoléon I 85, 110, 224 n.71, 230 n.14
    Code Civil 14, 20–1
Napoléon III 112, 129
needleworkers and needlework

Bouvier's social history of 206 n.18
Catherine, patron saint of 8
décente lingère 53
female pastime 50, 160, 190, 196
J. J.'s promotion of 97, 105
La Mode illustrée 127, 130, 145
prostitutes and 213 n.13
travaux des femmes 96, 108, 113
Nochlin, Linda 213 n.6, 230 n.14, 231 n.20
Noël, Gustave 229 n.4
Noël, Laure, *see* Colin, Laure
Numa 14, 208 n.33
"Phénomène vivant" 27–30, *28*

official art 39, 148, 150, 151, 231 n.21

painting
    genre 166, 229 n.4, 230 n.9
    plein air 178
    see also flower painting; miniature painting; watercolor
panoramic literature 3, 9, 26, 203 n.7
Parent-Duchâtelet, Alexandre 208–9 n.40, 213 n.13
Paris
    Bon Marché 227 n.119
    boulevard des Capucines 85, 183
    course des catherinettes 8
    course des midinettes 200
    "cris de Paris" 218 n.58
    fashion capital 3, 108, 220 n.2
    Haussmannization 129, 178
    Jardin des Tuileries 200
    Jardin du Luxembourg 236 n.81
    Louvre 109, 121
    map of, in *Madame Bovary* 116
    midinette strike 8, 202, 218 n.63
    Opéra 26, 89, 109, 115, 117
    Opéra-Comique 69
    passages 54
    place de la Bourse 26
    rue Saint-Honoré 85–6, 195
    rue Vivienne 9, 26, 27, 65, 68, 72, 84
    Siege of Paris 91, 127, 129
    Théâtre des Folies-Dramatiques 74
    Théâtre du Palais Royal 68
    Union des Femmes Peintres et Sculpteurs 230 n.14, 233 n.40
    see also Parisienne; Salon, Paris
Paris Commune 91, 129
Parisienne 9, 89, 220 n.3
    Emma Bovary as aspiring 89, 113, 116, 225 n.77
    Les Heures du jour 162, 234 n.55
    modistes as aspiring 86
    Raymond as 138
    Renneville as 112, 120
    La Sylphide as embodying and directed toward 95, 113
particule 111, 224 n.71
passementerie 186
Paul, S.
    "Ex-Modiste" 22, *23*, 27, 209–10 n.53
Pauquet, Hippolyte 148
Pauquet, Polydor 148
pélerine collar 162
pelisse 178, 184
Perrot, Michèle 78, 83, 218 n.72
Le Petit Courrier des dames
    "Walking Dress and Riding Dress" *158*
petite-bourgeoisie 129, 220 n.4
petites mains 5, 27, 41, 76, 83, 186
    anonymity 25, 160, 197
    original notion of, persisting in sweatshops 210 n.54, 234 n.52
    role of 25, 160, 190, 210 n.54, 234 n.52
Le Petit Journal
    "Le Course des Midinettes" 200, *201*
    fait divers 75–6, 218 n.69, 218 n.72
Le Petit Moniteur 81
petits métiers 58, 61
"Phénomène vivant" (Numa) 27–30, *28*
Philipon, Charles
    "L'Agaçante Modiste" *45*, 48, 53, 56, 216 n.35
photography 229 n.2, 233 n.48, 236 n.80
piecing system 21
Plaisir de France 148
plein air painting 178
Pollock, Griselda 162, 213 n.6, 234 n.59
poplin 85, 135, 138
pornographic prints 65–6, 68, 217 nn.50–1
"Porteuse de modes" (Gavarni) 58–61, *59*, 82
"Portrait d'une petite fille" (Héloïse Colin) *192*, 193
"Portraits d'Héloïse et Anaïs Colin par elles-mêmes" (Anaïs and Héloïse Colin) 153–68, *154*, 186, 188

gazes 160–2
hands 156, 159–60, 188, 190
Salon of 1840 165, 233 n.39, 235 n.70
snood 159, 234 n.51
poupée, see marotte
première modiste 10, 27, 71, 76, 210 n.64, 218 n.66
  elevation to 10, 205 n.6
  role of 10, 25, 32, 160
La Presse 148, 222 n.22
presse feminine, see fashion press
prêt-à-porter 129
print culture 3, 229 n.140
  bourgeois femininity 4
  calicot 210 n.64
  modiste 5, 24, 44, 47, 66–8, 86, 217 n.57
    vaudeville depictions compared to 48, 69, 74, 217 n.57
  presse féminine's separation from 220 n.6
prostitutes and prostitution 202, 213 n.3
  artifice 215 n.31
  color yellow 216 n.35
  fashion workers and/as 46–8, 52, 74, 77, 208–9 n.40, 213 n.13, 214 n.19, 215 n.33, 219 n.81
  femme isolée 208–9 n.40
  Parent-Duchâtelet's inquiry into 208–9 n.40, 213 n.13
  rue Vivienne 9
Prouté, Paul 239 n.120

Raymond, Emmeline 6, 91
  Bonne ménagère 226 n.107
  Harper's Bazaar 122
  Le Journal des demoiselles 122, 221 n.11, 222 n.27
  La Mode illustrée 37, 91, 94, 95, 121, 122–45, 221 n.11, 226 n.111, 228–9 n.140
    Der Bazar and 127
    bonne ménagère (good housewife) 92, 95, 140, 142
    craft projects, sewing patterns, and household tips 122, 125, 130–4, 131, 132, 133, 134
    description de toilettes 130, 135, 138
    fashion plates 16, 17, 35, 127, 130, 135, 137, 138–9; "Toilettes de Melle. Castel…" 135, 136
    frugality 126, 130, 138, 146
    large format 122–3
    modes 130, 135, 138–9, 140
    morality 127–9, 139, 142–4, 146
    objection to advertisements 135, 227 n.122
    price points 122, 123, 226 n.109
    prospectus 129, 226 n.113
    readership 122
    rébus 123, 126, 141
    renseignements 130, 135, 140–2, 142, 143, 212 n.88, 228 n.133
    sale of Raymond's portrait to subscribers 141, 144
    La Sylphide and 122
    usefulness 129–34, 138
  multilingual 127, 227 n.121
  unmarried 92, 145
"Rencontre des petites ouvrières" 57–8 57
Renken-Deshayes, Raphaëlle 139, 222 n.111, 228–9 n.140
Renneville, vicomtesse de (Olympe Valleé) 6, 37, 91, 94, 95, 221 n.11
  La Gazette rose 94, 117–21, 221 n.11, 222 n.29
    "newness" of 117–20, 224 n.74
    Second Empire and 94, 121
  gender dissimulation 111, 120
  obituary 121
  portrait of 111
  Raymond's persona compared with 122, 129, 138
  "la reine des chiffons" 224 n.61
  Second Empire and 91, 94, 112, 121, 129, 226 n.95
  separation from husband 92, 110, 112
  single parent 92, 110, 112
  La Sylphide 92, 95, 109–21, 122, 222 n.29
    Parisienne 95, 112, 113, 120
    shopping 112–13, 116–17, 120
    signing columns as "V. de Renneville" 114
    soft advertising 115, 117, 120
    vicomtesse de Renneville as invented title 94, 110–11, 120–1
  Villemessant and 94, 110–12, 117, 221 n.11
La République française 82
Restoration 93, 148, 216 n.44
La Révolte des modistes (play) 71–2
La Revue des deux mondes 204 n.1
Ribeyre, Félix 111
Rifelj, Carol 215 nn.32–3
Ringelberg, Kristen 152
"La robe de bal" 101, 102
Roche, Daniel 52, 213 n.5, 215 n.28

Romanticism 160, 175, 208 n.33, 230 n.9
    Alexandre Colin and 7, 153, 155, 160, 204 n.13
Rousseau, Jean-Jacques 50

Sainte-Colombe, Athénie de la 120–1
Sajou 113, 224 n.75
Salon, Paris
    Album du Salon de 1842 165, 235 n.68
    Alexandre Colin at 235 n.63
    Anaïs Colin at 165, 167, 175, 235 n.64, 239 n.124
        medal 165, 195, 235 n.69
    Héloïse Colin at 147, 165, 167, 175, 235 n.64, 239 n.124
        medal 147, 165
    Joséphine Colin at 232 n.26, 235 n.63
    Anaïs and Héloïse Colin's shared self-portrait at 165, 233 n.39, 235 n.70
    drawing 231 n.15, 237 n.87
    "lesser" or "minor" arts 151, 231 n.15, 237 n.88
    "Salon de 1857" 147–8, 150, 152, 165, 231 n.23
    watercolor 175, 231 n.15, 235 n.63
    women artists at 150, 151, 165, 230–1 n.15
Sapori, Michelle 50
Saran 115
Schor, Naomi 231 n.23
Schweitzer, Sylvie 10, 205 n.8, 209 n.46
Scott, Joan W. 18, 208–9 n.40
Scribe, Eugène 70, 74
seam 1–2, 4
seamlessness 1–2, 18, 25, 30, 38, 188
seamstresses 1, 2, 20, 21, 35, 99, 103, 135, 195, 216 n.44
    Coco Chanel's beginnings as 204 n.15
    couturier compared with 203 n.5
    expansion of work and rise in status 50
    femmes isolées 208–9 n.40
    guilds 50, 203 n.5, 214 n.23
    home 223 n.41
    midinette strike 22
    modistes as skilled 4, 215 n.32
    piquante couturière 53
    Victorian 210 n.65
    Madeleine Vionnet's beginnings as 204 n.15
    see also Jeanne Bouvier
Second Empire 48, 72, 87, 92, 96, 127, 148
    fashion print market 148
    La Gazette rose and 94

    Renneville and 91, 94, 112, 121, 226 n.95
    veil in 4
Sellèque, Jean-Baptiste 93, 221 n.14
Senneville, vicomtesse de 224 n.64
sewing 2, 202, 203 n.5
    dexterity required for 160
    female pastime 50, 96, 113
    images in fashion plates 178, 190
    instructions and patterns 96, 101, 105, 108, 116, 122, 129, 130, 224 n.75
    seam 1–2, 4
Le Siècle 82
Siege of Paris 91, 127, 129
Signac, Paul 229 n.4
silk 1, 32, 34, 47, 48, 85, 121, 177, 182
    dress 109, 186
    gray-lilac 135
    shawl 109
    skirt 58, 178
    stockings 99
"Si Madame vient la Poupée fera son jeu" (Valmont) 63–5, *64*
Simmel, Georg
    "On Fashion" 215 n.29
Simon, Jules
    L'Ouvrière 18–20, 208 n.39
    preface to *"Tu seras ouvrière"* 20, 21
"S.M. l'Impératrice Eugénie" (Anaïs Colin) 148, *149*
snood 159, 234 n.51
Solomon-Godeau, Abigail 55, 213 n.6
Soulier, Vincent 220 n.1
Sourrieu, Frédéric 165
"Story of a Bonnet" (Fontaney) 9–10, 22, 25–30, 43, 68, 211 n.70
    calicot 210 n.64
    hat as commodity fetish 9–10, 24–6, 27, 29, 38, 205 n.3, 206 n.13
    modiste as object of voyeurism 9, 27
strikes 8, 72, 202, 218 n.63
Sue, Eugène
    Le Juif errant 165
sweatshops 210 n.54, 211 n.75, 234 n.52
La Sylphide 92, 109–10, 120, 135
    advertisements page 117, *119*
    fashion plates 112
        "Chapeau de Mlle Soller" 117, *118*
    l'Epinay in 35–7, 110

Madame Bovary and 89, 117, 225 n.77, 226 nn.95–6
Raymond's borrowing from 122
readership 113
Renneville, columnist 110, 112–17, 221 n.11, 222 n.29, 226 n.95
    Parisienne 95, 112, 113, 120
    shopping 112–13, 116–17
    signing columns as "V. de Renneville" 114
    soft advertising 115, 117, 120
    vicomtesse de Renneville as invented title 94, 110–11, 120–1
    run 95
    Villemessant's founding of 109–10, 112, 116

taffeta 85, 121, 135, 138, 177, 178
Tamboukou, Maria 12, 206 n.18, 207 n.22
Ténint, Wilhelm
    Album du Salon de 1842 165, 235 n.68
Terni, Jennifer 68, 217 n.52, 217 n.57
Texier, Edmond 205 n.1
Thierry family 37, 94
Third Republic 48, 91, 94
Thomas, Dana 202
Tilburg, Patricia A. 13, 207 n.27, 210 n.65, 212 nn.89–90, 239 n.1
"Toilettes de Melle. Castel . . ." 135, *136*
"Toilettes d'enfants (. . .)" (Anaïs Colin), 183, *184*, 193
"Toiletttes de Mme Fladry . . ." (Héloïse Colin) 190–3, *191*
top hat 18
toque hat 22, 53
Toudouze, Anaïs Colin, *see* Colin, Anaïs
Toudouze, Édouard 151
Toudouze, Gabriel
    Anaïs Colin's collaboration with 165, 235 n.62
    Anaïs Colin's marriage to 151, 155, 229 n.4, 235 n.62
    death of 151, 165, 193, 235 n.62
Toudouze, Georges 151
Toudouze, Gustave 151, 156, 195, 232 n.31, 235 n.62
    Mademoiselle Lambelle 193–5
Toudouze, Isabelle 151, 193, 229 n.4
travaux des femmes 96, 113
trottin 41, 42, 61, 70, 71, 75, 76, 78, 200
    atelier hierarchy 44, 70, 76, 217 n.46
    "La Chausse au trottin" *60*, 61, 82, 200
    Les Modistes 70, 71

Le Trottin de la modiste (play) 75, 78, 218 n.66, n.68
tulle 115, 135, 138, 170, 173
    hat 25, 26
Turner, J. M. W. 175
"*Tu seras ouvrière*" (Desmaisons) 20–2, 24, 30, 32, 38, 73, 211 n.70, 218 n.61

Union des Femmes Peintres et Sculpteurs 230 n.14, 233 n.40
unmarried women 84, 209 n.40
    Catherine, patron saint of 8
    femme majeure 21
    Raymond as 92, 145
    relative autonomy of 20–1, 209 n.44, n.46
    vieille demoiselle 20

Valleé, Olympe, *see* Renneville, vicomtesse de
Valmont, A. de
    "Si Madame vient la Poupée fera son jeu" 63–5, *64*
Van Remoortel, Marianne 127, 221 n.10, 227 n.121, 228 n.140
vaudeville 3, 5, 8, 44, 48–50, 68–76, 86, 87, 214 n.21
    calicot 210 n.64
    happy ending 72, 74–5
    identity play/mistaken identity 69, 71, 72, 74
    modiste
        Un Chapeau de paille d'Italie 73–4
        fait divers and 75–6, 78, 80
        La Modiste au camp 72–3
        Modiste et modeste 74
        Les Modistes 70–1, 78
        La Révolte des modistes 71–2
        songs about 70, 216 n.38
        Le Trottin de la modiste 75, 78, 218 n.66, n.68
    modiste pastime 68, 69, 217 n.56
    origins of 218 n.58
    primary source material and scholarly topic 217 n.54, 217 n.57
    slapstick 69, 70, 71–2, 74, 75
Veblen, Thorstein 208 n.36
Vernet, Horace 148, 155, 230 n.9
Vernier, Charles
    "Les Grisettes" 55–7, *56*, 216 n.40
La Vie quotidienne 151
Villemessant, Hippolyte de
    Le Figaro 94

La Gazette rose 94, 117, 221 n.11
    Renneville and 94, 110–12, 117, 221 n.11
    La Sylphide 109–10, 112, 116
Vionnet, Madeleine 204 n.15
    bias-cut 202, 239 n.8
"La Voix de foule" 18, *19*

"Walking Dress and Riding Dress" *158*
Waller, Margaret 93
watercolor
    "minor" art form 147, 153, 174
    oil painting compared with 174–5
    "Salon de 1857" 147–8, 150, 152, 165, 231 n.23
    "Technique l'aquarelle" 174
    Traité d'aquarelle 177, 178, 180, 237 n.93
Wettlaufer, Alexandra 231 n.16, n.20
widows
    Anaïs Colin 21, 151, 156, 194, 237 n.97
    J. J. as "widow" 105
    modistes 82, 84
    relative autonomy of 20–1, 206 n.46, 209 n.44
    Renneville (Vallée) as "widow" 110
women artists 7, 35, 165, 233 n.48
    exclusion from École des Beaux-Arts 7, 150, 153
    exclusion from official art 150
    family members as subjects for 153–5
    fashion plate illustrators 7, 35
    "lesser" genres and 147
    marginalization of 150, 152, 207 n.20
    regarding of, as amateurs 231 n.16
    retouching of works by male artists, accusations of 157
    at the Salon 150, 151, 165, 230–1 n.15
    self-portraiture 157, 162
    Union des Femmes Peintres et Sculpteurs 230 n.14, 233 n.40
    watercolor and 147, 150
women's labor, concealment of 3–4, 10–12, 14, 24, 25, 38–9
women's press, *see* fashion press
women's wages 18, 46, 215 n.33
Worth, Charles Frederick 203 n.5, 215 n.26

Yvert, Fabienne 140

Zola, Émile
    Au Bonheur des Dames 209 n.43
    Pot-Bouille 218 n.69